Trade Agreements and Women

Trade Agreements and Women

Transcending Barriers

AMRITA BAHRI
Associate Professor of Law, Instituto Tecnológico Autónomo de México and Co-Chair for Mexico, WTO Chair Program

OXFORD
UNIVERSITY PRESS

OXFORD
UNIVERSITY PRESS

Great Clarendon Street, Oxford, OX2 6DP,
United Kingdom

Oxford University Press is a department of the University of Oxford.
It furthers the University's objective of excellence in research, scholarship,
and education by publishing worldwide. Oxford is a registered trade mark of
Oxford University Press in the UK and in certain other countries

Published in the United States of America by Oxford University Press
198 Madison Avenue, New York, NY 10016, United States of America

British Library Cataloguing in Publication Data

Data available

Library of Congress Control Number: 2024947769

ISBN 9780198935728

DOI: 10.1093/9780198935759.001.0001

Printed and bound by
CPI Group (UK) Ltd, Croydon, CR0 4YY

The manufacturer's authorised representative in the EU for product safety
is Oxford University Press España S.A. of el Parque Empresarial San
Fernando de Henares, Avenida de Castilla,
2 – 28830 Madrid (www.oup.es/en).

I dedicate this book to my dad, Professor Gurdip Singh, who has always motivated me to work with dedication and to create an impact. He left us for his heavenly abode four months before I completed working on this book, but he will always live through my work, in my thoughts, and in my heart. I dedicate this book to you, Dad. Sending you a big hug all the way to paradise!

Praise Page

This is a remarkable book as it courageously raises all the right, but sometimes uncomfortable, questions and masterly guides us in our own search for answers. What are the barriers to women's economic empowerment and how are they related to trade? Can trade agreements play a role in overcoming these barriers? What can be learned from efforts already made in this regard? What should/could be done next to ensure that trade genuinely works for all, particularly those who have been historically marginalized, as women have? Amrita Bahri's timely book makes an important contribution to the discussion on how trade agreements can maximize the benefits and minimize the negative impact that trade may have on women.

Peter L.H. Van den Bossche
Professor of International Economic Law, Faculty of Law, University of Bern

This book will serve as a major reference for any reader, expert or not, who intends to better comprehend the trade and gender nexus. It guides both negotiators and non-negotiators through the complexities of gender-responsive free trade agreements, providing a detailed legal analysis of gender provisions. This analysis makes previous publications on the topic from the last decade obsolete. Understanding how trade agreements incorporate gender equality is crucial, as they shape national trade policies and influence international approaches. This book is a much-needed and essential primer for anyone considering a deep dive into trade and gender equality.

Anoush der Boghossian
Head of the Trade and Gender Office, World Trade Organization (WTO)

Mainstreaming gender in trade agreements can play a key role in addressing the systemic challenges that women and other marginalized stakeholders face in cross-border and international trade. Amrita tackles this important agenda by investigating these systemic challenges and the impact of mainstreaming gender in trade agreements. The legal compact of the African Continental Free Trade Area (AfCFTA) includes a Protocol on Women and Youth in Trade. As state parties implement the AfCFTA, the lessons that Amrita draws from this comprehensive analysis provide an important resource for governments, business associations, and traders. I am very pleased to recommend this important contribution to the discourse, the analysis, and the practice of mainstreaming gender in trade agreements.

Trudi Hartzenberg
Executive Director, Trade Law Centre (tralac)

Foreword

The World Trade Organization (WTO) has been intensively engaged in developing institutional initiatives that promote dialogue and advance research on the intersection of trade and women, beginning with its 2017 Buenos Aires Declaration on Trade and Women's Economic Empowerment. In addition, the WTO Informal Working Group on Trade and Gender, established in 2020, serves as a crucial platform for WTO members to enhance women's participation in global trade and to exchange practices and perspectives to incorporate a 'gender lens' into the work of the WTO. Also notable is the WTO's Gender Research Hub, which continuously seeks out new research and data to deepen understanding of women's economic empowerment through trade, incubating new ideas and approaches on this vital topic.

In this context, Dr Amrita Bahri's *Trade Agreements and Women: Transcending Barriers* emerges as a groundbreaking book-length analysis of the relationship between women and trade agreements. Drawing on her years of research and practical experience as well as her knowledge of the WTO, Dr Bahri provides a comprehensive, analytical assessment of the international trade and gender framework. She offers keen insights into how international trade policies affect women, explores the challenges they face as they engage in trade, and evaluates existing tools and proposals to address these problems. Her in-depth analysis makes a compelling case for how women's economic empowerment, of profound value in its own right, can contribute to economic growth and development by enhancing trade outcomes to the benefit of women, men, families, and societies. As such, it complements the WTO's contributions and provides a solid basis to advance that work.

The book begins by outlining the social and economic barriers women face and discusses the potential benefits of increasing their participation in trade. Dr Bahri advocates for more inclusive international norms and explores existing frameworks that address women's concerns in trade, including a thorough assessment of WTO initiatives and free trade agreements. Her innovative approach to evaluating the gender-responsiveness of trade agreements showcases the progress already made and the capacity to advance the design of trade agreements and instruments to overcome the barriers that women encounter.

In examining current practices and proposing future directions, Dr Bahri not only underscores the potential of trade agreements to empower women but also addresses the limitations and challenges we have seen in their implementation. Highlighting the complexities of integrating gender considerations into trade policy, she offers practical recommendations for advancing women's economic opportunities through trade and thereby benefiting societies more broadly.

By offering a comprehensive perspective on leveraging trade agreements as tools for women's empowerment and presenting a roadmap for enhancing the global trading system, Dr Bahri's insightful analysis and recommendations are a valuable contribution to the discourse on gender and trade, both at the WTO and in national policymaking.

Angela Paolini Ellard,
Deputy Director-General,
World Trade Organization
Geneva
5 September 2024

Acknowledgments

Writing a book is a journey that doesn't happen alone. I am deeply grateful to all those who supported and encouraged me throughout this process.

First and foremost, I would like to express my heartfelt gratitude to my husband, Ankit Sharma, whose unwavering support and sometimes challenges that questioned my thoughts have kept me motivated during the highs and lows of writing this book. Ankit, your unwavering scepticism about my ideas forced me to sharpen my arguments and refine my work. Your devil's advocacy has truly been the secret sauce to this book—though I still maintain I was right most of the time!

Special thanks are also due to my mom, Anita Bahri, and my son, Ayaan Sharma Bahri, for their patience and understanding during the countless hours I spent immersed in this work. It was a challenging task to bring this book to its completion after I became a mom to my beautiful yet a very loud and demanding son, but the will to make him proud of his mom kept me going.

I would like to thank Instituto Tecnológico Autónomo de México (ITAM) which has always gone beyond my expectations to provide its support and encouragement throughout my academic ventures. Thanks to the understanding and encouragement from the leadership team at ITAM, particularly Professor Alejandro Hernández, Professor Miguel Messmacher, and Professor Joyce Sadka,working on this book became a pleasant journey even amidst the stormy phase for having recently lost my father and as a new mom juggling through sleepless nights and tiring days. I would also like to thank the WTO Chairs Program for providing the platform to exchange views with other experts and policymakers from across the world and to engage in multiple events and conferences that have played a tremendous role in shaping this book.

Thanks also go to my dear friends and colleagues who have encouraged me throughout the process of this writing and research. In particular, I cannot miss thanking Anoush der Boghossian for many 'stormy' brainstorming sessions we had on different findings in this book and her brilliant work in the field that served as an inspiration for this work. Thanks also go to my friend Olabisi Akinkugbe for helping me pick the right title for this book. I would also like to thank my research assistants—Harendra Singh, Shubhangi Sonpir, Josie Cope Granados, Harish Kesav, Guillermo Moad, and Dyuti Pandya—for their immense help with research, referencing, and editing.

Lastly, I want to thank the readers of this book. Your interest and enthusiasm inspire me to continue writing. This book invites you, the reader, to not only absorb its insights but to actively engage with them. Whether you are a policymaker, a scholar, a student, or a concerned citizen, your interaction with these ideas can contribute to a more inclusive and equitable global trade environment. Let this be a starting point for further exploration, discussion, and action in your respective spheres. Together, we can push for a global trade system that can genuinely work for all, particularly those who have been historically marginalized.

Thank you all for being part of this journey.

Amrita Bahri
Mexico City
30 July 2024

Contents

Figures

Abbreviations

A4AI	Alliance for Affordable Internet
A4T	Aid for Trade
AA	Association Agreement
AfCFTA	African Continental Free Trade Area
ANZCERTA	Australia–New Zealand Closer Economic Relations Trade Agreement
AoA	Agreement on Agriculture
ASEAN	Association of Southeast Asian Nations
BIT	Bilateral Investment Treaties
CCFTA	Canada–Chile FTA
CECA	Comprehensive Economic Cooperation Agreements
CEDAW	Convention on the Elimination of All Forms of Discrimination Against Women
CEO	Chief Executive Officer
CEPA	Comprehensive Economic Partnership Agreements
CETA	Comprehensive and Economic Trade Agreement
CIFTA	Canada–Israel Free Trade Agreement
COMESA	Common Market for Eastern and Southern Africa
Covid-19	Corona Virus Disease of 2019
CPTPP	Comprehensive and Progressive Agreement for Trans-Pacific Partnership
CSR	Corporate Social Responsibility
CU	Customs Union
EAC	East African Community
EAEU	Eurasian Economic Union
EC	European Communities Concerning Regulation
EEA	European Economic Area
EFTA	European Free Trade Association
EPA	Economic Partnership Agreement
EU	European Union
FAO	Food and Agriculture Organization
FOGE	Federal Office of Gender Equality
FTA	Free Trade Agreement
GATS	General Agreement on Trade in Services
GATT	General Agreement on Tariffs and Trade
GBA Plus or GBA +	Gender-Based Analysis Plus
GDDI	Gender Digital Divide Index
GDP	Gross Domestic Product
GNP	Gross National Product

GPA	Agreement on Government Procurement
GSP	Generalized System of Preferences
GTAGA	Global Trade and Gender Arrangement
GVC	Global Value Chain
IA	Integration agreement
ICESCR	International Covenant on Economic, Social and Cultural Rights
ICT	Information and Communications Technology
IFAD	International Fund for Agricultural Development
ILO	International Labour Organization
IMF	International Monetary Fund
IPR	Intellectual Property Right
ISDS	Investor–State Dispute Settlement
ISO	International Organization for Standardization
ITC	International Trade Centre
ITU	International Telecommunication Union
IWG	Informal Working Group
JSI	Joint Statement Initiative
KPFTA	Peru–Korea Free Trade Agreement
MC-12	Twelfth WTO Ministerial Conference
ME	Micro Enterprises
MECE	Mutually Exclusive and Collectively Exhaustive
MFN	Most Favoured Nation
MNE	Multinational Enterprises
MRA	Mutual Recognition Agreement
MSME	Micro, Small, and Medium-Sized Enterprises
NAFTA	North American Free Trade Agreement
NTM	Non-Tariff Measures
OCT	Overseas Countries and Territories
OECD	Organisation for Economic Co-operation and Development
PPP	Public–Private Partnerships
PTA	Preferential Trade Agreements
RTA	Regional Trade Agreement
SADC	Southern African Development Community
SDG	Sustainable Development Goals
SME	Small and Medium-Sized Enterprises
SPS	Sanitary and Phytosanitary Measures
STEM	Science, Technology, Engineering, and Mathematics
TBT	Technical Barriers to Trade
TFA	Trade Facilitation Agreement
TFEU	Treaty on the Functioning of the European Union
TPRM	Trade Policy Review Mechanism
TRIPS	Trade-Related Aspects of Intellectual Property Rights
TSD	Trade and Sustainable Development
TTIP	Trade and Investment Partnership
UK–Japan CEPA	UK–Japan Comprehensive Economic Partnership Agreement

UN	United Nations
UNCTAD	United Nations Conference on Trade and Development
UNDP	United Nations Development Programme
UNECA	United Nations Economic Commission for Africa
UNECE	United Nations Economic Commission for Europe
UNESCO	United Nations Educational, Scientific and Cultural Organization
UNFPA	United Nations Population Fund
UNFSS	United Nations Forum on Sustainability Standards
UNGA	United Nations General Assembly
UNICEF	United Nations Children's Fund
US	United States
USD	United States Dollar
USMCA	United States–Mexico–Canada Agreement
VCLT	Vienna Convention on the Law of Treaties
VSS	Voluntary Sustainability Standards
WBG	World Bank Group
WEF	World Economic Forum
WTO	World Trade Organization

Introduction

To many of us, the world seems to be falling apart. Just a couple of years ago, there was a broad consensus on the value of free markets, liberal trade, and globalization. Economic globalization as an unstoppable force was seen as a win-win equation for all—but that consensus has now been lost, and it is giving way to discussions and debates on how trade and globalization have in fact left many worse off.

The health pandemic and other subsequent crises, such as the acceleration of climate change and its devastating impact, wars, and unilateral actions, are driving many countries—some of which were once the architects and designers of the current world trading system—to further retreat from global economic integration.[1] This had led to proliferated discontent towards globalization and free trade, and the need to regulate them in a multilateral manner. Recent events have shown that long-established trade relationships can suddenly break down in extraordinary circumstances, exposing the risks of excessive reliance on international partners that may suddenly halt trade across their borders.

National security, public health, corporate power, workers' rights, the environment, food security, and many other concerns have become the breeding grounds for a retreat from globalization and a march towards protectionism. In response to the current crisis, countries seem poised to reinforce the movement towards de-globalization. However, a large part of the trade policy community continues to stress that re-globalization, not de-globalization, is the way to go forward. For re-globalization, we need to redefine the goals of our economies to ensure that globalization works for all. Hence, we are at a critical juncture: between a long period where globalization dominated and dictated everything and a period of dramatic flux.[2] However, one factor that remains constant and continues to bind the world together is 'international trade'.

Even though trade continues to bind nations together, one fact about it is abundantly clear: it has had its winners and losers, as it has benefited some and left others without benefits or even with negative ramifications. Recognizing this has led to the inclusion of social issues in trade policy instruments as countries are increasingly focusing on actors who have less access to international markets or those who receive disproportionately higher negative consequences from international

[1] Amrita Bahri, Weihuan Zhou, and Daria Boklan, *Rethinking, Repackaging, and Rescuing World Trade Law in the Post-Pandemic Era* (Hart Publishing 2021).

[2] Anthea Roberts and Nicolas Lamp, *Six Faces of Globalization: Who Wins, Who Loses and Why It Matters* (Harvard UP 2021).

Trade Agreements and Women. Amrita Bahri, Oxford University Press. © Amrita Bahri 2025.
DOI: 10.1093/9780198935759.003.0001

trade.[3] The expectation is that the integration of 'non-trade issues' in trade policies and agreements may encourage economic policies that can more forcefully protect human rights and the environment.[4] The text of free trade agreements (FTAs)[5] in all their intricate details thus matters: when trading rules are appropriately formulated, they can work as stepping stones for the formulation of inclusive trade policies. Even though they are primarily designed to play a pivotal role in shaping the global economic landscape, the influence of trade agreements extends beyond mere economic transactions as they impact the lives and well-being of people around the globe. Moreover, evidence shows that an increasing number of FTAs now seek to enforce better human rights practices, as these agreements can influence governments to make improvements in certain human rights behaviours.[6]

In recent years, FTAs have accommodated several sustainable development goals (SDGs) with countries using these instruments to align economic development with social justice, human rights, effective labour standards, and environmental protection. Regional and bilateral agreements have risen in number and scope over the years and most of the current agreements go much beyond reciprocal tariff concessions for goods and services as they also extend to rules on investments, competition, government procurement, labour standards, gender equality, and the environment. Provisions on so-called 'non-trade objectives' are now increasingly included in these agreements as they aim to protect disadvantaged groups from any harm that lowering trade barriers may cause. Among the myriad groups affected by these agreements, women are particularly vulnerable as the distributional outcomes of trade have varied between women and men.

The discussion on the inclusion of women-related provisions in trade agreements is not new. The first such provisions appeared in the 1957 Treaty of Rome establishing the European Economic Community, which required each member state to guarantee the application of the principle of equal pay for equal work for women and men.[7] Since then, women-related provisions have appeared in several

[3] Jean-Frédéric Morin, Andreas Dür, and Lisa Lechner, 'Mapping the Trade and Environment Nexus: Insights from a New Data Set' (2018) 18(1) Global Environmental Politics 122.

[4] OECD, 'How are trade and environmental sustainability compatible?' <www.oecd.org/trade/topics/trade-and-the-environment/> accessed 21 April 2024.

[5] The term FTA as used in the book encompasses several different types of arrangements. These include FTAs such as the United States–Mexico–Canada Agreement (USMCA), in which member countries have agreed to reduce or eliminate trade barriers among themselves, or customs unions (CU), such as the European Union (EU), which is a deeper form of economic integration arrangement in which member states also maintain common tariffs and trade policies with respect to the rest of the world. It can also include interim arrangements that can lead to either an FTA or CU. FTAs can be bilateral, plurilateral, regional, or mega-regional, and they can be drafted purely as trade agreements or as economic partnership agreements, association agreements, strategic partnership agreements, and such others.

[6] Emilie Hafner-Burton, 'Trading Human Rights: How Preferential Trade Agreements Influence Government Repression' (2005) 59(3) International Organization 593.

[7] European Union, Treaty Establishing the European Community (Consolidated Version), Rome Treaty (25 March 1957) <www.refworld.org/legal/agreements/eu/1957/en/40087> accessed 21 April 2024.

agreements. Currently, more than 20% of trade agreements contain at least one explicit provision relating to women's concerns.[8] These inclusions, however, only narrate half the story. The other half, as discussed in Chapter 2, is about the negative impact trade agreements and economic partnerships can have on women as they can also exacerbate existing inequalities and challenges for women.[9] As shown in Chapter 2, trade liberalization and its policy instruments such as trade agreements may not only put the livelihoods and employment of women at risk, but they can also disrupt economic sectors where women are most active, thereby depriving them of employment and business opportunities.[10] At the same time, Chapters 2 and 4 have shown that trade agreements—if negotiated with an inclusive lens—can translate into more job opportunities, better business connections, enhanced market access, and fewer barriers to accessing finance and other productive resources for women.[11]

The scholarship remains divided on how trade agreements impact women and we need more data and evidence to better understand the impact trade agreements have had on men and women in various sectors of different countries and regions.[12] Meanwhile, it is crucial to negotiate and implement trade agreements in an inclusive manner to ensure that such agreements do not perpetuate the existing inequalities between men and women. In other words, it is important that future

[8] Author's own calculations; FTAs listed at WTO Regional Trade Agreement (RTA) database and currently in force are counted in this estimation. Explicit provisions are those that are drafted with women- or gender-related language and use the following terms: *mujer, mujeres, género, niñas/niños, sexo, equidad, maternidad, paternidad, paternal, maternal, igualdad, atención infantil* [in Spanish]; women, girl, woman, girls, maternity, gender, childcare, sex, mother [in English]. Only those explicit provisions are included in this study that includes text that offers commitment, vision, or actions to challenge gender inequalities and empower women through international trade. Implicit provisions are those that do not contain women-specific language but nevertheless have the capacity to benefit women. Examples may include provisions on morals, human rights, social welfare, labour rights, poverty, corporate social responsibility, inclusive development, and so on.

[9] Marzia Fontana, 'Advocacy Tool: "Gender Justice in Trade Policy: The Gender Effects of Economic Partnership Agreements"' (One World Action 2009).

[10] Sheba Tejani and William Milberg, 'Global Defeminization? Industrial Upgrading, Occupational Segmentation and Manufacturing Employment in Middle-Income Countries' (April 2010) Schwartz Center for Economic Policy Analysis Working Paper; Marzia Fontana and Cristina Paciello, 'Gender Dimensions of Agricultural and Rural Employment: Differentiated Pathways Out of Poverty' (FAO, IFAD and ILO 2010); Elisa Gamberoni and José Guilherme Reis, 'Gender-Informing Aid for Trade: Entry Points and Initial Lessons Learned from the World Bank' (July 2011) 62 The World Bank.

[11] Jeni Klugman and Elisa Gamberoni, 'Gender and Trade: A Fresh Look at the Evidence' *International Trade Forum Magazine* (1 July 2012) <http://www.tradeforum.org/Gender-and-trade-A-fresh-look-at-the-evidence> accessed 20 April 2020. Eg following the implementation of the North American Free Trade Agreement (NAFTA), women in Mexico experienced increased wage rates, work autonomy, and professional capacity through enhanced infrastructure and skill development. Increased employment for women in Pakistan is discussed in Asma Hyder and Jere R Behrman, 'International Trade Openness and Gender Gaps in Pakistani Labor Force Participation Rates over 57 Years' (2012) 17(3) Journal of the Asia Pacific Economy 367; contrary evidence is discussed in Cirila Quintero-Ramírez, 'The North American Free Trade Agreement and Women' (2002) 4(2) International Feminist Journal of Politics 240.

[12] UNCTAD, 'Making Trade Agreements Work for Gender Equality—Data and Statistics' (18 June 2020) Policy Brief No 81 <https://unctad.org/en/pages/PublicationWebflyer.aspx?publicationid = 2795> accessed 1 July 2020.

trade negotiations can help maximize the benefits and minimize the negative impacts that trade agreements may have on women as employers, employees, and consumers.

The multilateral system and its actors, as discussed in Chapter 3, have also affirmed and reinforced the intersection between trade policies and women's interests. With the adoption of the World Trade Organization's (WTO's) Joint Declaration on Trade and Women's Economic Empowerment[13] and the creation of the Informal Group on Trade and Gender.[14] the WTO is seeking to play a fundamental role in ensuring that trade becomes sustainable and creates opportunities for all including women and men. The WTO has also created a research network, known as the 'Gender Research Hub', to deepen the understanding on women and trade by fostering further research and data collection efforts. However, serious questions remain about the suitability of the WTO as a forum to lead the *démarche* on women and international trade.

Although the WTO's multilateral space may not be fully prepared to embrace these issues, recent trends highlight the promising role that FTAs can play in addressing concerns related to sustainable and inclusive development. In 2011, a WTO study estimated that 75% of countries have negotiated FTAs that include provisions on human rights.[15] As per the 2016 report by the International Labour Organization (ILO), more than 30% of trade agreements in force include commitments on labour rights protection.[16] In addition, countries have increasingly used trade agreements to cooperate on environmental matters by including environment protection and climate change-related provisions in almost 18% of existing trade agreements and economic partnerships.[17] Currently, more than 21% of agreements have an explicit commitment on gender equality.[18] Moreover, around 27% of trade agreements currently in force contain at least one explicit

[13] Buenos Aires Joint Declaration on Trade and Women's Economic Empowerment, December 2017 ('Declaration 2017') <www.wto.org/english/thewto_e/minist_e/mc11_e/genderdeclarationmc11_e.pdf> accessed 1 July 2020.

[14] For details, see WTO, 'Interim Report Following the Buenos Aires Joint Declaration on Trade and Women's Economic Empowerment' (25 September 2020) WTO doc WT/L/1095/Rev.1 <https://docs.wto.org/dol2fe/Pages/SS/directdoc.aspx?filename=q:/WT/L/1095R1.pdf&Open=True> accessed 21 April 2024.

[15] Susan Ariel Aaronson and Jean Pierre Chauffour, 'The Wedding of Trade and Human Rights: Marriage of Convenience or Permanent Match?' (nd) WTO Research and Analysis <www.wto.org/english/res_e/publications_e/wtr11_forum_e/wtr11_15feb11_e.htm> accessed 21 April 2024.

[16] ILO, 'Labour Provisions in Trade Agreements don't Hurt Business' (18 July 2016) <www.ilo.org/global/about-the-ilo/newsroom/news/WCMS_499348/lang--en/index.htm> accessed 23 December 2021.

[17] Immaculate Martínez-Zarzoso, 'Assessing the Effectiveness of Environmental Provisions in Regional Trade Agreements: An Empirical Analysis' (2018) 2018/02 OECD Trade and Environment Working Papers <www.oecd-ilibrary.org/environment/assessing-the-effectiveness-of-environmental-provisions-in-regional-trade-agreements_5ffc615c-en> accessed 12 November 2021.

[18] Author's own analysis and calculations (details on record with the author).

provision that relates to disability inclusion interests.[19] These developments show that the global community is preparing to ensure that there remains harmony between trade and sustainable development. However, willingness and appetite in addressing these concerns vary by country and by issue. For example, countries have generally shown a greater inclination to include labour standards rather than women-related concerns in their trade agreements. This disparity may partly stem from the perception that labour—as one of the three primary manufacturing inputs along with capital and raw materials—is directly related to trade. In contrast, women-related issues are often viewed as 'supposedly' non-trade-germane social concerns.[20] Irrespective of such variations, there is now a growing realization that trade needs to be sustainable to ensure that countries can reconcile trade liberalization with their important national interests. It also needs to be inclusive to better include and benefit marginalized players.[21]

I.1 Scholarship's Take on Trade and Sustainable Development

The concept of 'development' remains a highly controversial and much-debated topic in international legal scholarship. According to some development scholars, the focus of development has traditionally been understood as a concept that relates to economic growth, which is generally measured by economic indicators such as a country's gross domestic product (GDP) and gross national product (GNP).[22] However, current scholarship is steadily moving away from this understanding as it is widely recognizing that economic development in itself cannot ensure the well-being of an individual or a society.[23] As a result, the concept of development is exponentially developing and gradually encompassing non-economic aspects.

[19] Amrita Bahri, 'Making Trade Agreements Work for People with Disabilities: What's Been Achieved and What Remains Undone?' (2022) United Kingdom Foreign, Commonwealth and Development Office.

[20] Desirée LeClercq, 'The Disparate Treatment of Rights in Trade' (2021) 90(1) Fordham Law Review 1. The author notes that this appetite largely depends on whether the non-trade concerns are related to trade and whether they impact production or trade costs.

[21] Mehraj Ahmad Sheikh, Mushtaq Ahmad Malik, and Rana Zehra Masood, 'Assessing the Effects of Trade Openness on Sustainable Development: Evidence from India' (2020) 5(1) Asian Journal of Sustainability and Social Responsibility; Inge Røpke, 'Trade, Development and Sustainability: A Critical Assessment of the "Free Trade Dogma"' (1994) 9(1) Ecological Economics 13; Arlo Poletti, Daniela Sicurelli, and Aydin B Yildirim, 'Promoting Sustainable Development Through Trade? EU Trade Agreements and Global Value Chains' (2020) 51(3) Italian Political Science Review/Rivista Italiana di Scienza Politica 339.

[22] Leila Choukroune and James J Nedumpara, *International Economic Law: Text, Cases and Materials* (CUP 2021).

[23] Betsey Stevenson and Justin Wolfers, 'Economic Growth and Subjective Well-Being: Reassessing the Easterlin Paradox (2008) NBER Working Papers 14282 <http://www.nber.org/papers/w14282> accessed 1 July 2020; J Allister McGregor and Nicky Pouw, 'Towards an Economics of Well-Being' (2016) 41(4) Cambridge Journal of Economics 1123.

Andrew Lang in his work observed that 'we should also be debating what "social purpose" we want the trade regime to embody (in addition to the economic purpose)'.[24] Lang explains that 'we need to reinvent embedded liberalism for the global age by finding new ways and new forms through which to combine social protection with a continuing commitment to liberal trade'.[25] These views are in line with Ruggie's concept of embedded liberalism that is grounded in two ideas, which may well have been historically apt when he expressed them in 1982. First, that international regimes are functionally isolated projects and, second, that they have discrete social purposes.[26] This understanding has further evolved over the past four decades and, as such, avoiding impediments to commerce is no longer considered to be a social purpose but instead a tool to achieve the broader purpose of enhanced welfare.

Numerous studies on trade and development have employed different approaches and methodologies to understand how trade can relate to sustainable development. Several quantitative studies largely undertaken by economists have identified various positive as well as negative impacts of sustainability provisions.[27] Another set of studies that have probed this relationship are the qualitative studies generally carried out by political scientists and legal scholars. These studies have used different research methods including case studies and other qualitative techniques such as in-depth interviews, focus groups, and participant observation. Most of the detailed studies have focused on the textual aspect of these agreements as they have identified and assessed the language and scope of provisions relating to trade and sustainable development.[28] Several studies have also mapped out trade agreements that contain sustainability provisions and have assessed or critiqued the ways in which such provisions are constructed.[29] This growing scholarship has

[24] Andrew Lang, 'Reconstructing Embedded Liberalism: John Gerard Ruggie and Constructivist Approaches to the Study of the International Trade Regime' (2006) 9(1) Journal of International Economic Law 81, 84.

[25] ibid 98.

[26] John Gerard Ruggie, 'International Regimes, Transactions and Change: Embedded Liberalism in the Postwar Economic Order' (1982) 36(2) International Organization 379; see also John Ruggie, 'Embedded Liberalism Revisited: Institutions and Progress in International Economic Relations' in Emanuel Adler and Beverly Crawford (eds), *Progress in Postwar Economic Relations* (Columbia UP 1991).

[27] See eg Ida Bastiaens and Evgeny Postnikov, 'Greening Up: The Effects of Environmental Standards in EU and US Trade Agreements' (2017) 26(5) Environmental Politics 847.

[28] James Harrison and others, 'Labour Standards Provisions in EU Free Trade Agreements: Reflections on the European Commission's Reform Agenda' (2019) 18(4) World Trade Review 635; Kristoffer Marslev and Cornelia Staritz, 'Towards a Stronger EU Approach on the Trade–Labor Nexus? The EU–Vietnam Free Trade Agreement, Social Struggles, and Labor Reforms in Vietnam' (2022) 30(3) Review of International Political Economy 1125.

[29] Jean-Frédéric Morin and Myriam Rochette, 'Transatlantic Convergence of Preferential Trade Agreements Environmental Clauses' (2017) 19(4) Business and Politics 621; Peter Draper, Nkululeko Khumalo, and Faith Tigere, 'Sustainability Provisions in Regional Trade Agreements: Can They be Multilateralised?' (21 July 2017) International Centre for Trade and Sustainable Development (ICTSD) and Inter-American Development Bank (IDB) <www.tralac.org/news/article/11916-sustainability-provisions-in-regional-trade-agreements-can-they-be-multilateralised.html> accessed 16 May 2022.

expanded our understanding of how trade agreements currently interact with different values of sustainable development, the real-world impact these agreements can have, and what remains to be done in respect of making these agreements work for everyone.[30]

The sustainability agenda in FTAs has been triggered by a range of proponents including civil society organizations, trade unions, business groups, and politicians. These proponents have pushed for various kinds of sustainability-related provisions in their respective trade agreements.[31] It is therefore not surprising that current sustainability provisions that have made their way into the negotiated and enforced FTAs are poised to achieve a range of different sustainability outcomes.

Traditionally, the type of sustainability provisions that have mostly featured in the academic literature have been those that have sought to impose obligations on signatory governments; these obligations, for instance, have included commitments to reaffirm and to effectively implement the obligations a country has already assumed under international instruments such as those relating to international human rights or labour standards or environmental treaties.[32] These legal obligations are generally based on the assumption that trade agreements can be utilized to encourage governments of other countries which are party to the FTA to take actions to address sustainability concerns, and hence these policy instruments can become an important vehicle for foreign policymaking with a sustainability lens.[33] Moreover, as discussed earlier in this introduction, targeting trade agreements from a sustainability perspective is also somewhat justified by the fact that their market-access-oriented provisions can themselves have negative environmental and social impacts which several studies are beginning to uncover.[34]

With time, modern-day trade agreements are becoming all-encompassing and the list of concerns they include is expanding into disciplines that have never been traditionally covered by such agreements. Concerns relating to the environment, climate change, clean energy, fisheries, rural development, poverty alleviation, and labour are constantly pushing the text of trade agreements for their acceptance.

[30] Sharon Anglin Treat, 'Trade agreements and sustainability: innovations and illusions in EU and US agreements' (Institute for Agriculture & Trade Policy 23 September 2021) <www.iatp.org/documents/trade-agreements-and-sustainability-innovations-and-illusions-eu-and-us-agreements> accessed 21 April 2024; also see Claire Guyot, 'Free trade agreements struggle to convince on social, environmental standards' (EURACTIV 23 March 2018) <www.euractiv.com/section/ceta/news/free-trade-agreements-struggle-to-convince-on-social-environmental-standards/> accessed 21 April 2024.

[31] Bart Kerremans and Myriam Martins-Gistelinck, 'Interest Aggregation, Political Parties, Labour Standards and Trade: Differences in the US and EU Approaches to the Inclusion of Labour Standards in International Trade Agreements,' (2009) 14(5) European Foreign Affairs Review 683.

[32] Evgeny Postnikov and Ida Bastiaens, 'Does Dialogue Work? The Effectiveness of Labor Standards in EU Preferential Trade Agreements' (2014) 21(6) Journal of European Public Policy 923.

[33] Flavia Jurje and Sandra Lavenex, 'Trade Agreements as Venues for "Market Power Europe"? The Case of Immigration Policy' (2013) 52(2) Journal of Common Market Studies 320.

[34] Ryan Abman and Clark Lundberg, 'Does Free Trade Increase Deforestation? The Effects of Regional Trade Agreements' (2020) 7(1) Journal of the Association of Environmental and Resource Economists 35.

While there is widespread commitment to achieving the SDGs, the current literature has observed that the reference to SDGs in trade agreements remains a contentious issue. There are several fundamental questions, such as: what is the role of 'sustainable development' in trade agreements? How can countries accommodate sustainable development concerns, especially when they often contradict trade interests? Is the current inclusion of sustainable development concerns merely focused on addressing negative externalities of trade or are they a window-dressing attempt to hide the adverse impact of trade liberalization?

Another crucial concern commonly shared by developing countries is that it is generally the more powerful developed countries that are pushing for sustainability provisions in trade agreements and poorer developing countries being the recipients of this new negotiating trend.[35] Hence, this can be seen as developed countries' agenda and for the developing world—a tool of disguised protectionism and/or neo-colonialism.[36] There is also a long-standing concern that trade and sustainability provisions are disproportionately burdensome on developing countries as they saddle them with resource-demanding responsibilities without offering any supportive measures to accomplish the same.[37] There is an underlying resentment that free trade and liberalized markets have resulted in some advanced countries losing their comparative advantages in manufacturing goods and hence, as an attempt to level the playing field, these countries are introducing such sustainability standards in their trade agreements.[38] In this sense, countries fear that sustainability provisions in trade agreements can be used as coercive instruments to enforce non-trade values and also negate their negotiated market access.[39]

These concerns have widened the trust deficit between developed and developing countries and have therefore undermined the legitimacy of the SDG agenda for many years. While it is true that the sustainability provisions are generally reciprocal in nature, it is also true that they are mostly being advocated and proposed by developed countries. Such is especially the case with labour provisions,[40] environmental standards,[41] gender equality concerns,[42] as well as those relating to

[35] Amrita Bahri and Renata Amaral, 'Gender Equality Provisions in Trade and Investment Agreements: Are They Widening the Negotiation Capacity Gap?' (2024) 23(1) World Trade Review 47.

[36] Jagdish N Bhagwati and 102 Other Signatories, 'Third World Intellectuals and NGOs Statement against Linkage' (TWIN-SAL) (CUTS 6 September 1999) <https://doi.org/10.7916/D8KD24KG> accessed 17 May 2022.

[37] Cosimo Beverelli, Jurgen Timothy Kurtz, and Damian Raess, *International Trade, Investment and the Sustainable Development Goals: World Trade Forum* (CUP 2020) 111–14.

[38] Steve Charnovitz, 'The Law of Environmental "PPMs" in the WTO: Debunking the Myth of Illegality' (2002) 27(59) Yale Journal of International Law.

[39] Evgeny Postnikov and Ida Bastiaens, 'Social Protectionist Bias: The Domestic Politics of North–South Trade Agreements' (2020) 22(2) The British Journal of Politics and International Relations 347.

[40] Axel Marx, Nicolás Brando, and Brecht Lein, 'Strengthening Labour Rights Provisions in Bilateral Trade Agreements: Making the Case for Voluntary Sustainability Standards' (2017) 8(3) Global Policy 78.

[41] Bastiaens and Postnikov (n 27).

[42] Bahri and Amaral (n 35).

disability inclusion.[43] These observations show why the inclusion of sustainability clauses in international trade remains more of a symbolic endeavour, is opposed by many, and can cause a steep divide between the developed and developing countries. Going forward, the inclusion of such concerns in trade agreements must be based on a careful, inclusive, and well-concerted approach.

I.2 About the Book

Trade agreements are not considered as an end in themselves; they are rather a means and a vehicle to achieve and further SDGs. While they can serve as an appropriate vehicle to achieve various SDGs, there are multiple challenges and constraints that a country may face in making their trade policy instruments work in that respect. Moreover, some sustainability concerns have over time become more acceptable than others, while yet others have continued to face resistance and backlash. One such contentious concern is that of women, which forms the subject matter of the book.

The relationship between trade agreements and women is perhaps a tale of two stories: the first is the result of pressure from civil society and certain political quarters over the perceived dominance of trade policy in international affairs at the expense of social values; the second is perhaps the growing interest and anxiety over the relationship between these legally equivalent but politically asymmetrical sets of international obligations. The book focuses on how these asymmetrical yet complementary sets of international obligations—women empowerment and trade liberalization—interact, overlap, and converge.

The book explores how trade agreements can strengthen women empowerment. To do so, it provides answers to several questions which remain unanswered in trade policy corridors. What role can trade agreements play in respect of women empowerment and what limitations do they have in that respect? How are current agreements accommodating such concerns? Are such inclusions merely symbolic and a 'tick-in-the-box' exercise or is there something more to them? What makes an agreement responsive to the needs of women and how can countries increase the responsiveness of their trade agreements towards the concerns that women face? What risks and challenges can a country encounter in using its trade agreements in this respect? How are other countries incorporating such provisions in their agreements and in what forms and with what scope? What options do countries have in testing out the potential of trade agreements in this respect and making future inclusion of women-related provisions more effective and meaningful for women? This book represents the first

[43] Bahri (n 19).

systematic attempt to address these questions as it examines how trade agreements might be altered to address women's interests more effectively. It offers description and analysis of whether trade agreements can further women empowerment, how can they can address the barriers that women face, and what different negotiating options countries have for including women's concerns in their future trade agreements.

The book draws from my review of all trade agreements currently in force, my experience of having prepared the first-ever methodology to assess gender-responsiveness of trade agreements,[44] as well as work over a number of years with several international organizations and policymakers on trade and gender projects, and deep empirical research based on semi-structured interviews and other interactions with the wider policy audience over the previous eight years. It presents a fascinating mix of scholarly interventions and insiders' insights as, in addition to literature review and assessment of trade agreements, experience and insight has been gathered through interviews and discussions with over 85 stakeholders engaged in trade negotiations in the capacity of negotiators, civil society representatives, practitioners, international diplomats, scholars, and researchers. These research methods make this study the first book-length legal analysis of women and trade agreements.

The path to achieving women's empowerment is difficult and necessitates sophisticated approaches that address different realities faced by women in different parts of the world, while recognizing the role that decision-makers can play in overcoming long-standing practices, laws, or processes that oppress or disenfranchise women and girls. The book explores the role that trade policymakers and leaders have played in respect of removing the barriers women face and the role they can potentially play in this respect going forward through international trade negotiations. Given the significance of its subject matter, and its rapidly evolving relevance for the international law community, the book serves as an invaluable source for academics, researchers, students, and policymakers in this critical time and beyond.

With more and more countries including provisions on women's concerns in their trade agreements and trade negotiation discussions, policymakers and negotiators are on the lookout for resources to expand their understanding of how best they can negotiate these provisions or deal with pressures from their trading partners who might want to include such provisions in their agreements. The book caters to a policy audience from a wide range of countries, including: (1) those who lead the inclusion of such provisions in their agreements; (2) those who are still considering the advantages or risks of such inclusions; and (3) those who are keen to stay away from such discussions and are therefore figuring out their options

[44] This framework is currently employed by the International Trade Centre, WTO/UNCTAD.

for dealing with pressures from their trade partners to incorporate women's concerns in future trade agreements. In addition, the book provides a literary basis for training government officials and trade negotiators across the globe on this subject. With a multitude of trade negotiations ongoing and an increasing demand for attention to non-trade issues on the verge of trade cooperation, the book presents a unique tool for trade negotiators and policymakers to address the topic of women empowerment. It provides timely contributions and guidance for policymakers to prepare, revise, and negotiate new norms to regulate trade in an inclusive manner and to ensure that they work for all, including women.

Researchers and scholars studying trade law, sustainable development, inclusion, and gender will find in the book the most topical issues concerning trade agreements and women's rights. It additionally provides scholars with abundant food for thought on major challenges in this field and how best to deal with them. It will also interest scholars of international law and feminism/women empowerment as the book seeks to fill a major gap in the feminist analysis of international law by adding in the angle of trade law and policy. The book can also provide a menu of research options and ideas for future research topics in the emerging field of trade inclusiveness and can serve as a teaching and learning resource for a growing number of courses and training programmes that are now focusing on gender studies in international law, including trade and investment, economic law, international relations, international business, and beyond.

I.3 The Buzzword of 'Gender Mainstreaming': What is it About?

When it comes to adding women's concerns into trade agreements, 'gender mainstreaming' has been the main buzzword for the past few years. It has been used frequently and widely by all trade and women enthusiasts—including trade negotiators, diplomats, international organizations, civil society representatives, and research scholars. Gender as such is a broad term; it includes women as well as men and traditional as well as non-traditional genders. The terms 'gender' and 'gender mainstreaming' have mostly been used in trade agreements and policies without any attempts by policymakers to define them or clarify their scope; however, it is possible to infer from a systemic assessment of the provisions containing these terms that they have mostly been used only to refer to the interests of women who identify themselves as *cisgender* women, thereby excluding—intentionally or unintentionally—concerns relating to men as well as non-*cisgender* women and men.

The book is not about 'gender equality' as a whole; it is about women and their empowerment through trade agreements. Hence, whenever terms such as 'gender' or 'gender equality' are used, they intend to refer to *cisgender* as well as transgender women, and their characteristics, norms, behaviours, and roles.[45]

Gender mainstreaming more broadly is defined as 'the (re)organization, improvement, development, and evaluation of policy processes so that a gender equality perspective is incorporated in all policies at all levels at all stages, by the actors normally involved in policy-making'.[46] When used in the context of FTAs, it mostly refers to the inclusion of concerns relating to women in the drafting and implementation of FTAs. This is a process by which parties seek to include women's perspectives in their trade liberalization efforts and policies. It should not be confused with the gender-impact assessment of trade agreements, which is a process to assess either the ex-ante or ex-post impact of trade agreements on women in certain countries. The process of mainstreaming affirms a member's commitment, understanding, and political will to empower women through trade policies and agreements. The process also aims to maximize the positive impact and minimize the negative impact of trade agreements on women empowerment goals. The term 'gender responsiveness' has also been used extensively in the scholarship; it has mostly been used to refer to a process that assesses how sensitive, informed, or committed the provisions of a trade agreement are to issues relating to women. In other words, the way and extent to which an agreement mainstreams women's concerns defines how responsive that agreement is to their concerns.

I.4 The Book's Structure

The book comprises nine chapters. Chapter 1 serves as an entry point by offering a detailed contextual background to the barriers women face, setting the stage for subsequent chapters that explore how trade policies can assist in overcoming these barriers. It provides a foundational understanding of key terms used throughout the book and discusses how internal and external barriers hinder women's economic empowerment, with examples from Asia, the Middle East, Africa, and South America.

Chapter 2 examines the bi-directional relationship between trade policies and women's empowerment, analysing how trade impacts women in various roles and how enhancing women's empowerment can boost trade

[45] Even though this book seeks to focus on women as a homogenous group, it raises reflections on where the differences can occur for *cis-women* and trans-women in terms of the barriers they face in trade, as these barriers may be different or even more formidable for women who may have other variables to consider such as transgender identity, a disability, race, or association with indigenous groups.

[46] Mieke Verloo, 'Displacement and Empowerment: Reflections on the Concept and Practice of the Council of Europe Approach to Gender Mainstreaming and Gender Equality' (2005) 12(3) Social Politics 344.

competitiveness and productivity. The chapter builds a case for inclusive international trade regulation. Chapter 3 discusses recent initiatives and developments in respect of trade and women empowerment within the framework of the WTO. With this focus, the chapter seeks to explore whether the WTO institutions and its rulebook are ready to regulate trade in a manner that can help minimize the negative repercussions trade liberalization and globalization can have on women.

Chapter 4 addresses the critical questions of whether and how FTAs can incorporate concerns related to women and assist in overcoming the barriers they face. It builds a case for using trade agreements to address women's concerns and explores the reasons behind the increasing number of FTAs negotiated to include women-related provisions. Chapter 5 identifies eight possible hesitations that countries—mainly developing ones—may have in advancing women's concerns through trade agreements, and it provides discussion on each of these hesitations, together with practical examples from several regions.

Following the discussions in the previous two chapters on how trade agreements can uphold women's empowerment and the hesitations policymakers may have in that respect, Chapter 6 introduces the International Trade Centre's Maturity Framework that I prepared to help trade negotiators measure the responsiveness of their trade agreements to women's concerns. Using this diagnostic approach, countries can develop a roadmap to achieve the desired level of responsiveness for their FTAs following their respective needs, willingness, and resources.

Chapter 7 provides a discussion of ten different approaches that are employed by countries to add women's perspectives to existing trade agreements with the help of multiple practice examples from different regions. With this, it prepares a detailed menu of negotiating options for trade negotiators from across the globe. After assessing the ways in which such provisions are currently added, Chapter 8 critically assesses the problems with the ways in which those provisions have so far been included. The critique focuses on how such provisions are drafted, their imprecise scope, their lack of enforcement potential, the absence of associated plans for their effective implementation, the disconnect between the solutions they offer and the barriers that women face in trade, and their focus on women in their traditional roles; it also discusses the reluctance of negotiators to step beyond their zone of familiarity and their use of a template approach to drafting such provisions. The chapter elaborates on this critical assessment and presents eight fundamental problems with the current inclusion of such provisions.

Chapter 9 proposes a roadmap for the future negotiations of trade and women-related provisions with the help of a five-dimensional framework that offers concrete recommendations on the following aspects: drafting, focus areas, location of provisions, nature, and types of provisions, and their implementation and enforcement processes. In this manner, the framework proposed in this chapter, titled 'The Pentagon Roadmap for Trade and Gender Negotiations', prepares a blueprint for future trade negotiations on women-related provisions. The recommendations provided are designed to be adaptable, reflecting the diverse political, economic, social, and legal contexts of different countries.

1
Barriers that Impede Women's Economic Empowerment

1.1 What is Women's Empowerment?

'Empowerment' is a contested concept with no single definition. It can have different meanings depending on different perspectives. Zimmerman defines it as the 'notion of people having the ability to understand and control themselves and their environments—including social, economic, and political factors—expanding their capabilities and horizons and elevating themselves to greater levels of achievement and satisfaction'.[1] Chamberlain employs a 'mental health' perspective in defining 'empowerment' and refers to it as a process that has a number of elements including decision-making power, access to information and resources, and access to opportunities.[2] Page and Czuba view empowerment as a 'multidimensional social process that helps people gain control over their own lives' and provides them with the power to employ it in 'their own lives, communities and society, by acting on issues they define as important'.[3]

The term 'women empowerment' refers to a 'socio-political concept that involves cognitive, psychological, economic and political dimensions'.[4] The cognitive dimension involves women's understanding of the factors that may result in their subordination and their ability to make choices that may go against cultural or social expectations. The psychological dimension focuses upon women's beliefs to improve their social and economic conditions. The economic dimension entails women's access to economic opportunities that can increase their economic independence. Finally, the political dimension is the ability to understand and appreciate one's situation and mobilize resources for social change. Women are disempowered if they are prevented from arriving at their actual potential, which can happen as a result of multifaceted barriers that create disadvantages for them. Women's empowerment can therefore be viewed as the process of correcting

[1] Marc Zimmerman, 'Taking Aim on Empowerment Research: On the Distinction Between Individual and Psychological Conceptions' (1984) 18(1) American Journal of Community Psychology 169, 177.

[2] Judi Chamberlin, 'A working definition on empowerment' (1997) <https://psycnet.apa.org/record/1997-05758-006> accessed 16 September 2022.

[3] Nanette Page and Cheryl E Czuba, 'Empowerment: What Is It?' (1999) 37(5) Journal of Extension 24, 32.

[4] PX Francina and Mary Venus Joseph, 'Women Empowerment: The Psychological Dimension' (2013) 5(2) Rajagiri Journal of Social Development 163, 170.

Trade Agreements and Women. Amrita Bahri, Oxford University Press. © Amrita Bahri 2025.
DOI: 10.1093/9780198935759.003.0002

gender disparity in a society to improve the condition and status of women in all spheres of their lives.[5]

Women are empowered when they have the liberty to take control and ownership of their lives and make choices. But what exactly is liberty?

1.2 What is Liberty?

'Liberty' is a powerful word. The twentieth-century political philosopher Isaiah Berlin conceptualized liberty as 'negative' and 'positive'.[6] Berlin defined negative liberty as freedom from (or absence of) constraints imposed by other people or external factors. A person is negatively free to the extent that other people do not restrict what that person can and wants to do. Positive liberty, on the other hand, is defined as freedom (including ability and opportunity) to pursue and achieve the 'willed goal'. Positive liberty is freedom from internal constraints such as fear, lack of courage, and self-confidence.

This conceptualization helps explain the barriers that impede women's participation in trade. The following sections explain the barriers that obstruct women's positive and negative freedom to engage in economic activities. However, women cannot be considered as a homogenous group as women operate in different conditions and in the multiplicity of their roles. Like broader society, women as a group can be seen as a collection of various subgroups, with some being affected more deeply than others owing to certain compounding factors. These compounding factors could include, but are not limited to, race, colour, region, physical condition, gender, location, and so on. For example, some of the barriers discussed in the following sections may be more severe and may present themselves in a different manner for indigenous women, women with disability, and black or transgender women.

The factor of race, for example, could exacerbate the discriminatory experience of a black woman compared to her white counterpart. Feminists also contend that the factor of location, particularly for women in developing and least developed countries, can compound the oppression of women.[7] If one were to identify the most oppressed group of women, one would turn to the developing world. Similar observations can be made in respect of transgender and

[5] UNFPA (Addis Ababa), 'Gender Inequality and Women's Empowerment Ethiopian Society of Population Studies, In-depth Analysis of the Ethiopia Demographic and Health Survey' (2008) <www.semanticscholar.org/paper/Gender-Inequality-and-Women-%E2%80%99-s-Empowerment-1-of-%E2%80%99-Ababa/17c3a0548b1942b868b03fc51dee22817dbabfcd> accessed 17 September 2022

[6] Isaiah Berlin, 'Two Concepts of Liberty' in Henry Hardy (ed), *Liberty* (OUP 2002).

[7] Emezat Mengesha, 'Rethinking the Rules and Principles of the International Trade Regime: Feminist Perspectives' (2008) 22(78) Engendering National & Global Economic Policies 13, 26.

non-binary women who may face heightened barriers against both negative and positive liberty.[8]

For the sake of clarity and structure, this chapter will mostly treat women as a homogenous group; however, it will in relevant places raise reflections on where the differences can occur as a result of compounding factors.

1.3 Barriers that Impede Positive Freedom

As per the feminist psychology scholarship, women are not positively free if they allow internal constraints to impede their professional goals such as self-doubt, acceptance of cultural stereotypes, lack of confidence, and fear of societal perceptions.[9] Lack of self-esteem and self-efficacy may also act as internal constraints. Theorists define self-esteem as a person's beliefs about self-worth and self-acceptance; self-efficacy is defined as a person's beliefs about their ability to perform successfully.[10] Sandberg describes these inner barriers in the following words: 'Fear is at the root of so many of the barriers that women face. Fear of not being liked. Fear of making the wrong choice. Fear of drawing negative attention. Fear of overreaching. Fear of being judged. Fear of failure. And the holy trinity of fear: the fear of being a bad mother/wife/daughter.'[11] These psychological barriers are rarely discussed as they are mostly underplayed, yet they can significantly disrupt a woman's professional endeavours and ambitions.

In a research interview, the female CEO of a leading multinational firm confirmed that the biggest barrier she faced in her professional journey was internal; it was the mental dialogue she had with herself while being surrounded by gender-based societal pressures and family expectations.[12] To lead a multinational company as the CEO, she had to go through a 'fundamental identity shift' as she had always believed that she was 'simply not cut out to be a leader'.[13] Another female entrepreneur confirms that lack of self-confidence was a significant barrier she faced and she could only overcome that barrier when she 'removed herself from

[8] Kristi E Gamarel and others, 'Community-Led Response to Address Economic Vulnerability due to COVID-19 with, for, and by Transgender Women of Color: A Qualitative Pilot Evaluation' (2023) 8(2) Transgender Health 195.

[9] Amy K Kiefer and Denise Sekaquaptewa, 'Implicit Stereotypes, Gender Identification, and Math-Related Outcomes: A Prospective Study of Female College Students' (2007) 18(1) Psychological Science 13, 18; Mellanie C Steffens, Petra Jelenec, and Peter Noack, 'On the Leaky Math Pipeline: Comparing Implicit Math-Gender Stereotypes and Math Withdrawal in Female and Male Children and Adolescents' (2010) 102(4) Journal of Educational Psychology 947.

[10] Albert Bandura, 'Self-Efficacy: Toward a Unifying Theory of Behavioral Change' (1977) 84(2) Psychological Review 191.

[11] Sheryl Sandberg, *Lean In: Women, Work, and the Will to Lead* (Alfred A Knopf 2013).

[12] Interview with the CEO of a leading financial technology company in Latin America (details withheld, 9 September 2020).

[13] ibid; confirmed in an interview with the chief financial officer of a leading Latin American bank (details withheld, 12 August 2020).

her gender' as she had to 'start acting as a man' to be able to run a business.[14] Fear of acting against societal pressures and predetermined gender-specific expectations is a significant obstacle. These societal expectations and gender roles are formed and perpetuated by our interactions with the surrounding social environment.

Here, I am tempted to go against academic stereotypes and share with readers some of my personal experience to further illustrate this problem. I have had to overcome many such obstacles myself to get here and be able to write this book. There have been many instances but I will share one of them here. When I wrote my first book, I was frowned upon by some family members and friends who clearly told me that my foremost responsibility as a married woman was to produce babies and not books.[15] That conversation triggered an internal dialogue within me on whether I should really give in to societal expectations to maintain my norm-abiding image and likeability. I feared losing the respect of my family members. I feared I would risk my likeability for my professional success. I found this competence–likability trade-off to be self-defeating. Caught between my traditional roles and career ambitions, I realized that I was experiencing an internal barrier framed by theorists as the 'fear of success syndrome'.[16] After engaging in this dialogue with myself for several months, I decided not to give in to what others expected of me; I went ahead and fulfilled what I expected of myself.

Stereotyped gender roles dictate that a woman's primary responsibilities are limited to household management, reproduction, and childcare. Acceptance of these norms and roles puts women a step further away from economic empowerment. Women tend to accept a significantly larger portion of domestic responsibilities, such as cleaning, cooking, and care-giving, as compared to men, making them time-poor.[17] Time poverty is one of the main barriers that impede women's participation in economies, as it implies for them paucity of time to receive education, skill development, vocational training, employment prospects, and business opportunities.[18] Moreover, most household work is largely invisible and unpaid.[19] These society-fabricated gender roles result in diminishing the confidence

[14] Interview with the managing director of a small e-marketplace business based in Mexico (details withheld, 19 September 2020).

[15] Author's personal conversations with a family member (details withheld).

[16] Sally M Reiss, 'External Barriers Experienced by Gifted and Talented Girls and Women' (2001) 4 Gifted Child Today 24 27, 66 <https://gifted.uconn.edu/schoolwide-enrichment-model/external_barriers/#> accessed 17 September 2022.

[17] Matthias Doepke and Fabian Kindermann, 'Bargaining over Babies: Theory, Evidence, and Policy Implications' (2019) 109(9) American Economic Review 32, 64 (the authors observe that women provide the majority of childcare even if both spouses are working).

[18] Maria Floro, 'Economic Restructuring, Gender and the Allocation of Time' (1995) 23(11) World Development 1913. (Note that trade liberalization can reduce the cost of products and services to help women save time.)

[19] Discussion on the gross distribution of unpaid care work between women and men discussed in ECLAC, 'Repository of information on time use in Latin America and the Caribbean' (2019) <https://oig.cepal.org/sites/default/files/2019-10_repositorio_uso_del_tiempo_eng.pdf> accessed 21 April 2020.

required to excel in a profession or business. Women's risk-averse behaviour, as confirmed by behavioural economics, can also be a barrier to starting, running, or expanding a business due to the caution they exert in decision-making, particularly in respect of investments and market expansion.[20]

The 'Cinderella complex'—a psychological barrier influenced by cultural and societal expectations—reflects a desire to avoid responsibility and rely on others.[21] This can lead to anxiety about success, fear of failure, and societal pressure to maintain femininity. A different internal barrier is the 'imposter phenomenon', which means that a sense of 'not being good enough' constrains some women and that this constraint limits their human capabilities to achieve their goals.[22] At times, women are more than 'victims' as they become 'active resistors' of positive change and inadvertently employ a self-restricting culture which plays a role in holding them back in various ways.

These internal barriers can be more intense and can pose a larger risk for women who may also be disadvantaged or marginalized for other reasons such as colour, gender, location, and physical condition. For example, women of colour may have a lower self-esteem and self-confidence compared to their white female counterparts due to the ongoing burden of prejudice and discrimination that can negatively impact their ability to perform.[23] Similar observations can be made for women with disabilities who have faced barriers in various aspects of their lives due to bias, stereotypes, and cultural norms.[24] Such conditions may also have a multiplying impact in terms of the disadvantages they can produce as women with disabilities can, for example, experience multiple layers of discrimination as a result of their race, age, gender, and sexual orientation, as well as their disability.

Finally, these internal barriers are not innate but are linked to external factors like educational and financial limitations, patriarchal structures, cultural beliefs, and discriminatory laws. Hence, addressing external barriers can help reduce the internal barriers, thereby enhancing women's economic independence and professional success. The next section will explore these external barriers to women's negative freedom.

[20] Jiekun Huang and Darren J Kisgen, 'Gender and Corporate Finance: Are Male Executives Overconfident Relative to Female Executives?' (2013) 108(3) Journal of Financial Economics 822, 839. These findings are challenged by other scholars, see eg Julie A Nelson, *Gender and Risk-Taking: Economics, Evidence, and Why the Answer Matters* (Routledge 2018).

[21] Colette Dowling, *The Cinderella Complex: Women's Hidden Fear of Independence* (Summit Books 1981).

[22] Pauline Rose Clance and Suzanne Imes, 'The Imposter Phenomenon in High Achieving Women: Dynamics and Therapeutic Intervention' (1978) 15(3) Psychotherapy Theory, Research and Practice 241, 247.

[23] Deborah M Wilson and others, 'The Self-Esteem of African American Women: The Impact of Black Church Attendance' (2022) 23(2) The Journal of the Research Association of Minority Professors 1.

[24] Amrita Bahri, 'Making Trade Agreements Work for People with Disabilities: What's Been Achieved and What Remains Undone?' (2023), UK FCDO and Cowater International Inc <www.genderandtrade.com/_files/ugd/86d8f7_a4ebc789a1ae4c81b51d725cbc31bfa3.pdf> accessed 6 June 2024.

1.4 Barriers that Impede Negative Freedom

Several external barriers impede women's negative freedom. For ease of understanding, this section divides these barriers into three categories: barriers within borders, barriers at borders, and barriers across borders. These categories are not mutually exclusive, as some barriers may fit under more than one of the following categories.

1.4.1 Barriers within borders

1.4.1.1 Domestic laws and regulations

As per the World Bank report entitled 'Women, Business and the Law 2022', there are only 18 countries that do not have laws that discriminate against women.[25] According to the study, 90% of the 190 countries studied had at least one law impeding women's access to economic opportunities. The laws that limit women's access to economic opportunities are different in their nature and scope. These legal and regulatory barriers mainly manifest themselves in three forms: (1) laws that impede women's access to finance and other productive resources; (2) laws that constrain employment and business opportunities; and (3) laws that affect women's social status and physical safety.

1.4.1.1.1 Domestic laws and regulations impeding access to finance and other productive resources

Access to finance refers to the ability to access basic financial services and institutions that allow a person or an entity to make formal payments, deposit money, and apply for loans.[26] It is a critical factor for business initiation and survival. Approximately 50% of the women in the world do not have a bank account or access to other financial services.[27] In the rural areas of low-income countries, only about 20% of bank account holders are women.[28] The International Finance Corporation estimates that almost 70% of women-owned small and medium-sized enterprises (SMEs) in developing countries do not have access to financial institutions and services.[29] International surveys have shown that women-led businesses

[25] The World Bank, 'Women, Business and the Law 2022' (2022) <https://openknowledge.worldbank.org/handle/10986/36945> accessed 6 June 2024.

[26] The World Bank, 'Financial Access' (2016) <www.worldbank.org/en/publication/gfdr/gfdr-2016/background/financial-access> accessed 23 September 2023.

[27] Asli Demirgüç-Kunt and others, *The Global Findex Database, 2021: Financial Inclusion, Digital Payments, and Resilience in the Age of Covid-19* (World Bank Publications 2021).

[28] UN Women, 'Innovation for Gender Equality' (2019) 5 <http://www.unwomen.org/-/media/headquarters/attachments/sections/library/publications/2019/innovation-for-gender-equality-en.pdf?la=en&vs=733> accessed 17 September 2022.

[29] IFC, 'Women-Owned SMEs: A Business Opportunity for Financial Institutions' <www.ifc.org/wps/wcm/connect/44b004b2-ed46-48fc-8ade-aa0f485069a1/WomenOwnedSMes+Report-Final.pdf?MOD=AJPERES&CVID=kiiZZDZ> accessed 17 September 2022.

have a much lower probability of obtaining credit and are charged higher interest rates for loans upon approval as compared to their men-led counterparts.[30]

Several laws and regulations can be seen as impeding women's access to finance and other productive resources. One example is that of the Democratic Republic of Congo, which, until 2017, had laws that forbade women from opening a bank account, registering a business, and even signing simple contracts.[31] Certain other countries such as Bolivia, Malawi, the Maldives, and Mauritius have recently repealed similar discriminatory laws. Yet, it is still possible to find such laws in other countries such as Bahrain and Uzbekistan. In Bahrain, for instance, the law designates the husband as head of the family and requires the wife to obtain his permission for any task such as opening a bank account or registering a business. In Chad, Guinea-Bissau, and Niger, married women need their husband's permission to open a bank account.[32]

Without a bank account, women cannot engage in financial transactions. Furthermore, they also cannot build a track record of their creditworthiness. Without such a record, women are unable to apply for capital. This barrier is exacerbated for women in countries with inheritance laws that favour men.

According to the Women, Business and the Lawreport, 33 countries have laws that do not provide the same inheritance rights to sons and daughters.[33] Unequal inheritance rights limit women's access to start-up capital and productive assets. The Civil Code of Iran, for example, provides for blatantly discriminatory inheritance laws that require the inheritance of sons to be twice as much as that of daughters.[34] Married women are particularly disadvantaged in several countries. In Iran, the law excludes real estate from the properties that a surviving wife may inherit.[35]

Article 145 of Algeria's Family Code puts married women in a position of disadvantage when it comes to succession and inheriting from their husbands. It establishes that married women only have the right to a quarter of the succession when their husbands have no descendants, while married men under the exact same circumstances have a right to half of the succession. Such a rule complicates widows' financial independence and reinforces prejudices against women owning property or wealth.[36] Limited rights to family assets imply that women wishing to start a

[30] Alexander Muravyev, Dorothea Schäfer, and Oleksandr Talavera, 'Entrepreneurs' gender and financial constraints: Evidence from international data' (2009) <https://econpapers.repec.org/article/eeejcecon/v_3a37_3ay_3a2009_3ai_3a2_3ap_3a270-286.htm> accessed 17 September 2022.

[31] World Bank Group, 'Women, Business and the Law 2019: A Decade of Reform' (2019) 11 <https://thedocs.worldbank.org/en/doc/702301554216687135005002 2019/original/WBLDECADEOFREFORM2019WEB0401.pdf> accessed 17 September 2022.

[32] The World Bank, 'Women's Financial Inclusion and the Law' <http://pubdocs.worldbank.org/en/610311522241094348/Financial-Inclusion.pdf> accessed 17 September 2022.

[33] The World Bank (n 31).

[34] The Civil Code of Iran 1928, s 6(1) art 907.

[35] Since 2009, a wife can receive the value of her share of an inheritance from the land of her deceased husband. However, she still cannot inherit the land itself. (The Civil Code of Iran 1928, s 6(4) arts 946, 948.)

[36] The People's Democratic Republic of Algeria Code de Famille 1984.

business may not have any collateral to access the credit needed to start or expand a business. Lack of collateral due to unfavourable inheritance laws and lack of a track record to reflect creditworthiness can erect formidable barriers for women to access finance. Inadequate physical and reputational collateral explains why most businesses owned by women are concentrated in less capital-intensive sectors.

Despite legislative advancements, a gender gap in land rights persists, with only 52 of 164 nations ensuring women's land rights in practice. Discriminatory religious and customary laws also hinder women's ability to inherit or acquire land, perpetuating their subordinate status.[37] This barrier is particularly severe for transgender women, as financial exclusion is prevalent among the transgender community. This is primarily because transgender women have historically faced significantly more restricted access to financial products and services from formal financial institutions compared to non-transgender women. Multiple factors can be blamed for this, some of which are their low financial literacy and awareness, lack of formal employment, unfriendly behaviour of bank staff and officers, insufficient provision of legal documents from the government, lack of access to relevant information, and lack of financial literacy programmes.[38] These challenges may be very similar for women with other compounding factors such as women with a disability.[39]

1.4.1.1.2 Domestic laws and regulations constraining employment and business opportunities

Gender biases in domestic laws affect women's participation in the paid economy, resulting mostly in 'horizontal' segregation of men and women in the labour market. 'Horizontal gender segregation' refers to the pattern where women are concentrated in fewer sectors or industries than men—such as tourism, agriculture, textiles and garments, and care services.[40] In turn, 'vertical gender segregation' (also known as the 'glass ceiling effect') refers to women's lack of representation in leadership and decision-making roles. Domestic laws, such as Article 85 of Madagascar's Labour Code, contribute to gender segregation by restricting women's employment in certain industries, particularly night work in industrial establishments. This restriction impedes women from working in certain industries but the law does not impose a similar restriction if women work with their

[37] Social Institutions and Gender Index (SIGI), 'SIGI 2019 Global Report: Transforming Challenges into Opportunities' (8 March 2019) <www.oecd.org/dev/sigi-2019-global-report-bc56d212-en.htm> accessed 6 June 2024.

[38] Rajesh Barik and Pritee Sharma, 'What Constraints Financial Inclusion for the Transgender Community? Field-Based Evidences from Odisha (India)' (2021) 13(1) Contemporary Voice of Dalit 66, 80.

[39] James Atta Peprah, Eric Atsu Avorkpo, and Evans Kulu, 'People with Disability and Access to Financial Services: Evidence from Ghana' (2023) 15(6) Regional Science Policy & Practice 1198.

[40] UNCTAD, 'Trade and Gender Linkages: The Gender Impact of Technological Upgrading in Agriculture' (2020) UNCTAD/DITC/2020/1 <https://unctad.org/webflyer/gender-impact-technological-upgrading-agriculture> accessed 17 September 2022.

family members. This waiver encourages women to seek employment within their families thus increasing women's dependency on family members.

Similar work restrictions are found in other countries—including Bangladesh,[41] Egypt,[42] Niger,[43] Malaysia,[44] India,[45] Pakistan,[46] and Croatia[47]—where labour laws prohibit women from working at night time.[48] These laws directly infringe on women's economic freedom to practise a career of their choosing. This significantly downplays women's ability to engage in various lucrative work that may require night working hours such as the entertainment industry. Another example is the Belarus Labour Code, which prohibits the employment of women in jobs considered to be strenuous or hazardous.[49] Article 60 of the code also prohibits women from working at night, except in cases of nursing, domestic labour, and such other activities, which are mainly low-paid professions. These laws reinforce the stereotypes that identify certain occupations as appropriate mainly for men; the problem lies in the fact that most professions associated with men attract better pay and social recognition. Moreover, such regulations ensure that female labour force participation remains concentrated in low-skilled activities, with little chance to access higher-value-added, male-dominated jobs. This gives rise to the phenomenon of 'feminization of labour', which refers to an increase in female employment typically in labour-intensive, low-value-added, low-wage activities that are only available with insecure working conditions.[50]

In many cases, women are the only provider for a household and such restrictive laws could disproportionately affect them by denying them the possibility to work at night and earn an extra income. These challenges are not only limited to cisgender women and are even worse for women who identify as transgender as they may face many adverse job outcomes due to workplace inequity. This lack of equity may be blamed on lack of trans-inclusive, non-discrimination policies and laws, trans-inclusive organizational cultures, and personal biases and stereotypes.[51] Studies have also reported that more than one in four transgender

[41] Bangladesh Factories Act 1965, art 65(1b); Shops and Establishments Act 1965, art 23.

[42] Labour Code of Egypt 1981 (Act No 137), art 152 (the prohibition does not apply, however, to 'female workers purely engaged in agriculture'); Labour Code for Overseas Territories 1952 (Law No 52-1322), art 159.

[43] Labour Code of Niger 1996 (Ordinance No 96-039), art 98; and Labour Code of Niger 1967 (Decree No 67-126/MFP/T), art 107.

[44] Malaysian Employment Act 1981 (No 265), s 34(1), 36 art 2B.

[45] Indian Factories Act 1948 (No 63), art 66(1b).

[46] Pakistan Factories Act 1923 (Amendment of 1987), s 23C(2); Pakistan Factories Act of 1934 (Amendment of 1987), s 45(1b).

[47] Croatian Labour Act 1995 (Text No 758), art 52.

[48] ILO, 'A Compendium of National Law and Practice' <www.ilo.org/public/english/standards/relm/ilc/ilc89/pdf/rep-iii-1b-c3.pdf> accessed 17 September 2020.

[49] Republic of Belarus Labour Code 1999, arts 262, 60.

[50] Guy Standing, 'Global Feminization Through Flexible Labor: A Theme Revisited' (1999) 27(3) World Development Elsevier 583, 602.

[51] Nickolas B Davis and Stephen T Yeung, 'Transgender Equity in the Workplace: A Systematic Review' (2022) 12(1) Sage Open <https://journals.sagepub.com/doi/10.1177/21582440221082863> accessed 6 June 2024.

people worldwide have lost their job due to bias and more than three-quarters have experienced some form of workplace discrimination in the form of refusal to hire, privacy violations, harassment, and physical and sexual violence, and that these are experienced at even higher rates by transgender people of colour.[52]

Such legal restrictions also extend to impeding women's access to business opportunities. One relevant example is found in Equatorial Guinea where a wife needs her husband's permission to sign a contract.[53] This severely impugns the agency of a woman to start a business as her consent is vitiated and directly hinged on the whim of her husband. Under the Eswatini Personal Law, a married woman cannot conclude a contract without her husband's permission, cannot be represented in civil suits, and cannot administer property.[54] This restriction on the right to conclude contracts includes restrictions on the ability to access bank loans, mortgages, and financial credit generally. These laws in a way relegate married women to the legal status of minors as they can only operate under the guardianship of their husbands.

Finally, lack of proper maternity benefits also restricts women's ability to avail themselves of economic opportunities. Several countries do not provide sufficient maternity and childcare leave thus exposing the female workforce to the risk of losing their employment or business opportunities. The United States ranks particularly low in this area as it is the only member of the Organisation for Economic Co-operation and Development (OECD) with no federally mandated paid maternity leave policy at the national level.[55] However, companies with over 50 employees have a legal obligation to offer up to 12 weeks of unpaid leave for 'expanding family' reasons under the Family and Medical Leave Act.[56] This falls short of the stipulated 14 weeks prescribed and recommended by the International Labour Organization (ILO) guidelines.[57] Insufficient leave allowance and lack of a national paid leave policy have resulted in women being fired from their jobs due to extended periods of absence or the flexibility required to manage work with childcare.[58]

[52] Brandon J Hill and others, 'Exploring Individual and Structural Factors Associated with Employment Among Young Transgender Women of Color Using a No-Cost Transgender Legal Resource Center' (2017) 2(1) Transgender Health 29.

[53] The World Bank (n 32).

[54] Eswatini Personal Status Law 2019 (No 15), art 61.

[55] Pew Research Center, 'Among 41 countries, only US lacks paid parental leave' <www.pewresearch.org/fact-tank/2019/12/16/u-s-lacks-mandated-paid-parental-leave/> accessed 17 September 2022.

[56] United States Family and Medical Leave Act 1993, s 102 (apart from a few companies that have amended their polices or certain state laws extending the scope to paid leave, the only exception at the federal level is the Federal Employee Paid Leave Act (FEPLA), which offers 12 weeks of paid parental leave for federal workers).

[57] ILO, 'Maternity Protection Convention' 183 (2000) <www.ilo.org/dyn/normlex/en/f?p=NORMLEXPUB:55:0::NO::P55_TYPE,P55_LANG,P55_DOCUMENT,P55_NODE:REV,en,C183,/Document> accessed 17 September 2022.

[58] *Myers v Hope Healthcare LLC*, Case no 2:13-cv-14459-SFC-MKM; *Panattony v Village of Frankfurt*, Case no 1:17-cv-06710; *Kimberlie Michelle Durham v. Rural/Metro Corporation*, Case no 4:16-CV-01604-ACA.

In the Democratic Republic of Congo, labour law restricts women from taking annual leave in the same year that they have taken maternity leave, which, although recognizing maternity rights, can have punitive effects on working mothers.[59] Annual and maternity leave have different purposes; annual leave allows employees to carry out further studies or have a rest period and maternity leave allows women to dedicate themselves completely to their childbearing responsibilities. For working mothers, the period of maternity leave is not a period of rest or leisure; it is, in fact, a period that requires women to engage in intense hard work and care-giving responsibilities. The possibility to take annual leave in the same year as maternity leave may allow working mothers a much-needed period of rest or an extended period to provide unpaid childcare.

1.4.1.1.3 Laws affecting women's social status

Iran's Civil Code grants the position of head of the family exclusively to husbands.[60] In addition, the code obliges women to fulfil the sexual needs of their husbands at all times.[61] These laws objectify women and discriminate against them in the most blatant manner. In Bahrain, a rapist may avoid punishment if he agrees to marry his victim.[62] Although this law is intended to protect women from the social stigma that may come from this bodily harm, the psychological effects of such a policy can be grave for women. This law allows the rapist to unilaterally initiate a divorce at a later point in time; hence, marrying the victim (even for a short period of time) is a straightforward way to avoid punishment. These considerations make women less likely to report rape and lead their lives with psychological scars that may jeopardize their self-esteem or confidence that is required to succeed or progress in their professional endeavours.

Women of colour, including Asian, black, and Hispanic women, may have an even deeper social disadvantage than racially/ethnically white women as studies have found that women with darker skin tones may face greater exposure to problems such as discrimination, abuse, poverty, negative perceptions and beliefs, and economic hardship. These problems are worsened when skin colour and gender are considered in conjunction with other compounding factors such as race and ethnicity.[63]

[59] Labour Code, Law No. 015/2002, s 130.

[60] Civil Code of Iran 1928.

[61] This is known as the requirement of *tamkin* (submission). A woman's refusal to engage in sexual activity with her husband constitutes *noshuz* (disobedience) and can disqualify her for maintenance rights.

[62] Bahrain Penal Code 1976, art 353.

[63] Krista M Perreira, Joshua Wassink, and Kathleen Mullan Harris, 'Beyond Race/Ethnicity: Skin Color, Gender, and the Health of Young Adults in the United States' (2019) 38(2) Popul Res Policy Rev 271.

1.4.1.2 Cultural and religious norms

Cultural and religious norms impact women in different ways in different countries. Some of these norms impact women's social status, while others directly infringe upon their employment or educational prospects. The cultural set-up in Jordan exemplifies how cultural perceptions can take precedence over the benefits of education. Jordanian women are among the most educated in the Middle East; they have even surpassed men, accounting for 53% of the country's university graduates.[64] However, these successes in education have not translated into their higher participation in the country's labour force or country's leadership roles. In 2018, Jordan had the lowest female labour participation rate of any country in the world which was not at war.[65]

Cultural factors, such as patriarchal family dynamics in Jordanian society, reinforce gender roles that limit women's involvement in decision-making and emphasize their domestic responsibilities.[66] A World Bank study has shown that around 60% of men disapprove of their wives working in mixed-gender environments; 70% of men disapprove of their wives returning after 5 pm; and 44% believe that working women expose themselves to unnecessary harassment.[67] Harassment in public spaces and a larger share of responsibilities at home, together with this cultural set-up, explain the very low female labour participation in Jordan.

Cultural norms can also mitigate women's access to productive resources. In Nigeria, 80% of dispositions of property are carried out under customary law.[68] Three major ethnic groups in Nigeria are the Igbo, Yoruba, and Hausa; each of them has a different set of rules regarding women's inheritance rights. In Igbo customary law, daughters and wives are considered personal property and therefore they have no right to succession regarding their father's movable or immovable property. In Yoruba customary law, daughters are entitled to their deceased father's property on the same terms as their brothers but widows cannot inherit their husband's estate as it is passed on to his heirs. As per Hausa customary norms, each daughter receives half the share of a son.[69] The common factor of these

[64] OECD, 'Women's Political Participation in Jordan: Barriers, Opportunities and Gender Sensitivity of Select Political Institutions' (2018) <www.oecd.org/mena/governance/womens-political-participation-in-jordan.pdf> accessed 6 June 2024.

[65] The World Bank, 'Hashemite Kingdom of Jordan: Understanding how gender norms in MNA impact female employment outcomes' (2018) <https://openknowledge.worldbank.org/bitstream/handle/10986/30947/ACS25170-PUBLIC-FULL-REPORT-Jordan-Social-Norms-June-1-2018-with-titlepg.pdf?sequence = 1&isAllowed=y> accessed 17 September 2022.

[66] Semiray Kasoolu and others, 'Female Labor in Jordan: A Systematic Approach to the Exclusion Puzzle' (Center for International Development at Harvard University) <https://growthlab.cid.harvard.edu/publications/female-labor-jordan-systematic-approach-exclusion-puzzle> accessed 17 September 2022.

[67] The World Bank (n 65).

[68] Joy Ezeilo, 'Law and practices relating to women's inheritance rights in Nigeria: an overview' (WomenAid Collective) <https://silo.tips/download/laws-and-practices-relating-to-womens-inheritance-rights-in-nigeria-an-overview> accessed 17 September 2022.

[69] Popoola Sulaiman Akorede and others, 'Abuses of Women in Inheritance Across Cultures: An Exploratory Study of Its Prevalence and Religious Panacea' (2017) 16(12) Chinese Business Review 620.

customary norms is that women do not enjoy the same inheritance rights as their male counterparts.

Moreover, families in some regions continue to marry off their minor daughters due to various cultural factors such as sanctions from their communities, family honour, and the increased dowry earnings received for marrying girls at an early age. Besides exposing girls to physical and sexual violence, child marriages cut short their academic and professional prospects as they are expected to take over family and household chores from a very young age leading to myriad struggles. Child marriages can also lead to early pregnancy, further blocking their ability to learn new skills, seek further education, or explore economic opportunities to gain financial independence. Without an income of their own, they are tied to a lifetime of dependency on their husbands.[70]

Religion, alongside culture, can limit women's financial independence, with gender-based physical segregation being a religious norm that separates women from men in public spaces.[71] Countries practising this religious norm maintain a strict system of physical segregation in every aspect of public life, including in public transportation and medical establishments.[72] This physical segregation largely impacts the ability of women to access public spheres and participate in business and economic activities. It bars women from participating in markets that are largely operated and regulated by men. It can also deteriorate women's self-confidence and esteem to venture out and explore educational or economic opportunities.

One prevalent form of social segregation is the observance of purdah. In Bangladesh, for example, purdah prescribes the pattern of exchange between men and women. It has three direct implications: the exclusion of women from almost all labour markets, their confinement within the household, and containment of their freedom to dress up or lead their lives the way they wish to do so. Purdah's restrictions on women's freedom of movement limit their access to employment opportunities, continuation of education, and creation of business networks.[73] Community purdah norms (mostly those mandating seclusion), along with a traditional division of labour assigning domestic work to women, are the reasons why women are less likely than men to participate in paid work in certain countries. This can be seen directly in Bangladesh where, despite the trade liberalization of

[70] UNICEF, 'Child marriage around the world' <www.unicef.org/stories/child-marriage-around-world> accessed 18 September 2022.

[71] US Department of State, 'Saudi Arabia Country Specific Information' <https://web.archive.org/web/20131211183846/http://travel.state.gov/travel/cis_pa_tw/cis/cis_1012.html> accessed 18 September 2022.

[72] Centre for Human Rights in Iran, 'Gender Segregation Violates the Rights of Women in Iran' <www.iranhumanrights.org/2014/09/gender-segregation/> accessed 18 September 2022.

[73] Souad Adnane, 'Moving freely: Moving closer to gender equality' (*World Bank Blogs*, 2019) <https://blogs.worldbank.org/opendata/moving-freely-moving-closer-gender-equality> accessed 28 September 2020.

the 1990s, the growth of the garment industry, and successful campaigns to close the gap between men and women in primary and secondary education, female labour force participation has improved only modestly and is among the lowest in developing countries.[74]

1.4.1.3 Social and behavioural constrains

In most countries, women primarily handle reproductive and unpaid work, spending at least twice as much time on unpaid work as men. This time poverty hinders their economic opportunities and slows their progress as they juggle family and professional responsibilities.[75]

In Japan, for instance, while women spend an average of 7 hours and 34 minutes on household chores each day, men spend only 1 hour and 23 minutes on an average.[76] These numbers show that women are expected to perform most of the household work. Balancing home and work responsibilities was seen as a significant barrier by 44% of women business owners in Nigeria and 37% in Argentina.[77] According to a study by the ILO, women in Tanzania tend to withdraw from employment at an earlier age than men due to their care-giving responsibilities. In many countries and households, women are still expected to leave their jobs once they get married or once they have children.[78] More than any other factor, marital status seems to represent the biggest barrier when it comes to women's economic integration.[79] In traditional societies, strong prejudices due to lack of affordable childcare and social services reinforce the notion that a man should be the main source of family income, while the woman should devote her time to domestic tasks.

Japan's female labour force participation rate has increased from one of the lowest in the 1990s to above the OECD average at 52.7% in 2018, thanks to its government policies promoting women empowerment, such as expanding childcare

[74] Niaz Asadullah and Zaki Wahhaj, 'Missing from the Market: *Purdah* Norm and Women's Paid Work Participation in Bangladesh' (IZA Institute of Labour Economics 2016) <www.iza.org/publications/dp/10463/missing-from-the-market-purdah-norm-and-womens-paid-work-participation-in-bangladesh> accessed 18 September 2022.

[75] Diane Whitmore Schanzenbach and Ryan Nunn, 'The 51%: Driving Growth Through Women's Economic Participation' (Brookings 2017) <www.brookings.edu/multi-chapter-report/the-51-percent-driving-growth-through-womens-economic-participation/> accessed 4 October 2022.

[76] Editorial, 'Social norms hinder women's career growth' *The Japan Times* (2019) <www.japantimes.co.jp/news/2019/03/22/national/social-norms-hinder-womens-career-growth/> accessed 18 September 2022.

[77] OECD, 'Unlocking Markets for Women to Trade' (2015) <www.oecd-ilibrary.org/content/publication/aa9eaa55-en> accessed 18 September 2022.

[78] Deniz Kagniciouglu, 'The Role of Women in Working Life in Turkey' (2017) 226 WIT Transactions on Ecology and The Environment 349, 358.

[79] Ipek Ilkkaracan, 'Analysis of Istanbul Labour Market from a Gender Equality Perspective' (International Labour Organization 2016) <www.ilo.org/wcmsp5/groups/public/---europe/---ro-geneva/---ilo-ankara/documents/publication/wcms_490144.pdf> accessed 18 September 2022.

facilities and removing tax deductions that discouraged full-time employment.[80] However, challenges persist for women's full integration into the economy. For example, despite Japan's flexible paid childcare leave policy for fathers, only 2% of fathers take such leave as compared to 83% of mothers. Moreover, around 68% of women quit their jobs fully after marriage or birth. Cultural and societal expectations are the main reasons that explain these numbers as procuring employment is seen as an additional task for women.[81]

Women engaged in businesses also experience a lack of respect from their male business partners; many have observed that their male business partners' or male clients' behaviour towards them reflects a degree of chauvinism. At times, women have felt that they are not taken seriously merely because of their gender and have received refusals from clients to do business with them due to lack trust of their skills, capacity, and dedication to their businesses. A female entrepreneur based in Mexico affirms that investors sometimes discard the possibility of investing in a women-owned business because they are not confident that a woman would be able to keep up with the demands of the business due to her family responsibilities and pressures.[82] In addition, for transgender women business owners, additional hurdles and unique obstacles can arise as they face greater levels of discrimination, social stigma, hostility from others, and even more limited access to resources and information.[83]

1.4.1.4 Access to education

According to UNESCO, around 132 million girls in the world are still out of school, including 34.3 million of primary school age, 30 million of lower-secondary school age, and 67.4 million of upper-secondary school age.[84] Despite decades of progress, girls around the world are still unable to go to school at the same rate as boys due to a range of barriers. A UNESCO report notes that only 66% of countries have achieved parity among boys and girls in primary school education. The problem worsens as girls grow older, as only 45% of countries have parity in lower secondary schools, and this number reduces to about 25% in upper secondary schools. These disparities highlight the failure of countries throughout the world to enforce the commitments they have made under international treaties that mandate gender

[80] The World Bank, 'Labour force participation rate, female (% of female population ages 15+) (modelled ILO estimate)—Japan, OECD members' (2020) <https://data.worldbank.org/indicator/SL.TLF.CACT.FE.ZS?locations = JP-OE> accessed 1 October 2020.

[81] OECD, 'Closing the Gender Gap: Act Now' (2016) <www.oecd-ilibrary.org/social-issues-migration-health/close-the-gender-gap-now_9789264179370-en> accessed 18 September 2022.

[82] Interview with a Mexico City business owner (details withheld, 15 October 2020).

[83] Christian N Thoroughgood, Katina Sawyer, and Jennica R Webster, 'Creating a Trans-Inclusive Workplace', Harvard Business Review (March–April 2020) <https://hbr.org/2020/03/creating-a-trans-inclusive-workplace> accessed 6 June 2024.

[84] UNESCO, 'Girls' education Gender equality in education benefits every child' <www.unicef.org/education/girls-education> accessed 18 September 2022.

parity in education.[85] The reasons for this disparity are many, including poverty, child marriage, lack of infrastructure and safety in schools, and gender-based violence. Lack of educational opportunities impedes women's participation in labour markets; it keeps them away from gaining the socio-emotional life skills necessary to navigate and adapt to a changing world; it restricts their ability to make decisions about their lives and families; and it diminishes their capability to contribute to their communities and economies.

Despite achieving positive results such as an 18% increase in net primary school enrolment of girls between 2000 and 2012, the Republic of Ghana still has socio-cultural and economic factors that impede girls' full access to basic education.[86] For every three boys who complete senior high school, only two girls do so. Besides, the transition rate from junior high to senior high for girls is only 51.2%, as compared to 65.1% for boys. Although several factors play into this reality, the societal favouring of boys' over girls' education is one of the main drivers for this gap between men and women, and it widens as students progress to higher levels.[87] In Ghana, patrilineal family structures and poverty lead to a preference for sons' education over daughters', with many families viewing girls' education as unnecessary and a distraction from household chores.[88]

A World Trade Organization (WTO) study confirms that when parents cannot finance the schooling costs for all their children, they prefer to save on the cost by keeping their girl child out of school.[89] This is mainly because of cultural stereotypes and the lack of job opportunities for women. In certain countries, boys are seen as an asset, whereas girls are seen to belong to their husband's family after they are married. Hence, investing in boys is considered a good investment. In addition, in countries where job opportunities for women are scarce, restricted, or low-paid, the opportunity cost of schooling is perceived to outweigh the potential returns from their education. Studies have shown that parents have higher expectations from boys than from girls to eventually work in high-paid science, technology, engineering, and mathematics (STEM) jobs, independent of the academic performance of their children.[90]

[85] Eg UNESCO, 'Global Education Monitoring Report Gender Review: Meeting our commitments to gender equality in education' (2018) <https://en.unesco.org/gem-report/2018_gender_review> accessed 18 September 2022.

[86] Sharon Wolf and others, 'Barriers to School Attendance and Gender Inequality: Empirical Evidence From a Sample of Ghanaian Schoolchildren' (2016) 11(2) Research in Comparative & International Education <https://journals.sagepub.com/doi/10.1177/1745499916632424> accessed 6 June 2024.

[87] George Prince, 'Education Inequality: How Patriarchy and Policy Collide in Ghana' (2015) 5(7) International Journal of Humanities and Social Science 11.

[88] Aurora Rubio, 'Factors that Impact Girls' Education in Ghana' (2018) 9(1) Leadership Research <https://viurrspace.ca/bitstream/handle/10613/6204/Rubio.pdf?sequence=1> accessed 18 September 2022.

[89] WTO, 'Women and Trade 2020' (2020) <www.wto.org/english/tratop_e/womenandtrade_e/womenandtrade_e.htm> accessed 18 September 2022.

[90] Victor Lavy and Edith Sand, 'On the origins of gender gaps in human capital: Short- and long-term consequences of teachers' biases' (2018) <www.sciencedirect.com/science/article/abs/pii/S004727271

Biases against women permeate through and pervade the content of education as well. In Kuwait, for instance, girls are taught about the roles of women as wives and mothers as part of their educational curricula.[91] A course on household management is taught to girls in primary and secondary public schools with the module mainly focused on learning household chores such as cooking, cleaning, and sewing.[92] Schools make these modules an essential or a highly desirable requirement for female students, while boys are discouraged or even laughed at if they choose to study that module. On the other hand, a girl's entry into a STEM-related module can be frowned on or looked down on.

These reasons ensure that women remain under-represented in the STEM disciplines. Lack of access to STEM educational opportunities reduces potential job opportunities for women, mainly in lucrative sectors. Without an increase in their educational and skill levels, women cannot increase their employment share in higher productivity trading firms that pay more, have better working conditions, and provide safety nets and benefits including health insurance and pensions.

1.4.1.5 Digital divide between women and men

In an increasingly digitally enabled society, a significant challenge that remains is the digital inclusion of women. The gender digital divide is the 'measurable gap between women and men in their access to, use of and ability to influence, contribute to and benefit from ICTs (information and communication technologies)'.[93] This includes access to and use of the internet, ownership of a computer or mobile phone, and representation in the technology sector.

As per the Gender Digital Divide Index (GDDI), which is a metric that measures the extent to which the internet is accessible and affordable to all in a way that contributes to social and economic progress, in developing countries, the socio-economic gaps between men and women have deepened as a result of digital transformation. According to the GDDI report of 2022, the ITU (International

8301750> accessed 18 September 2022; Maaike van der Vleuten, Stephanie Steinmetz, and Herman van de Werfhorst, 'Gender norms and STEM: the importance of friends for stopping leakage from the STEM pipeline' (2019) <www.researchgate.net/publication/331764798_Gender_norms_and_STEM_the_importance_of_friends_for_stopping_leakage_from_the_STEM_pipeline> accessed 18 September 2022.

[91] CEDAW, 'Concluding observations of the Committee on the Elimination of Discrimination against Women (Kuwait)' (United Nations Committee on the Elimination of Discrimination against Women 2011) <www2.ohchr.org/english/bodies/cedaw/docs/co/KUWAITCO30.pdf> accessed 18 September 2022.

[92] Human Rights Council, 'Report of the Working Group on the issue of discrimination against women in law and in practice on its mission to Kuwait' (United Nations Office of the High Commissioner for Human Rights 2017) <www.refworld.org/docid/5947d4ec4.html> accessed 18 September 2022.

[93] Tina Power, 'The gender digital divide and COVID-19: Towards feminist internet regulations in Southern Africa' (African Declaration on Internet Rights and Freedoms 2020) <https://africaninternetrights.org/sites/default/files/Tina_Power.pdf> accessed 18 September 2022.

Telecommunication Union) found that in 2021, 'nearly two-thirds of the world-wide population had used the internet and digital technologies to access social media, education, healthcare, jobs, financial services, civic engagement, government services, and much more'.[94] However, the ITU also estimated that over 2.9 billion people are still offline and 96% of them live in developing countries. Additionally, the report found that while the gender digital divide is narrowing on a global scale and has been almost eliminated in most developed countries (89% of men and 88% of women online), the gap between men and women persists and is in fact much larger in poorer countries (31% of men compared to 19% of women) and in landlocked developing countries (38% of men compared to 27% of women). The regions with the most pronounced gender digital divide are Africa (35% of women compared to 24% of men) and the Arab states (68% of men compared to 56% of women).[95]

These inequalities present significant barriers to women's economic empowerment and equality. ICTs offer women access to the new digital economy, financial inclusion opportunities through financial technologies such as open banking, training and educational opportunities, inclusion in political processes, access to e-commerce opportunities, health care, and even medical information.[96] With a steep learning curve and the high costs of internet access in many developing countries, women find it harder to continue working remotely and are therefore further excluded from the economy.[97]

There are many contributing factors that lead to this divide. One of these factors is the cultural set-up. In India, many local governance bodies (panchayats) have banned the use of mobile phones for women, especially for girls under the age of 18, citing reasons such as distraction from studies.[98] Another factor is affordability, which remains the biggest barrier to access to technology.[99] Women employed in lesser paying jobs may not be able to afford access to the internet and smart phones. Moreover, women are generally less likely to be digitally literate, not only for technical activities (eg coding and designing) but also for simple tasks (eg

[94] Gender Digital Divide Index (GDDI) Report 2022, 7 <https://gddindex.com/wp-content/uploads/2022/02/GDDI-Report-2022.pdf> accessed 18 September 2022.

[95] Press release ITU, '2.9 billion people still offline' (30 November 2021) <www.itu.int/en/mediacentre/Pages/PR-2021-11-29-FactsFigures.aspx> accessed 18 September 2022.

[96] Hayet Kerras, 'The Impact of the Gender Digital Divide on Sustainable Development: Comparative Analysis between the European Union and the Maghreb' (2020) 12(8) Sustainability 3347.

[97] Media Institute of Southern Africa Zimbabwe, 'Internet access a fundamental human right—data must fall!' (MISA Zimbabwe 2020) <http://zimbabwe.misa.org/2020/04/08/internet-access-a-fundamental-human-right-data-must-fall> accessed 29 September 2020.

[98] Al Jazeera and Reuters, 'India: Banning women from owning mobile phones' (Al Jazeera 2016) <www.aljazeera.com/news/2016/02/26/india-banning-women-from-owning-mobile-phones/> accessed 18 September 2022.

[99] A4AI, 'Affordability Report 2019' (World Wide Web Foundation 2019) <https://a4ai.org/research/affordability-report/affordability-report-2019/> accessed 18 September 2022.

using applications, sending or receiving emails, and searching for information).[100] According to cross-national skills assessments women in numerous countries are 25% less likely than men to know how to leverage ICTs for basic purposes, such as using simple arithmetic formulas in a spreadsheet and men are around four times more likely than women to have advanced ICT skills such as the ability to programme computers or code a language.[101] In some cases, women prefer to stay away from online platforms or accessing the internet as they are increasingly exposed to all forms of online harassment, bullying, and violence. The latest studies show that during the global health pandemic of 2020, there was a surge in online violence and bullying against women.[102] Owing to these factors, ICTs and related sectors continue to be male-dominated, and the onset of the global health pandemic has only made it worse.

1.4.2 Barriers at borders

1.4.2.1 Lack of access to trade-related information

Trade information is a precondition for empowering small businesses and maintaining profitable cross-border operations through informed decision-making. In several countries, mainly in the developing world, information on rules and regulations is neither clear nor easily available. The unavailability of resources in vernacular languages creates a problem, especially for those with limited access to education and technology.[103] Research shows that lack of knowledge about cross-border trade regulations and procedures is more prevalent among female than male traders.[104] Women traders face particular constraints in accessing information regarding compliance with complicated border procedures, tariffs, exchange-rate fluctuations, customs procedures, product standards, and other

[100] UNESCO, 'I'd blush if I could. Closing Gender Divides in Digital Skills through Education' (2019) <https://2b37021f0f4a464083520a3c1b7c2aab.filesusr.com/ugd/04bfff_06ba0716e0604f51a40b4474d4829ba8.pdf> accessed 18 September 2022.

[101] UNESCO, 'Accountability in Education: Meeting Our Commitments', Global Education Monitoring Report (2017) <https://unesdoc.unesco.org/ark:/48223/pf0000259338> accessed 18 September 2022.

[102] Ingrid Brudvig, Chenai Chair, and Adriane van der Wilk, 'Covid-19 and increasing domestic violence against women: The pandemic of online gender-based violence' (World Wide Web Foundation) <http://webfoundation.org/docs/2020/07/WWWF-Submission-COVID-19-and-the-increase-of-domestic-violence-against-women-1.pdf> accessed 18 September 2022.

[103] Rae Lesser Blumberg, Joyce Malaba, and Lis Meyers, 'Women Cross-Border Traders in Southern Africa: Contributions, Constraints, and Opportunities in Malawi and Botswana' <www.agrilinks.org/sites/default/files/resource/files/ICBT%20Gender%20Assessment%20Report_Final_4-30-2016.pdf> accessed 18 September 2022.

[104] Deutsche Gesellschaft für Internationale Zusammenarbeit (GIZ) GmbH, 'Trade and Gender—exploring a reciprocal relationship: Approaches to mitigate and measure gender-related trade impacts' (German Cooperation 2014) <www.oecd.org/dac/gender-development/GIZ_Trade%20and%20Gender_Exploring%20a%20reciprocal%20relationship.pdf> accessed 18 September 2022.

regulations. Information relating to border taxes and procedures is critical for businesses to make economically sound and well-informed business decisions. Lack of this information for businesses implies that decisions may be made without full knowledge of the market realities; this can reduce their profit margins or result in a complete loss of earnings if they are dealing in perishable goods.[105] Hence, this information is essential if trade is to be used as a tool for economic empowerment and for increasing women's participation in the global market.

Lack of information exacerbates the chances of economic exploitation and coercion as border officials often take advantage of this information asymmetry. Border officials can exploit the lack of transparency surrounding trade procedures to generate uncertainty and coerce traders to pay informal fees at the risk of having their goods seized. Due to low access to ICTs among traders in Tanzania, for example, women traders often do not have timely access to valuable price and product information, which exposes them to the risk of exploitation by better informed intermediaries.[106] However, Tanzanian women are not alone in this struggle. The inability to access information prior to arriving at a border-crossing can compel cross-border traders to rely on border agents to provide this information.

Low rates of education, the digital divide, and lack of access to business networks can also be blamed for this barrier. In Bangladesh and India, women are often excluded from and even discouraged from participating in trade associations, trade chambers, trade fairs, and trade promotion training, all of which are often a significant source of such information for traders.[107] Women traders and employees are discouraged (due to cultural reasons or heavy household responsibilities) from leveraging information from business networking opportunities that cater in most countries to businesses owned and managed by men. This barrier is even more formidable for women traders with visual impairment, who cannot access information published in print form or on digital platforms that are not available to them in an accessible format. This is not merely an inconvenience for them but also a significant barrier that can hinder their capacity to access trade-related information.

1.4.2.2 Tariff and non-tariff barriers to trade in goods as well as services

High tariffs disproportionately impact women businesses, consumers, and employees. Evidence from the United States suggests that women consumers face

[105] Chelsea Ruiter, Lance Hadley and Queena Li, 'Impacts of Non-Tariff Barriers for Women Small Scale Cross-Border Traders on the Kenya-Uganda Border' (Sauti Africa 2017) <https://sautiafrica.org/wp-content/uploads/2017/03/REV-4-Web-Impacts-of-Non-Tariff-Barriers-for-Women-Small-Scale-Cross-Border-Traders-on-the-Kenya-Uganda-Border.pdf> accessed 18 September 2022.

[106] UNCTAD, 'BORDERLINE: Women in informal cross-border trade in Malawi, the United Republic of Tanzania and Zambia' (2018) UNCTAD/DITC/2018/3 <https://unctad.org/en/PublicationsLibrary/ditc2018d3_en.pdf> accessed 18 September 2022.

[107] Talajeh Livani, Nadeem Rizwan, and Sanjay Kathuria, 'Inclusive Regional Trade: Promoting the Economic Empowerment of Women in the BBIN Region' (2019) 4(1) ANTYAJAA: Indian Journal of Women and Social Change <https://journals.sagepub.com/doi/10.1177/2455632719836801> accessed 6 June 2024.

higher border tariffs than male consumers.[108] The average applied tariff rates on women-specific products are higher than the average applied tariff rates on men-specific products. One such product is apparel, a product with most consumers being women and which amounts to about 75% of the total tariff burden on US households. A WTO study found that custom duties on the import of garments remain stubbornly high compared to other manufactured goods. This tax disparity—that disproportionately impacts industries where both the majority of the workforce and the consumers are women—is referred to as the 'pink tariff'.[109] The differentiation in tariffs is not designed with the purpose of harming women; yet textiles and agriculture continue to face higher tariffs perhaps because these industries mainly employ low-wage workers and hence tariffs are used to reduce their comparative advantage in that respect. The majority of these workers are women as they hold a disproportionate number of jobs in the garment industry, particularly in the developing world.[110]

The majority of women-owned or women-managed SMEs are engaged in the disproportionately taxed textiles, clothing, and agricultural sectors. A study from India shows that products produced largely by women face on average 6 percentage point higher tariffs than products produced by men in export markets. In 2012, goods produced by women in India had an average tariff of 13%, whereas those produced by men had an average tariff of 7.8%. This gap in tariffs faced by Indian women exporters is, to a large extent, driven by women's high employment share in the agriculture and textiles sectors.[111]

In addition to tariff barriers, modern barriers to trade often take the form of non-tariff measures (NTMs). NTMs, such as sanitary and phytosanitary standards (SPS) or technical barriers to trade (TBT), tend to have a significant impact on the industries that are relevant for women's businesses, such as agriculture and textiles.[112] These barriers can be imposed in the form of certification costs, customs paperwork and delays, lack of transparency in the regulatory environment, shipping procedures and delays, and supply chain governance issues. A WTO report confirms that about 66% of women-owned exporting companies reported facing difficulties with NTMs, as compared to 51% of men-owned firms.[113] The most cited problems by women-owned SMEs are the arbitrary behaviour of customs

[108] Arthur Gailes and others, 'Gender and Income Inequality in United States Tariff Burden' (US International Trade Commission 2018) <www.usitc.gov/publications/332/working_papers/ggst_-_gender_and_income_inequality_in_tariffs.pdf> accessed 18 September 2022.

[109] WTO (n 89).

[110] ibid.

[111] Adelina Mendoza, Gaurav Nayyar, and Roberta Piermartini, 'Are the "Poor" Getting Globalized?' (World Bank 2018) <https://openknowledge.worldbank.org/handle/10986/30576> accessed 18 September 2022.

[112] Ghada Ahmed, 'Global Value Chains, Economic Upgrading and Gender in the Call Center Industry' in Cornelia Startiz and José G Reis (eds), *Global Value Chains, Economic Upgrading and Gender in the Call Center Industry* (Duke 2013).

[113] WTO (n 89).

officers, reckless handling of goods during inspections, unnecessary delays during inspections, demands for bribes or other informal payments, and the need to submit a large number of different documents.

The main problem with NTMs is that they often lead to fixed costs which do not vary with the number of products exported by a business. NTMs increase the compliance costs associated with procedures, regulations, and standards and these costs can be particularly burdensome for SMEs with little experience in foreign trade and scarce resources to bear the additional cost burden.[114] As compared to large multinational firms, SMEs with their smaller basket of exports and imports tend to have fewer resources and a lower threshold for absorbing trade costs and the associated risks. This implies that fixed trade costs often make up a larger share of the unit cost of their goods when compared to their rivals who export larger volumes. SMEs often do not have specialized teams to handle border procedures and are even more exposed to costs derived from cumbersome and lengthy administrative procedures. This, together with the finding that women are more likely to own SMEs with smaller profit margins compared to large multinational companies, suggests that NTMs affect women's businesses more severely than businesses owned by men. Given that female-owned businesses are usually smaller and less capital-intensive than male-owned businesses, female-owned businesses tend to suffer disproportionally from NTMs.[115]

Moreover, women working in service-based industries continue to face high and formidable barriers especially involving their temporary movement from one country to another as low-skilled workers. This challenge is significant as almost 30% of the women workforce is employed in service-based industries and trade in services faces much higher barriers than trade in goods. In addition, women are mostly employed in labour-intensive services that require physical proximity between providers and consumers, which means that women face a high proximity burden when offering cross-border services. These services require the presence of a service provider in the importing country. This mode of supply via the presence of natural persons continues to face significant trade barriers. Temporary mobility offers enormous opportunities for women's participation; however, most of the services that are liberalized under the WTO's General Agreement on Trade in Services (GATS) framework through Mode 4[116] are mainly reserved for highly

[114] WTO, 'Financial Inclusion and the GATS: Barriers to Financial Inclusion and Trade in Services' (2014) Note by the Secretariat, Committee on Trade in Financial Services, S/FIN/W/88/Add.1, 13 <https://docs.wto.org/dol2fe/Pages/SS/directdoc.aspx?filename = q:/S/FIN/W88.pdf&Open=True> accessed 18 September 2022.

[115] OECD, 'Women's Entrepreneurship: Issues and Policies' (2nd OECD Conference of Ministers Responsible for Small and Medium-Sized Enterprises, 2004) <chrome-extension://efaidnbmnnnibpcajpcglclefindmkaj/https://www.oecd.org/cfe/smes/31919215.pdf> accessed 24 September 2023.

[116] For more details on GATS Mode 4, see WTO, 'Movement of natural persons (mode 4)' <www.wto.org/english/tratop_e/serv_e/mouvement_persons_e/mouvement_persons_e.htm#:~:text=Under%20the%20General%20Agreement%20on,in%20the%20territory%20of%20another> accessed 6 June 2024.

qualified professionals and senior business categories.[117] With the majority of these roles going to men, multiple restrictions such as immigration, administrative, procedural, eligibility, and licensing requirements still impede this mode of delivery, and these restrictions by their very nature are often changeable or arbitrary and cannot lead to predictable market access.

Many service sectors are female-dominated; one such sector is care-giving and nursing, which requires a specific type of accreditation (the accreditation requirement changes depending on the country where the employment is being offered). Therefore, even skilled migrant women in OECD countries experience poor labour market integration despite their educational attainment.[118] Mutual Recognition Agreements (MRAs), either bilaterally or plurilaterally, represent an instrument to harmonize these standards for professional qualifications. They are allowed under WTO's GATS as a deviation from the most-favoured-nation requirement (which prohibits discrimination between trading partners). However, most developed countries have had very limited participation in MRAs and continue to act as standard-setters with respect to setting the requirements for qualifications and credentials.[119]

1.4.2.3 Physical and economic violence

Cross-border women traders experience economic coercion at borders. Women face economic coercion in various forms; these range from gender-based discrimination in the processing of documentation, delays in releasing consignments, and unwarranted impounding of goods, to bribery and corruption including demands for informal fees. One study reports that over half of female cross-border traders experience economic violence by border officials, police officials, and third-party intermediaries.[120] Violence against women can also be manifested in physical and sexual forms. Studies have found that women experience physical violence in various forms, such as rape and sexual harassment (sexual touching, groping, stripping), abusive behaviour (insults and spitting by police officials), verbal threats of harassment and rape, and demands for sexual favours in exchange for favoured treatment at the border.

[117] Inter-agency Network on Women and Gender Equality, 'Gender Equality & Trade Policy' (2011) Women Watch 10 <www.un.org/womenwatch/feature/trade/gender_equality_and_trade_policy.pdf> accessed 1 April 2020.

[118] International Organization for Migration, 'Harnessing Knowledge on the Migration of Highly Skilled Women' (2014) <https://publications.iom.int/books/harnessing-knowledge-migration-highly-skilled-women> accessed 18 September 2022.

[119] Simonetta Zarrilli, 'Moving professionals beyond national borders: mutual recognition agreements and the GATS' (UNCTAD 2005) <https://unctad.org/system/files/official-document/ditctncd20052_en.pdf> accessed 18 September 2022.

[120] Jessica Jacobson and Susan Joekes, 'Violence Against Women Traders at Border Crossings' (UK Aid Work and Opportunities for Women 2019) <chrome-extension://efaidnbmnnnibpcajpcglclefindmkaj/https://assets.publishing.service.gov.uk/government/uploads/system/uploads/attachment_data/file/876256/Query-31-VAW-Traders.pdf> accessed 24 September 2023.

A study from Southern Africa describes how women are at times forced to create transactional sexual relationships with border officials as a 'coping mechanism' to mitigate the risks of sexual violence and harassment by different perpetrators.[121] This refers to an arrangement where women traders are forced to develop 'romantic' relationships with border officials to protect themselves from sexual violence by other men at the border and economic coercion by border officials.[122] Another study in Africa found that more than 70% of cross-border women traders face physical threats on a daily basis.[123]

A World Bank study confirms that in Africa's Great Lakes region, women traders have reported feeling physically threatened by male officials or pressured to offer unofficial payments to male customs officials and third-party intermediaries. At border crossings, the study shows that female traders pay noticeably higher taxes and bribes than their male counterparts; the goods are delayed for longer than goods being traded at border crossings; and they spend more money on transportation to get through the border crossings as they opt for safer means to do so.[124] Women business owners in many countries have reported that corruption is pervasive at border crossings. While this impacts both men and women, it can expose women to harassment or abuse to a greater extent.

There can be different perpetrators of such violence at borders, ranging from border and customs officials, police officials, and third-party intermediaries (agents, smugglers, transport workers), to other male traders. The key reasons that trigger this violence at border crossings include stereotypical behaviours imposing stigma on women for trading across borders, women's lack of access to information about taxes and fees, information asymmetries around fluctuating exchange rates or border taxes, lack of familiarity with procedures and complexities with different financing instruments, and lack of mechanisms to enforce required regulations.[125] Another reason can be the unsafe infrastructure and facilities at borders. In developing countries, inadequate and unsafe infrastructure means poor lighting, unsafe accommodation for overnight stays if required, unsafe and unhygienic sanitation services (eg women-only toilets with lockable doors), and lack of maternity-related facilities such as feeding, family rooms, and childcare facilities. Other infrastructural deficiencies can include lack of banking facilities, poorly equipped help desks,

[121] USAID, 'Toolkit for Integrating GBV Prevention and Response into Economic Growth Projects' (2014) <www.usaid.gov/sites/default/files/documents/1865/USAID%20Toolkit%20GBV%20EG%20Final%209-22-14.pdf> accessed 18 September 2022.

[122] Blumberg, Malaba, and Meyers (n 103).

[123] Ruiter, Hadley and Li (n 105).

[124] Heidi Stensland Warren, Maria Liungman, and Aileen Yang, 'What's it like for women to trade across borders?' (World Bank 2019) <https://blogs.worldbank.org/trade/whats-it-women-trade-across-borders> accessed 18 September 2022.

[125] Kate Higgins and Liz Turner, 'Brief 3: Integrating poverty and social analysis into Aid for Trade programmes: trade facilitation and trade-related infrastructure' (UK DFID Aid for Trade: Promoting Inclusive Growth and Poverty Reduction Programme 2010) <https://assets.publishing.service.gov.uk/media/57a08b1f40f0b652dd000aee/trade-brief3.pdf> accessed 18 September 2022.

and the absence of female security forces for physical inspections and security issues. For instance, there are once-a-week makeshift bazaars/markets at certain specified points on zero lines of the India–Bangladesh border known as '*haats*', that allow people residing near the border of both countries to trade with each other without having to pay any customs duties. Women who predominately engage in this exchange find hurdles due to the predominance of male supervising officers and security personnel in these areas.[126] The almost complete absence of women officials at these border points is a powerful deterrent for most women in the region.

Inadequate transportation facilities to and from borders also constitute a significant difficulty. Women experience a range of violent acts during travel to and from borders. These instances usually take place on buses, 'lifts', trains, and kombis/mini-vans and happen in the form of theft of goods and cash, sexual harassment, verbal abuse from touts and drivers, extortion by police and customs officials, and harassment and theft by transport operators.[127] These difficulties deter women from engaging in formal cross-border trading and force them to opt instead for informal routes of trading or leaving the trade altogether. This explains why a vast majority of informal cross-border traders in many developing countries are women. In Southern Africa, this number is as high as approximately 70% and 60% in Western Africa.[128] Engagement in informal routes worsens the problems that women face, as informal border crossings pose heightened risks of coercion and violence by smugglers and intermediaries. All these difficulties can lead to women giving up their economic activities or working with male colleagues that then cuts their profit margin. Hiring porters or trusting a male business partner can eat into profits and prevent women from acting independently, especially if doing so requires going out at night.

1.4.3 Barriers across borders

1.4.3.1 Mobility restrictions

A WTO study confirms that women are significantly less likely to move out of their country of residence for economic and professional reasons and that family migration patterns show that women's mobility is largely dominated by men's professional prospects.[129] Inherently patriarchal legal systems explain this finding.

[126] Nisha Taneja and others, 'Trade Facilitation Measures to Enhance Participation of Women in Cross-border Trade in BBIN' (Crier 2018) <chrome-extension://efaidnbmnnnibpcajpcglclefindmkaj/https://www.icrier.org/pdf/Cross-border_Trade_in_BBIN-Jan-2018.pdf> accessed 24 September 2023.

[127] Olga Sasunkevich, *Informal Trade, Gender and the Border Experience* (Routledge 2015).

[128] Centre for International Governance Innovation, 'Reshaping Trade through Women's Economic Empowerment: Mainstreaming Gender in the Face of Pervasive Inequality' (2018) <www.cigionline.org/sites/default/files/documents/Women%20and%20Trade.pdf> accessed 18 September 2022.

[129] WTO (n 89).

Several countries have imposed restrictions on the international mobility of women; these restrictions impede their access to economic opportunities outside their country of residence. In Iran, for example, women must obtain their husband's approval to travel abroad or even to secure a passport.[130] Articles 1005 and 1114 of the Civil Code in Iran state that men reserve the exclusive right to determine the place of their wives' residence.[131] Article 18 of the Passport Law in Iran requires women to obtain written consent from their husbands to be issued with a passport. Moreover, Article 19 of the Passport Law reinforces this limitation by providing that men are entitled to impose a travel ban on their wives and request that their passports be confiscated. Despite a reform in 2017 that established several exceptions whereby women could travel out of the country under special circumstances (academics, diplomats, athletes, pilgrims, and others), married women still require permission from either a prosecutor or their husbands.[132] Besides limiting women's ability to study, do business, or work abroad, this regulation does not allow Iran to benefit from the potentially large income flows that female migrants could send back home.[133] Similar laws can be observed in the legislation of Oman[134] and Qatar.[135]

There are certain countries that do not have any legal restrictions for women to apply for passports but procedural requirements make it difficult for women to do so. In India, for instance, women applying for passports find that even after the introduction of a national identification system (called *Aadhaar* cards), passport application, renewal, and re-issuance processes often require women to provide documents establishing their spouses' or parents' identity or to submit additional documents if there is a change in their marital status—even if their husband's name was not even mentioned in their previous passport. Moreover, passport offices usually demand that once women are married, they must seek an amendment in their passport to reflect their husband's name.[136] These requirements for unnecessary documentation or procedural complications cause delays and harassment,

[130] The Family Law of Iran 1975, art 18; Human Rights Watch, 'World Report 2017: Iran' (2017) <www.hrw.org/world-report/2017/country-chapters/iran> accessed 18 September 2022.

[131] The Civil Code of Iran 1928. (A wife will be considered *nashezeh* (disobedient) and unworthy of spousal maintenance rights if she leaves her husband's home against his will, even if it is for escaping a situation of domestic violence.)

[132] Center for Human Rights in Iran, 'Married Women in Iran Still Need "Permission" to Travel Abroad Under Amendment to Passport Law' (2017) <www.iranhumanrights.org/2017/07/married-women-in-iran-still-need-permission-to-travel-abroad-under-amendment-to-passport-law/> accessed 5 October 2020.

[133] Empower Women, 'Freedom of movement and women's economic empowerment' (2016) <www.empowerwomen.org/en/who-we-are/news/2016/2/freedom-of-movement-and-womens-economic-empowerment> accessed 7 October 2020.

[134] Oman Personal Status Law 1997 (Royal Decree No 32/97), art 54(5); Oman Passport Law 1997 (Royal Decree No 69/97).

[135] Law No 22 of 2006 Promulgating 'The Family Law' (2006).

[136] Gaurav Vivek Bhatnagar, 'At Passport Office, Women Encounter Discriminatory, Humiliating Procedures' (The Wire 2016) <https://thewire.in/gender/passport-procedures-discriminatory-humiliating-especially-women> accessed 18 September 2022.

evidencing how the system continues to perceive women as dependent on either their father or husband. Unless reformed or repealed, such legal norms and procedures will continue to limit women's rights to seek opportunities for employment, business, or education beyond borders.

1.4.3.2 Access to official identification documents

Around a billion people across the world face challenges to prove their identity but women and girls (especially those living below the poverty line) are most affected. According to the World Bank, women in developing countries are less likely than men to hold an official identification document such as a birth certificate, passport, national identity card, or driving licence.[137] Around 45% of women in low-income countries do not have access to official identification documents.[138] Without an official identification document, women cannot enter into contracts, register businesses, open bank accounts, secure credit, or apply for work visas or travel documents. Women are effectively 'invisible' if they do not have an official identity document; this becomes a fundamental barrier to their societal and economic participation.[139] The lack of legal gender recognition procedures in many countries creates further barriers for transgender people in employment, health, education, and access to banking as they cannot access official identification documents. In many regions, transgender individuals have barriers in even getting their births registered or obtaining a birth certificate. In many regions, transgender individuals also face barriers in registering their gender 'change' in official documents or obtaining a modified birth certificate. Acknowledging this barrier, the UN Sustainable Development Goal 16 has set the target of providing everyone (regardless of their gender) with a legal identity document by 2030.[140]

This barrier can be blamed on a variety of reasons, including unaffordable fees and formalities attached to seeking the issue of formal identity documents, culturally embedded practices and biases where hospitals do not issue birth certificates for girls, or the general reluctance of families to apply for a birth certificate for a girl who is unlikely to enter the education system or attain employment.[141]

[137] Lucia Hanmer and Mariana Dahan, 'Identification for Development: Its Potential for Empowering Women and Girls' (*World Bank Blogs*, 2015) <https://blogs.worldbank.org/voices/identification-development-its-potential-empowering-women-and-girls> accessed 18 September 2022.

[138] Lucia Hanmer, 'Refugee women face complex barriers to proving identity' (*World Bank Blogs*, 2020) <https://blogs.worldbank.org/dev4peace/refugee-women-face-complex-barriers-proving-identity> accessed 7 October 2020.

[139] Identification for Development, '2019 Annual Report' (World Bank Group 2019) 2 <http://documents1.worldbank.org/curated/en/566431581578116247/pdf/Identification-for-Development-ID4D-2019-Annual-Report.pdf> accessed 18 September 2022.

[140] United Nations General Assembly, 'Transforming our world: the 2030 Agenda for Sustainable Development' (2015) UN Doc A/Res/70/1, 16 <https://sdgs.un.org/2030agenda> accessed 18 September 2022.

[141] Megan O'Donnell, 'Why Registration and ID Are Gender Equality Issues' (Center for Global Development 2016) <www.cgdev.org/blog/why-registration-and-id-are-gender-equality-issues> accessed 7 October 2020.

In Indonesia, surveys have found that the costs and difficulty of travel to the public authorities that issue these documents are a significant constraint for poor rural women. Women are tied to their household responsibilities and may not have sufficient time and available transportation to travel to such offices (often from villages to cities) to apply for official identification documents. In countries such as Egypt and Algeria, women face different requirements than their male counterparts in order to apply for an identification document; for example, married women must provide the name of their husband on their application for the issue of an identification document.[142] Hence, although the law may not bar women from applying for a birth certificate, gender-based procedures and discrepancies in practice disproportionately increase the hurdles for women.

1.4.3.3 Poor working conditions, employment restrictions, and physical safety concerns for female migrants

The World Bank has found that the inadequacies of legal and social conditions in some countries discourage women from other countries from seeking job opportunities in those economies.[143] The possibility of being exposed to poor and exploitative working conditions deters women workers from finding economic opportunities abroad. These conditions vary from country to country but are found to be worse in countries that do not grant adequate labour law protection to immigrants. Approximately 48% of the 281 million international migrants are estimated to be women. Roughly 13% of migrant women are employed in domestic work, while the vast majority—constituting 81%—are engaged in informal employment without social or labour protections.[144]

For instance, Lebanon is home to more than 250,000 migrant domestic workers. Most of them migrate from African and Asian countries such as Ethiopia, the Philippines, and Bangladesh. In November 2018, 186,429 of migrants were women, the majority of whom entered the country through authorized recruitment agencies.[145] Instead of being regulated by Lebanon's Labour Law, migrant domestic workers in Lebanon are subject to the kafala system, whereby the primary responsibility of regulating the relationship between

[142] International Bank for Reconstruction and Development, 'Achieving Universal Access to ID: Gender-based legal barriers against women and good practice reforms' (World Bank Group 2019) <https://openknowledge.worldbank.org/handle/10986/32474> accessed 18 September 2022.

[143] The World Bank, 'Women, Business and the Law: Afghanistan' (2022) <https://wbl.worldbank.org/en/data/exploreeconomies/afghanistan/2020#wbl_gpd> accessed 18 September 2022.

[144] India Centre for Migration and UN Women, 'Towards Safe Migration For Aspiring Women Domestic Workers' (UN Women 2018) <https://asiapacific.unwomen.org/en/digital-library/publications/2018/01/for-aspiring-women-domestic-workers> accessed 18 September 2022.

[145] Amnesty International, 'Their House is My Prison: Exploitation of Migrant Domestic Workers in Lebanon' (2019) <www.amnesty.org/en/documents/mde18/0022/2019/en/#:~:text=Careers-,Lebanon%3A%20'Their%20house%20is%20my%20prison'%3A%20Exploitation%20of,migrant%20domestic%20workers%20in%20Lebanon&text=Lebanon%20is%20home%20to%20over,of%20these%20workers%20are%20women> accessed 18 September 2022.

worker and employer rests in the hands of the employer, who exercises control over the worker's immigration and legal residency status. Under this system, domestic workers cannot enter the country, resign from their jobs, change employment, or leave the country without explicit permission from their employer.[146] This leads to situations in which women feel that the only escape from abusive employers is to run away.[147] However, given that under kafala most employers confiscate their workers' passports and residency permits, these women risk suffering detention or being deported if they abscond from their work.[148] The economic crisis which stemmed from both the Covid-19 pandemic and the August 2020 port explosion further aggravated these issues, leading to hundreds of domestic workers being abandoned by their financially strained employers and therefore left homeless.[149]

Besides Lebanon, other countries where the kafala system is practised include the Gulf Cooperation Council members (Bahrain, Kuwait, Oman, Qatar, Saudi Arabia, and the United Arab Emirates) and Jordan. Several countries have implemented limited reforms aimed at enhancing the rights and legal protection of domestic workers. For instance, in 2008, Jordan included domestic workers in their labour laws and, in 2003, Oman enacted legislation to make it illegal for employers to loan workers to other employers. In 2017, Qatar and the United Arab Emirates passed promising legislation on domestic workers' rights but these two countries have not changed their widespread use of the kafala system itself.[150] According to a regional media source, there are approximately 9.4 million foreign workers—roughly 29% of the total population—in Saudi Arabia. Women, primarily from Southeast Asia and Africa, migrate to Saudi Arabia to work in a variety of sectors, including construction and domestic service. In the past few years, many of these workers have been subjected to forced labour under the kafala system.[151] In addition to poor working conditions, as previously discussed, female migrants in

[146] International Labour Organization, 'Employer–Migrant worker relationships in the Middle East: Exploring scope for internal labour market mobility and fair migration' (2017) <www.ilo.org/beirut/publications/WCMS_552697/lang--en/index.htm> accessed 18 September 2022.

[147] Roshan De Stone and David L Suber, 'Women migrant workers come together against the kafala system in Lebanon' (Middle East Monitor 2018) <www.middleeastmonitor.com/20180508-women-migrant-workers-come-together-against-the-kafala-system-in-lebanon/> accessed 18 September 2022. (In 2017, two migrant domestic workers died every week in Lebanon.)

[148] Morgan Meaker, 'The Middle East's Kafala System Imprisons Millions of Women' (Medium 2018) <https://gen.medium.com/the-middle-easts-kafala-system-imprisons-millions-of-women-172d191a1fa1> accessed 18 September 2022.

[149] Michelle Lonnquist, 'Hardships for Lebanon's Migrant Domestic Workers Rise' (Human Rights Watch 2020) <www.hrw.org/news/2020/09/14/hardships-lebanons-migrant-domestic-workers-rise> accessed 6 October 2020.

[150] Migrant Forum in Asia Secretariat, 'Reform of the Kafala (sponsorship) system' (International Labour Organization) <www.ilo.org/dyn/migpractice/docs/132/PB2.pdf> accessed 18 September 2022.

[151] USDOS, '2019 Trafficking in Persons Report: Saudi Arabia' (2019) <www.ecoi.net/en/document/2010898.html> accessed 18 September 2022.

many countries have fewer job options to choose from as a result of laws that limit women from doing jobs that are deemed 'inappropriate' or 'dangerous'.[152]

Another factor that may discourage women from seeking employment abroad is the heightened risk of human trafficking. Human trafficking can be understood as a modern form of slavery in which people are recruited or obtained to work against their will through force, fraud, or coercion.[153] Women and girls account for around 71% of those subject to modern slavery around the world.[154] The problem remains persistent in industries where there is lack of government regulation and oversight. Risk factors for human trafficking include working in high-risk sectors like domestic work, working under live-in systems (living in the employer's household), and migration regimes that link employment with rights to legal residence or work permits.[155] These risk factors are particularly present in female-dominated industries including domestic service and hotel work.

In various countries, there are countless incidents of women being taken to foreign countries under the promise of lucrative employment prospects.[156] However, reports show that some female migrants end up being exploited into sex rackets and prostitution. Many female migrants become victims of sexual abuse and struggle, most of whom are unaccounted for, in foreign countries. This is common, especially for women travelling abroad for the purpose of finding work in domestic care settings.[157] The fear of being exposed to unsafe conditions deters women from seeking and accepting foreign jobs.

The internet and digital technologies have led to new trends in human trafficking.[158] Women from Sierra Leone, for example, have been found to enter Kuwait on the promise of jobs as nurses, only to find upon arrival that they are being sold as housemaids.[159] Different social media platforms and websites have

[152] Johnny Wood, '104 Countries have laws that prevent women from working in some jobs' (World Economic Forum 2018) <www.weforum.org/agenda/2018/08/104-countries-have-laws-that-prevent-women-from-working-in-some-jobs/> accessed 18 September 2022.

[153] Fiona David and others, 'Migrants and their vulnerability to human trafficking, modern slavery and forced labour' (IOM Publications 2019) <https://publications.iom.int/books/migrants-and-their-vulnerability-human-trafficking-modern-slavery-and-forced-labour> accessed 18 September 2022.

[154] ibid.

[155] Gudrun Greve and others, *Migrant Women and Human Trafficking. Handbook for Professionals* (La Strada Česká republika 2016) <www.ban-ying.de/fileadmin/banying/publikationen/Handbook_FinalwithAuthors.pdf> accessed 18 September 2022.

[156] AS Shan, '50 Malayali women enmeshed in sex racket stranded in Bahrain' *The New Indian Express* (2019) <www.newindianexpress.com/states/kerala/2019/feb/23/50-malayali-women-enmeshed-in-sex-racket-stranded-in-bahrain-1942440.html> accessed 18 September 2022.

[157] UNODC, 'Global Report on Trafficking in Persons 2018' (2018) <www.unodc.org/documents/data-and-analysis/glotip/2018/GLOTiP_2018_BOOK_web_small.pdf> accessed 18 September 2022.

[158] Brittany Anthony, 'On-Ramps, Intersections, and Exit Routes: A roadmap for Systems and Industries to Prevent and Disrupt Human Trafficking' (Polaris 2018) <https://polarisproject.org/resources/on-ramps-intersections-and-exit-routes-a-roadmap-for-systems-and-industries-to-prevent-and-disrupt-human-trafficking/> accessed 18 September 2022.

[159] Pete Pattisson, 'Women from Sierra Leone "sold like slaves" into domestic work in Kuwait' *The Guardian* (2015) <www.theguardian.com/global-development/2015/apr/02/women-sierra-leone-sold-like-slaves-domestic-work-kuwait#:~:text=Women%20from%20Sierra%20Leone%20formerly,and%20then%20resold%20multiple%20times.> accessed 18 September 2022.

been found to host black markets for human trafficking and the search for domestic workers. For example, sponsors of foreign domestic workers in Saudi Arabia can avoid complicated transfer laws and fees, if they want to dismiss a worker who they have sponsored, by selling or transferring their workers online. This way, they avoid penalties for breaking their contractual obligations and can also earn a fee for the sale of their former employee.[160] An undercover investigation by the BBC found similar practices in Kuwait, where apps such as '4Sale' and 'Instagram' allow employers to sell the sponsorship of their domestic workers to others for financial gain.[161]

These challenges are even more formidable for transgender women who experience violence worldwide at alarmingly high rates. Research shows that transgender people are over four times more likely than cisgender people to be victims of violent crime, including rape and assault. Moreover, this violence and abuse amplifies notably for women who migrate beyond international borders for work or their livelihood. Transgender women who migrate to work also face high rates of hate crimes and discrimination in several countries.[162]

1.4.4 Negative freedom is a means to achieve positive freedom

Removal of external barriers for attaining negative freedom can help women achieve positive freedom. Overcoming external barriers gives women profound insights into themselves and their capabilities, enabling them to chart a more effective course to their economic independence and professional success. Anchoring to a specific professional purpose can enable women to redirect their attention towards who they need to be and what they need to learn in order to achieve their professional goals. 'Instead of defining themselves in relation to gender stereotypes—whether rejecting stereotypically masculine approaches because they feel inauthentic or rejecting stereotypically feminine ones for fear that they convey incompetence—female leaders can focus on behaving in ways that advance the purposes for which they stand.'[163] Focusing on a purpose can also lead women to take up activities that are critical to their success, such as seeking education or skill development. Economic empowerment can cultivate self-confidence

[160] France 24, 'In Saudi Arabia, domestic workers are auctioned online' (2018) <https://observers.france24.com/en/20180315-saudi-arabia-domestic-workers-are-auctioned-online> accessed 18 September 2022.

[161] Owen Pinnell and Jess Kelly, 'Slave markets found on Instagram and other apps' (BBC News 2019) <www.bbc.com/news/technology-50228549> accessed 18 September 2023.

[162] Oxfam America and the Tahirih Justice Centre, 'Surviving Deterrence: How US Asylum Deterrence Policies Normalise Gender-Based Violence' (2023) <www.tahirih.org/news/transgender-asylum-seekers-the-impact-of-gender-based-violence-and-deterrence-policies-at-the-border/> accessed 18 September 2023.

[163] Herminia Ibarra, Robin J Ely, and Deborah M Kolb, 'Women Rising: The Unseen' (2013) 91(9) Harvard Business Review 60.

and self-esteem in women and can elevate their social status in their families and societies. Access to information, decision-making positions, productive resources, and employment opportunities enables women to overcome internal barriers.[164] Gaining control, having decision-making power, becoming self-reliant and assertive, attaining the ability to articulate opinions, and gaining a wider view of the world beyond their families or villages helps women achieve physiological independence.

Hence, negative freedom leads to positive freedom, but positive freedom is an important precondition for the attainment of negative freedom. Psychological (or internal) empowerment is a blend of self-esteem, self-efficacy, self-determination, self-confidence, self-awareness, and positive thinking. Ryff identifies six areas of psychological well-being: having self-autonomy, attaining environmental mastery, experiencing personal growth, creating positive relations with others, having a purpose in life, and the feeling of self-acceptance. These areas are directly linked and heavily influenced by economic empowerment. Empowerment is not a top-down process; it is essentially a bottom-up process that starts from within. External forces can play a significant role in empowering women with women themselves playing the fundamental role of empowering themselves.

Psychological empowerment increases women's sense of personal control and motivates them to engage in productive work. Nelson and Quick observe that empowerment gives a sense of 'belongingness and job enrichment' to women employees as well as the ability and confidence to take on work responsibilities. 'Women workforce that is psychologically empowered is motivated and accelerated to participate in innovative strategies.'[165] Women professionals who are positively empowered can perform challenging roles, effectively accomplish meaningful work-related tasks, and confidently influence decision-making processes.[166]

The discussion in this chapter also shows that all forms of freedom from external barriers are intricately related to each other and mainly to the economic empowerment of women.[167] Denial of social rights, for example, may not directly present

[164] Gunman Mishra, 'The Psychological Facets of Women Empowerment at Workplace' (2016) 2(1) International Journal of Recent Trends in Engineering & Research <www.semanticscholar.org/paper/The-Psychological-Facets-of-Women-Empowerment-at-Mishra/a938a5169abcf8a9b1b3f85062f85b50bf0e34d0> accessed 6 June 2024.

[165] Debra L Nelson and James Campbell Quick, *Principles of Organizational Behavior: Realities and Challenges* (South-Western 2012).

[166] Ayelet Makarosand Haya Itzhaky, 'Work-Related Stress and Social Workers' Perceptions of Effectiveness in Light of the Recent Changes in Social and Economic Policies in Israel' (2008) 30(2) Social Development Issues 45, 58.

[167] Yin-Zu Chen and Hiromi Tanaka, 'Women's Empowerment' in Alex C Michalos (ed), *Encyclopedia of Quality of Life and Well-Being Research* (Springer 2014). (For this study, '"women's empowerment" refers to the process of increasing women's access to control over the strategic life choices affecting them and allowing access to the opportunities to help realize their capacities. Women's empowerment as an economic, political, and sociocultural process challenges the system of sexual stratification that has resulted in women's subordination and marginalization to improve women's quality of life.')

an immediate threat to a woman's ability to be employed or start a business, but it may put women a few steps further away from attaining economic independence. For example, women can be psychologically scarred due to increased domestic violence and household responsibilities; this could jeopardize their confidence or psychological make-up to succeed or progress in their professional endeavours.[168] On the other hand, barriers that directly impede women's access to productive resources (eg capital, property-ownership, or employment markets) not only negatively impact women's economic independence but also impact women's societal independence. The denial of economic rights may not necessarily present an immediate threat to human life or health but it does significantly affect the ability of women to exercise essential human capabilities. For example, working women with access to financial resources may be less exposed to domestic violence or family subjugation as compared to women who are not economic actors themselves and are hence dependent on others.[169] This is where international trade can play a significant role as it can create economic opportunities that may not only impact women's economic empowerment but also can have a positive influence on other areas such as their social and psychological empowerment.

[168] Naila Kabeer, 'Gender Mainstreaming in Poverty Eradication and the Millenium Development Goals: A Handbook for Policymakers and Other Stakeholders' (2003) 1 Commonwealth Secretariat 39, 44.

[169] Leslie Kurshan, 'Rethinking Property Rights as Human Rights: Acquiring Equal Property Rights for Women Using International Human Rights Treaties' (2000) 8(2) Journal of Gender, Social Policy & the Law, 353 357, 358 (describing discriminatory practices and provisions in nations of the Organization of American States which deprive women of their property rights but which could be challenged by women under international human rights law).

2
Trade and Women
Understanding the Nexus

2.1 Introduction

Empowering women can take place through two different, yet complementary, approaches: the bottom-up or top-down approach. The bottom-up approach calls for efforts to amend national laws, procedures, institutions, culture, and social norms at the domestic level to reduce barriers that impede women's empowerment. Prioritizing domestic policies and regulations is crucial for advancing women's economic empowerment as they can directly impact the conditions of women as employees, entrepreneurs, and consumers. However, as discussed in the previous chapter, this approach may not work for various countries that have discriminatory laws or patriarchal social set-ups that create formidable barriers and challenges for women. On the other hand, the top-down approach calls for employing international laws or institutions to incentivize changes at the domestic level. This book is based on the top-down approach as it builds understanding on why and how international trade agreements, policies, and institutions can help in reducing the barriers that impede women's access to economic opportunities.

The focus on the nexus between international trade and sustainable development predates the establishment of the World Trade Organization (WTO). One of the first acknowledgements of the relationship between women empowerment and commerce can be traced back to the Treaty on the Functioning of the European Union (TFEU), which included provisions for equal pay and equal representation in trade.[1] In 1995, the WTO's Marrakesh Agreement enshrined the objective of sustainable development in its Preamble.[2] A quarter of a century later, the discussions in policy circles have evolved dramatically and the term 'sustainable development' has become far better understood and accepted as a concept that relates to trade. The Addis Ababa Agenda of Action builds a clear network between international trade and women's empowerment. It reads as follows: 'Recognizing the critical role of women as producers and traders, we will address their specific challenges to facilitate women's equal and active participation in domestic,

[1] Consolidated versions of the Treaty on European Union and the Treaty on the Functioning of the European Union [2016] OJ C202/1 (TFEU), art 157.

[2] Marrakesh Agreement Establishing the World Trade Organization (1994), 1867 UNTS 154, 33 ILM 1144, Preamble ('WTO Agreement').

Trade Agreements and Women. Amrita Bahri, Oxford University Press.
DOI: 10.1093/9780198935759.003.0003

regional and international trade.'[3] The UN General Assembly (UNGA) has called upon the WTO, the World Bank Group (WBG), and other international and regional bodies to support governmental initiatives and develop complementary programmes to help countries achieve the full implementation of the Beijing Declaration and Platform for Action to protect women's rights.[4] The 2030 Agenda for Sustainable Development recognizes international trade as an engine for inclusive and sustainable economic growth and an important means to achieve the UN's 2030 Sustainable Development Goals (SDGs).[5]

Another multilateral instrument that reinforces this view is the WTO's Joint Declaration on Trade and Women's Economic Empowerment.[6] This declaration, signed in December 2017 in Buenos Aires by almost 70% of WTO members, reaffirms that 'international trade and investment are engines of economic growth for both developing and developed countries, and that improving women's access to opportunities and removing barriers to their participation in national and international economies contributes to sustainable economic development'.[7]

Although there is no explicit mention of women-related concerns in the WTO's rulebook, there has been a significant upsurge in free trade agreements (FTAs) that are carving out space for concerns related to women's empowerment.[8] In addition to FTAs, explicit provisions relating to women's concerns are finding their way into some bilateral investment treaties (BITs)[9] and non-reciprocal preferential trade access schemes.[10] Moreover, in recent years, WTO members have reported in their

[3] UN General Assembly, Addis Ababa Action Agenda of the Third International Conference on Financing Development, A/RES/69/313, Addis Ababa Action Agenda (2015) <https://sustainabledevelopment.un.org/content/documents/2051AAAA_Outcome.pdf> accessed 9 September 2022.

[4] UN Women, 'On the 25th Anniversary of landmark Beijing Declaration on Women's rights, UN Women calls for accelerating its unfinished business' (2020) <www.unwomen.org/en/news/stories/2020/9/press-release-25th-anniversary-of-the-beijing-declaration-on-womens-rights> accessed 17 August 2021.

[5] UN General Assembly, 'Transforming our world: the 2030 Agenda for Sustainable Development' (21 October 2015) A/RES/70/1 <www.refworld.org/docid/57b6e3e44.html> accessed 13 November 2020.

[6] WTO, 'Buenos Aires Joint Declaration on Trade and Women's Economic Empowerment' (WTO Ministerial Conference, 2017) <www.wto.org/english/tratop_e/womenandtrade_e/buenos_aires_declaration_e.htm> accessed 18 October 2022 ('Declaration 2017').

[7] ibid.

[8] International Trade Centre, 'Mainstreaming Gender in Free Trade Agreements' (2020) <www.intracen.org/uploadedFiles/intracenorg/Content/Publications/ITC%20Mainstream%20Gender_FTA_20200707_web.pdf> accessed 17 August 2021.

[9] Renata Vargas Amaral and Lillyana Daza Jaller, 'The Role of Regulation and MNEs in Ensuring Equal Opportunities for Women' (2020) 27(3) Transnational Corporations 183.

[10] General Agreement on Tariffs and Trade, 'Decision on differential and more favourable treatment reciprocity and fuller participation of developing countries' (1979) L/4903 <www.wto.org/gatt_docs/English/SULPDF/90970166.pdf> accessed 1 September 2021. The Generalized System of Preferences (GSP) is a trade programme, enabled by the GATT/WTO trading system, designed to promote growth in developing countries by allowing developed countries to offer non-reciprocal preferential treatment (eg zero or low duties on imports) to products originating in developing countries. The international legal basis for this system is an 'enabling clause', 72 adopted in 1979, which allows derogations to WTO rules on non-discrimination (ie most-favoured-nation (MFN) status). For details on how the EU has plans to further support equality between men and women through its GSP regulation, see European Parliament, 'Implementation of the Generalized Scheme Preferences (GSP) Regulation (EU) No 978/

trade policy review reports, the various trade policies they have put in place to foster women's economic empowerment in their respective jurisdictions.[11] These developments reflect the acknowledgement within the trade community that trade policy can serve as a tool for empowering women.

Women's economic empowerment and international trade share an intricate and complex relationship as the former can be enhanced through the effective regulation of the latter.[12] This relation is often described as a 'bi-directional relationship' as, in addition to the impact international trade can have on women, the empowerment of women can also have a significant impact on international trade. The following two sections explain this bi-directional relationship between trade and women empowerment.

2.2 Trade and Women Empowerment: A Bi-Directional Relationship

There is a bi-directional relationship between international trade and women empowerment. On the one hand, trade affects women as employees, employers, and consumers. On the other hand, women's empowerment affects the performance, competitiveness, and productivity of international trade.

2.2.1 International trade impacts women's empowerment

Trade liberalization has had a different distributive impact on women and men, and this impact has been both negative and positive. The factors that mediate this effect include resource endowments, labour market institutions, systems of property rights, and other socio-economic characteristics.[13] Women tend to be more affected by the negative effects of trade liberalization and face more barriers than men when it comes to taking advantage of the opportunities offered by trade. This is mainly because of the biases against women in education and training, wage

2012 (2018/2109(INI))' (2019) European Parliament Resolution 9 <www.europarl.europa.eu/doceo/document/TA-8-2019-0207_EN.pdf> accessed 1 September 2021.

[11] Anoush der Boghossian, 'Trade Policies Supporting Women's Economic Empowerment: Trends in WTO Members' (2019) WTO Staff Working Paper ERSD-2019-07 <www.wto.org/english/res_e/reser_e/ersd201907_e.pdf> accessed 18 October 2022. From 2014–18, the trade policies of 111 WTO members were under trade policy review. About 70% of them reported at least one trade policy targeting women's economic empowerment.

[12] Anna Hutchens, 'Empowering Women through Fair Trade? Lessons from Asia' (2010) 31(3) Third World Quarterly 449.

[13] Marzia Fontana, 'The Gender Effects of Trade Liberalization in Developing Countries: A Review of Literature' (University of Sussex 2003) <www.ciedur.org.uy/adm/archivos/publicacion_200.pdf> accessed 12 September 2022.

inequalities, and inequalities in the distribution of resources, as well as unequal access to productive inputs such as credit, land, and technology.[14] This section explains the way in which international trade can impact women in three different categories: the impact of trade on women as employees, the impact of trade on women as business actors, and the impact of trade on women as consumers.[15]

2.2.1.1 Trade's impact on women employees

As per the Heckscher-Ohlin-Stolper-Samuelson models, conventional trade theory has shown that a country's comparative advantage is based on its factors that are in abundant supply.[16] A country with an endowment of low-skill and low-wage labour will export the commodities that use that abundance of labour supply. With trade liberalization, the demand for labour-intensive commodities has risen; it has also increased the demand for labour and hence increased wages.[17] This effect is particularly felt in developing countries where unskilled labour is found in abundance and a significant part of the unskilled labour force is made up of females. Studies have shown that trade liberalization increases women's wages due to competitive pressures and thereby reduces the scope for employers to discriminate against the women workforce.[18] However, there is insufficient evidence to establish with certainty whether the increase in women's wages is linked to opportunities created by international trade, more women attaining education, or men's declining wage rates.[19]

A study of formal sector employment in manufacturing, conducted in both developed and developing countries, has shown a positive correlation between increased exports and increased female employment.[20] Hence, based on the conventional theory, trade liberalization can increase the demand for financial compensation for the women's workforce. The Heterodox economic theory contradicts these observations as it observes that the business model of international firms

[14] UNCTAD, 'Mainstreaming Gender in Trade Policy' (2009) Note by the UNCTAD Secretariat TD/B/C.I/EM.2/2/Rev.1 <http://www.unctad.org/en/docs/ciem2d2_en.pdf> accessed 1 September 2021.

[15] Don Flynn and Eleonore Kofman, 'Women, Trade, and Migration' (2004) 12 Gender & Development 66.

[16] Edward E Leamer, 'The Heckscher-Ohlin Model in Theory and Practice' (1995) 77 Princeton Studies in International Finance <https://ies.princeton.edu/pdf/S77.pdf> accessed 17 August 2020.

[17] Eddy Lee, 'Trade liberalization and employment' (2005) DESA Working Paper No 5, UN.org <chrome-extension://efaidnbmnnnibpcajpcglclefindmkaj/https://www.un.org/en/ecosoc/meetings/2005/docs/Eddy%20Lee.pdf> accessed 5 October 2023.

[18] Janneke Pieters, 'Can Free Trade Policies help to reduce Gender Equalities in Employment and Wages' (IZA World of Labour 2018) <https://wol.iza.org/uploads/articles/455/pdfs/trade-liberalization-and-gender-inequality.pdf> accessed 17 August 2021.

[19] Günseli Berik, 'Mature Export-Led Growth and Gender Wage Inequality in Taiwan' (2000) 6(3) Feminist Economics 1 <www.tandfonline.com/doi/abs/10.1080/135457000750020119> accessed 19 October 2022; Remco H Oostendorp, 'Does Globalization Reduce the Gender Wage Gap?' (World Bank workshop on 'Gender, growth and poverty', 2002) <https://openknowledge.worldbank.org/handle/10986/13887> accessed 19 October 2022.

[20] Adrian Wood, 'North–South Trade and Female Labour in Manufacturing: An Asymmetry' (1991) 27(2) Journal of Development Studies 168.

dealing in foreign trade is based on absolute production costs[21] (rather than relative costs, as argued by conventional theory).[22] This would mean that in developing countries, where women constitute a significant portion of the unskilled labour force, there exists a competitive advantage for export-oriented firms to maintain their absolute labour costs at low levels.[23] Hence, trade liberalization may cause a rise in demand for women's labour but not necessarily an increase in their wages or an improvement in their working conditions. On the contrary, such companies have strong financial incentives to keep these wages as low as possible. Thus, rather than promoting women's interests, trade liberalization can lead to the exploitation of the female workforce and further widen the existing divide between men and women.[24]

Empirical data has also shown that the overall wage gap between men and women remains large in countries that rely on female labour, especially where there has been a rapid growth in exports. Due to trade liberalization, female workers and producers are more likely to contribute to the unskilled labour force in export-oriented industries and remain concentrated in low-skilled activities with little chance to access high-value-added jobs that remain male-dominated.[25] This explains why almost 80% of women globally still occupy low-skill jobs.[26] It also explains why there is an over-representation of women in the informal economy and non-tradable sectors. This phenomenon is also known as the 'feminization of

[21] Arthur S Alderson, 'Explaining the Upswing in Direct Investment: A Test of Mainstream and Heterodox Theories of Globalization' (2004) 83(1) Social Forces 81.

[22] Absolute costs refer to the level of production costs, which are used as a measure of efficiency. Lower production costs indicate higher efficiency. Relative costs are based on the concept of opportunity cost, which is defined as the value of the next-best alternative to the current use of the available economic resources. Lower opportunity cost indicates higher relative efficiency.

[23] Thi Anh-Dao Tran, 'The Feminization of Employment through Export-Led Strategies: Evidence from Viet Nam' (2019) 25 Revue de la regulation 1. The principle of comparative advantage, which is at the core of standard trade theory, suggests that countries compete based on relative unit costs. In contrast, the concept of competitive advantage states that countries compete based on absolute unit costs (rather than relative costs).

[24] Chinhui Juhn, Gergely Ujhelyi, and Carolina Villegas-Sanchez, 'Men, Women, and Machines: How Trade Impacts Gender Inequality' (2012) Working Paper 18106 <https://papers.ssrn.com/sol3/papers.cfm?abstract_id=2066403> accessed 19 October 2022 (the authors observe that trade liberalization has increased the ratio of female blue-collar worker to male blue-collars workers as well as the relative wage of female blue-collar workers, but there is little evidence of an increasing female share in white-collar occupations). See also Lilia Domínguez-Villalobos and Flor Brown-Grossman, 'Trade Liberalization and Gender Wage Inequality in Mexico' (2010) 15(4) Feminist Economics 53 (the authors observe that NAFTA's effect on rural employment brought a general increase in the ratio of women workers in export crops but did not improve the quality of life of rural workers. Also, in the case of Mexico's maquiladoras, located in Tijuana, employers hire married women, women with children, and women with low levels of education who constitute a low-wage sector of the labour force with very few other employment alternatives. Thus, the manufacturers have taken advantage of this low-wage labour force, making women accept 'flexible' terms of employment).

[25] Guy Standing, 'Global Feminization through Flexible Labour: World Development' (1989) 17(7) Science Direct 10775.

[26] The World Bank and the World Trade Organization, 'The Role of Trade in Promoting Gender Equality' (World Bank Publications 2020) <www.worldbank.org/en/topic/trade/publication/women-and-trade-the-role-of-trade-in-promoting-womens-equality> accessed 6 June 2024.

labour', which refers to both an increase in female employment (typically in labour-intensive, low-value-added, and low-wage activities) and a worsening of their working conditions.[27] An example of this is the feminization of the manufacturing labour force in developing countries. 'The greater the share of garments, textiles and electronics in a country's exports, the greater the employment-creating impact of trade has been for women.'[28]

When working as a labour force, women are perceived as secondary workers as they are relatively easier to lay off due to their low bargaining power thus making them more vulnerable. Women's weaker property rights and access to other resources, coupled with other barriers that obstruct their employment opportunities, reduce their bargaining power. Another constraint that prevents women from seizing new opportunities is the heavy burden of household responsibilities and surplus female labour available to work at low cost and in poor working conditions.[29] In addition, increased competition further reduces the bargaining power of women wage earners, especially if they are heavily employed in sectors competing internationally based on low-cost labour. Their bargaining power is further compromised by the cultural and social barriers they face (as explained in the previous chapter). Therefore, the expansion of women's trade-related employment does not automatically imply better job quality, better earnings for women, or reduced wage gaps between men and women.

Studies have shown that over the past decade the number of women working in export-dependent firms has visibly increased but there are still more men than women in export-dependent jobs.[30] Moreover, women work in sectors that are less engaged in trade.[31] Increasing their engagement in trade can help women work towards better and more competitive salaries.[32] Evidence also indicates that trade can facilitate women's transition from the informal into the formal economy thus

[27] Guy Standing, 'Global Feminization through Flexible Labour: A Theme Revisited' (1999) 27(3) World Development 583.

[28] Fontana (n 13).

[29] International Labour Organization, 'Gender in employment policies and programmes: What works for women?' (2017) Working Paper No 235 <chrome-extension://efaidnbmnnnibpcajpcglclefindmkaj/https://www.ilo.org/wcmsp5/groups/public/---ed_emp/documents/publication/wcms_613536.pdf> accessed 5 October 2023.

[30] Jayati Ghosh, 'Globalization, Export-Oriented Employment for Women and Social Policy: A Case Study of India' (2002) 30(11) Social Scientist 17.

[31] OECD, 'Trade and Gender: A Framework of Analysis' (2021) OECD Trade Policy Papers No 246, 11, 12 <www.oecd-ilibrary.org/docserver/6db59d80-en.pdf?expires=1663215197&id=id&accname=guest&checksum=2251E66982BBB62F6D4AF9E9340C66D5> accessed 11 September 2022. Across all OECD countries, women are much less likely than men to work in manufacturing, a highly traded sector. On average, only 30% of the manufacturing workforce is made up of women.

[32] Many studies have found that there exists an exporter wage premium—that exporters pay higher wages than non-exporters. See Esther Ann Bøler, Beata Javorcik, and Karen Helene Ulltveit-Moe, 'Working Across Time Zones: Exporters and the Gender Wage Gap' (2018) 111 Journal of International Economics 122; Zornitsa Kutlina-Dimitrova and others, 'How Important are EU Exports for Jobs in the EU?' (2018) 4 Chief Economist Note <https://trade.ec.europa.eu/doclib/docs/2018/november/tradoc_157551.pdf> accessed 9 September 2022.

offering improved working conditions and access to various benefits.[33] Trade creates better jobs for women. In sectors with high levels of exports, women workers are more likely to be formally employed in a job with better benefits, training, and security. Studies conducted by the World Bank and WTO have shown that women workers are less likely to be employed in the informal sector if they work in sectors that are more engaged in trade or are more integrated into global value chains.[34] Additionally, other studies have indicated that foreign trade can lead to increased wages for women as exporting firms tend to offer higher pay and better working conditions compared to non-exporting firms.[35]

2.2.1.2 Trade's impact on women entrepreneurs

As business stakeholders, women are more likely to own more informal, smaller, and less profitable businesses than their male counterparts.[36] This is mainly because of the barriers they face in accessing productive resources such as land, capital, technical skills, business information, and education. In particular, these barriers may include, but are not limited to: a lack of access to educational opportunities including business training; the digital divide between men and women caused by a lack of affordability and digital know-how; a lack of access to productive resources such as land, finances, and other assets; the disproportionately high tariff and non-tariff barriers faced by women-owned businesses engaged in agriculture and textiles; a lack of access to trade-related information and business networks; and the disproportionately high burden involved in discharging their household responsibilities.[37]

Women own close to 10 million of the world's micro, small, and medium-sized enterprises (MSMEs).[38] This means that more than 30% of MSMEs in the world

[33] Informal workers are defined as workers who neither benefit from a social security scheme nor have a working contract. Contrary view in Mélika Ben Salem and Chahir Zaki, 'Revisiting the Impact of Trade Openness on Informal and Irregular Employment in Egypt' (2019) 34(3) Journal of Economic Integration 465.

[34] WBG and WTO, 'Women and Trade: The Role of Trade in Promoting Gender Equality' (World Bank 2020) <https://openknowledge.worldbank.org/handle/10986/34140> accessed 1 September 2021 ('WTO and World Bank Report 2020').

[35] ibid. Developing countries that double their manufacturing exports—a typical increase for developing countries that open themselves to trade—would see women increase their share of total manufacturing wages from 24% to 30% through a combination of increased employment and higher salaries.

[36] ILO, 'Women and Men in the Informal Economy: A Statistical Picture' (2018) <www.ilo.org/wcmsp5/groups/public/---dgreports/---dcomm/documents/publication/wcms_626831.pdf> accessed 17 August 2021.

[37] International Trade Centre, 'Women Entrepreneurs: An Action Plan to "Build Back Better"' (2020) <https://edse.org.za/wp-content/uploads/2020/11/W20-Policy-brief_Bejing25_20201021_web.pdf> accessed 19 October 2022.

[38] In 2011, the IFC reported that women-owned enterprises accounted for approximately 30% to 37% (8–10 million) of all MSMEs in emerging markets. The WTO Regional Surveys 2019–20 data showed that 46.3% of them had less than ten employees and 27% between 11 and 30 employees. The percentage dropped when looking at larger firms: only 4.6% of women-owned businesses employed between 51 and 100 staff and only 3.3% of them owned companies with more than 100 employees.

are owned by women entrepreneurs. The micro size of most MSMEs owned by women means that when a crisis strikes, downsizing their businesses becomes challenging.[39] For many, downsizing would entail closing their businesses, as was the case during the Covid-19 crisis.[40] Moreover, women business owners are disproportionately affected by trade compared to men-owned MSMEs, primarily because the former tend to be smaller than the latter.[41] As business size increases, the presence of women as owners decreases. Additionally, women-owned businesses typically generate substantially less revenue than men-owned businesses.[42]

One reason why women's businesses remain smaller is that women entrepreneurs are not sufficiently integrated in international trade. This is a direct consequence of the small(er) size of their businesses, which makes competing in international markets difficult. In the WTO Regional Surveys 2019–20, 49% of businesswomen explained that their reason for not exporting was linked to the small size of their companies, which consequently limited their capacity.[43] Focusing their activities and resources at the domestic level rather than exporting also impacts their business model, making them easy prey for economic crises. Since women-owned firms export less, they do not fully capitalize on the increased opportunities for expansion and economies of scale offered by direct engagement in international markets.

This is also the case in developed countries. Eg in Canada, 92.7% of women-owned firms employ less than 20 staff members. (WTO survey, 'Assessing Women Entrepreneurs' Knowledge Gap on Trade in East Africa, South Asia, and Latin America. 2019–2020', unpublished but highlighted at <www.wto.org/english/tratop_e/womenandtrade_e/womenandtrade_e.htm>. More than 800 women entrepreneurs were surveyed in Latin America, South Asia, and East Africa between 2019 and 2020; Wendy Cukier and others, 'The State of Women's Entrepreneurship in Canada: 2020' (Women Entrepreneurship Knowledge Hub 2020).)

[39] IWA 34:2021, 'Women's entrepreneurship—Key definitions and general criteria' (ISO.org 2021) <www.iso.org/obp/ui/#iso:std:iso:iwa:34:ed-1:v1:en> accessed 1 September 2021. A women-owned business is defined as one that is more than 50% owned by one or more women, with its management and control held by one or more women. Additionally, a woman must be a signatory of the business's legal documents and financial accounts and the business must operate independently from businesses that are not owned by women. A women-led business is defined as one that is at least 25% owned by one or more women, whose management and control lie with one or more women. If a board exists, at least one-third of its members should be women and a woman must be a signatory of the business's legal documents and financial accounts. Finally, the business must operate independently from those that are neither led nor owned by women.

[40] John Schneider, 'Global State of Small Business Report' (Data for Good, Facebook 2021) <https://about.fb.com/wp-content/uploads/2021/04/Global-State-of-Small-Business-Report-March-2021.pdf> accessed 9 July 2021; OED and Facebook, '2020 Global State of Small Businesses' (World Bank 2021) <https://dataforgood.fb.com/global-state-of-smb/> accessed 9 July 2021.

[41] Markus Goldstein and others, 'The Global State of Small Business during COVID-19: Gender Inequalities' (*World Bank Blogs*, 2020) <https://blogs.worldbank.org/developmenttalk/global-state-small-business-during-covid-19-gender-inequalities> accessed 9 July 2021 (the article notes that female-owned businesses were 5.9 percentage points more likely to have closed their businesses than male-owned businesses).

[42] OECD (n 31).

[43] More than 800 women entrepreneurs were surveyed in Latin America, South Asia, and East Africa between 2019 and 2020, WTO survey (OECD, n 37).

Trade is an agent of diversity: diversity of markets, clients, products, and services.[44] Therefore, lack of presence in international markets prevents women entrepreneurs from using trade to fuel business expansion and as a tool to weather the occasional economic storm. Consequently, the lack of diversity in women entrepreneurs' activities becomes a reason why they are mostly small and hence remain relatively more vulnerable to economic crises compared to male-owned businesses.[45] Another factor contributing to the smaller size of women's businesses is that women entrepreneurs tend to have less experience in owning and managing a business compared to men. Lack of access to suitable educational opportunities, such as business training, may also be to blame in this regard.

Trade liberalization fosters international competition. While this may increase opportunities for employment for individuals and business for firms, it also intensifies the need to expand the size of a business and upgrade technologically.[46] This may be burdensome for women-run enterprises that have limited access to market networks, credit, and digital knowledge. However, trade liberalization has led to the introduction of new technologies that can benefit women-owned businesses. The use of new technology, such as blockchain-based applications, and online platforms to engage in e-commerce can provide women's businesses with relatively easy and cost-effective ways to enter foreign markets and also expand their businesses.[47]

With the significant rise in e-commerce, women entrepreneurs are transforming their traditional business model as they are going digital and fostering their businesses' online presence.[48] However, this growing trend needs to be accompanied by supportive policies and training for women as the digital divide between men and women continues to persist.[49] To allow women's businesses to profit from the

[44] WTO, 'Levelling the Trading Field for SMEs' (2016) World Trade Report 58 <www.wto.org/english/res_e/booksp_e/world_trade_report16_e.pdf> accessed 9 July 2021.

[45] ILO (n 36).

[46] UNCTAD (n 14).

[47] Amrita Bahri, 'Blockchaining International Trade: A Way Forward for Women's Economic Empowerment?' in Maarten Smeets (ed), *Adapting to the Digital Trade Era: Challenges and Opportunities* (WTO Publications 2021) <www.wto.org/english/res_e/booksp_e/adtera_e.pdf> accessed 8 September 2023.

[48] Accenture, 'COVID-19: Consumer Change How They Shop, Work and Live' (2020) <www.accenture.com/us-en/insights/retail/coronavirus-consumer-behavior-research> accessed 19 October 2022 (according to a global survey conducted by Accenture, 160% is the expected future increase in e-commerce purchases from new or low frequency users); Dotcom Distribution, '2020 Dotcom Distribution eCommerce Consumer Study: Adapting to the Rapidly Changing eCommerce Landscape' (2020) <https://dotcomdist.com/2020-dotcom-distribution-ecommerce-consumer-study-adapting-to-the-rapidly-changing-ecommerce-landscape/> accessed 26 October 2022; Global Entrepreneurship Monitor, '2018/2019 Women's Entrepreneurship Report' (2019) <www.gemconsortium.org/report/gem-20182019-womens-entrepreneurship-report> accessed 8 September 2022 (in the US, about 31% of shoppers believe that they will purchase more online now than before Covid-19).

[49] International Telecommunications Union (ITU), 'Bridging the Gender Divide' <www.itu.int/en/mediacentre/backgrounders/Pages/bridging-the-gender-divide.aspx> accessed 9 July 2021. In 2019, the proportion of women using the internet globally was 48% compared to 58% of men in the same year. The proportion of women using the internet is higher than that of men in only 8% of countries.

available digital solutions, it is important to ensure that women have access to digital solutions and that they have the skills required to benefit from such technologies in their businesses. However, this digital transformation may not apply to all sectors and all women entrepreneurs equally. The question therefore remains as to whether digitalization and setting up an online platform on the internet or through social media is enough to support women entrepreneurs. Owing to the digital divide between men and women, men are more likely to work in the platform economy and are four times more likely than women to avail themselves of the opportunities offered by trade digitalization.[50]

2.2.1.3 Trade impacts women consumers and their households

Trade liberalization tends to delegitimize state intervention.[51] This can be particularly problematic for women as it diminishes a government's ability to rectify the maldistribution of resources that trade liberalization has perpetuated against women. With women in vulnerable positions due to the multifaceted barriers they face, state intervention is particularly crucial for them as it can rectify the imbalances created in the markets.[52] However, trade liberalization is antagonistic towards such intervention.[53] Trade rules restrict and even prohibit state intervention in various fields regulated under trade agreements, including benefits that states can provide to women consumers in the form of subsidies or tax waivers.

Moreover, when trade is liberalized, tariffs are reduced. Reduced tariffs can negatively impact government revenue, compelling a government to reduce or withdraw the provision of social services that are otherwise subsidized or financed by that government.[54] In some cases, this might lead to the privatization of certain social services that are relevant for women, such as provisions of medical care, childcare, and education. Privatization of social services can also increase costs, making them unaffordable, or less affordable, for working women without medical cover or working mothers with childcare needs.[55] A lack of affordable social services impacts women more than men as women professionals tend to bear a larger

In Latin America, 49% of women entrepreneurs received support and training during the Covid pandemic. Of those, 57% received training on digital transformation including e-commerce, 40% on innovation and creativity, 24% on online payment solutions, and 25% on e-market places.

[50] OECD, 'Bridging the Digital Gender Divide' (2018) <www.oecd.org/digital/bridging-the-digital-gender-divide.pdf> accessed 17 August 2021.

[51] IMF Staff, 'Global Trade Liberalization and the Developing Countries' (2001) <www.imf.org/external/np/exr/ib/2001/110801.htm#ii> accessed on 7 October 2023.

[52] Zo Randriamaro, *Gender and Trade* (Institute of Development Studies 2006).

[53] This can be seen in the WTO core principles, eg MFN, National Treatment, and Reciprocity.

[54] OECD, 'Covid-19 and International Trade: Issues and Actions' (2020) <www.oecd.org/coronavirus/policy-responses/covid-19-and-international-trade-issues-and-actions-494da2fa/> accessed 17 August 2021.

[55] In The Public Interest (ITPI), 'How Privatization Increases Inequality' (2016) <www.inthepublicinterest.org/wp-content/uploads/InthePublicInterest_InequalityReport_Sept2016.pdf> accessed 17 August 2021.

portion of domestic responsibilities, even during their working hours.[56] Hence, this can make women more time-poor as it implies an increase in their childcare duties which they could otherwise delegate if they were able to access affordable childcare.[57]

Time poverty is one of the barriers that impedes women's participation in economies as it implies a lack of time for receiving education, skill development, vocational training, employment prospects, and business opportunities.[58] In addition, most household and domestic work is largely invisible and unpaid.[59] This puts women a step further from being economically empowered. On the other hand, trade liberalization measures can alleviate the burden of unpaid domestic work that women undertake. Foreign trade can transform these tasks into services, potentially provided by non-nationals and sold in formal markets. Women may become users of these services and thus trade in services can liberate time for women to enter formal employment.[60] Additionally, another potential time-saving impact of foreign trade can be realized through lower costs and greater availability of labour-saving household appliances such as washing machines, blenders, and dishwashers.[61]

At the household level, trade liberalization can either reduce or increase female control over household spending. One of the factors that determine this control is whether trade liberalization creates more sources of independent income for women. Trade liberalization can change the employment opportunities and consumption patterns of women and men. If these changes are positive for women, they are likely to influence the allocation of roles, time, and resources among household members in a manner that favours women. For example, an increase in the economic value of a woman's time might result in the reallocation of some of her household responsibilities to her husband. This also impacts her ability to control resources and make decisions relating to what food items to buy for family consumption, in what quantities, and how these are to be distributed among family

[56] Matthias Doepke and Fabian Kindermann, 'Bargaining over Babies: Theory, Evidence, and Policy Implications' (2019) 109(9) American Economic Review 3264 (the authors observe that women provide the majority of childcare even if both spouses are working).

[57] Titan Alon and others, 'The Impact of Covid-19 on Gender Equality' (2020) NBER Working Paper 26947 <www.nber.org/system/files/working_papers/w26947/w26947.pdf> accessed 19 October 2022.

[58] Maria Floro, 'Economic Restructuring, Gender and the Allocation of Time' (1995) 23(11) World Development 1913 (the author notes that trade liberalization can reduce the cost of products and services to help women save time).

[59] UN, 'Repository of information on time use in Latin America and the Caribbean' (Discussion on gross distribution of unpaid care work between and men in ECLAC, 2019) <https://oig.cepal.org/sites/default/files/2019-10_repositorio_uso_del_tiempo_eng.pdf> accessed 21 April 2020.

[60] National Board of Trade Sweden, 'Trade and Social Sustainability: An Overview and Analysis' (2017) <www.kommerskollegium.se/globalassets/publikationer/rapporter/2017/publ-trade-and-social-sustainability-webb.pdf> accessed 8 September 2022.

[61] Nilüfer Çagatay, 'Trade, Gender and Poverty' (United Nations Development Programme 2001) <www.researchgate.net/publication/49464683_Trade_Gender_and_Poverty> accessed 8 September 2022.

members.[62] Moreover, newly created jobs for women can challenge stereotypes.[63] With more power over their decisions and economic independence, women also gain heightened confidence and self-esteem.[64]

Another way to understand how trade impacts women and men differently is to look at variations in their purchasing power. As discussed in the previous sections, women are more likely to be represented in lower-income quintiles than men. Trade can have a positive impact on women consumers in low-income quintiles as the lower price of goods enables them to purchase and thereby increase their real incomes. Hence, trade liberalizing reforms can impact consumers by lowering prices and providing access to a wider variety of goods and services.[65] This aligns with conventional wisdom, which suggests that trade lowers prices by fostering greater competition and trade liberalization, thereby reducing both non-tariff and tariff trade barriers. However, studies have shown that tariff and non-tariff barriers are generally higher on essential goods such as food staples, clothing, and footwear.[66]

Moreover, because trade agreements have strengthened intellectual property rights (IPRs) for the protection of several products, including pharmaceutical goods and medicines, this has negatively impacted the vulnerable sections of society that have low purchasing power, such as women. These problems become worse for women with other disadvantageous compounding factors, such as women with a disability. One example to illustrate this problem is the strengthened IPR commitments in trade agreements, which have increased the cost of access to assistive equipment (such as wheelchairs, walking aids, and prosthetics) for people with disabilities.[67] This is particularly concerning, given that an adequate supply of such equipment is crucial for the safety, independence, and quality of life of women with disabilities. This disadvantage is further exacerbated by the fact that the majority of people living with disabilities are women. In addition, the imposition of heavy taxes on assistive devices and other related equipment has compounded the challenge of accessing these resources for individuals with

[62] Allan Winters, Neil McCulloch, and Andrew McKay, 'Trade Liberalization and Poverty: The Evidence So Far' (2004) 42(1) Journal of Economic Literature 72.

[63] Petia Topalova, 'Immobility and Regional Impacts of Trade Liberalization: Evidence on Poverty from India' (2010) 2(4) American Economic Journal: Applied Economics 1.

[64] UNCTAD, 'The Effects of Trade on Women's Well-Being and Economic Empowerment: Evidence and Research Methodologies' (2021) <https://vi.unctad.org/tag/docs/vol1/vol1m2.pdf> accessed 17 August 2021.

[65] Christian Broda and David E Weinstein, 'Globalization and the Gains from Variety' (2006) 121(2) Quarterly Journal of Economics 541.

[66] Alan V Deardorff and Robert M Stern, 'Measurement of Non-Tariff Barriers' (1997) 179 OECD Working Paper <www.oecd.org/economy/growth/1863859.pdf> accessed 17 August 2021.

[67] For more information, see Amrita Bahri, 'Trade Agreements and Disability Inclusion: Demystifying the Disconnect between Barriers and Policy Solutions', United Kingdom Foreign, Commonwealth and Development Office and Cowater International Inc (2023).

disabilities, particularly affecting disabled women who often have lower real incomes and purchasing power.

Higher tariffs affect all consumers equally but they disproportionately burden low-income consumers who are forced to allocate a larger share of their income to these tariffs, thereby negatively impacting their real income and affordability. Furthermore, recent reports have shown that tariffs are generally higher on goods destined for women compared to those that are destined for men, leading to what is known as 'pink taxes'.[68] The goods that face these considerably higher pink taxes include clothing, handbags, and sanitary products such as pads and tampons.[69] One study found that between 2006 and 2016 the tariff burden on women's apparel in the United States was US$2.77 billion higher than on men's clothing. This gender gap grew about 11% in real terms over that period.[70] Another study by the New York City Department of Consumer Affairs of the gender pricing of nearly 800 products revealed that, on average, women's products cost 7% more than similar products for men.[71] This highlights how trade policy can inadvertently exhibit bias against women consumers, suggesting that trade liberalization may not necessarily benefit female consumers if it does not prioritize products consumed by women and low-income groups.

2.2.2 Women's empowerment impacts international trade

There is a compelling business case for women's empowerment as there seems to be a positive correlation between women's empowerment and a country's GDP. A study conducted by McKinsey estimated that achieving equality in economic opportunities for women and men could increase global Gross Domestic Product (GDP) by US$28 trillion in the next ten years.[72] International Labour Organization (ILO) studies have confirmed these estimates as they have shown that reducing the

[68] New York City Department of Consumer Affairs, 'From Cradle to Cane: The cost of being a female consumer, a study of gender pricing in New York City' (2015) <www1.nyc.gov/assets/dca/downloads/pdf/partners/Study-of-Gender-Pricing-in-NYC.pdf> accessed 1 September 2021. Goods destined for women and girls were found to be 7% higher in price on average than those destined for men and boys in New York City, even after correcting for potential differences in quality.

[69] Mackenzi Lafferty, 'The Pink Tax: The Persistence of Gender Price Disparity' (2019) 11 Midwest Journal of Undergraduate Research 56.

[70] The World Bank and the World Trade Organization, 'The Role of Trade in Promoting Gender Equality' (World Bank Publications 2020) <www.worldbank.org/en/topic/trade/publication/women-and-trade-the-role-of-trade-in-promoting-womens-equality> accessed 17 August 2023.

[71] New York City Department of Consumer Affairs (n 68). In some cases, there were negligible differences between the products. Eg two toy scooters of the same brand but with different colours, red for boys and pink for girls, were valued at $24.99 and $49.99 respectively.

[72] McKinsey & Co, 'The Power of Parity: How Advancing Women's Equality Can Add $12 Trillion To Global Growth' (2015) <www.mckinsey.com/~/media/mckinsey/featured%20insights/employment%20and%20growth/how%20advancing%20womens%20equality%20can%20add%2012%20trillion%20to%20global%20growth/mgi%20power%20of%20parity_full%20report_september%202015.pdf> accessed 17 August 2021.

gap in labour participation rates between men and women by 25% would raise global GDP in 2025 by 3.9%.[73] Hence, there are clear economic gains for economies that can be achieved by engaging more women in the labour force and providing them with more business opportunities.

There are two dimensions to be considered for understanding the impact of women empowerment on trade. The first dimension is how women's empowerment is used to promote export competitiveness and economic growth.[74] The second dimension is how that empowerment may foster more empowerment of women with the creation of new economic opportunities.

Women's empowerment can have a positive impact on economic growth through greater accumulation of human capital as more women and girls access educational opportunities. This is a crucial factor for the development of national productivity and sustainable development.[75] Moreover, a more productive, skilled, and educated workforce in a country increases the rates of return on investments and attracts more foreign investment.[76] Studies have also found a positive correlation between women's education and an increase in their employment opportunities, the size of export-focused manufacturing sectors in that country, and the country's economic growth.[77] However, as observed in the previous section, female employees are a source of competitive advantage for firms facing international competition. This is because such companies tend to exploit the existing wage gap between men and women by paying lower wages to women compared to men in order to keep their labour costs as low as possible. As a result, women in the workforce face low wage rates, poor working conditions, and lack of social security benefits.[78] As van Staveren and others and Elson observe, female employees constitute a 'source of competitive advantage' and female businesses are typically 'underachievers of competitive advantage'.[79] This is why a large unskilled women's

[73] ILO, 'World Employment and Social Outlook Trends 2020' (2020) <www.ilo.org/wcmsp5/groups/public/---dgreports/---dcomm/publ/documents/publication/wcms_734455.pdf> accessed 17 August 2023.

[74] Marzia Fontana, 'Gender Equality in Trade Agreements' (2016) Study for the FEMM Committee, Brussels, European Parliament <www.europarl.europa.eu/RegData/etudes/STUD/2016/571388/IPOL_STU(2016)571388_EN.pdf> accessed 10 September 2022; Marzia Fontana, 'Women's Work: The Impact of Trade on Gender Equality' (World Politics Review 2014) <www.worldpoliticsreview.com/insights/13687/womens-work-the-impactof-trade-on-gender-equality> accessed 1 September 2021.

[75] Manuel Santos Silva and Stephan Klasen, 'Gender Inequality as a Barrier to Economic Growth: A Review of the Theoretical Literature' (2021) 19 Review of the Economics of the Household 581.

[76] Alessandro Cigno, 'Trade, Foreign Investment, and Wage Inequality in Developing Countries' (IZA World of Labour 2015) 193 <https://wol.iza.org/articles/trade-foreign-investment-and-wage-inequality-in-developing-countries/long> accessed 17 August 2021.

[77] Chatham House and Vivid Economics, 'Evidence for Action: Gender Equality and Economic Growth' (Chatham House 2010) <http://www.chathamhouse.org.uk/files/17416_0910gender.pdf> accessed 1 September 2021.

[78] Gurushri Swamy, 'International Trade and Women' (2004) 39(45) Economic and Political Weekly 4885.

[79] Irene van Staveren and others, 'The Feminist Economics of Trade' in Irene van Staveren and others (eds), *The Feminist Economics of Trade* (Routledge 2007) 1.

workforce in developing countries constitutes a key source of competitiveness in labour-intensive industries. These conditions contradict the obligations countries have assumed under various international instruments, such as the Convention on the Elimination of All Forms of Discrimination Against Women (CEDAW) 1979, the ILO's core labour standards, and the UN SDGs.

The rationale behind keeping the women's workforce concentrated in low-skilled and low-value-added jobs also contradicts business interests as studies have shown that increasing women's participation in senior decision-making positions in companies can increase their economic efficiency and productivity.[80] Companies with women in leadership positions are more profitable than those without as firms with women in executive and directorial positions have, in the last two decades, reported higher annual profit margins than those without female leaders.[81] Moreover, more women in trade helps to diversify trade as women employees and entrepreneurs can bring new products, processes, and concepts to the markets.[82]

Business opportunities for women can have a positive spill-over impact on women employees, families, and communities. It can increase employment opportunities for women as MSMEs (one-third of which in the world are owned by women) employ more than two-thirds of the global population.[83] In fact, businesswomen tend to employ more women compared to businesses owned by men.[84] As per a WTO survey, in companies with less than ten employees, 57% of workers are female.[85] For firms with between 11 and 30 employees, 18% of workers are female. When women start earning money, their bargaining power in the family increases. With increased bargaining power, the family has a better status and a better quality of life. This is sometimes known as the 'power of the purse'.[86] In addition, the economic empowerment of women leads to more prosperity, reduced poverty, and positive impacts on the ecosystems that operate in and on their families. This is

[80] ILO, 'Beyond the Glass Ceiling: Why Businesses Need Women at the Top' (2019) <www.ilo.org/infostories/en-GB/Stories/Employment/beyond-the-glass-ceiling> accessed 17 August 2021.

[81] Soyoung Han and Marcus Noland, 'Companies with women in leadership positions are more profitable than those without' (PIIE 2020) <www.piie.com/research/piie-charts/companies-women-leadership-positions-are-more-profitable-those-without> accessed 1 September 2021.

[82] Ben Shepherd and Susan Stone, 'Trade and Women', ADBI Working Papers 648, Asian Development Bank Institute <https://ideas.repec.org/p/ris/adbiwp/0648.html> accessed 25 September 2023.

[83] UNCTAD, 'Global Initiative Towards Post-Covid-19 Resurgence of the MSME Sector' <https://unctad.org/project/global-initiative-towards-post-covid-19-resurgence-msme-sector> accessed 9 July 2021.

[84] Kimberly Weisul, 'Report: Female Entrepreneurs Much More Likely to Employ Women' (Women Entrepreneurship Report 2018) <www.inc.com/kimberly-weisul/these-entrepreneurs-hired-very-few-men.html> accessed 1 September 2021.

[85] Anoush Der Boghossian and Amrita Bahri, 'Finding Feet on Trade Agreements: Empowering Women Entrepreneurs Amidst a Pandemic' (2023) 50(1) Legal Issues of Economic Integration 13.

[86] WTO, 'Gender Aware trade policy: A Springboard for Women's Economic Empowerment' (2019) 4 <www.empowerwomen.org/en/resources/documents/2019/10/gender-aware-trade-policy-a-springboard-for-womens-economic-empowerment?lang=en> accessed 10 September 2022.

because women invest most of their income back into their families, notably in education, food, and health care, as well as into their communities as they prefer to buy local products. Increasing women's economic power therefore has a 'snowball effect' on their families and their societies by increasing living standards for all and, hence, reducing poverty.[87]

2.3 Conclusion

Trade is a tool to achieve development, yet it is inadvertently non-neutral in terms of its distributive impacts on men and women. Trade liberalization affects men differently from women and it is therefore important for trade policymakers to engage in the negotiation and implementation of trade agreements with that consideration in mind. This nexus creates a case for the formulation and implementation of inclusive trade policies, which are not *de jure* discriminatory; however, they impact women and men differently due to dissimilar initial conditions. It is at the same time crucial to note that an inclusive trade policy is not an alternative to inclusive domestic policies and regulations; it must work in tandem with domestic policy to support women's economic empowerment. The following chapters will explore the possibilities of deploying international trade policies to incentivize changes at the domestic level that can help create a level playing field for both women and men.

[87] Jane Korinek, 'Trade and Gender: Issues and Interactions' (2005) 24 OECD Trade Policy Papers <www.oecd-ilibrary.org/docserver/826133710302.pdf?expires=1663237033&id=id&accname=guest&checksum=6321C322B67874ECFAD5FCC35C20D2A8> accessed 10 September 2022 (the author observes that jobs bring more household resources under women's control, which in turn has a positive effect on investments in the health and education of future generations).

3

Can WTO Laws and Institutions Empower Women?

3.1 Introduction

The website of the World Trade Organization (WTO) has a dedicated webpage on 'Women and Trade'. It starts with the following phrase: 'Trade can play an important role in driving women's economic empowerment. The WTO therefore seeks to build a more inclusive trading system that will allow more women to participate in trade and to reap the economic benefits of global trading.'[1] The question is: how? How can the WTO contribute to building a more inclusive trading system?

To date, the WTO rulebook remains gender-blind, in the sense that it does not contain a single explicit provision that relates to women. Moreover, scholars have observed that the WTO makes a difficult case for the representation of women and their interests as its multilateral framework is perhaps not ready to take on this additional issue over and above the 'legacy' issues lingering on the negotiation waiting list (eg agriculture, fisheries, and services).[2] For these and other reasons, despite the many strides taken to advance women's issues at the multilateral level, questions remain about the suitability of the WTO as a forum to lead the *démarche* on women and international trade. However, recent developments have shown that WTO has the potential to contribute to several aspects of enhancing women's interests by using trade policies.

In 2017, 118 members and observers of the WTO agreed to a joint declaration enhancing women's empowerment in international trade.[3] This was a landmark initiative by WTO members in which they acknowledged the high degree of interconnectedness between trade and women, and the need to have inclusive trade policies that are geared towards women empowerment. This declaration, which is a soft law instrument and a forum for sharing policy practices, reinforces the

[1] WTO, 'Women and trade' <www.wto.org/english/tratop_e/womenandtrade_e/womenandtrade_e.htm> accessed 18 September 2021.

[2] Judit Fabian, 'Global Economic Governance and Women: Why Is the WTO a Difficult Case for Women's Representation?' in Amrita Bahri, Dorotea López, and Jan Remy (eds), *Trade Policy and Gender Equality* (CUP 2023) 65.

[3] By 2020, 127 WTO members had signed the Buenos Aires Declaration, 'Buenos Aires Joint Declaration on Trade and Women's Economic Empowerment' (2017). For more details on WTO initiatives, see Anoush der Boghossian, 'Gender Responsive WTO: Trade Rules and Policies Work for Women' in Bahri, López, and Remy, ibid 65.

Trade Agreements and Women. Amrita Bahri, Oxford University Press.
DOI: 10.1093/9780198935759.003.0004

importance of augmenting women's access to economic opportunities through international trade. Other notable efforts by the WTO include various outreach events[4] and research outputs[5] that have contributed to the enhancement of understanding how trade is related to women's concerns.

In addition, the WTO nominated a specialized division in 2017 that is responsible for handling trade and gender issues.[6] This trade and gender division (now known as the WTO's Trade and Gender Office) is responsible for coordinating work among divisions, taking stock of what the WTO is doing and considering opportunities for new initiatives and further work to promote inclusive trade. It has four key functions: (1) raising awareness and understanding of the relationship between trade and women; (2) facilitating WTO members' actions and policies on enhancing women's empowerment using trade; (3) generating new data to better understand the impact of trade on women; and (4) capacity-building through the provision of training to public and private stakeholders on issues concerning trade and equality among men and women.

Another important institutional development in this respect took place on 23 September 2020, when a group of WTO members agreed to establish an Informal Working Group on Trade and Gender.[7] The Informal Working Group's objectives are threefold: (1) sharing best practices among members on increasing women's participation in trade; (2) considering and clarifying the meaning of a 'gender lens' in the context of international trade and expounding on how such a perspective could usefully be applied to the work of the WTO; and (3) reviewing and discussing relevant analytical work produced by the WTO Secretariat and exploring how best to support the delivery of the WTO Aid for Trade work programme.[8]

The WTO has also created a research hub—known as the Gender Research Hub—to deepen understanding of the intersection between women and trade by fostering further research and data-collection efforts. The Hub serves as an information-sharing platform where researchers and experts from around the

[4] For details, see WTO (n 1). Outreach efforts include conferences, seminars, round table discussions, and workshops on trade and women empowerment.

[5] eg see the World Bank, 'Women and Trade: The role of trade in promoting gender equality' (World Bank Group and WTO 2020) <www.worldbank.org/en/topic/trade/publication/women-and-trade-the-role-of-trade-in-promoting-womens-equality> accessed 18 September 2021; José-Antonio Monteiro, 'Gender-related provisions in Regional Trade Agreements' (WTO, Economic Research and Statistics Division 2018) <chrome-extension://efaidnbmnnnibpcajpcglclefindmkaj/https://www.wto.org/english/res_e/reser_e/ersd201815_e.pdf> accessed 6 October 2023; WTO, 'Making trade work for women: key findings from the World Trade Congress on Gender' (2023).

[6] WTO, 'WTO Action Plan on Trade and Gender 2021–2026' <chrome-extension://efaidnbmnnnibpcajpcglclefindmkaj/https://www.wto.org/english/tratop_e/womenandtrade_e/action_plan_21-26.pdf> accessed 6 October 2023.

[7] WTO, 'Informal Working Group on Trade and Gender' <www.wto.org/english/tratop_e/womenandtrade_e/iwg_trade_gender_e.htm> accessed 6 October 2023.

[8] For details, see WTO, 'Interim Report Following the Buenos Aires Joint Declaration on Trade and Women's Economic Empowerment' (25 September 2020) WT/L/1095/Rev.1 <chrome-extension://efaidnbmnnnibpcajpcglclefindmkaj/https://docs.wto.org/dol2fe/Pages/SS/directdoc.aspx?filename=q:/WT/L/1095R1.pdf&Open=True> accessed 7 October 2023.

globe can exchange research and collaborate on the topic. It also aims to foster research partnerships, helps gather research for easier access to experts' findings, and brings visibility to the academic work on trade and women to promote the topic as a recognized field of research and learning.[9] Moreover, the Hub serves as a collaborative platform as it facilitates dialogues and discussions on the topic among different stakeholders since its members are from academia, international organizations, think tanks, and government offices. The WTO members' continued work and vision in respect of furthering women's interests also became somewhat more visible in the Twelfth and Thirteenth Ministerial Conferences, as members at those meetings adopted an Outcome Document[10] and a Declaration[11] respectively, through which they recognized the importance of achieving women's empowerment for sustainable economic growth.

These recent developments and initiatives reaffirm the intention and willingness of the WTO as an organization willing to engage in making trade more inclusive. With nearly universal membership, and given its expertise in global rulemaking on trade issues and the institutional role it can play in advancing that agenda, the WTO could naturally lead the campaign in this area; in particular, its current trade agreements have the potential to contribute to women empowerment. This chapter will offer reflections on how the following trade agreements and initiatives can enhance women's concerns: the General Agreement on Trade in Services,[12] the Agreement on Agriculture,[13] the Aid for Trade programme,[14] the Trade Policy Review Mechanism,[15] GATT's General Exceptions,[16] the Trade Facilitation Agreement,[17] and the Revised Agreement on Government Procurement.[18] These agreements and mechanisms do not contain a single explicit commitment or provision regarding women's empowerment, yet the discussion in this chapter shows how an inclusive interpretation and implementation of these agreements can foster women's empowerment and increase their participation in trade. Some other disciplines under the WTO ambit (not discussed in this chapter) may also help women, such as Trade-Related Aspects of Intellectual Property Rights (TRIPS),[19], Sanitary and Phytosanitary Measures

[9] For more information, see the WTO Gender Research Hub, <www.wto.org/english/tratop_e/womenandtrade_e/gender_research_hub_members_e.htm> accessed 7 May 2024.

[10] WTO, 'MC12 Outcome Document' (22 June 2022) WT/MIN(22)/24, para 13.

[11] WTO, Abu Dhabi Ministerial Declaration (adopted on 2 March 2024) WT/MIN(24)/DEC, para 16.

[12] General Agreement on Trade in Services (15 April 1994) 1869 UNTS 183.

[13] Agreement on Agriculture (15 April 1994) LT/UR/A-1A/2 <http://docsonline.wto.org>.

[14] WTO, 'Nairobi Ministerial Declaration' (19 December 2015) WT/MIN(15)/DEC.

[15] Marrakesh Agreement Establishing the World Trade Organization (15 April 1994) 1867 UNTS 154, Annex 3 ('Marrakesh Agreement' or 'WTO Agreement').

[16] General Agreement on Tariffs and Trade 1994 (15 April 1994) 1876 UNTS 187, art XX (a).

[17] Agreement on Trade Facilitation (22 February 2017) 1915 UNTS 103, art X:3.

[18] Revised Agreement on Government Procurement (30 March 2012) 1915 UNTS 103, Annex 4(b).

[19] Agreement on Trade-Related Aspects of Intellectual Property Rights (15 April 1994) 1869 UNTS 299.

(SPSs),[20] Technical Barriers to Trade (TBTs),[21] and the Enabling Clause.[22] However, this chapter will not provide a discussion on how these disciplines could contribute because even though these cross-cutting issues may have some impact on the participation of women in trade, that impact is not clear due to a lack of data and scholarship on the issue. In addition, there are no clear best practice examples from WTO members employing these disciplines to boost women empowerment.

Taking that as the context, Sections 3.2 to 3.7 of the chapter will provide a discussion on how the abovementioned instruments, if seen through an inclusive lens, can contribute in this respect. Sections 3.8 and 3.9 offer reflections on recent examples that highlight the institutional and procedural limitations the WTO has in this respect and why it might not be an appropriate forum for this discussion.

3.2 General Agreement on Trade in Services (GATS)

Globally, almost 30% of the female workforce are employed in service-based industries.[23] Foreign trade is steadily shifting towards services and trade in services employs a larger share of women than the trade in goods sectors such as agriculture, textiles, and manufacturing.[24] According to the International Labour Organization (ILO), in 2000, 46% of all service sector workers were women, which rose to 58% by 2020.[25] Moreover, trade in services is expanding faster than trade in goods and therefore it has a greater potential to provide more employment and business opportunities for women. In the business world, women are more likely to lead and own companies in the service sectors. However, women often work in services that are mostly domestic in nature and are not traded across borders, such as health, education, and public administration; this is mainly because such services are more costly to provide across borders and there are higher barriers to trade in services than barriers to trade in goods.[26]

Women are also more likely to be employed in labour-intensive services that require physical proximity between providers and consumers, and such industries continue to face heavy non-tariff barriers to trade. Moreover, in a health crisis

[20] Agreement on the Application of Sanitary and Phytosanitary Measures (15 April 1994) 1867 UNTS 493.

[21] Agreement on Technical Barriers to Trade (15 April 1994) 1868 UNTS 120.

[22] 1979 Decision on Differential and More Favourable Treatment, Reciprocity and Fuller Participation of Developing Countries (28 November 1979) L/4903, para 2c.

[23] World Economic Forum, 'The Industry Gender Gap' (2016) 5 <http://www3.weforum.org/docs/WEF_FOJ_Executive_Summary_GenderGap.pdf> accessed 21 April 2020.

[24] Jane Korinek, Annabelle Mourougane, and Elisabeth van Lieshout, 'Women are less engaged in trade: Why, and what to do about it' (2023) <https://cepr.org/voxeu/columns/women-are-less-engaged-trade-why-and-what-do-about-it#footnote2_0tkosln> accessed 21 April 2024.

[25] ILO, 'Statistics on Women' <https://ilostat.ilo.org/topics/women/> accessed 21 April 2024.

[26] Sebastian Benz and Alexander Jaax, 'The costs of regulatory barriers to trade in services: New estimates of ad valorem tariff equivalents' (2020) OECD Trade Policy Papers, fn 238.

such as the Covid-19 pandemic where social distancing became a global norm, service industries such as tourism, finance, and education suffer significant loss of revenue.[27] Therefore women workers employed in those sectors are in an economically vulnerable position, especially in situations of crisis. Women are also over-represented in low-paid, part-time, and temporary employment, often without job protection, maternity benefits, health benefits, or pensions commensurate with their working life.[28] In any industry that is hit hard by a crisis—be it financial, environmental, or health-related—women are more likely to feel a more significant impact as compared to men who tend to have higher representation in senior positions and benefit from well-paid and permanent roles (often with stronger job protection and employment benefits) than women.[29] The WTO's GATS can help mitigate some of these losses and enhance women's access to better opportunities in the services industry.

The introduction to the GATS contains a clear statement that the agreement is 'aimed at promoting the interests of all participants on a mutually advantageous basis and at securing an overall balance of rights and obligations while giving due respect to national policy objectives'.[30] The participants of trade in services, as identified in this statement, include women employees, businesses, and consumers and hence the agreement should seek to protect and enhance their interests through the implementation of the agreement. The statement also acknowledges that it is important to respect the national policy objectives of WTO members, which may include women's empowerment or equality between men and women. Likewise, GATS seeks to increase the predictability of regulatory environments, which in turn makes it easier to export and import services for service-based industries.[31] Predictable regulatory environments particularly benefit small and micro firms, which are a significant source of employment and business opportunities for women employees and entrepreneurs.

Several legal provisions in GATS can be seen as implicitly beneficial towards the need to empower women. Article IV.1 seeks to increase the participation of

[27] Joan Faus, 'This is how coronavirus could affect the travel and tourism industry' (World Economic Forum 2020) <www.weforum.org/agenda/2020/03/world-travel-coronavirus-covid19-jobs-pandemic-tourism-aviation/> accessed 21 April 2020; UNESCO, 'COVID-19 Educational Disruption and Response' (2020) <https://en.unesco.org/covid19/educationresponse> accessed 21 April 2020.

[28] Linda Shields, Jenny Hall, and Abdulla A Mamun, 'The "Gender Gap" in Authorship in Nursing Literature' (2011) 104(11) Journal of the Royal Society of Medicine 457; Thomas Baum, 'International perspectives on women and work in hotels, catering and tourism' (ILO, 2013) 39–40 <www.ilo.org/wcmsp5/groups/public/@dgreports/@gender/documents/publication/wcms_209867.pdf> accessed 21 March 2020.

[29] Günseli Berik, 'Mature Export-Led Growth and Gender Wage Inequality in Taiwan' in Irene Van Staveren and others (eds), *The Feminist Economics of Trade* (Routledge 2007) 141.

[30] GATS, Preamble.

[31] Von Rudolf Adlung and Marta Soprana, 'SMEs in Services Trade—A GATS Perspective' (2013) 48(1) Intereconomics 41; Communication from Canada, 'Working to Ensure Benefits from the GATS for Members' Small and Medium Sized Enterprises (SMEs)', TN/S/W/36 (Council for Trade in Services Special Session, 2005)

developing countries in world trade by strengthening the capacity and competitiveness of their domestic services.[32] It aims to achieve this by enhancing developing countries' stakeholders' access to technology. This provision could be used to enhance the capacity and competitiveness of services in those sectors that provide significant employment and business opportunities for women. It could also be used to provide better technological support to women service providers to help them offer their services remotely in different markets without having the need to travel or face technical barriers such as immigration restrictions.[33]

Article IV.2 of GATS provides that WTO members (mainly developed countries) shall establish contact points to facilitate access to information related to developing countries' markets. Through this provision, WTO members can provide information that is relevant for women exporters, such as information regarding women's business networks in their respective countries and industries. Women entrepreneurs or employees could use this information to forge better connections with other entrepreneurs. In turn, this increased connectivity could help them find local partners, potential customers, or favourable government procurement opportunities in different foreign markets.

Article VI further seeks to foster developing countries' access to information networks.[34] This provision could also be beneficial for female service providers as it could help them secure timely information regarding market-entry barriers such as immigration-related restrictions and a plethora of administrative, procedural, eligibility-related, and licensing requirements in different foreign markets. The provision also seeks to encourage further liberalization of market access in sectors and modes of supply that are of export interest to developing countries. This Article, read together with Article XVI, could be deployed to expand market access for female service providers. Article XVI restricts members from imposing limitations on access to their service markets, provided that such restrictions are agreed upon and specified in their schedules.

Liberalization efforts in respect Mode 4 of supply[35] (ie presence of natural persons) can, in particular, enhance women's participation in the export and import of services. Mode 4 delivery involves the temporary movement of service suppliers

[32] Anh-Nga Tran-Nguyen and Americo Beviglia Zampetti (eds), *Trade and Gender: Opportunities and Challenges for Developing Countries*, UNCTAD/EDM/2004/2 (United Nations, 2004).

[33] Support for this argument can be found in Jan Yves Remy, 'Closing the Digital Gender Divide through Trade Rules' (Centre for International Governance Innovation 2019) <www.cigionline.org/articles/closing-digital-gender-divide-through-trade-rules> accessed 28 April 2020.

[34] Article VI requires members to provide objective and transparent criteria and procedures regarding competence, qualification requirements, technical standards, and licensing requirements to ensure that they do not constitute unnecessary barriers to trade in services. In addition, in cases where specific commitments are undertaken by a member, that member is obliged to ensure that all measures of general application affecting trade in services are administered in a reasonable, objective, and impartial manner.

[35] WTO, 'Movement of natural persons' <www.wto.org/english/tratop_e/serv_e/mouvement_persons_e/mouvement_persons_e.htm> accessed 18 September 2021.

from one country to the territory of another country. Female service providers' ability to work in foreign markets presents an opportunity to boost their employment. Temporary mobility offers enormous opportunities for women's participation; however, most of the services that are liberalized under the GATS framework through Mode 4 are mainly reserved for highly qualified professionals and senior business categories.[36] A majority of these roles are often held by men. Hence, there is an obvious need to revisit the quality and quantity of multilateral commitments in this respect. Multiple restrictions such as immigration, administrative, procedural, eligibility-related, and licensing requirements still impede this mode of delivery. By their very nature, these restrictions are often changeable or arbitrary and thus cannot lead to predictable market access.[37]

Mode 4 movements have a particular significance as they can enable women to enhance their level of education, skills, and work experience. This Mode can become particularly useful when national unemployment rates for women suffer a significant plunge, both in absolute terms and in relation to men, due to a natural calamity, a financial crisis, or a health pandemic.[38] Due to lack of employment opportunities domestically, and the time that might be required to revive an economy (eg after a pandemic-inflicted recession), identifying employment opportunities abroad could become a viable alternative. This could especially be the case in the health-care, education, and hospitality sectors. Scholarship has found that women employed under Mode 4 are not only able to support their families; they also create jobs for others by employing them for household responsibilities such as childcare.[39] Their increased collective spending on consumer goods and services provides new employment opportunities in national economies. This in turn can help in reducing poverty.[40] Gains from the liberalization of this mode of delivery could thus make a significant contribution to the achievement of the Sustainable Development Goals, especially through poverty reduction and the promotion of women's economic empowerment.

Article VII could also be of importance in reducing existing barriers to the movement of natural persons from one country to another. It encourages members

[36] Inter-agency Network on Women and Gender Equality, 'Gender Equality & Trade Policy' (Women Watch 2011) 10 <www.un.org/womenwatch/feature/trade/gender_equality_and_trade_policy.pdf> accessed 1 April 2020.

[37] United Nations Economic and Social Council, 'Draft Training Materia on streamlining formalities and documentary procedures connected with importation, exportation and transit' (Centre for Trade Facilitation and Electronic Business, 25th Session, 2019) ECE/TRADE/C/CEFACT/2019/20, 8–9.

[38] Amrita Bahri, 'Women at the Frontline of COVID-19: Can Gender Mainstreaming in Free Trade Agreements Help?' (2020) 23(3) Journal of International Economic Law 563.

[39] Martha Chen and others, 'Progress of the World's Women' (UNIFEM 2005) <www.unwomen.org/en/digital-library/publications/2005/1/progress-of-the-world-s-women-2005-women-work-and-poverty#view> accessed 1 April 2020.

[40] Sununtar Setboonsarng, 'Transport Infrastructure and Poverty Reduction', Policy Brief No 21, Asian Development Bank, 9; Anirudh Shingal, 'Liberalizing versus Facilitating Mode 4 Trade in Services' (2020) Policy Research Working Paper 9227, World Bank Group, 5.

to recognize the certifications, licences, education, or experience granted by another country. Such recognition, in full or in part, could be based on agreements or arrangements between the given countries or they may be accorded autonomously by country. For faster economic recovery in a post-pandemic world, especially for women in service industries, WTO members can agree to provide complete recognition of the professional credentials of service providers in a specific industry from its top five or top three import markets. This would mainly be the case for sectors in which women are highly represented such as health, education, tourism, retail, and distribution.

Article XIV (a) could also to some extent be useful in this respect. It allows members to pursue otherwise GATS-inconsistent measures if they are necessary to protect public morals. This exception could allow a member to pursue an otherwise GATS-inconsistent measure if it were necessary to protect or empower female service providers. This seems to be a very ambitious interpretation of Article XIV (a) and there is no jurisprudence which supports such an interpretation. However, arguments can be found in favour of this interpretation in several WTO cases that have invoked Article XX (a) of the General Agreement on Tariffs and Trade 1994 (GATT 1994).[41] In *US—Gambling*,[42] the Panel found that the term 'public morality' denoted standards of good and bad conduct on the part of or on behalf of a community or nation and that the meaning of the concept for members may vary over time and space, depending on various factors, including prevailing social, cultural, ethical, and religious values. The Panel also stated that members should be given a certain amount of freedom to define and apply the concept of 'public morality' in their respective territories by their own systems and scale of values.[43] In *EC—Seals*,[44] the Appellate Body found that the term 'to protect', when used in relation to 'public morals', did not require the Panel to identify the existence of a risk to EU public morals regarding seal welfare.[45] In light of these interpretations, a country could argue that the protection of or empowerment of female service providers, especially when they are hit by a particular crisis, is a public morality concern for its nation. The defending country could argue that the protection of or empowerment of female service providers amounts to a clear legitimate objective, provided that the 'design, architecture, and revealing structure' of the measure reflects a genuine public moral concern in that respect.[46]

[41] GATT 1994, art 11.

[42] WTO Appellate Body Report, *United States—Measures Affecting the Cross-Border Supply of Gambling and Betting Services* (20 April 2005) WT/DS285/AB/R, 5797.

[43] ibid.

[44] WTO Appellate Body Reports, *European Communities—Measures Prohibiting the Importation and Marketing of Seal Products* (18 June 2014) WT/DS400/AB/R and WT/DS401/AB/R, 7.

[45] ibid 5.167, 5.199–5.201.

[46] ibid 5.302.

3.3 Agreement on Agriculture (AoA)

Women grow much of the world's food and, according to the Food and Agriculture Organization (FAO), they represent more than 43% of the world's agricultural workforce. The percentage is significantly higher in developing countries where the majority of workers in agricultural sectors are women.[47] In most developing countries, women are predominantly engaged in the agricultural sector and mainly in subsistence farming. The experience in developing countries over the previous decades has shown that subsistence agriculture has not benefited from trade liberalization as it has been geared towards increasing export production, leading to the ignorance and displacement of women farmers in the subsistence sector.[48] Trade liberalization has had the effect of increasing the production of export crops, which has led to an increase in imports of food crops that compete with locally produced crops. This competition has depressed the prices of locally produced food crops and made small-scale farm production less profitable. In this way, trade in agriculture has so far affected men and women differently, as women are usually small-scale food-crop farmers working in subsistence farming, while men are typically more actively engaged in the production and marketing of agricultural commodities traded in the international markets.

As discussed in the first chapter, women face severe barriers accessing productive resources in the agriculture sector. The UN's FAO estimates that if women had the same access to productive resources as men, they could increase yields on their farms by 20–30%.[49] This could raise the agricultural output in developing countries by up to 4%, which could in turn reduce the number of hungry people in the world by 12–17%. In other words, around 100–50 million more hungry people could be fed.[50] Women's participation in the labour force as farmers indicates that agriculture offers a significant source of employment for women, yet this employment is often poorly paid and women are subjected to poor working conditions.[51] This shows how agriculture is not only a source of employment but could also be a source of exploitation for women. This is where the WTO's AoA can play a fundamental role in regulating agricultural trade sustainably and inclusively.

[47] ILO, 'Employment in agriculture, female (% of female employment) (modeled ILO estimate)' (2020) <https://data.worldbank.org/indicator/SL.AGR.EMPL.FE.ZS> accessed 11 April 2020.

[48] The World Bank, FAO, and IFAD, *Gender in Agriculture: Sourcebook* (2009) <http://siteresources.worldbank.org/INTGENAGRLIVSOUBOOK/Resources/CompleteBook.pdf> accessed 18 September 2021.

[49] FAO, 'Women could feed millions more people if given access to means of production—UN' (UN News 7 March 2011) <https://news.un.org/en/story/2011/03/368252-women-could-feed-millions-more-people-if-given-access-means-production-un> accessed 18 September 2021.

[50] FAO, 'The State of Food and Agriculture, Women in Agriculture—Closing the Gender Gap for Development' (2011) <http://www.fao.org/3/a-i2050e.pdf> accessed 11 April 2020.

[51] ILO, 'Women Work More, But are Still Paid Less' (ILO/95/22, ILO Press Release, 25 August 1995) <www.ilo.org/global/about-the-ilo/newsroom/news/WCMS_008091/lang--en/index.htm> accessed 18 September 2021.

The AoA's Green Box measures can allow members to employ support measures in favour of women to mitigate and compensate for the disproportionate impact of trade liberalization on women farmers. These measures, for example, can allow members to invest in subsistence agriculture and rural farming communities. They could create funds which could then be used to support women farmers through the implementation of various activities focused on training, research, and advisory services.[52] The use of such funds in other areas of investment that could help female farmers by increasing their productivity and income include the provision of marketing or promotion advice, an increase in access to information about better farming practices, and the enhancement of infrastructure such as electricity, roads, transport, and water supply.[53] Such measures can target specific barriers that impede the integration of women in the economy such as the lack of access to education, training, infrastructure, and information.

Some WTO members have employed these measures for the benefit of female farmers. For example, the Dominican Republic notified WTO of its measures to provide advisory services which aim to integrate rural women into productive and commercial agricultural activities. Guatemala has also reported the use of Green Box measures to provide credit assistance to small producers in its rural areas; the programme's direct beneficiaries were reported to be 5,200 producers, most of whom were intended to be women.

Another gender-responsive provision could be Article 6.2 of AoA, which is often referred to as the AoA's 'Development Box' as it allows WTO members to provide agricultural input subsidies to resource-poor farmers, a majority of whom. especially in developing economies, are women. This provision aims to allow developing members to encourage agricultural and rural development and support low-income and resource-poor producers. This can therefore support women farmers who, in particular, lack access to the required resources, work in informal sectors, and often do not own the land on which they work. Gambia once used the flexibility of this provision to provide free fertilizer to its female farmers.[54]

Another suitable tool may be the Generalized System of Preferences (GSP),[55] through which developed countries can offer non-reciprocal preferential treatment (eg zero or low duties on imports) to products originating in developing countries. Using GSP, developed countries can lower tariffs and non-tariff barriers

[52] GATS, Annex 2 (Green box measure defined in Annex 2); Agreement on Agriculture, art 6.2 (the AoA allows developing countries additional flexibilities in providing domestic support).

[53] Government services programmes allowed as per para 2 of Annex 2 as long as the programme satisfies the general criteria provided under para 1. The use of these services programmes should be considered by WTO members irrespective of any pandemic, but the ongoing situation makes their invocation in the interest of women even more indispensable.

[54] Anoush der Boghossian, 'Trade Policies Supporting Women's Economic Empowerment: Trends in WTO Members' (2019) World Trade Organization Staff Working Paper ERSD-2019-07.

[55] 'Decision on Differential and More Favourable Treatment, Reciprocity and Fuller Participation of Developing Countries' (Enabling Clause), Decision of 28 November 1979, L/4903.

for the import of food crops as well as cash crops that are most relevant for women farmers, producers, marketers, and business owners. These favourable interpretations and proposals are promising; however, the real elephant in the room before ensuring that the AoA can mitigate future harm to women is to address the long-standing constraints faced by women in terms of their lack of access to productive resources (land, credit, inputs, transport, extension services, storage, technical assistance, market opportunities, and know-how), because strengthened access over these resources will enable women to shield themselves from the negative effects of trade liberalization or to take advantage of the possible positive effects. With the help of incentives created by GSP schemes, and even the Aid for Trade programme, developed WTO members can help developing members to mobilize resources towards addressing some of these challenges.

3.4 Aid for Trade (A4T) Programme and Trade Policy Review Mechanism (TPRM)

The WTO's Aid for Trade (A4T) programme aims to provide support to developing and least-developed WTO members to assist them in building their trade capacity by converting market access opportunities into market presence. It does so by addressing four key areas: (1) creation of trade policy and regulations; (2) improvement in economic infrastructure; (3) building productive capacity; and (4) promotion of trade-related adjustments. Economic empowerment of women has long been a focus area for the WTO's A4T programme. The A4T initiative was created at the Hong Kong Ministerial Conference in 2005. In 2006, the A4T Task Force was created to kickstart the initiative's implementation. The final report of the Task Force, released in July 2006, includes an explicit mandate on gender equality.[56] Recommendations provide that A4T 'should take full account of the gender perspective and other goals of sustainable development'.[57] Moreover, in paragraph 5 of the WTO Declaration of 2017, the WTO members recognize that 'Aid for Trade supports tools and know-how for analysing, designing and implementing more gender-responsive trade policies.'[58]

The 2019 Monitoring and Evaluation Exercise found that women's economic empowerment now occupies a prominent position in the agendas of donor and partner countries. The Exercise found that about 84% of donors' A4T strategies and 85% of partner countries' national or regional development strategies seek to

[56] WTO, 'Recommendations of the Task Force on Aid for Trade' (Aid for Trade Task Force, 27 July 2006) WT/AFT/1 <https://docs.wto.org/dol2fe/Pages/FE_Search/FE_S_S009-DP.aspx?language=E&CatalogueIdList=58379&CurrentCatalogueIdIndex=0&FullTextHash=&HasEnglishRecord=True&HasFrenchRecord=True&HasSpanishRecord=True> accessed 18 September 2021.

[57] ibid section F.2.

[58] WTO (n 8) 5.

promote women's economic empowerment.[59] It also found that the main target group for gender-related A4T actions is that of women entrepreneurs.

Many donors have given considerable importance to issues concerning women's empowerment in their list of objectives. Many have also identified gender equality as a key instrument for achieving other Sustainable Development Goals including poverty reduction and economic growth. Yet, gender was not mentioned as an A4T priority until a few years ago. However, this has changed as donors and partner countries have gradually integrated women's concerns into their A4T objectives. In 2022, 92% of developing countries and 90% of donors included women's economic empowerment as a priority in their national or regional development plans or trade-related development aid.[60] Moreover, even though the main focus of trade priorities has been on export diversification, trade-related infrastructure, trade policy and regulations, competitiveness, access to global value chains, and trade facilitation, it is possible to argue that women empowerment can nevertheless be enhanced through effective and inclusive regulation of these priority areas.

One case study illustrates how infrastructure-building projects can have an impact on women's livelihoods. In Uganda, the A4T project titled 'Kalangala Infrastructure Services and Renewables Project' generated US$1 million in government revenue and created more than 300 jobs. It also empowered women by providing them with basic infrastructure such as electricity and creating more and better job opportunities for them.[61] This example shows that even though the A4T initiative is geared towards helping governments to build their trade capacity, access global markets, and increase their exports, it can also contribute to women's economic empowerment by lifting some of the obstacles women face, particularly with regard to trade-related infrastructure. Another example to illustrate this point is the case of Canada, an A4T donor that supports Burkina Faso in electrifying its rural areas using solar energy. The project targets the empowerment of businesswomen, increasing their production, and improving their processing and storage options in specific sectors which are predominantly female-led. Women's groups were also involved to ensure that the project fitted their needs.[62]

Thus, the following question arises: what more can be done to leverage the A4T programme in this respect? The A4T work programme 2018–19 provides some guidance on how it can contribute to the design of a trade agenda that is more

[59] Anoush der Boghossian, 'Women's economic empowerment: an inherent part of Aid for Trade' (World Trade Organization, Economic Research and Statistics Division, 2019).

[60] Aid for Trade Global Review, 'Empowering connected, sustainable trade', ch 4 <www.wto.org/english/res_e/booksp_e/aid4trade22_e.pdf> accessed 28 September 2022.

[61] WTO, 'Aid for Trade at a Glance 2011: Showing Results' (2011) <www.wto.org/english/res_e/publications_e/aid4trade11_e.htm> accessed 18 September 2021 (derived from Boghossian (n 59)).

[62] Marianne Musumeci and Kaori Miyamoto, 'Strengthening the gender dimension of aid for trade in the least developed countries' (Enhanced Integrated Framework 2019) <https://trade4devnews.enhancedif.org/en/news/strengthening-gender-dimension-aid-trade-least-developed-countries> accessed 8 May 2022.

responsive to women.[63] Focusing on economic diversification and empowerment, the programme outlines the WTO's role in providing youth and women with training in required skills, access to financing, and bridging the digital divide between men and women and between developed and developing countries. It also emphasizes the need to increase the competitiveness of small and medium-sized enterprises (SMEs), connecting them to global value chains and organizing thematic workshops on digital connectivity, e-commerce, and access to finance.

In addition, the WTO can offer an advantage through enhanced funding to countries that show a willingness to work on women's concerns through their trade policies and agreements. The A4T programme can encourage members to negotiate commitments within the scope of their trade policies and agreements on enhancing women's access to productive resources as well as their participation in education and skill development in those areas that can translate to highly paid job and business opportunities. A4T could also be used as a soft enforcement tool for trade policies, whereby the programme could withhold or reduce funding to those recipient countries that have violated their women-related obligations under a specific trade agreement or may not have reported their plans on implementing them in the previous five years or more. Employing a 'carrot and stick' approach (offering incentives to motivate countries to adhere to prescribed behaviours or actions, or some sort of punishment or disadvantage if they do not comply) can create incentives for A4T recipient countries to consider women's concerns when they formulate trade policies and agreements in the future or conduct impact assessments or reviews of their trade agreements. In this respect, the Enhanced Integrated Framework could be employed to bring together and exchange know-how and experience on this subject among the governments, organizations, civil society, and academia in least-developed countries.[64]

The Trade Policy Review Mechanism (TPRM) seeks improved adherence of WTO members to rules and commitments established in multilateral trade agreements by monitoring and reviewing their trade policies and measures.[65] It was found that, up until 2015, 70% of WTO members whose policies and measures were reviewed had incorporated considerations relating to women into their 'national or regional trade strategies, mostly to enhance women's participation in the workforce'.[66] Members have crafted these initiatives in the form of financial and non-financial incentives given to women-owned micro, small, and medium-sized

[63] Committee on Trade and Development, 'Aid-For-Trade Work Programme 2018–2019: Supporting Economic Diversification and Empowerment for Inclusive, Sustainable Development through Aid for Trade' (World Trade Organisation Committee on Trade and Development, Aid for Trade, 7 May 2018) WT/COMTD/AFT/W/75.

[64] WTO, 'Enhanced Integrated Framework' <www.wto.org/english/tratop_e/devel_e/teccop_e/if_e.htm> accessed 18 September 2021.

[65] Trade Policy Review Mechanism (1 January 2019) 1869 UNTS 480.

[66] Rohini Acharya and others, 'Trade and Women—Opportunities for Women in the Framework of the World Trade Organisation' (2019) 22(3) Journal of International Economic Law 323.

enterprises (MSMEs), the creation of women-favouring agriculture and fisheries policies, and the employment of women-favouring government procurement schemes. In the future, the TPRM can continue to monitor policies and measures undertaken by WTO members and assess whether such policies and measures are blind or responsive to the concerns of women. Based on this assessment, through its A4T programme, the WTO can provide additional incentives to countries that have made notable attempts to create or implement their trade policies using an inclusive approach towards women.

3.5 Article XX of GATT 1994 and Article XIV of GATS: The Public Morality Defence

Article XX of GATT and Article XIV of GATS allows WTO members to use trade-restrictive measures to protect particular non-trade values like human, animal, or plant life, public morals, or health, if certain conditions and qualifications are met.[67] Under these provisions, WTO members can restrict trade for a number of social reasons, including protection of the environment, animal health and life, human health and life, prevention of prison labour, and promotion of public morals. The public morals exception operates as a 'catch-all' for measures that do not neatly fit under any of the other exceptions.[68] Hence, a country may argue that the imposition of a measure or trade restriction to protect women's economic interests amounts to the protection of a country's moral interests. The existing morality exception may allow a country to take a measure that might otherwise be inconsistent with obligations under a trade agreement. Therefore, what kind of measures can be justified under the public morality exception? According to Steve Charnovitz, trade measures fall into two categories: those classified as 'outwardly directed' and those that are 'inwardly directed'.[69] Outwardly directed trade measures are those that are aimed at protecting the societal interests of people in a foreign country, whereas inwardly directed trade measures are those that protect the societal interests of people in their own country.

Outwardly directed trade measures can be taken against a targeted country to oppose a particular practice it might be engaging in. For example, bans or restrictions on exports and imports of goods or services can be seen as outwardly directed if they are taken to oppose the poor observance of commitments that

[67] Regis Y Simo, 'Trade and Morality: Balancing between the Pursuit of Non-Trade Concerns and the Fear of Opening the Floodgates' (2019) 51(3) George Washington International Law Review 407, 414, 460.

[68] Liane M Jarvis, 'Women's Rights and the Public Morals Exception of GATT Article 20' (2000) 22(1) Michigan Journal of International Law 219.

[69] Steve Charnovitz, 'The Moral Exception in Trade Policy' (1998) 38 Virginia Journal of International Law 689, 695, 716.

a country has agreed under the Convention on the Elimination of All Forms of Discrimination Against Women (CEDAW) 1979 or ILO Conventions. The aim of these measures may be to protect foreign female workers as they could be invoked to prevent the importation of goods from a nation that engages in human rights abuses against women. Inwardly directed measures can be taken to protect or empower women in the jurisdiction of the country invoking the measure. These measures become particularly relevant in times of uncertainty and hardship, such as during a health pandemic. During such uncertain situations, governments may offer various support schemes to domestic industries or small businesses that have a specific impact on women employees and entrepreneurs. These schemes could take the shape of state-aid, government bail-outs, loans, or subsidies. Some of the outwardly directed and inwardly directed measures may violate the commitments countries may have undertaken in multilateral, regional, and bilateral trade agreements. However, countries can justify these violations by invoking the exception of public morality that is found in almost every multilateral, bilateral, or regional trade agreement.

This may seem to be an ambitious interpretation of Article XX (a) of GATT, yet it is possible to find some support in favour of such an interpretation in existing jurisprudence and scholarship. The concept of public morals encompasses a wide spectrum of values and beliefs,[70] ranging from religious[71] and human rights principles[72] to societal attitudes regarding alcohol,[73] drugs, and corruption in business and politics,[74] gambling,[75] consumer protection,[76] and the treatment of nature and animals.[77] Literature suggests that a very stringent approach to the application of public morals exceptions may even infringe upon the legitimate interests and sovereign rights of a state to protect the values its society regards as important.[78]

[70] Nicolas F Diebold, 'The Morals and Order Exceptions in WTO Law: Balancing the Toothless Tiger and Undermining Mole' (2007) 11(1) Journal of International Economic Law 43, 49–50.

[71] WTO Secretariat, 'Report of the WTO Secretariat on the Trade Policy Review of Israel' (13 August 1999) WT/TPR/S/58, 24. Israel restricted importation of non-Kosher meat products.

[72] Treasury and General Government Appropriations Act of 1998, Pub L No 105-61, § 634, 111 Stat 1272, 1316 (1997). The United States restricted importation of products made by indentured child labour.

[73] WTO Secretariat, 'Report on the Trade Policy Review of Indonesia' (23 May 2007) WT/TPR/S/184, 30. Indonesia restricted importation of alcohol for moral reasons.

[74] WTO Panel Report, *Colombia—Measures Relating to the Importation of Textiles, Apparel and Footwear* (22 June 2016) WT/DS461/R, paras 7.338–7.339. In *Colombia—Textiles*, Colombia established a direct link between money laundering and drug trafficking and other criminal activities, including internal armed conflict. This led the Panel to conclude that combating money laundering was a 'policy designed' to protect public morals thereby accepting that the 'compound tariff', which was designed to prevent money laundering, had the objective of protecting public morals.

[75] WTO Panel Report, *United States—Measures Affecting the Cross-Border Supply of Gambling and Betting Services* (20 April 2005) WT/DS285/R.

[76] WTO Appellate Body Report, *Brazil—Certain Measures Concerning Taxation and Charges* (11 January 2019) WT/DS472/AB/R.

[77] WTO Appellate Body Report, *European Communities—Measures Prohibiting the Importation and Marketing of Seal Products* (18 June 2014) WT/DS400/AB/R and WT/DS401/AB/R.

[78] ibid 44, 74.

Certain moral norms are shared universally, as opposed to being state-specific.[79] Gender equality is considered to be a fundamental moral norm by most WTO members that have assumed commitments in this respect in multiple international conventions and treaties.[80]

The *US—Gambling* and *EC—Seals* cases have clarified that the concept of 'public morality' may vary over time and space.[81] The Panel has recently reinforced this view in *US—Tariff Measures on Certain Goods from China*, as it reiterates that members should be granted a certain degree of their own policy space to define their own public morals objectives as each member may have its own concept of morality.[82] In light of these interpretations, a country could argue that the protection of women's business and employment prospects in a particular industry that might have been severely hit by a crisis, such as the Covid-19 pandemic, is a public morals concern for its nation. It could be argued that this concern amidst a pandemic amounts to a clear legitimate objective, provided it survives the strictures under the requirements of necessity, nexus, and chapeau.[83]

The assessment of defence under Article XX involves a two-tiered analysis in which a measure must first be provisionally justified under one of the subparagraphs of Article XX before it is examined under the chapeau of Article XX.[84] Provisional justification under one of the subparagraphs requires that the challenged measure must 'address the particular interest specified in that paragraph' and that there must 'be a sufficient nexus between the measure and the interest protected'.[85] In the context of Article XX (a), this means that a member wishing to justify a measure must demonstrate that it has adopted or enforced a measure 'to protect public morals' and that the measure is 'necessary' to protect such public morals. As a result, WTO members have not only faced the tough standard of the chapeau but the overwhelming majority of respondents have also failed to prove that the trade-restricting measure at issue was necessary to achieve the goal for which it was

[79] Mark Wu, 'Free Trade and the Protection of Public Morals: An Analysis of the Newly Emerging Public Morals Clause Doctrine' (2008) 33 Yale Journal of International Law 215, 240.

[80] UN, Charter of the United Nations (24 October 1945) 1 UNTS XVI, art 1; UN, Convention on the Elimination on All Forms of Discrimination against Women (18 December 1979) 1249 UNTS 13. More observations in Tyler M Smith, 'Much Needed Reform in the Realm of Public Morals: A Proposed Addition to the GATT Article XX(A) Public Morals Framework, Resulting from China—Audiovisual' (2011) 19 Cardozo Journal of International and Competition Law 733, 759.

[81] For details, see text corresponding to nn 42, 44, and 45.

[82] WTO Panel Report, *United States—Tariff Measures on Certain Goods from China* (2020) WT/DS543, para 7.130.

[83] WTO Appellate Body Reports, *European Communities—Measures Prohibiting the Importation and Marketing of Seal Products* (18 June 2014) WT/DS400/AB/R and WT/DS401/AB/R, para 5.302.

[84] WTO Appellate Body Report, *United States—Standards for Reformulated and Conventional Gasoline* (20 May 1996) WT/DS2/AB/R, 20–22.

[85] WTO Appellate Body Report, *United States—Measures Affecting the Cross-Border Supply of Gambling and Betting Services* (20 April 2005) WT/DS285/AB/R, para 292. The Appellate Body stated that the two-tier analysis set out in WTO jurisprudence is contemplated under both art XIV of GATS and art XX of GATT 1994.

designed. As a result, no measure seeking a defence under the morality exception has so far survived the strictures of the necessity and the chapeau tests which can act as serious impediments to invoking protection under the general exceptions.[86] Hence, given the high threshold set by Article XX, achieving favourable support for women through such exceptions seems very unlikely.[87]

3.6 Trade Facilitation Agreement

Trade facilitation is about simplifying and streamlining the processes we use to move goods across borders. It aims to introduce processes which can reduce the time and cost implications of trade faced by traders at borders. The WTO's Trade Facilitation Agreement (TFA) creates binding obligations for WTO members to improve their customs procedures by making them more transparent and efficient in cooperation with border regulatory agencies and the private sector.[88] The Agreement also contains provisions for technical assistance and capacity building to support its implementation in developing and least developed countries.[89] Generally speaking, with reduced trade costs and complexities linked to handling imports and exports, the TFA can significantly benefit small businesses owned or managed by women. Moreover, the Agreement contains precise provisions that can target and reduce several barriers that women traders and women-owned businesses face at the borders.[90]

[86] In seven cases where the respondent invoked the morality exception to justify GATT- or GATS-inconsistent measures, it failed to satisfy the morality exception test established in WTO jurisprudence. WTO Appellate Body Report, *United States—Measures Affecting the Cross-Border Supply of Gambling and Betting Services* (20 April 2005) WT/DS285/AB/R; WTO Panel Report, *China—Measures Affecting Trading Rights and Distribution Services for Certain Publications and Audiovisual Entertainment Products* (19 January 2010) WT/DS363; WTO Panel Report, *European Communities—Measures Prohibiting the Importation and Marketing of Seal Products* (16 June 2014) WT/DS401; WTO Panel and Appellate Body Report, *Colombia—Measures Relating to the Importation of Textiles, Apparel and Footwear* (22 June 2016) WT/DS461/R and WT/DS461/R/AB; WTO Appellate Body Report, *Indonesia—Importation of Horticultural Products, Animals and Animal Products* (22 November 2017) WT/DS477/R/AB; WTO Panel and Appellate Body Report, *Brazil—Certain Measures Concerning Taxation and Charges* (11 January 2019) WT/DS472/R and WT/DS472/R/AB; WTO Panel Report, *United States—Tariff Measures on Certain Goods from China* (15 September 2020) WT/DS543. The Panel Report issued on 15 September 2020 in *United States—Tariff Measures on Certain Goods from China* reinforces this difficulty as the United States unsuccessfully justified its tariffs imposed against Chinese goods on the grounds of morality. The Panel found that the United States could not establish the requirement of necessity and nexus in this case and hence failed to even preliminarily justify its measure under this exception.

[87] This subsection is adapted from Amrita Bahri and Daria Boklan, 'Not Just Sea Turtles, Let's Protect Women Too: Invoking Public Morality Exception or Negotiating a New Gender Exception in Trade Agreements?' (2022) 33(1) European Journal of International Law 237.

[88] Agreement on Trade Facilitation art V.

[89] ibid art XIII:2.

[90] Global Alliance for Trade Facilitation, 'The World Trade Organization's Trade Facilitation Agreement through a Gender Lens' <www.tradefacilitation.org/global-alliance-publications/the-tfa-through-a-gender-lens/> accessed 18 September 2021.

Article 1 obliges members to establish enquiry points that can provide information in a timely and transparent manner. Therefore, this provision deals directly with information access problems faced by many cross-border women traders. Article 5 seeks to ensure that TBTs such as procedural controls applied at the border to protect human, animal, or plant life or health are not applied in a discretionary and arbitrary manner. It provides that if customs officials detain any import, they shall promptly inform the carrier, the importer, or its agent. This provision would allow cross-border women traders or businesses to save the time they might have otherwise lost waiting in being notified of any such detention. With time, they can also save the cost of border control procedures.

Article 5, read with Article 6, can in addition save women from discriminatory fees, charges, or informal favours (financial or non-financial) that may be imposed on women traders at the border, as these provisions contain measures to enhance impartiality, non-discrimination, and transparency, along with the associated charges and penalties. However, to ensure that this happens, it is crucial to propagate awareness among women traders about the rights these provisions create in their favour. Without awareness, these concerns could go unchallenged in the future.

Article 7 facilitates the expedited release of goods by allowing for the provision of electronic documents and acceptance of electronic payment of duties, taxes, and other kinds of financial charges. Other procedures, such as post-clearance audit and timely publication of release time information, also support the expedited release of goods. In this manner, the provision enhances access to information and saves women traders and businesses the investment they would have had to make in the release of goods without such procedures. In addition to the cost dimension, it can also save women traders from the discrimination they may otherwise face from customs officials at the border in the process of getting the goods released. However, for this provision to be effective, the information needs to be made available in a user-friendly and accessible manner and the provision needs to be supported by relevant and effective domestic policies.

The TFA also provides that, when possible, governments should establish a '*de minimis* shipment value or dutiable amount for which customs duties and taxes will not be collected'.[91] This provision would be useful for women entrepreneurs engaged in e-commerce as it would reduce trade costs for small businesses. Considering that the global small parcel market is expected to more than double from 103 billion parcels in 2019 to between 220 and 262 billion parcels by 2026, implementing this measure could support many women-owned MSMEs.[92] In

[91] Agreement on Trade Facilitation, art VII.8.2 (d).

[92] Cathy Morrow Roberson, 'Global parcel volumes expected to double by 2026 on e-commerce boom' (Journal of Commerce Online 2020) <www.joc.com/international-logistics/global-parcel-volumes-expected-double-2026-e-commerce-boom_20201012.html> accessed 9 July 2021.

particular, this provision can support the 'suitcase trade' of informal women entrepreneurs; however, one of its drawbacks could be that it can encourage women entrepreneurs not to scale up their businesses or formalize them so that they can continue to avail themselves of the benefits of the *de minimis* threshold.

Finally, Article 10 can be recognized as an implicit provision to empower women and can help them to minimize the cost and complications of doing business as it seeks to keep the formalities connected with the import, export, and transit of goods at the minimum possible level. A regular review of procedures, uniform documentation requirements and procedures, creation of a single window for border formalities, and use of international standards can help minimize costs and complications and may facilitate women's access to relevant information about border procedures, paperwork, licences, penalties, and other related formalities. The provision obliges members not to have a mandatory requirement for the use of customs brokers and so the elimination of untrained customs brokers from the process can further mitigate the possibility of harassment and discrimination against women businesses and women employees at the border. In addition, Article 8 might help cross-border women traders to minimize unsafe conditions and instances of harassment they may face at the borders as it encourages cooperation across national border agencies that share a common border.

The discussion in this section has demonstrated that effective implementation of the TFA could help women traders overcome three of the most formidable barriers, that is, access to information, cost, and complexity of doing business, and both harassment and discrimination based on sex. Women traders are often at a disadvantage in meeting the high cost and time demands of complex trading requirements, especially in developing countries where procedures may be cumbersome and not always transparent. Discrimination or harassment against women by border officials or third-party intermediaries (eg untrained agents/brokers) can also make trade more costly and discourage women from trading internationally. An action that is crucial for the inclusive implementation of TFA would be to develop border infrastructures whilst keeping in mind women's security concerns. This could include investing in proper lighting, separate sanitation facilities, safe and well-lit waiting rooms, feeding and family rooms, trained security personnel, and provision of banking, foreign exchange, and other services in very close proximity to border stations.[93] It may also be useful to create specialized help desks for women to report any wrongdoing or to obtain any required information from officers specially trained to deal with such concerns.

Achievement of these objectives would require the effective implementation of the Agreement. For this to happen, implementation will have to accompany

[93] Nisha Taneja and others, 'Trade facilitation measures to enhance women's participation in cross-border trade in BBIN' (2018) Indian Council for Research on International Economic Relations Working Paper No 350 <http://hdl.handle.net/10419/176377> accessed 18 September 2021.

or follow various requirements that do not fall directly within the Agreement's scope. These requirements could include the development of infrastructure at the border, enhancing the ability of private stakeholders to comply with border requirements, and creating intra-country channels that allow members to share and learn from their best practices and experiences. Other requirements may include the provision of appropriate training to authorized brokers and border officials, preparing women to be border officials or customs brokers, and imparting training on digital skills to border officials, brokers, and cross-border women traders so that they can optimize the use of a single window concept.[94] International organizations can take up the role of providing training to customs officials and brokers regarding the procedures, formalities, and information that businesses need to operate and deal with different stakeholders such as large and small enterprises and women traders.[95] This training could also comprise sessions that explain how officials can use the World Customs Organization's Gender Equality Organizational Assessment Tool to assess their border policies, practices, and activities.[96] In addition, international organizations could also help in gathering sex-disaggregated and industry-specific data to better identify the number of women entrepreneurs and traders engaged in cross-border businesses in different sectors.

Finally, it is also crucial to create a procedure that can allow for smooth coordination between public and private stakeholders so that public stakeholders can convey information to businesses promptly and the businesses can provide inputs and convey their concerns to the public officials. Moreover, public–private partnerships (PPP) may be crucial for developing countries as they may not have the necessary resources and capacity to fully modernize their customs operations. PPP arrangements could help governments gain access to resources they might not otherwise have, such as the finances required for infrastructure work and digital expertise to modernize border procedures. Private stakeholders—the real victims and beneficiaries of this change—could provide these resources to help governments overcome the resource constraints they may otherwise face when implementing the requirements provided in the Agreement. An example of such collaboration is the Global Alliance for Trade Facilitation, which seeks to ensure that the TFA works to reduce non-tariff trade barriers and red tape so that women-owned businesses can secure the benefits of trade. The Alliance is a mechanism

[94] The single window concept denotes a facility enabling trade and transport stakeholders to submit standardized information and documents through a singular point of entry thus streamlining compliance with import, export, and transit regulations.

[95] ITC, 'TFA Implementation' <www.intracen.org/itc/trade-facilitation-programme/TFA-Implementation/> accessed 18 September 2021. The ITC is carrying out research in this area.

[96] World Customs Organization, 'WCO promotes Gender Equality and Diversity' <http://www.wcoomd.org/en/topics/capacity-building/activities-and-programmes/gender-equality.aspx> accessed 18 September 2021.

that brings governments and businesses together to help countries implement the TFA.[97]

3.7 The Revised Agreement on Government Procurement (GPA)

Public procurement accounts for around one-fifth of global gross domestic product (GDP).[98] Up to this point, women entrepreneurs have not been able to participate in this market due to the nature of their businesses;[99] however, there is no concrete data to confirm the extent to which women are excluded from government procurement opportunities. International Trade Centre (ITC) estimations show that women entrepreneurs supply only 1% of that market. This low participation rate can be attributed to various barriers, such as limited access to information about bidding opportunities and processes, inability to meet the bidding requirements due to lack of time, expensive standards, and certification requirements, the substantial and capital-intensive nature of contracts, and bureaucratic hurdles associated with the bidding and selection processes.[100]

Governments are both market regulators and market participants and, thus, they are best placed to make procurement procedures inclusive and supportive of women's businesses by minimizing the barriers that impede their access. Governments can take several steps in this direction as they can provide procurement-related assistance to SMEs to encourage their participation in public tenders. This assistance could be provided through capacity-building training programmes or through the provision of subsidies or preferential pricing mechanisms. Article V.3 (a) of the WTO's GPA explicitly allows developing countries to provide a price preference programme under certain conditions and for certain procurement processes. Governments could also endeavour to reduce entry barriers (eg heavy licensing requirements) that may deter small businesses' access to this market. They can provide quotas or set-asides for SMEs in general or exclusively for women-owned businesses. Creating reservations or set-asides is perhaps the most controversial form of assistance and its application may invoke a legal challenge on its inconsistency with the WTO's GPA. It could be argued that

[97] Global Alliance for Trade Facilitation, 'Who we are: The Alliance' <www.tradefacilitation.org/who-we-are/about-us/> accessed 18 September 2021.

[98] ITC, 'Empowering women through public procurement' (2014) <www.intracen.org/publication/Empowering-Women-Through-Public-Procurement/> accessed 18 September 2021.

[99] Erin Kepler and Shane Scott, 'Are Male and Female Entrepreneurs Really That Different?' (SBA Office of Advocacy September 2007) <https://cmapsconverted.ihmc.us/rid=1225646682718_310554911_6940/Erin%20kepler%26scotte%20Shane%20-%20are%20male%20and%20female%20entrepreneurs%20really%20that%20different.pdf> accessed 18 September 2021.

[100] Eliza Niewiadomska, 'Facilitating participation of women-owned small and medium-sized enterprises in local and global public procurement markets' (Workshop on Enhancing the Participation of Women Entrepreneurs and Traders in Government Procurement, 25 June 2018) <www.wto.org/english/tratop_e/womenandtrade_e/programme_workshop_e.htm> accessed 18 September 2021.

preferences, reservations, and set-asides may discriminate against foreign companies. Even though these strategies could constitute a violation of the GPA, such actions could be defended as a public morality concern under Article III.2 (a) of the Agreement, particularly concerning the empowerment of women-owned businesses. That being said, advocating for a process which is conducive for women businesses is not solely a moral imperative; it also presents a business case. Mainstreaming women's interests in public procurement processes may not merely help women businesses to participate in this market, it can also help governments enlarge their pool of potential suppliers for every bidding process. The less complicated and 'low-hanging' measures in this respect could include increasing transparency in procurement processes and simplifying the application process by reducing the documentation requirements.

The GPA built on the WTO's fundamental principles of non-discrimination, transparency, and predictability to promote good governance mechanisms in government procurement practices and policies.[101] It has several legal provisions that can help governments create conducive conditions for women-led businesses. Article XIV of the Agreement, for example, encourages the use of e-procurement tools that can further enhance the accessibility and efficiency of procurement systems. Moreover, prompt publication and notice requirements under Articles VI and VII respectively can ensure that businesses (including small, women-owned businesses) obtain information about the bidding process in good time to prepare their applications. Articles VIII, IX, and X also play a role in this respect as they seek to streamline and standardize the conditions of participation, qualification requirements for suppliers, technical specifications, and tender documentation requirements. Complicated, burdensome, and resource-demanding public procurement procedures can dissuade women business owners from participating in public procurement markets, especially because they may have less experience and fewer resources to draw upon than other businesses.[102] By minimizing the differences and streamlining procedures and practices that foster predictability and fairness, governments can ensure that women businesses are not left out of this process due to sex-based discrimination, unfairness, or unpredictability that causes small businesses to stay out of public procurement.

Article XI prescribes 40 days as a general minimum period for submission of tenders, leaving the suppliers with sufficient time to prepare and submit their requests for participation. This provision directly helps women-owned businesses that often struggle with meeting the bidding requirements due to lack of time to

[101] Bedri Kamil Onur Tas and others, 'Does the WTO Government Procurement Agreement Deliver What It Promises?' (2018) 18 World Trade Review 609.

[102] FreshMinds, 'Evaluating SME Experiences of Government Procurement' (2008) <http://shared.freshminds.co.uk/marketing/SME_Procurement_Report.pdf> accessed 18 September 2021.

submit their applications. Article XV of the GPA may also be helpful as it ensures that the treatment of tenders and awarding of contracts take place in a simple and fair manner. The GPA's requirement for domestic review of procurement decisions provides women business owners with a crucial platform to voice their concerns if they face any unfair or discriminatory treatment that puts them at a disadvantage in the procurement market. Hence, the Agreement has several provisions that can enable governments to enhance the participation of women entrepreneurs in this sector. An inclusive interpretation of the Agreement can therefore help countries rethink how they can boost the participation of women in the public procurement market.

However, the Agreement has its own constraints as it remains a plurilateral agreement, meaning that not all WTO members are part of the accord. In addition, it does not contain any explicit provisions relating to women that may oblige a party to take inclusive and supportive measures in their respective jurisdictions. Nevertheless, several GPA members have used various government procurement policies to foster MSMEs' and women entrepreneurs' participation in the economy. These policies are crafted in different forms including quotas for women-owned businesses, gender-neutral allocation of contracts, or the extension of preference to companies that have women-favouring and non-discriminatory policies and practices.[103] For instance, Switzerland is an example of practice in this respect as it uses its public procurement market as a lever to deter the private sector from engaging in gender-biased practices.[104] The Swiss government has put in place a procurement policy that gives preference to companies that respect equal pay and non-discrimination during contract allocation.[105] To fulfil this commitment, the country has established 'Logib', an online tool designed to evaluate the records of companies to confirm whether they have adhered to equal pay and non-discrimination commitments. Furthermore, the Federal Office of Gender Equality (FOGE) conducts independent investigations to verify whether such companies are complying with equal pay requirements. If wage discrimination is identified

[103] WTO, 'Trade Policies Supporting Women's Economic Empowerment: Trends in WTO Members' (20 May 2019) Economic Research and Statistics Division Staff Working Paper ERSD-2019-07.

[104] SN Nyeck, '(Out)bidding Women: Public Procurement Reform Diffusion and Gender Equality in Africa' (2015) 13 Wagadu 24.

[105] This commitment is grounded in art 8.1(c) of the Federal Act on Public Procurement (FAPP) which reads as follows:

> The following principles shall be respected in awarding public contracts:
>
> ...
>
> c. Contracts shall only be awarded to suppliers that guarantee equal treatment of men and women in respect of pay for workers performing services in Switzerland.

This provision derives from the Federal Act on Gender Equality (Gender Equality Act, GEA) of 24 March 1995. Article 3.2 Prohibition of discrimination reads: 'This prohibition applies in particular to hiring, allocation of duties, setting of working conditions, pay, basic and advanced training, promotion and dismissal.'

in a company, its tender can be revoked or a penalty for breach of contract can be issued.[106]

Other countries like the United States have also taken steps in this regard, including the mandate of preferential set-asides for women suppliers, especially in industries where the rate of engagement of women-run companies is low.[107] However, Chile is a clear front runner in this respect, as it has taken multiple steps to enhance women's participation in its government procurement market. It has implemented e-procurement tools to facilitate application processes and has introduced a simplified and inclusive selection criteria. Its other efforts include the provision of training for women-owned businesses on how they can improve their capacities, certifying them as eligible suppliers, establishing women associations and networks, and creating digital tools to disseminate information in a transparent and timely manner.[108] The ITC has found that the e-marketplace has been particularly useful in pulling more women-owned companies into the procurement market because of the ease of doing business online. Yet, digitalization of these procedures could have some negative ramifications for women businesses that do not have enough technological expertise to be able to make use of such platforms. Article V.8 of the GPA could help mitigate this challenge as it allows developing countries to request technical cooperation and capacity building for the implementation of the Agreement. Therefore, by invoking this provision, the WTO can offer training on digital processes and platforms to both public and private stakeholders.

3.8 The Plurilateral Initiatives: Joint Statement Initiative on Services Domestic Regulation and Joint Declaration on Trade and Women's Economic Empowerment

The discussions in the previous sections demonstrate the crucial role of the WTO's multilateral and plurilateral agreements in the protection and enhancement of

[106] Swiss Confederation, 'Ordinance on Public Procurement' (12 February 2020) SR 172.056.11, art 6.4 (presently derived from the presentation by Patric Aeberhard, Equal Pay Expert, Federal Office for Gender Equality, Switzerland at the WTO Workshop on 'Workshop on Enhancing the Participation of Women Entrepreneurs and Traders in Government Procurement', 25 June 2018).

[107] For details on gender-smart procurement policies in the EU, the United States, Australia, and Chile, see Susan Harris Rimmer (ed), 'Gender-smart Procurement Policies for Driving Change' (Chatham House, 2017) 25.

[108] eg ChileCompra oversees Mercado Publico—an e-marketplace for selling products and services primarily composed of MSMEs. ChileCompra has also launched Sello Empresa Mujer, a Women Supplier Certification that helps procurement agencies identify women-owned enterprises that have more than half female employees. ChileCompra has also developed a 'commercial management' programme as well as a mentorship programme that trained women state suppliers with leadership tools, provided them with the certification, and formed a women's association of state suppliers known as the Associación de Mujeres Empresarias Provedores del Estado (AMEPE).

women's empowerment within trade, particularly when they are interpreted and implemented with an inclusive approach. Moreover, there has been an emerging interest in understanding how other plurilateral initiatives are increasingly becoming an alternative path to revitalize the WTO's much needed negotiating function.[109] In December 2021, a number of WTO members adopted a declaration announcing the successful conclusion of negotiations for the Joint Statement Initiative (JSI) on Services Domestic Regulation. This JSI aims to increase the transparency, predictability, and efficiency of the authorization procedures of service providers. In February 2024, the disciplines of JSI entered into force for 45 WTO members, following the conclusion of certification procedures under the GATS. Interestingly, this JSI includes a binding provision on non-discrimination between men and women in the context of authorization procedures for service supplies. Therefore, it demonstrates how women-related considerations can be addressed by WTO members using plurilateral initiatives.

The WTO's Joint Declaration on Trade and Women's Economic Empowerment, signed in December 2017 in Buenos Aires by almost 70% of the WTO membership, further reaffirms that improving women's access to opportunities and removing barriers to their participation in national and international economies can contribute to sustainable economic development. This multilateral initiative aligns with and complements CEDAW 1979 and Goal 5 of the Sustainable Development Goals in the 2030 UN Agenda for Sustainable Development.

This is a promising development in the multilateral trading system as it marks a concrete starting point for future deliberations and discussions on how trade can accommodate gender equality concerns. The Declaration is an anchoring commitment agreed upon in a multilateral setting. Although the commitments included in the Declaration were not bold enough to unleash any daring changes, the relevance of the Declaration is undisputed because, for the very first time, gender equality was discussed at a high-level meeting in the context of trade policy and a direct and explicit link was established between women's economic empowerment and trade. Moreover, the ambitions of the Declaration were followed up by the creation of an Informal Working Group on Trade and Gender (IWG) at the WTO in September 2020. Yet, we cannot ignore its limitations. First, the declaration is neither binding in nature nor does it impose any obligation on signatory members to undertake actions or confer any right on any member to justify an otherwise WTO-inconsistent measure. Second, it seeks to prepare a framework to guide its members to reformulate their trade policies in a gender-responsive manner, yet it does not contain any action plan or proposed measures or strategies for its implementation nor does it provide any guidance to its signatories on how to implement the instrument into their domestic laws and procedures. Third, it has no

[109] Daria Boklan, Olga Starshinova, and Amrita Bahri, 'Joint Statement Initiatives: A Legitimate End to "Until Everything is Agreed"?' (2023) 57(2) Journal of World Trade 339.

enforcement or implementation mechanism, relying entirely on the good intentions and best endeavours of its signatory members.[110] Some critics have called the Declaration a 'Trojan horse' that may be used to bring in more contentious issues to the already stalled multilateral trade negotiations,[111] and noted that it can 'allow developed countries to use the advantage of more forward gender policies to obstruct exports from underdeveloped nations'.[112]

3.9 The Results from Twelfth and Thirteenth Ministerial Conferences Are Not Promising

At the WTO's Twelfth Ministerial Conference (MC12), trade and gender enthusiasts were awaiting another significant advance in this field as there were high expectations that the WTO members would sign a more ambitious declaration, entitled 'The Joint Ministerial Declaration on the Advancement of Gender Equality and Women's Economic Empowerment within Trade'. Its draft was launched months before the conference in December 2021. A glance through the then available draft showed that the Declaration aimed at seeking the collaboration of WTO members on a number of concrete activities including: (1) to review, develop, and improve the collection of gender-disaggregated data on trade and gender as the basis for gender-responsive policies; (2) to utilize the findings of research initiatives to inform trade policy to support women's economic empowerment; (3) to explore and analyse ender perspective and women's economic empowerment issues in the work of the WTO; and (4) to promote collaboration among international and regional organizations and national authorities for gender mainstreaming in the Aid for Trade programme. Unlike the 2017 Buenos Aires Declaration which was informal in nature, the new Declaration was meant to be a formal Ministerial Declaration and was being supported by 125 members as at May 2022. Given that its objective was to 'explore and analyze a gender perspective and women's economic empowerment issues in the work of the WTO', some scholars believed that it had the potential to instigate significant change within the WTO as it could have had the impact of gender equality being permeated across all WTO work.[113]

[110] Discussed in Amrita Bahri, 'Measuring the Gender-Responsiveness of Free Trade Agreements: Using a Self-Evaluation Maturity Framework' (2019) 14 (11) Global Trade & Customs Journal 517.

[111] Roberto Bissio, 'Is "gender" a Trojan horse to introduce new issues at WTO?' (Third World Network 11 December 2017) <https://twnetwork.org/wto/%E2%80%9Cgender%E2%80%9D-trojan-horse-introduce-new-issues-wto> accessed 18 September 2021.

[112] Ananya Singh, 'Explained: India's refusal to back WTO declaration on gender equality in trade' (QRIUS 15 December 2017) <https://qrius.com/explained-india-refusal-gender-equality-trade/> accessed 18 September 2021.

[113] Simonetta Zarrilli, 'If at first you do not succeed, try women's economic empowerment through trade' <www.tradeexperettes.org/blog/articles/if-at-first-you-do-not-succeed-try-womens-economic-empowerment-through-trade?rq=simonetta> accessed 18 September 2023.

Unsurprisingly to many, the Declaration did not materialize and the hopes and aspirations of its adoption faded alongside the memories of the Twelfth Ministerial Conference. Some believe that it did not go through because it faced intense opposition from many members and that most members were not ready to take such a leap in terms of assuming affirmative or concrete actions in respect of gender equality. Opposition also stemmed from lack of evidence on how trade relates to women and the general belief that trade policy is not the most effective instrument to empower women. Furthermore, the considerable challenge of integrating women's concerns into trade governance was underscored by the MC12 Outcome Document, in which members 'recognized' women's economic empowerment and 'took note' of the efforts of the WTO, the United Nations Conference on Trade and Development (UNCTAD), and the ITC on the subject. Many viewed the paragraph as a substitute for the Joint Ministerial Declaration mentioned earlier which, instead of being approved at MC12 as expected, was put on hold.

At the most recent Thirteenth Ministerial Conference, WTO members included, or rather repeated, a very similar reference to women's empowerment in the Ministerial Declaration.[114] The inclusion reads as follows: 'We recognise that women's economic empowerment and women's participation in trade contributes to economic growth and sustainable development. We take note of WTO work, including in collaboration with other relevant international organizations, through activities such as capacity-building initiatives and sharing experience to facilitate women's participation in trade.'[115] This statement comes with an associated footnote that reads: 'These are general messages on cross-cutting issues that do not change the rights or obligations of WTO Members and do not relate to any Joint Statement Initiatives.'[116] There are several important things to note here. The WTO members in this reference do not go beyond showing awareness or recognition as they merely seek to 'recognize' how women contribute and 'take note' of the WTO activities in respect of facilitating women's participation in trade. This means that the members in this document do not assume any affirmative commitments in respect of women empowerment. Moreover, the WTO members do not even express an intention to continue working in this respect as the statement merely reads that they 'take note of' the existing work. It cannot be said with certainty whether the members support it, oppose it, would like it to continue, or would rather prefer its discontinuation in the future. One can counterargue and infer an indirect intention of the WTO members to carry out more work in this respect as the statement contains their 'recognition' of the importance of women's empowerment and participation in trade. However, what comes as a more disappointing addition is the accompanying footnote in which the members clarify beyond any doubt that these

[114] Abu Dhabi Ministerial Declaration (n 11).
[115] ibid para 16.
[116] ibid para 16, fn 2.

statements are merely 'general messages' and cannot serve as the basis for any legal right or obligation, or even future plurilateral initiatives.

3.10 Conclusion

Many WTO members have argued that the WTO is not the appropriate forum to discuss issues related to women as 'gender does not relate to trade, and hence WTO should refrain from bringing in non-trade issues' on its agenda.[117] Critics have raised questions regarding the use of the WTO framework to drive social changes like women's empowerment and there is a notable reluctance among WTO members to include issues relating to women in the multilateral space, as opposed to the inclusion of other contemporary issues such as digital trade, e-commerce, labour, and intellectual property.

This unease underscores a clear reality: it is probably impractical to propose changes in the WTO's rulebook to make it explicitly responsive to women's concerns. If WTO members struggled to reach a consensus on completely non-binding declarations with various best endeavour promises, it is inconceivable, or rather impractical, to expect them to agree on explicitly including women's concerns in WTO texts. Furthermore, aside from a multilaterally negotiated outcome, WTO members have continued to oppose or have shown indifference to institutional or outreach efforts by the organization in this respect. This resistance can be attributed to four possible reasons:

(1) If used as a sword, women-related concerns in trade instruments can usher in a new generation of protectionist actions against selected countries.
(2) If used as a shield, defending countries can justify anything under an exception favouring women because the definition and scope of the terms 'gender equality' and 'women empowerment' are as broad and as ambiguous as the scope of the public morality exception.
(3) Countries may lack the political will to improve women's situations in their respective jurisdictions. A general lack of political willingness could be attributed to a country's lack of understanding about the inter-relationship between trade and women.
(4) Countries may believe that women's empowerment is not directly related to trade and hence should not be included in trade instruments. This view is in line with feminist scholars who argue that trade law and feminist studies are two different fields of study and should therefore be kept separate to avoid possible conflicts of law and jurisdictions. The fear is that such inclusions

[117] Suresh Prabhu, 'Indian Minister of Industry and Commerce' (Indian Press Conference, WTO Ministerial Conference, Buenos Aires, 11 December 2017).

may invoke a potential conflict of law between the WTO norms and guiding principles usually found in domestic laws or international instruments such as ILO and CEDAW.[118]

These initial observations show that the WTO's multilateral space has various limitations that impede its potential to mainstream concerns relating to women. The multilateral trading system may not be fully prepared to sign on to these issues but recent trends show the promising role that free trade agreements (FTAs) can play in this respect. The following chapter provides an in-depth discussion on how and why FTAs can respond to women's concerns.

[118] Martha C Nussbaum, *Women and Human Development: The Capabilities Approach* (CUP 2007) 5–6, 70.

4

Can Trade Agreements Empower Women?

4.1 Introduction

The number of free trade agreements (FTAs) has skyrocketed over the past two decades. They have become an effective instrument among selected negotiating parties to reflect rapidly changing societies and economies as they enable parties to reach a consensus in a timely manner and on traditionally contentious subjects, such as digital trade, labour standards, or artificial intelligence. With the growing understanding that FTAs have had disproportionately negative effects on women, the next obvious question to address is whether FTAs can accommodate concerns relating to women and help them address the barriers they face. Because FTAs can reach so deeply into regulatory areas traditionally reserved for national governments—such as competition policy, investment, environment protection, core labour standards, immigration, etc—it is possible to argue that they may also have the apparent potential to reach the regulations and procedures impacting gender equality.[1]

The inclusion of women-specific language has recently been viewed as a building block to ensure that trade agreements can empower women by helping them overcome the barriers they face and by creating new opportunities for them.[2] There is a growing understanding in the trade policy world that trade agreements can provide a basis for translating commitments relating to gender equality from international understandings into national trade policies. As a result, in recent years there has been a sharp increase in the number of FTAs mainstreaming women's concerns and challenges, to the extent that such inclusions are gradually emerging as a policy norm in trade agreements.[3] Certain countries are seen as champions of this approach as they have included ambitious, broad, and multiple commitments to empower women in their trade agreements.[4] However, many other countries have so far stayed away from this trend or have been passive or indifferent to it.

[1] Constance Z Wagner, 'Looking at Regional Trade Agreements through the Lens of Gender' (2012) 31 St Louis University Public Library Review 497.

[2] Rohini Acharya and others, 'Trade and Women—Opportunities for Women in the Framework of the World Trade Organization' (2019) 22(3) Journal of International Economic Law 323.

[3] José-Antonio Monteiro, 'Gender-Related Provisions in regional Trade Agreements' (WTO Economic Research and Statistics Division 18 December 2018) <www.wto.org/english/res_e/reser_e/ersd201815_e.pdf> accessed 8 April 2021.

[4] Amrita Bahri, 'Measuring the Gender-Responsiveness of Free Trade Agreements: Using a Self-Evaluation Maturity Framework' (2019) 14(11) Global Trade & Customs Journal 517.

Trade Agreements and Women. Amrita Bahri, Oxford University Press. © Amrita Bahri 2025.
DOI: 10.1093/9780198935759.003.0005

The last few years have been phenomenal in this respect. In 2018, the European Parliament passed a resolution to include gender equality consideration in all future EU trade agreements.[5] By doing this, the EU committed itself to ensuring that trade-related aspects of women's interests are adequately addressed in its future trade agreements.[6] In 2019, two FTAs with a dedicated chapter on trade and gender were entered into.[7] In 2023, the EU and Chile negotiated a stand-alone and very comprehensive chapter entitled 'Trade and gender equality' in the Interim Agreement on Trade, in which they added a number of commitments in the form of reaffirmations, cooperation activities, minimum legal standards, common commitments relating to their laws and procedures, institutional arrangements, procedures on review and implementation, and procedures on dispute settlement.[8] The parties to the African Continental Free Trade Area (AfCFTA) Agreement also negotiated a stand-alone Protocol on Women and Youth in Trade, which aims to operationalize the Agreement's commitment relating to women and to promote equal opportunities for women in intra-African trade.[9] In addition, beyond bilateral negotiations, key initiatives such as the Global Trade and Gender Agreement (GTAGA) have been instrumental in translating the importance that countries give to the issue of gender equality in their trade policy contexts.[10] These developments challenge the long-standing assumption that trade and women's interests are not related. They affirm that neither international trade nor gender equality is a zero-sum game. Everyone benefits from making trade more inclusive.

FTAs can play an important role in empowering women in several ways. They can help women deal with the barriers they face as countries can encourage their trade partners to create or change domestic laws and procedures that can reduce the challenges that hinder women's interests, thereby fostering favourable conditions for women's participation in trade and commerce. FTAs can also encourage countries to carry out ex-post and ex-ante impact assessments of trade agreements to which they are party, which can then help in gathering evidence on how trade agreements can and have impacted women in different countries and regions.[11]

[5] European Parliament, 'Gender equality in EU trade agreements' (13 March 2018) 2017/2015(INI) <www.europarl.europa.eu/doceo/document/TA-8-2018-0066_EN.html> accessed 8 April 2020.

[6] European Commission, 'Communication from the Commission to the European Parliament, the Council, the European Economic and Social Committee and the Committee of the Regions, A Union of Equality: Gender Equality Strategy 2020–2025' (5 March 2020).

[7] Modernized Canada–Chile Free Trade Agreement (CCFTA) (2019); Modernized Canada–Israel Free Trade Agreement (CIFTA) (2019).

[8] Interim Agreement on Trade between the European Union and the Republic of Chile Agreement (2023) ch 27.

[9] Maxime Houinato 'AfCFTA: Upcoming Protocol on Women and Youth in Trade a chance to empower women' (UN Africa Renewal 22 February 2024) <www.un.org/africarenewal/magazine/february-2024/afcfta-upcoming-protocol-women-and-youth-trade-chance-empower-women> accessed 8 April 2024.

[10] Global Trade and Gender Arrangement (2020).

[11] Countries can use the United Nations Conference on Trade and Development (UNCTAD) toolbox on trade and gender for conducting these assessments. More details at UNCTAD, 'UNCTAD

Countries can bind themselves to certain minimum legal standards for improving the employment conditions of women or prohibiting sex-based discrimination.[12] Countries can also endeavour to increase women's access to health services, education, and skill development. They can additionally create encouraging conditions for women's businesses to flourish, for example through the creation of business networks and improved infrastructure in relevant sectors and industries. Countries entering into FTAs can also commit to increasing the representation of women in decision-making and policymaking roles. Provisions in such agreements can be directed toward increasing women's market access in specific industries that are most relevant for women from employment as well as business perspectives.[13] Countries entering into these agreements can also negotiate commitments to encourage or mandate their respective business stakeholders to assume voluntary sustainable standards on equal pay, flexible working conditions, or maternity protection for their women employees.

The baseline is that countries can use trade agreements as laboratories where they can experiment with different legal provisions that touch upon or deal with a range of concerns that relate to women. However, trade agreements are traditionally market access instruments, thus making it difficult for countries to understand why they should use such policy instruments to support women empowerment in the first place. If trade agreements are merely 'market access instruments', why should policymakers consider negotiating a range of societal concerns that are not related to market access? The following sections deal with this question as they first explain how trade agreements interact with women's concerns and then prepare a case for why such agreements can work for the benefit of women.

4.2 International Trade: Both a Friend and a Foe

Chapter 2 has shown how international trade can have both positive as well as negative impacts on women in their various roles. The flowchart in Figure 4.1 reaffirms a number of these observations as it identifies possible positive ways in which trade agreements in particular can impact women, followed by several ways in which trade agreements can negatively impact women.

As shown in Figure 4.1, trade liberalization and trade agreements can assist women in overcoming barriers they encounter within, at, and beyond borders;

Trade and Gender Tool Box' (2017) <https://unctad.org/en/pages/PublicationWebflyer.aspx?publicationid=1877> accessed 8 September 2019.

[12] Ida Bastiaens, Evgeny Postnikov, and Anne-Kathrin Kreft 'Labour Provisions in Trade Agreements and Women's Rights in the Global South' (2023) 14(5) Global Policy 702.

[13] Naila Kabeer, 'Globalization, Labor Standards, and Women's Rights: Dilemmas of Collective (In) Action in an Interdependent World' (2004) 10(3) Feminist Economics 35.

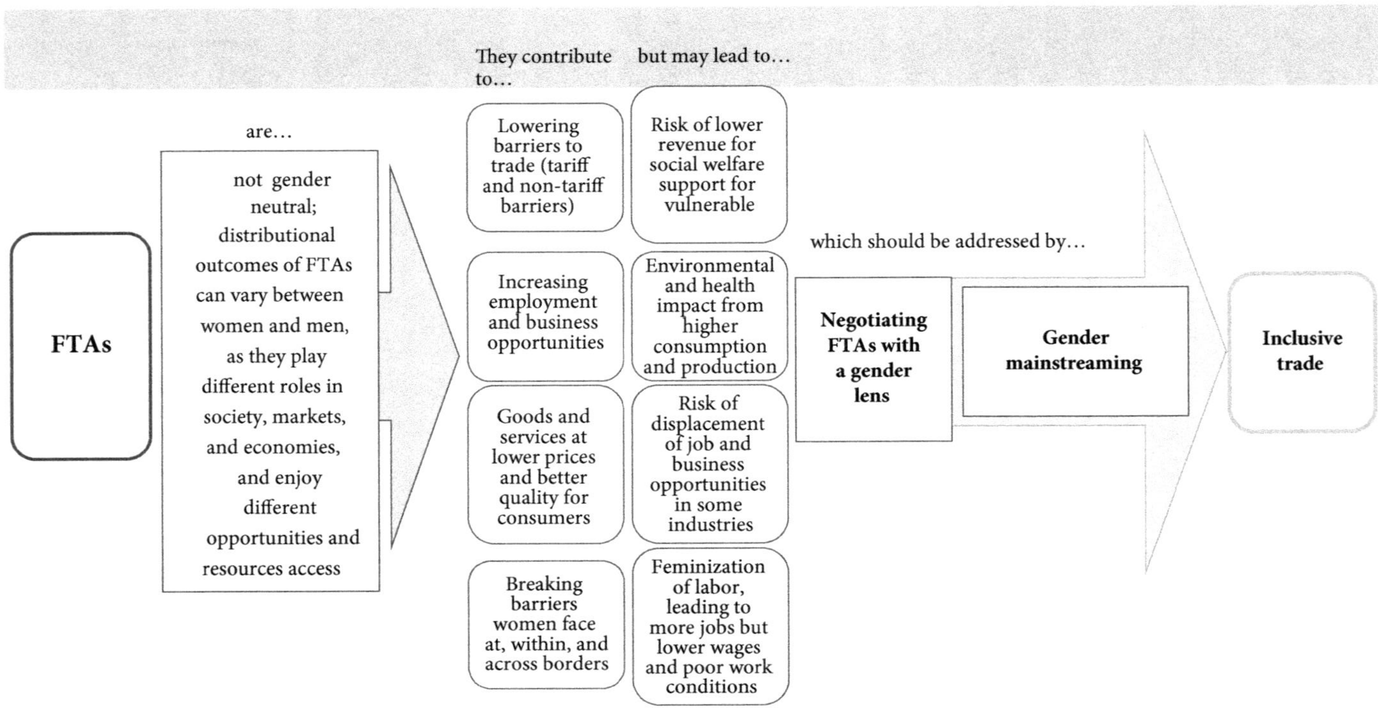

Figure 4.1 How trade agreements interact with women-related concerns?

they can lower the prices and increase the quality of goods and services available in markets, particularly those that are most relevant for women in their various roles, mainly as consumers; they can increase employment and business opportunities for all including women; and they can help reduce tariff and non-tariff barriers to trade, which are even more formidable for women businesses and consumers.[14] However, the impact of international trade on women is not so straightforward as it can also cause a range of complications and challenges.

As the flowchart shows, trade agreements that foster liberalization can increase the risk of lower revenue being available for social welfare support, which is most crucial for marginalized groups such as women. It can cause environmental and health damage due to high rates of consumption and production, which can then increase the vulnerability of women who are already more vulnerable to such changes than men.[15] It can also result in increased displacement of job and business opportunities in many industries. Evidence has shown that this displacement has predominantly impacted women, both as employees and employers. Furthermore, the findings in the previous chapter have also shown that trade liberalization can lead to the feminization of labour, resulting in an increase in jobs for women, albeit at low wage rates and in poor working conditions. It is therefore crucial that policymakers consider these externalities and negotiate trade agreements with commitments that can help reduce such issues. Nevertheless, several scholars have opposed such inclusions. One such scholar is Sengupta, who has concluded that trade agreements are unreliable agents of gender equality.[16] According to Sengupta, trade negotiations are driven entirely by commercial interests and trade agreements advocate for a more aggressive liberalization agenda. This is mainly because such agreements place exclusive emphasis on commercial interests, resulting in a lack of consideration for the social consequences that may derive from them. It is for this reason that they cannot sufficiently tackle the issue of gender inequality. LeClercq concurs that commercial interests dominate trade negotiations and that rights-based provisions will be incorporated into trade agreements only if they create fair trade conditions and directly impact the costs of production and trade.[17]

While Sengupta and LeClercq question the utility of gender-rights provisions in trade agreements, albeit for different reasons, Raj Bhala and Cody N Wood

[14] Fiona Colgan and Sue Ledwith, 'Diversity, Identities and Strategies of Women Trade Union Activists' (2000) 7(4) Gender, Work and Organization 242.

[15] Puyang Sun, Yong Tan, and Guang Yang, 'Export, FDI and the Welfare Gains from Trade Liberalization' (2020) 92 Economic Modelling 230.

[16] Ranja Sengupta, 'Addressing Gender and Trade Issues in Trade Agreements: Creating more problems than solutions?' (DAWN Publications 2018) <https://dawnnet.org/publication/addressing-gender-and-trade-issues-in-trade-agreements-creating-more-problems-than-solutions/> accessed 4 June 2024.

[17] Desirée LeClercq, 'The Disparate Treatment of Rights in US Trade' (2021) 90 Fordham Law Review 1.

strongly support incorporating such provisions. They contend that concerns relating to gender and sexual orientation should be effectively addressed through hard law mechanisms (eg trade agreements), using hard law language resulting in binding legal obligations for all parties.[18] Put differently, they advocate for 'hard-hard' law obligations—obligations entrenched in binding international agreements that include monitoring and dispute-settlement mechanisms and are expressed in binding, unambiguous terms. In determining the hardness of law, these authors have identified two dimensions: structural and textual hardness. Structural hardness is marked by the following factors: (1) whether the instrument containing the rules is incorporated into domestic law; (2) whether the rules apply to states and individuals; (3) whether there is a monitoring mechanism to ensure implementation of the rules and obligations (eg committees); (4) whether there is a dispute-settlement system in place to investigate and deal with violations; and (5) whether there is an enforcement mechanism with clear, step-by-step procedures that sanctions the violators through appropriate remedies. Textually, a law is hard if (1) it is expressed using mandatory verb constructions (shall, must, etc); (2) the language is not vague; (3) the language is not ambiguous; (4) the written rules compel parties to meet specific criteria by specific deadlines; and (5) the rules promulgate clear standards which domestic laws must meet.[19] The less a given provision or text meets these requirements, the softer the obligation contained in that provision.

Feminist trade economists have articulated at least two arguments supporting the incorporation of women-related concerns in trade agreements. The first is an economic argument that underscores the imperative of addressing gender disparities. Given that the goal of trade liberalization is to promote economic development among nations, and considering that numerous regional and multilateral agreements explicitly state in their preamble their commitment to achieving sustainable development, gender inequality poses a significant obstacle to these objectives. Multiple scholarly works indicate that gender inequality inhibits sustainable economic development. Conversely, evidence suggests that fostering gender equality facilitates economic growth and development.[20] The second argument is a human rights argument. Gender equality across all spheres of life constitutes a fundamental human right, recognized by the world community in several multilateral treaties and declarations. These include the Convention on the Elimination of All Forms of Discrimination against Women (CEDAW), the UN Charter and the International Bill of Human Rights, the Universal Declaration of Human Rights, the International Covenant on Economic, Social and Cultural

[18] Raj Bhala and Cody N Wood, 'Two Dimensional Hard-Soft Law Theory and the Advancement of Women's and LGBTQ + Rights Through Free Trade Agreements' (2019) 47 Georgia Journal of International and Comparative Law 2.

[19] ibid.

[20] Jane Korinek, 'Trade and Gender: Issues and Interactions' (2005) OECD Working Paper No 24, 7–8 <http://www.oecd.org/dataoecd/38/50/35770606.pdf> accessed 4 June 2024.

Rights, the International Covenant on Civil and Political Rights, and the two optional protocols.[21]

Korinek takes this discussion forward as she emphasizes that addressing the impacts of trade on women or increasing their participation in trade lies primarily in the domain of domestic policies; yet, trade policies and trade promotion can play an important role in supporting such domestic policies for more inclusive outcomes for women.[22] Korinek observes that FTAs can play a role in promoting inclusiveness not only because of the potential influence of trade on women as workers, entrepreneurs, or consumers but also because trade policies and agreements can contribute to identifying and diffusing novel ideas and policy concepts beyond the jurisdiction where they first appeared. Countries may thus include women-related provisions in their FTAs to ensure that they do not aggravate the existing gender gap and such inclusions can seek to improve gender-equalizing trends and ensure that women participate more widely and draw more benefits from international trade than is currently the case. In agreement with these views, Zarrilli notes that the inclusion of women's interests in trade agreements is to minimize the 'collateral damages' of trade reforms and international trade which have led to women's dismissals and marginalization. She argues that trade agreements can play a role in prioritizing women's well-being in two possible ways. First, countries can include specific references to gender equality and women's economic empowerment in trade agreements. Second, countries can assess the potential impact of trade reform, not only on a country but also on specific segments of the population, including women.[23]

Supporting the argument that trade agreements should indeed support women empowerment, Boghossian and Bahri observe that trade agreements can foster change for two specific reasons.[24] First, trade agreements between countries can increase trade flows and hence lead to more economic opportunities for all, including women. Second, through multilateral, regional, or bilateral trade accords, countries can encourage their trade partners to reduce trade barriers and create a conducive environment for women as entrepreneurs, employees, and consumers. Using the lure of enhanced market access and freer trade, countries can use trade agreements to bring about change. These domestic changes can be aimed at reducing barriers that women face as employees, entrepreneurs, and consumers.

[21] Elizabeth Evatt, 'Finding a Voice for Women's Rights: The Early Days of CEDAW' (2002) 34(3) George Washington International Law Review 515; Constance Z Wagner, 'Looking at Regional Trade Agreements through the Lens of Gender' (2012) 31 St Louis University Public Law Review 497.

[22] Jane Korinek, Evdokia Moïsé, and Jakob Tange, 'Trade and Gender: A Framework of Analysis' (2021) OECD Trade Policy Papers No 246, 39 <https://doi.org/10.1787/6db59d80-en> accessed 4 April 2024.

[23] Simonetta Zarrilli, 'International Trade Is at Risk of Leaving Women Behind' (CIGI 2018) <www.cigionline.org/articles/international-trade-risk-leaving-women-behind/> accessed 4 April 2024.

[24] Anoush Der Boghossian and Amrita Bahri, 'Finding Feet on Trade Agreements: Empowering Women Entrepreneurs Amidst a Pandemic' (2023) 50(1) Legal Issues of Economic Integration 13.

I concur with these arguments and advocate that trade agreements are suitable instruments to address the inequalities exacerbated by trade. If trade agreements, as some authors have concluded, are unreliable agents of gender equality since they are generally dominated by commercial interests, and if trade negotiations have so far been driven entirely by commercial interests, thus harming the interests of many including women, then what better instrument to rectify those wrongs than by trade agreements themselves. In other words, the negative impact of trade on women can effectively be mitigated by changing how trade agreements, which are the legal and policy instruments of trade, have so far been negotiated and implemented. The following section builds on this case as it delves further into the question of why trade agreements can be used to empower women.

4.3 Why Use Trade Agreements to Empower Women?

International institutions can influence a government's human rights actions through two principal mechanisms: coercion and persuasion.[25] However, in the case of international trade, international policy institutions and instruments can influence domestic actions and rectify domestic conditions through three possible mechanisms: coercion, persuasion, and motivation.

In the case of persuasion, institutions can provide targeted information to convince other actors of new ideas or norms that they may not otherwise adhere to.[26] It is, therefore, a process of changing actors' preferences and understandings of appropriate social behaviour to create new social facts. In the case of negotiation of trade agreements, countries can provide specific information on how trade has impacted different communities and how it can empower marginalized groups through the inclusion of targeted commitments in the text of a given agreement.

Coercion is defined as a threat or act by a government to disrupt commercial exchange with another state unless that state complies with a given demand or requirement.[27] Coercion can change behaviours by increasing the rewards of compliance or costs of defection through material rewards and punishments. During a trade agreement's negotiation, countries can compel the inclusion of social issues in the agreement's text, threatening withdrawal from such negotiations if their trade partners are unwilling to assume certain social commitments. Following negotiations, once an agreement is in force countries can enforce compliance with provisions on social commitments from their trade partners by threatening to suspend trade benefits or by offering rewards of extending additional benefits.

[25] Emilie M Hafner-Burton, 'Trading Human Rights: How Preferential Trade Agreements Influence Government Repression' (2005) 59(3) International Organization 593.

[26] Jean G Jones and Herbert W Simons, *Persuasion in Society* (Routledge 2017).

[27] Linda D Molm, *Coercive Power in Social Exchange* (CUP 1997).

Motivation refers to the process of inducing certain behaviour to achieve desired goals and, by using trade agreements, countries can impact domestic behaviour though motivation.[28] As such, governments can use these negotiating instruments to incentivize changes at the domestic level in other countries in exchange for enhanced or unfettered market access. In short, the lure of market access to important markets can be used as an incentive through trade agreements.

Countries may use one or more of these mechanisms to influence change; however, the use of persuasion and motivation is more inclusive than the use of coercion in this context. Moreover, trade agreements are increasingly going beyond their traditional subject matter of market access and are seeking to incorporate women-related concerns for several other reasons, including the following:

(1) The scope of trade agreements has broadened as they are now increasingly looking beyond mere market access concerns, covering various objectives including 'importing higher policy standards, strengthening regional policy coordination, locking-in domestic reforms, and even addressing foreign policy issues'.[29] In this sense, such agreements have included a range of concerns including, but not limited to, labour standards, environment protection, disability rights, and rights of indigenous peoples. These inclusions demonstrate how trade agreements have been used as a top-down mechanism to influence domestic conditions and regulations. Similarly, countries implementing such agreements can impact domestic conditions and regulations relating to women's rights and concerns by adding such commitments to an agreement's scope.

(2) Trade liberalization and trade agreements, which are instruments of trade liberalization, cannot be treated in isolation from their effects, effects which can go beyond mere economic consequences. For this reason, scholars have observed that 'human rights intuitively should prevail over trade norms, which, at the bottom, govern the movement of widgets across borders, not the right treatment of the individual in society'.[30] Scholars also observe that foreign trade is not a separate realm from that of human rights. If policy instruments regulating trade do not take into consideration their possible impact on different groups, especially in regard to human rights, this could possibly lead to countries opting for non-regulation of these undesirable impacts.

[28] Dale H Schunk and Maria K DiBenedetto, 'Motivation and Social Cognitive Theory' (2020) 60 Contemporary Educational Psychology 101832.

[29] Jean-Pierre Chauffour and Jean-Christophe Maur, *Preferential Trade Agreement Policies for Development: A Handbook* (World Bank, 2014).

[30] Berta Esperanza Hernández-Truyol and Stephen Joseph Powell, *Just Trade* (New York UP 2009).

(3) Commitments to the empowerment of women have already been agreed in a universal setting, with several international instruments calling on countries to cooperate for that purpose. Some of the international policy instruments where countries have assumed commitments to gender equality are the following: CEDAW, the Platform for Action, the UN 2030 Sustainable Development Goals (SDGs), the International Labour Organization's (ILO's) Conventions 100 and 111, the World Trade Organization's (WTO's) 2017 Declaration, and others. Hence, incorporating such commitments in trade agreements can serve as a way for countries to reaffirm their commitments under other instruments and heighten their likelihood of domestic implementation through the ratification of a given trade agreement.[31]

(4) Trade agreements can provide a platform for countries to cooperate. This argument makes more sense if we explore the nature of barriers that women face, mainly those pertaining to their participation in the workforce and the economy, discrimination in accessing social services and financial assistance, restricted access to productive resources, problems in accessing markets, cross-border challenges, etc. These concerns are not social in nature and most of them relate directly to business or economic interests. Hence, trade agreements can impact such economic-oriented concerns, mainly those pertaining to labour standards, workplace safety, workers' treatment, wages and work standards, security benefits, trade facilitation, provision of maternity-related facilities in the workplace, and government protection programmes. As such, they can serve as useful tools, or rather complementary tools, in addition to domestic changes and other instruments of international law and politics (eg human rights treaties and conventions). These standards can significantly help women address or overcome several barriers they face, especially regarding their economic independence.[32]

These points demonstrate why trade agreements can be used to enhance the interests of women. Moreover, the integration of women-related concerns in trade agreements can help maximize the positive impact and minimize the negative impact that trade agreements can have on the rights and interests of women. However, this integration needs to be meaningful and the approach to integration should be designed in the light of the barriers that women face.

[31] Beate Rudolf, 'Freedom from Violence, Full Access to Resources, Equal Participation, and Empowerment: The Relevance of CEDAW for the Implementation of the SDGs' (2019) Interdisciplinary Studies in Human Rights <https://link.springer.com/chapter/10.1007/978-3-030-30469-0_5> accessed 3 April 2024.

[32] Charlotte May-Simera, 'Reconsidering Sheltered Workshops in Light of the United Nations Convention on the Rights of Persons with Disabilities' (2006) (2018) 7(1) Laws 6.

4.4 What Triggered a Surge in the Inclusion of Women-Related Concerns in Trade Agreements?

The current surge in the inclusion of women-related commitments in trade agreements can be attributed to a number of factors.[33] More women have recently acquired decision-making roles at senior levels in trade policymaking and trade negotiations and more women entrepreneurs are now engaged in cross-border trade. In addition, civil society and advocacy groups, in cooperation with scholars, have showcased the negative impacts that trade liberalization has had on women in various countries. This has led to the realization of the importance of monitoring the non-economic impact of trade agreements.[34] Recent studies have also shown that economic growth depends on the economic empowerment of women and their inclusion in trade and commerce. A 2015 report by the McKinsey Global Institute showed that advancing gender equality could add nearly US$28 trillion to global annual GDP.[35] These findings sparked a significant discussion at national and international forums, prompting countries' political willingness to understand the nexus.

The extent to which FTAs embrace women's concerns largely depends on the political willingness of the administration in power. This can best be exemplified by the Chilean example, wherein women-related commitments became an explicit component of Chile's trade policy during President Michelle Bachelet's second administration from 2014 to 2018.[36] Another example is the growing political appetite for such concerns in Europe, which is evident from its dedicated parliamentary sessions on the topic, adoption of parliamentary resolutions, and production of in-house or commissioned studies to better understand the interconnection between trade and women.[37] Canada also presents an interesting example as its recent

[33] Simonetta Zarilli, 'The gender chapters in trade agreements: A true revolution?' (ICTSD 14 November 2017) <http://www.ictsd.org/opinion/the-gender-chapters-in-trade-agreements-a-true-revolution> accessed 13 August 2019; UNCTAD, 'The New Way of Addressing Gender Equality Issues in Trade Agreements: Is It A True Revolution?' (October 2017) Policy Brief No 53 <https://unctad.org/en/PublicationsLibrary/presspb2017d2_en.pdf> accessed 13 August 2019.

[34] Nilufer Cagatay, *Trade, Gender, and Poverty* (UNDP 2011); Kate Lappin, 'Free Trade or Women's Rights?' (Strategic Review 12 January 2018) <https://worldview.stratfor.com/article/free-trade-or-womens-rights> accessed 13 August 2019.

[35] McKinsey Global Institute, 'The Power of Parity: How Advancing Women's Equality Can Add $12 Trillion to Global Growth' (September 2015) <www.mckinsey.com/~/media/McKinsey/Industries/Public%20and%20Social%20Sector/Our%20Insights/How%20advancing%20womens%20equality%20can%20add%2012%20trillion%20to%20global%20growth/MGI%20Power%20of%20parity_Executive%20summary_September%202015.pdf> accessed 13 August 2019.

[36] Dorotea López, Felipe Muñoz, and Javiera Cáceres Bustamante, 'Gender Inclusion in Chilean Free Trade Agreements' (Working Paper), 14 (on record with the author). Bachelet's administration is widely known for its works and accomplishments relating to gender issues. For more information, see also Linda Stevenson, 'The Bachelet Effect on Gender-Equity Policies' (2012) 39(4) Latin American Perspectives 129.

[37] European Commission, 'Communication from the Commission to the European Parliament, the Council, the European Economic and Social Committee and the Committee of the Regions, A Union of Equality: Gender Equality Strategy 2020–2025' (2020) COM/2020/152; European Parliament, 'Gender mainstreaming in EU trade agreements' <www.europarl.europa.eu/thinktank/en/document/

approach to negotiating FTAs has been influenced by political debates on trade and the overall political will of the administration. In response to public perceptions concerning the lack of transparency in the negotiating process of trade agreements and the negative effects they have had on certain population groups, the government of Canada has recognized that trade policies need to respond more meaningfully to domestic, economic, social, and environmental policy priorities, including its Feminist International Assistance Policy.[38]

A country's cultural and religious norms, which often assign specific gender roles to women, can also determine the extent to which trade agreements and trade policies are responsive to women.[39] Middle Eastern countries' approaches towards including women's perspectives in trade agreements clearly illustrate this point. While countries in the Americas, Europe, and East Africa have included commitments in many of their agreement that envisage women in their economic and leadership roles, Middle Eastern countries have either stayed away from adding women-related commitments altogether or have mainly added such provisions to bolster and develop their countries' family planning and mother and child protection programmes.[40] These factors explain, at least in part, the varying levels of responsiveness towards women in different FTAs signed by various countries.

More broadly, the Covid-19 health pandemic intensified the ever-mounting concerns about the sustainability of economic growth and international trade.[41] After the pandemic, governments reiterated the fundamental importance of ensuring that trade rules go hand in hand with sustainable and inclusive development, ensuring that no group is left behind or is worse off.[42] The pandemic highlighted the vulnerabilities of women in trade as its economic and social ramifications disproportionately affected them.[43] It is therefore the right time

EPRS_BRI(2024)760388>; EU Monitor, 'EP Press conference Gender Equality in EU trade agreements report vote' (13 March 2018) INTA/FEMM, Strasbourg <www.eumonitor.eu/9353000/1/j9vvik7m1c3gyxp/vkmmbscygkt7?ctx = vhekc59myknp&tab=1> accessed 13 August 2023.

[38] Government of Canada, 'Canada's Feminist International Assistance Policy' <www.international.gc.ca/world-monde/issues_development-enjeux_developpement/priorities-priorites/policy-politique.aspx?lang=eng> accessed 8 May 2022.

[39] Jeni Klugman and Elisa Gamberoni, 'Gender and Trade: A Fresh Look at the Evidence' *International Trade Forum Magazine* (2 July 2012) <http://www.tradeforum.org/Gender-and-trade-A-fresh-look-at-the-evidence/> accessed 15 August 2019.

[40] Euro-Mediterranean Agreement establishing an association between the European Communities and their Member States and the Hashemite Kingdom of Jordan (2002), Title VI: Cooperation in social and cultural matters, ch 2: Social cooperation actions, art 82.

[41] Pallavi Panda, 'COVID-19, Trade Disruptions, and Gender: A Survey of the Potential Interactions and Consequences for Economic Development in Sub-Saharan Africa' (2022) 23(2) Journal of African Development 347.

[42] Amrita Bahri, Weihuan Zhou, and Daria Boklan, *Rethinking, Repackaging, and Rescuing World Trade Law in the Post-Pandemic Era* (Hart Publishing 2023).

[43] Amrita Bahri, 'Women at the Frontline of COVID-19: Can Gender Mainstreaming in Free Trade Agreements Help?' (2020) 23(3) Journal of International Economic Law 563.

to rethink the nexus between trade and women and to explore how trade agreements can contribute to 'building back together' with women in the post-Covid-19 world.

4.5 Regional Practices: Differences and Similarities

Even though we are yet to see concrete evidence of the benefits that including women's concerns in trade agreements can have, more and more countries are embracing this approach. However, countries have included women-related concerns in varied ways, with different language and levels of commitment, and with a focus on very different roles of women. In most agreements, such provisions are added as non-binding affirmations as they are drafted with non-mandatory verbs and 'soft' permissive grammatical constructions; on the other hand, several countries have drafted such provisions with legally binding expressions, while others are giving due consideration to the idea of negotiating binding commitments in the near future.[44] There is also a significant variation in the level of understanding, readiness, and appetite among countries to discuss and negotiate such commitments. On the one hand, some countries—especially in North and South America and Eastern and Southern Africa—are leading gender mainstreaming efforts; on the other hand, many countries—particularly those in the Asia Pacific region, the Middle East, and the Caribbean—have yet to take significant steps, or even their first step, in this regard.[45] The topics addressed in women-related provisions also vary from one region to another as some regions have included provisions on social and health-care concerns of women, while others have grounded such provisions in purely economic and market-oriented interests.[46]

This section highlights the contrast between how women-related concerns are included in existing trade agreements by countries in North and South America, the EU, Africa, and the Asia Pacific region. There are different modalities to mainstream women-related concerns in trade agreements and Figure 4.2 provides a

[44] See eg Treaty Establishing the Common Market for Eastern and Southern Africa (1993); Southern African Development Community Protocol on Gender and Development (2008); Agreement on Labour Cooperation between Canada and Jordan) (adopted 28 June 2009, entered into force 1 October 2012) ch 11 Labour, art 1(11); Free Trade Agreement between the Republic of Nicaragua and the Republic of China) (adopted 16 June 2006, entered into force 1 January 2008), ch 18 Labour, art 18(18); Interview with a trade negotiator (details withheld, on file with the author).

[45] Research findings from Amrita Bahri, 'Gender Mainstreaming in Free Trade Agreements: A Regional Analysis and Good Practice Examples', Gender, Social Inclusion and Trade Knowledge Product Series (2021) <https://wtochairs.org/sites/default/files/7.%20Gender%20mainstreaming%20in%20FTAs_final%20%286%29.pdf> accessed 13 August 2023.

[46] Karin Ulmer, 'Are Trade Agreements with the EU Beneficial to Women in Africa, the Caribbean, and the Pacific?' (2004) 12(2) Gender & Development 53.

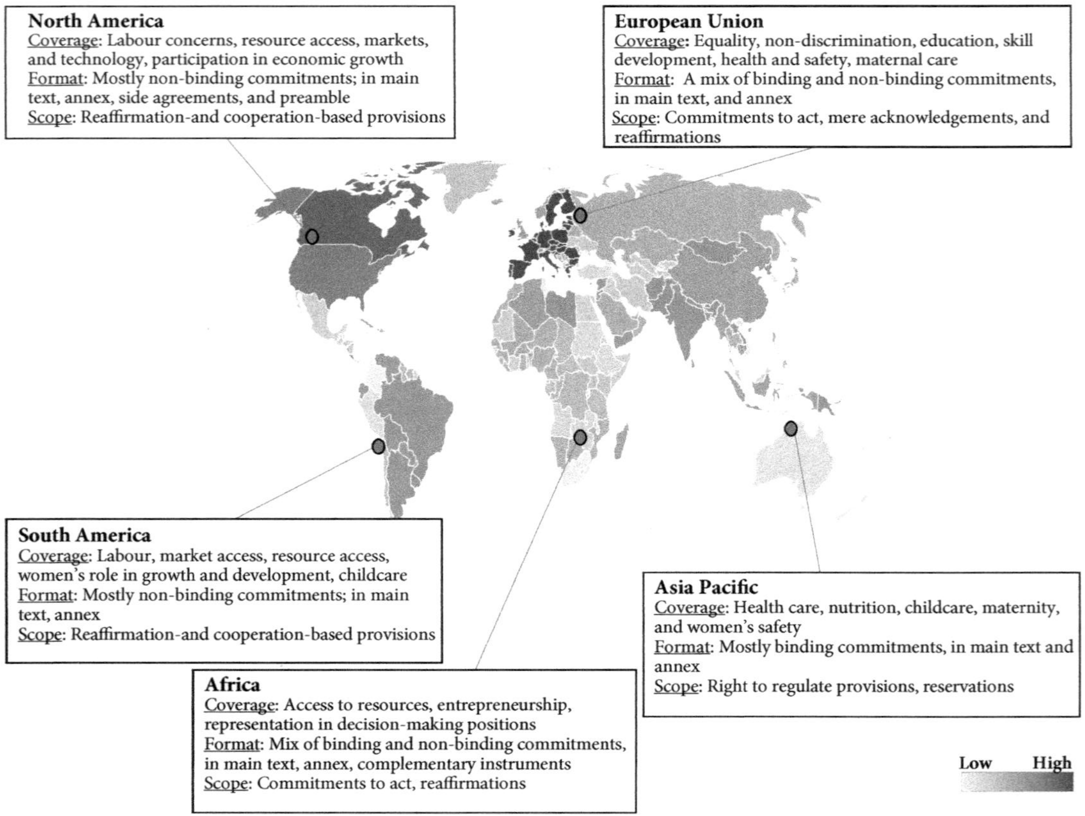

Figure 4.2 Women-related provisions in trade agreements: a bird's-eye view of trends in the EU, North and South America, Africa, and Asia Pacific

Notes: * The colour code reflects the aggregation of the number of times women-explicit words are used in all WTO-notified FTAs signed by each country. The darker the colour, the higher the frequency of women-explicit words included in FTAs. ** Only FTAs with women-explicit provisions were considered for the illustration. Some FTAs are included in the assessment of more than one country, depending on the countries that are party to those agreements. *** Gender-explicit words used for listing products or entities are not included in this assessment. **** Only trade agreements notified to the WTO and in force as of 15 June 2024 are included in this assessment.

Source: Bahri, 2021.

bird's-eye view of the differences (and at times similarities) observed from one region to another.[47]

The illustration identifies the countries that have led the inclusion of women-explicit commitments in their trade agreements.[48] The darker a territory of a country or region is shown on the map, the higher the number of provisions it has included in its FTAs that contain women-explicit wording. The content of women-related provisions is much more relevant than the number of times women-related words are mentioned in a specific agreement; a look at the number of times women-explicit words are mentioned does not reveal the scope of the commitments. However, the number of words included in an agreement can provide an initial indication of whether a given trade agreement includes women concerns and the extent to which those concerns are included. The underlying assumption is that the higher the usage of women-explicit words, the higher the number of legal provisions focused on women concerns in each agreement. The countries or regions that lead this count are Canada, Chile, and the EU, which shows that they have included an impressive number of women-explicit provisions in their recent trade agreements. Several African countries follow this direction as they have signed some agreements (eg the East African Community (EAC) and Common Market for Eastern and Southern Africa (COMESA)) with multiple women-explicit terms included in each.

The following subsections assess the differences and similarities observed in the way women-related commitments are included in existing trade agreements. This analysis is divided into three different categories: topic coverage, format, and scope. Topic coverage refers to the subjects (topics or themes) covered by the provisions and these topics are categorized as per the barriers they seek to address or the type of empowerment they seek to promote. Format refers to the location and language of these provisions. Scope refers to the nature of women-related provisions (eg affirmations, reaffirmations, cooperation-based commitments, general statements of intent, reservations, or legal standards).

4.5.1 Topic coverage

Differences can be observed in how the topics covered by such provisions change from one region to another. For instance, in the case of North America, most women-explicit trade agreements signed by Canada, the United States, and

[47] WTO RTA Database <https://rtais.wto.org/UI/PublicMaintainRTAHome.aspx>. Only FTAs with explicit gender provisions were considered for the purpose of this illustration. Only agreements in force at the time of writing on 15 June 2024 and notified to WTO are considered for this assessment.

[48] The explicit expressions included in this assessment are: women, girl, woman, girls, maternity, gender, childcare, sex, mother (in English); *mujer, mujeres, género, niñas, niños, sexo, equidad, maternidad, paternidad, paternal, maternal, igualdad, atencion infantil* (in Spanish).

Mexico treat women-related concerns from an economic perspective. These provisions mainly focus on labour standards, women's access to productive resources, market access and access to technology, skill development, and participation in economic growth.

The EU's mainstreaming approach includes these issues but is oriented towards a wider range of concerns on gender equality, non-discrimination, labour standards, education and skill development, health and safety, and maternal care, with a significant focus on cooperation. Another contrast can be seen in the areas covered by countries in the Asia Pacific area. As observed in Chapter 7, many of the inclusions in this region are made in the form of the right to regulate provisions, wherein countries reserve policy space to regulate specific areas that may impact women's health and maternal concerns, such as health care, nutrition, childcare, and women's safety.

South America's approach mostly resembles that of North America (without the underlying concern about lax standards that could serve as a source of unfair competitive advantage), but some agreements in this region include women-related considerations with topics similar to those in the Asia Pacific region. Women-related provisions negotiated by countries in that region focus on labour concerns, market and resource access, and women's role in growth and development. However, the agreements that South American countries have signed with Asian and Central American countries also include childcare concerns. Finally, the women-explicit provisions found in FTAs signed by African countries primarily seek to integrate women into the region's development process by enhancing their access to resources, promoting female entrepreneurship, and increasing women's representation and participation in political and decision-making positions.

4.5.2 Format

The location of such provisions in the text varies from one agreement to another. Several agreements include these provisions in their main text, while others put them in a side agreement, an annex, or a protocol. The agreements that accommodate these provisions in their main text place the provisions in the preamble, the objectives, the general principles clause, or in different chapters of their operative sections (eg chapters on labour, investment, small and medium-sized enterprises (SMEs), social and cultural development, and sustainable development). Some countries have also negotiated dedicated trade and gender chapters for inclusion in the agreement's main text with countries in North and South America being the pioneers in this trend. These chapters comprise acknowledgements of women's role in international trade, commitments to cooperate on reducing economic barriers for women, procedures and institutions to implement these commitments, and reaffirmation of joint commitments under international conventions and declarations.

The EU has employed a different approach in respect of format as it has frequently included women-explicit provisions in its chapters or provisions on trade and sustainable development or on the social, cultural, and education sections of its ‘Association Agreements’ or ‘Integration Agreements’. Most recently, the EU has negotiated side instruments alongside or subsequent to the negotiation of main agreements. One such example is the Comprehensive Economic and Trade Agreement (CETA) Trade and Gender Recommendation, which is a supplementary document containing recommendations on empowering women through CETA. Both Canada and the EU adopted this document after the signature and enforcement of CETA.[49] Some African countries have employed a similar approach as they have negotiated protocols and declarations wherein parties have assumed commitments on making international trade work for the benefit of women’s empowerment.[50]

In regard to the use of specific language, women-centric provisions in trade agreements are drafted in different ways. Most agreements use best-endeavour expressions, particularly in relation to cooperation activities.[51] In exceptional cases, they are drafted in mandatory language.[52] Mostly, these provisions are crafted using non-mandatory verbs and ‘soft’ permissive grammatical constructions. This trend has become somewhat of a rule in this regard. However, several countries, such as South Korea and New Zealand, have negotiated agreements with legally binding ‘right to regulate’ provisions regarding, for example, social services and employment standards. In such provisions, parties reserve the right to ensure that trade liberalization under a given FTA will not limit their policy space to regulate, for example, the provision of social services (eg childcare) in their respective jurisdictions.

4.5.3 Scope

There are marked differences across regions when it comes to the number of times agreements use women-explicit expressions in the main text or side instruments.

[49] CETA Trade and Gender Recommendation: EU–Canada Work Plan 2020–2021’ <www.international.gc.ca/trade-commerce/trade-agreements-accords-commerciaux/agr-acc/ceta-aecg/CETA_work_plan-AECG_plan_travail-2020-2021.aspx?lang=eng> accessed 13 August 2023.

[50] SADC Protocol on Gender and Development (2008) and Declaration on Gender & Development (1997) <www.sadc.int/issues/gender/0> accessed 13 August 2023.

[51] eg Canada–Israel FTA, art 13.3 reads: ‘Parties shall encourage the involvement of their respective government institutions, businesses, labour unions, education and research organizations, other non-governmental organizations, and their representatives, as appropriate, in the cooperation activities decided upon by the Parties.’

[52] eg USMCA’s art 23.9 reads: ‘each Party shall implement policies that it considers appropriate to protect workers against employment discrimination on the basis of sex . . . ’.

As shown in Figure 4.2, the region leading this trend is the EU, closely followed by North America, and then South America. Moreover, many countries in some regions—such as Southeast Asia and the Middle East—have stayed away from such inclusions or at best included related commitments indirectly or implicitly.

The scope and nature of these provisions differ depending on the agreements. In the agreements signed by the EU, most of the references are found in provisions relating to trade and sustainable development, the agreement's general objectives and principles, binding reservations, sections on social, cultural, and education-related cooperation, and reaffirmations of other international instruments. In contrast, agreements negotiated by North and South American countries have generally drafted their women-explicit provisions in the form of commitments relating to cooperation activities, reaffirmation of international instruments concerning women's rights, and general statements in an agreement's preamble. In addition, some countries include provisions on corporate social responsibility—that is, voluntary standards relating to women empowerment that enterprises operating within their territory or subject to their jurisdiction are encouraged to follow. In several instances, Peru has negotiated reservations to regulate various social services including childcare. In agreements negotiated by African countries, these mentions are typically found in provisions styled as general objectives and principles, general undertakings, provisions establishing or clarifying the components of regional institutions, and capacity-building and cooperation-related provisions. Finally, the most employed provisions in the Asia Pacific area are those in which countries reserve policy space to adopt or maintain regulations concerning social services including childcare, maternity benefits, health care, and physical safety.

4.6 Conclusion

While women empowerment can lead to more economic growth, the converse is not true; economic growth does not automatically lead to the empowerment of women. Hence, efforts need to be made to make that happen. Trade policy instruments can provide a relevant intervention. As discussed in the previous sections, several trade agreements include women concerns in distinctly unique ways; however, these inclusions are not revolutionary and have many gaps, mainly because a number of countries continue to be sceptical about using FTAs to advance women-related concerns. The following chapter provides a discussion on the hesitations that countries can face in using their trade agreements to achieve women empowerment goals and how these hesitations might deter such efforts in the context of trade negotiations and policy formulations.

5

Hesitations and Pitfalls that Impede the Inclusion of Women's Concerns in FTAs

5.1 Introduction

As discussed in the previous chapter, free trade agreements (FTAs) provide an entry point to enhance market access, encourage cooperation and elimination of discriminatory laws, remove barriers, and support countries to legislate on legal standards and practices including sustainable standards. As we have seen, several FTAs accommodate women's concerns in their own unique ways. However, with very few exceptions, almost no FTA so far has contemplated how women-related commitments can be implemented, financed, or enforced. For the implementation of such commitments, countries in their future FTAs need to create dedicated procedures and institutions that can put their long list of commitments into action. Moreover, countries have shown a clear preference for assuming these commitments (with very few exceptions) on a voluntary and permissive basis, using permissive grammatical constructions and soft verbs (eg 'may', 'could', 'consider', 'endeavour', 'promote', 'encourage', or 'cooperate') for their drafting.[1] Countries also leave these provisions out of the scope of their agreements' dispute-settlement mechanisms, which ensures that non-compliance with such provisions does not attract any type of legal repercussions. Another important consideration in this regard is to provide for associated provisions that outline how parties plan to mobilize resources to finance the activities they seek to assume in such agreements if they genuinely intend these commitments to be put into action. As of today, policymakers have not considered this aspect when negotiating and adding women-related provisions into their agreements. These findings show that there is a half-open door in FTAs that countries need to push further open by exploring different methods of implementing, financing, or enforcing their women-related commitments.[2]

[1] Raj Bhala and Cody N Wood, 'Two-Dimensional Hard–Soft Law Theory and the Advancement of Women's and LGBTQ + Rights Through Free Trade Agreements' (2020) 47(2) Georgia Journal of International and Comparative Law 306 (the authors point out that most gender-related commitments in the United States–Mexico–Canada Agreement (USMCA) and the Comprehensive and Progressive Agreement for Trans-Pacific Partnership (CPTPP) are aspirational and non-binding, and hence non-enforceable, and are sometimes drafted with vagueness and ambiguity and so are susceptible to myriad interpretations).

[2] Originally discussed in and adapted from Amrita Bahri, 'Women at the Frontline of COVID-19: Can Gender Mainstreaming in Free Trade Agreements Help?' (2020) 23(3) Journal of International Economic Law 563.

Trade Agreements and Women. Amrita Bahri, Oxford University Press. © Amrita Bahri 2025.
DOI: 10.1093/9780198935759.003.0006

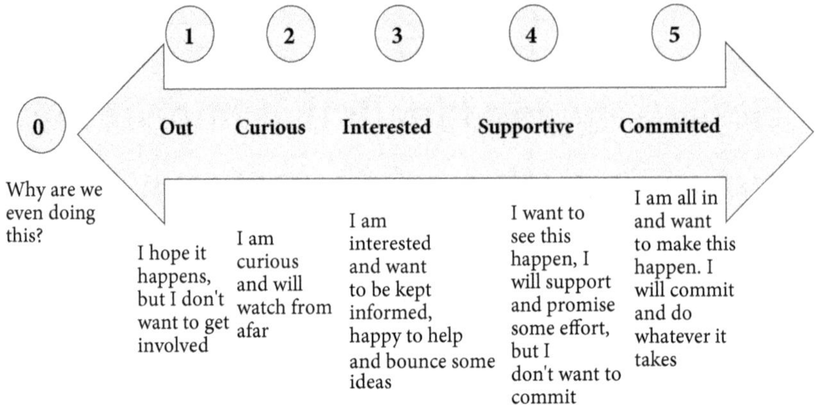

Figure 5.1 Countries' states of readiness and appetite for including women's concerns in FTAs

There is also a significant variation in the level of readiness and appetite countries have developed over the years to discuss and negotiate such concerns in a trade policy context.[3] On the one hand, various countries in North and South America, Africa, and the EU are leading efforts in this respect. Whereas, on the other hand, many countries in Southeast Asia or the Middle East, for example, are yet to take their first steps in this regard. At the same time, several countries in the Asia Pacific region have either opposed the inclusion of women's concerns in trade policy instruments or have shown reluctance to engage in such negotiations without fully comprehending the impact such provisions can have on their trade, economy, sovereignty, and social concerns. There are, too, then many countries positioned closer to the fence, finding themselves in between the two extremes of complete rejection and complete acceptance.

Figure 5.1 shows different states of readiness and appetite representing this variation. The figure shows six states of acceptance, from 'state 0' to 'state 5'. The design of these states of acceptance is based on a country's reaction or response to discussions on negotiating trade agreements aimed at furthering women's empowerment at national and international forums.

Several countries find themselves at the '0' state of readiness and appetite in terms of amending women's conditions through trade agreements as they have consistently opposed or entirely dismissed using trade agreements to address concerns that relate to women. Such countries have either stayed away from any trade

[3] Katrin Kuhlmann and others, 'Re-conceptualizing Free Trade Agreements Through a Sustainable Development Lens' (UNESCAP 27 July 2020) <www.unescap.org/sites/default/files/145%20Final-Team%20Katrin%20Kuhlmann-USA.pdf> accessed 10 October 2023.

discourse on women's interests or have explicitly and emphatically resisted such discourse or discussion.[4]

There are then a few countries in an 'out' state, meaning they have not engaged in actions, negotiations, or discussions on this matter. They have silently maintained their distance without openly opposing or criticizing such developments. In most instances, the countries found at this level of acceptance have several hesitations grounded in various reasons. These reasons may include a general belief that trade policies should focus solely on trade and not on resolving social problems, paucity of relevant data, a lack of political will, and fears that more developed countries will use such provisions in a protectionist manner to reduce their comparative advantage or impose their own moral standards on other countries.[5]

The third state of readiness can be labelled as 'curious'. In this state, countries, similarly to the second state, have largely refrained from this discourse and have avoided any developments or discussions on the matter. However, they have begun to develop an interest in observing what other countries might be doing in this regard.[6] They might be curious about how discussions on the inclusion of women's interests in trade agreements may unfold and take shape but they prefer to maintain their distance and observe how other nations integrate such commitments in their agreements.[7] Most countries in this state are hesitant to participate in such negotiations without fully comprehending the impact such provisions can have on their trade, economy, sovereignty, and social conditions.

Most countries today are found to be at the state of being 'interested'; they have shown some active interest in understanding the interaction between trade and women and they are keen to be kept informed of such developments. At this state, they are walking closer to the line of acceptance as they have increasing interest in knowing more and expanding their understanding of negotiating trade agreements together with commitments on women empowerment, including the benefits, risks, and limitations that are associated with inculcating such commitments. These countries may not have taken action or assumed concrete promises in respect of addressing women's concerns in the context of trade negotiations but they are keen to observe, learn from others' experiences in this respect, and at best engage in the exchange of ideas or discussions with others on the subject, unlike state

[4] Edmé Domínguez Reyes, 'Women Organizing against Free Trade in Latin America, Latin American Policy' (2014) 5(2) Latin American Policy 193, 203.

[5] Amrita Bahri, 'Gender Mainstreaming in Free Trade Agreements: A Regional Analysis and Good Practice Examples' (Gender, Social Inclusion and Trade Knowledge Product Series, funded by UK Aid, 2021) <https://wtochairs.org/sites/default/files/7.%20Gender%20mainstreaming%20in%20FTAs_final%20%286%29.pdf> accessed 10 October 2023.

[6] Interviews with policymakers from developing and developed country governments (details withheld, on file with the author).

[7] William Alan Reinsch, Jasmine Lim, and Ally Brodsky, 'Negotiating Trade Agreements: Gender as a Priority?' (CSIS 2021) <www.csis.org/analysis/negotiating-trade-agreements-gender-priority> accessed 10 October 2023.

2 where countries are merely observing the new domain.[8] Hence, their readiness to invest their efforts, resources, and time in developing the discourse on trade and gender may be minimal or even negligible but they have generally been interested in awareness or capacity-building initiatives such as participation in conferences and other events where such topics are discussed without any country being required to assume any obligation or task in that respect.

Then, another important state of readiness for countries is the state of being 'supportive' and most of the countries that have negotiated women-related or women-explicit provisions in their trade agreements are found to be in this state.[9] Such countries have more interest and a higher appetite for engaging in discussions on the subject and they are willing to support or engage in actions that can lead to making trade agreements work for women's empowerment. These countries have included or even mainstreamed women's concerns in their trade agreements. Some have even negotiated a whole stand-alone chapter on trade and women including a range of commitments in that respect; however, they have stayed away from assuming binding and enforceable obligations. These countries have shown an unequivocal belief and understanding of how trade can impact women and, hence, how trade agreements can accommodate concerns to ensure that they can benefit women. However, these countries still face hesitations that impede their efforts to assume legally binding obligations in that regard. Today, most of the current agreements that include provisions related to women include such provisions on the spirit of cooperation in which they hold back the right to deal with the soft commitments they assume in accordance with their preference and discretion.[10] By entering into such non-binding commitments, countries recognize that trade policies can carve out a space for furthering women's interests but they do not want to 'tie their own hands' through the international agreements they are signing with their trade partners.[11] Voluntary provisions, therefore, have provided a safe haven for countries in this state of acceptance.[12]

The final state of acceptance, state 5, represents the highest level of commitment a country can achieve for the inclusion of provisions that address women's concerns. In this state, countries are wholly committed that they want to assume

[8] Andrew T Guzman, 'The Design of International Agreements' (2005) 16(4) European Journal of International Law 579.

[9] Amrita Bahri, 'Making Trade Agreements Work for Women Empowerment: How Does It Help, What Has Been Done, and What Remains Undone?' (2021) 4(11) Latin American Journal of Trade Policy 6.

[10] José-Antonio Monteiro, 'The evolution of gender-related provisions in Regional Trade Agreements' (WTO.org 2021) <www.wto.org/english/res_e/reser_e/ersd202108_e.htm> accessed 11 October 2023.

[11] Kim, Soo Yeon and Hicks, Raymond, 'Credible Commitment Through PTAs and their Effects on Trade: A Study of Asia's Reciprocal Trade Agreements' (2009) APSA 2009 Toronto Meeting Paper <https://ssrn.com/abstract=1449204> accessed 11 October 2023.

[12] For multiple examples of trade agreements that feature such cooperation-based soft provisions, see Chapter 7.

commitments—soft as well as hard—to ensure that trade agreements can be made to work for the benefit of everyone, including women. In this state, countries can assume legally binding and fully enforceable commitments in respect of women's concerns in their agreements. However, a look at existing trade agreements and how they have accommodated women-related concerns reveals that hardly any country has reached this state in terms of including women's concerns in trade agreements. At best, some countries have come close to it as they have included binding commitments, minimum legal standards, waivers, or reservations with mechanisms for implementation and enforcement.[13] Even those that are considered pioneers or front runners in the gender mainstreaming approach have chosen to stay away from this state of commitment.[14]

Such different levels of readiness raise a plethora of questions about the discourse on trade and women: what reasons are to blame for the extreme variation in the level of readiness and appetite that countries have developed towards this approach? Why are countries reluctant to incorporate binding obligations in this regard or consider provisions that can ensure that such commitments are enforced and implemented? Moreover, why are several countries opposed or remain indifferent to such inclusions and how can we understand their concerns? Recent developments indicate that the trade policy world is gradually recognizing that trade policy can be used as a tool to empower women. This represents a drastic change in the trade policymaking mindset. However, to ensure that all countries—developing and developed—develop the appetite and understanding to participate in such discussions and negotiation attempts, it is crucial to address the hesitations and challenges that can impede such efforts. This chapter is an attempt in this direction as it identifies and provides discussion on eight possible hesitations that could be blamed for impeding efforts that can make trade agreements work for women.

5.2 Fears of Protectionism

Critics and policymakers from developing countries have observed that countries may hesitate to include women-responsive provisions in their trade agreements fearing that such provisions could enable developed countries to leverage their more progressive policies on women as a pretext for blocking imports from developing countries.[15] If binding commitments on women's concerns are included in

[13] Bahri (n 5).

[14] Amrita Bahri and Renata Amaral, 'Gender Equality Provisions in Trade and Investment Agreements: Are They Widening the Negotiation Capacity Gap?' (2024) 23(1) World Trade Review 47.

[15] Interviews with policymakers from developing country governments (details withheld, on file with the author); Ananya Singh, 'Explained: India's refusal to back WTO declaration on gender equality in trade' (QRIUS 15 December 2017) <https://qrius.com/explained-india-refusal-gender-equality-trade/> accessed 21 May 2024.

trade agreements, it may leave a large escape hatch wide open. Once opened, these commitments could allow countries to evade the obligations they have undertaken under a trade agreement for reasons that may only remotely relate to gender equality considerations.[16] By using provisions based on vaguely-defined expressions such as 'gender equality' or 'women empowerment', members could justify various retreats from their market access promises. Hence, fears of protectionism deter countries with wide gender inequality, discriminatory laws, cultural barriers, and lack of willingness to improve the situation of women domestically or internationally.

Trade agreements and trade negotiations have historically focused on economic issues, reduction of tariffs, and facilitation of trade, excluding social issues, amongst them, gender. FTAs were largely considered neutral in this respect as they did not appear to treat men and women differently or disadvantage women.[17] The different distributive impacts of trade and FTAs on women and men were therefore neither considered nor understood. However, this understanding has now changed and recent studies have shown how trade agreements can impact countries beyond their markets; they can impact the conditions of labour, employment, environment, and social welfare, and the condition of women as employers, employees, and customers.[18] Moreover, the inclusion of ambitious non-economic issues such as climate change and labour standard commitments in new-generation trade agreements shows that the clear line of separation that once existed between the economic and the non-economic perspective of trade has started to blur. Yet, there seems to be a greater unease towards the inclusion of women-related issues in the trade policy space as compared to the inclusion of other new-generation issues such as climate change, corruption, discrimination, and child labour. One of the reasons might be attributed to the broad nature with which such women-related provisions are currently drafted. Charnovitz observes that 'virtually anything can be characterized as a moral issue',[19] and the same can be said for gender equality as it lacks a universally-accepted definition. The broad and undefined scope of 'gender equality' can result in a shift towards unilateralism and may allow countries to disguise an illegal protectionist measure as a policy objective.

An associated concern could be the risk of eliminating a country's competitive advantage, given the low cost of women's labour in that country's labour-intensive industries.[20] The use of gender standards for the protection of domestic industries

[16] Roger Alford, 'The Self-Judging WTO Security Exception' (2011) 697 Utah Law Review 698.

[17] Constance Wagner, 'Looking at Regional Trade Agreements Through the Lens of Gender '(2012) 31 St Louis University Public Law Review 497.

[18] Steve Charnovitz, 'The Moral Exception in Trade Policy' (1998) 38 Virginia Journal of International Law 689.

[19] ibid.

[20] Elizabeth Whitsitt, 'A Comment on the Public Morals Exception in International Trade and the EC—Seal Products Case: Moral Imperialism and Other Concerns' (2014) 3(4) Cambridge Journal of International and Comparative Law 1376, 1390.

is the main concern several countries have voiced when they have resisted or opposed any development in this respect at multilateral forums. This includes instances such as the signing of the World Trade Organization (WTO) Declaration in 2017, the unsuccessful discussions on signing a formal joint declaration at the Twelfth WTO Ministerial Conference, and the unwilling or insufficient participation of WTO members at the Trade and Gender Informal Group to discuss these matters further.[21]

One might question how some countries with large trading stakes have signed trade accords with women-related commitments when the risk of 'reduced competitive advantage' could have acted as a limiting factor. Perhaps the explanation lies in the confidence countries can gain when they negotiate FTAs with other countries that have similar conditions to their own. This reason seems to be particularly apt in the case of the UK–Japan Comprehensive Economic Partnership Agreement (CEPA), where both parties share similar levels of human development (eg they are both highly developed free market economies).[22] This finding is in line with a recent study that has shown that parties are more willing to accept women-related commitments when they are negotiating such provisions with countries that are similarly situated in terms of their gender development levels (as measured by the gender development index).[23] Having trade partners with similar domestic conditions minimizes such fears of trade protectionism. In the Asia Pacific region, Japan is the only country that has signed a trade agreement (the UK–Japan CEPA) with a stand-alone chapter on trade and gender and a set of best practice provisions that seek to empower women economically within their trade policy space. Japan and the UK were both willing to negotiate such provisions and the chapter, which shows that an important factor which allows countries to forge ahead in this respect is whether both trading partners in a particular agreement are willing and able to assume such commitments within their trade policy context.[24] This reason explains why a number of developing countries have been left behind in such endeavours and advances.

[21] Roberto Bissio, 'Is "gender" a Trojan horse to introduce new issues at WTO?' (Third World Network 11 December 2017) <https://twnetwork.org/wto/%E2%80%9Cgender%E2%80%9D-trojan-horse-introduce-new-issues-wto> accessed 9 July 2021.

[22] United Nations, 'World Economic Situation and Prospects 2014: Country Classification' (2014) <www.un.org/en/development/desa/policy/wesp/wesp_current/2014wesp_country_classification.pdf> accessed 9 July 2021.

[23] José-Antonio Monteiro, 'Gender-related provisions in regional trade agreements' (2021) WTO Staff Working Papers ERSD-2018-15.

[24] The UK government has committed to formulating a post-Brexit trade policy that will uphold gender equality. (More information in 'Gender sensitive trade policy' (UK Policy Briefings September 2019) <https://wbg.org.uk/analysis/uk-policy-briefings/gender-impacts-of-trade-and-investment-agreements/> accessed 9 July 2021.) For more information on the UK government's commitments to 'gender-responsive trade', see 'Export Strategy: supporting and connecting businesses to grow on the world stage' (21 August 2018) gov.uk Policy Paper <www.gov.uk/government/publications/export-strategy-supporting-and-connecting-businesses-to-grow-on-the-world-stage/export-strategy-supporting-and-connecting-businesses-to-grow-on-the-world-stage> accessed 9 July 2021.

Developing countries have long been wary of the intentions of the developed world when it comes to negotiating non-market-access-related issues as part of trade negotiation endeavours. They have generally employed a defensive position while engaging in gender and other sustainability issues, especially so when they are negotiating or dealing with a developed country which has different domestic conditions than their own. This hesitation is linked to their past experiences with the developed world that relate to trade negotiations that have happened in the multilateral space.[25] In the words of one trade negotiator, 'They [developing countries] were taken for a ride on some progressive issues by the developed world.'[26] This statement shows that there is a trust deficit when it comes to discussions on trade policies and women. Some policymakers from the developing world consider these developments and initiatives as 'Trojan horse' moves as they believe that such moves can derail developing nations' hitherto achieved progress.[27] Therefore, any global initiative to add women-related provisions into trade agreements cannot be successful unless that trust deficit is addressed.[28] Unless consensus and comfort zones are built around these discussions, it is difficult to achieve common ground.

5.3 Under-Representation of Women in Policymaking Roles

Another possible reason holding back the upsurge of such inclusions or, rather, meaningful inclusion of such commitments is the under-representation of women in policymaking and decision-making roles. Although trade negotiations have increased in scope and scale, this has not resulted in a concomitant increase in the representation of women as experts, negotiators, and diplomats. The forums where trade negotiations take place involve large numbers of public and private stakeholders and hence they are prone to reproducing existing inequalities at policymaking and decision-making levels. This is mainly because women are often under-represented in high leadership roles in politics, government offices, and in businesses.[29] The higher the decision-making or policymaking forum, the more likely it is that women will be absent or under-represented. A recent study has shown, using quantitative empirical research, that women are largely absent from

[25] One such negotiation related to climate change. For more information, see Olivia Rumble, 'No Place to Discuss the CBAM, not even the WTO' (African Climate Wire 11 March 2024) <https://africanclimatewire.org/2024/03/no-place-to-discuss-the-cbam-not-even-the-wto/> accessed 9 July 2023.

[26] Interview with a trade negotiator (details withheld, on file with the author).

[27] Balakrishnan Rajagopal, 'Women and Trade at the WTO: Pink Herring, Trojan Horse or Historic Advance?' (CIGI Reshaping Trade Through Women's Economic Empowerment 9 April 2018) <www.cigionline.org/articles/women-and-trade-wto-pink-herring-trojan-horse-or-historic-advance/> accessed 9 July 2023.

[28] Interview with a trade negotiator (details withheld, on file with the author).

[29] Marzia Fontana, 'Gender Justice in Trade Policy: The Gender Effects of Economic Partnership Agreements. Synthesis Report' (One World Action 2009) <www.oecd.org/social/gender-development/47566754.pdf> accessed 9 July 2023.

important high-level decision-making processes at trade negotiating forums.[30] Hence, one effective way to add women's perspectives to future trade negotiations is to appoint more women to negotiating and policymaking roles. Women should be included in the trade policymaking agenda setting and negotiating roles because they are best placed to understand and find solutions to the problems that only they have faced.[31]

Appointment of women in senior negotiating roles in trade forums may be vital for ensuring that future trade agreements are gender-considerate for several reasons. First, women at the negotiating tables may add a different perspective to the overall process of negotiations and make the process responsive towards the needs of women negotiators who may simultaneously have childcare or other family responsibilities. Second, an increase in the number of senior female negotiators participating in negotiation processes may ensure frontloading of the women's issues on the trade agenda and arriving at provisions that can lead to clear benefits for women.[32] Third, female trade negotiators who reach high levels of responsibility within global trade negotiating forums have greater motivation to gain a robust understanding of gender analysis and gender implications along with the strong technical skills required for the job. Given the experience they have had in their lives, and the gender-specific barriers they might have faced, they are more likely to bring positions of equitable and inclusive trade outcomes to the negotiating table.[33]

Studies have shown how 'women's increased voice and agency in parliaments and national development processes confirm that gender-equitable targeted interventions typically increase with women's greater involvement, leading to transformative change . . . '.[34] Several examples reinforce this observation. During her term from 2014 and 2019, former EU Trade Commissioner Anna Cecilia Malmström addressed the need to empower women through trade by capitalizing on gender equality efforts in all aspects of EU policymaking. The theme of gender

30 Maria V Sokolova and Matthew Wilson, 'Setting Up the Table Right: Women's Representation Meets Women's Inclusion in Trade Negotiations' in Amrita Bahri, Dorotea López, and Jan Yves Remy (eds), *Trade Policy and Gender Equality* (CUP 2023).

31 Olayinka Bandele, 'An Equal Seat at the Table: Gendering Trade Negotiations' (2016) International Trade Working Paper 2016/14 Commonwealth Secretariat London. (Some trade experts from the United States, Canada, and Chile have provided contradictory views, arguing that a greater number of women in the negotiating room does not necessarily translate into more gender provisions in trade agreements. 'For example, evidence suggests that the Office of the United States Trade Representative (USTR) has been staffed with at least 50 percent women since the late 1980s, but the United States' first FTA gender provisions did not appear until the United States–Mexico–Canada Agreement (USMCA) entered into force in 2020—more than 30 years later.' William Alan Reinsch, Jasmine Lim, and Ally Brodsky, 'Negotiating Trade Agreements: Gender as a Priority?' (CSIS 24 May 2021) <www.csis.org/analysis/negotiating-trade-agreements-gender-priority> accessed 12 June 2024.)

32 London Chamber of Commerce and Industries, 'Inclusion of Women in the Negotiation of Free Trade Agreements' <www.londonchamber.co.uk/LCCI/media/media/Inclusion-of-Women-in-the-Negotiation-of-Free-Trade-Agreements.pdf> accessed 12 June 2024.

33 Interview with trade negotiator (details withheld, on file with the author).

34 Bandele (n 31).

equality in EU trade agreements and parliamentary resolutions gained significant momentum during her tenure and the momentum has continued since then.[35] Another example is the appointment of Dr Ngozi Okonjo-Iweala as the first female Director-General of the WTO who, since her arrival, has opened more doors for the members of the organization to engage and exchange on these issues.[36] At the WTO's Twelfth and Thirteenth Ministerial Conferences held in 2022 and 2024 respectively, the highest number of women participants was observed, negotiating on a range of issues including food security, health, and other trade policy themes. This also shows that the representation of women has increased in leadership roles in government as well as in permanent missions. These are promising developments and we can expect these developments to render more favourable results for women in the multilateral space.

5.4 Lack of Political Will

Lack of political will to leverage trade agreements to empower women is one of the key factors impeding efforts to negotiate women-related concerns for their inclusion in trade agreements. Gender equality matters do not enjoy political priority in the trade agendas of many countries and these issues have been further sidelined amidst growing health and economic concerns of countries across the world. To see real advancement in this respect, commitment to these issues needs to come from the highest levels of administration, including political stakeholders such as legislators and parliamentary members.[37]

Political will at the highest level can frontload women-centric considerations in national and international discussions. The political salience of a particular concern plays a vital role in determining whether that concern is addressed in the negotiating room. A country's lawmakers' views may factor into the negotiators' calculus when considering the content and scope of an agreement's language as that agreement will require the lawmakers' approval for its ratification.[38] The resolutions adopted by the European Parliament on mainstreaming gender concerns in

[35] Samira Rafaela, 'Incorporating gender in trade policy to benefit all Stakeholder' (EUobserver 12 April 2021) <https://euobserver.com/stakeholders/151507> accessed 12 June 2024; Maïa De La Baume, 'Malmström urges "male-dominated" OECD to do better on gender' (Politico 8 March 2021) <www.politico.eu/article/cecilia-malmstrom-male-dominated-oecd-better-on-gender/> accessed 12 June 2024.

[36] For recent initiatives, see WTO, 'Women and Trade' <www.wto.org/english/tratop_e/womenandtrade_e/womenandtrade_e.htm> accessed 12 June 2024.

[37] Elina Viilup, 'EU Trade Policy: Gender-Sensitive or Gender Blind?' (2016/2017) 5(6) GREAT Insights <https://ecdpm.org/work/shifts-in-trade-development-volume-5-issue-6-december-2016-january-2017/eu-trade-policy-gender-sensitive-or-gender-blind> accessed 12 June 2024.

[38] William Alan Reinsch, Jasmine Lim, and Ally Brodsky, 'Negotiating Trade Agreements: Gender as a Priority?' (CSIS 24 May 2021) <www.csis.org/analysis/negotiating-trade-agreements-gender-priority> accessed 12 June 2024.

trade agreements, the creation of a gender mainstreaming team in the Parliament's International Trade Committee, the commissioning of work on trade, and dedicated parliamentary debates on negotiating gender-responsive agreements are a result of the emerging political willingness to encourage inclusive and sustainable trade policies in the region.[39] The 2018 Resolution on gender equality in EU trade agreements was adopted with 512 votes in favour and 107 against, endorsing a resolution that would allow the consideration of women's interests in trade agreements.[40] The 2019 Resolution on mainstreaming women's concerns in policy instruments was adopted by 492 in favour and 126 against.[41] The massive support of Members of the European Parliament in favour of empowering women reflects the institution's readiness to strengthen women's empowerment and use policy instruments to achieve that goal. These examples show that a strong political will is the key to using trade agreements for women's empowerment.

Another example is that of Canada where gender equality is an aspect of its priorities in trade policymaking and negotiations. In the early years, this objective was implemented by the inclusion of language regarding the elimination of employment discrimination in labour cooperation agreements and labour chapters in FTAs.[42] More recently, Canada has sought to mainstream women-explicit considerations beyond labour standards throughout its FTAs. This is based on a commitment made in Canada's 2018 federal budget that established that more FTAs would be subject to gender-based analysis using Canada's analysis tool called Gender-based Analysis Plus (GBA+).[43] On 5 June 2017, Canada became the first G20 country to include a trade and gender chapter in an FTA, with its modernized Canada–Chile FTA. Since then, it has included women-related provisions in FTAs with several countries including Mexico, EU, Israel, and others. Canada's political will and expertise in the negotiation of women-related provisions in trade agreements is the key propeller behind this approach.[44]

[39] Claire Guyot, 'EP wants to include gender equality in free-trade agreements' (EURACTIV.fr 14 March 2018) <www.euractiv.com/section/politics/news/ep-wants-to-include-gender-equality-in-free-trade-agreements/> accessed 12 June 2024; also see Ina Opartyová and Justin Lindeboom, 'Towards a gender-sensitive EU external trade policy' (EJIL Talk 9 November 2023) <www.ejiltalk.org/towards-a-gender-sensitive-eu-external-trade-policy/> accessed 12 June 2024.

[40] European Parliament resolution of 13 March 2018 on gender equality in EU trade agreements, 2017/2015(INI) <www.europarl.europa.eu/doceo/document/TA-8-2018-0066_EN.html> accessed 12 June 2024.

[41] European Parliament resolution of 15 January 2019 on gender mainstreaming in the European Parliament, 2018/2162(INI) <www.europarl.europa.eu/doceo/document/TA-8-2019-0010_EN.html> accessed 12 June 2024.

[42] See eg Annex 13-A of the Canada–Ukraine FTA. Similar provisions can be found in the Canada–Honduras FTA (in force 1 October 2014); Canada–Columbia FTA (in force 15 August 2011); Canada–Panama FTA (in force 1 April 2013).

[43] Employment and Social Development Canada, 'Employment and Social Development Canada 2018–2019 Departmental plan—Supplementary information—Annex 1.7: Gender-Based Analysis (GBA+)' <www.canada.ca/en/employment-social-development/corporate/reports/departmental-plan/2018-2019/gender-based-analysis.html> accessed 12 June 2024.

[44] Interview with trade negotiators (details withheld, on file with the author).

The South American political appetite for these concerns can be further exemplified by the regional developments that have facilitated various integration mechanisms. The Pacific Alliance, an integration mechanism that includes Chile, Colombia, Mexico, and Peru, is one such example. During the Tenth Presidential Summit in 2015, the parties created a technical group on gender to ensure that gender became a cross-cutting issue in the region's agenda. At the Fifteenth Pacific Alliance Summit held in 2020 in Santiago, Chile, the four countries signed a Presidential Declaration on Gender Equality. Through this Declaration, the parties agreed on a roadmap to promote the economic empowerment of women in the Pacific Alliance and strengthen the protection of women's rights.[45] Other efforts have also been employed within the framework of regional integration mechanisms such as MERCOSUR, the Andean Community, and the Central American Common Market.

A clear difference can be seen in the approach of countries in which political administrations have issued mandates from the top to include women's perspectives as a strategic component of their governance. The Chilean example also testifies to the power of this as gender became an explicit component of Chile's trade policy during Michelle Bachelet's second administration from 2014 to 2018. Chile, alongside Uruguay, became the first country to negotiate a trade agreement with a dedicated chapter on trade and gender.[46] Another interesting example can be observed in India where under the administration of Prime Minister Narendra Modi an informal directive was issued to all government divisions to consider women's perspectives in their functioning. This directive was mentioned in the Prime Minister's speech as '*Nari Shakti*', which means 'women empowerment' or 'women's strength' in Hindi. *Nari Shakti* is an initiative focused on improving the lives of women in India and removing any constraints they might face in their overall development.[47] Since the issuance of this directive in 2023, women empowerment has been considered an important component of governance in India, which includes the governance of economic and trade concerns. This can be seen in several efforts including India's negotiation of its first-ever trade agreement with a notable provision on women

[45] Alianza del Pacífico, 'With Declaration on Gender Equality and the Digital Market of the bloc concludes the Pacific Alliance Summit' (Alianza del Pacífico 11 December 2020) <https://alianzapacifico.net/en/with-declaration-on-gender-equality-and-the-digital-market-of-the-bloc-concludes-the-pacific-alliance-summit/> accessed 12 June 2024.

[46] Dorotea López, Felipe Muñoz, and Javiera Cáceres, 'Gender Inclusion in Chilean Free Trade Agreements', Working Paper, 14 (on file with the author); Bachelet's administration is widely known for its works and accomplishments relating to gender issues. For more information, see Linda Stevenson, 'The Bachelet Effect on Gender-Equity Policies' (2012) 39(4) Latin American Perspectives 129.

[47] For details on other relevant initiatives in India, see Nari Shakti, 'From Women Development to Women-led Development' (Research Unit, Press Information Bureau, Government of India 7 March 2023) <https://static.pib.gov.in/WriteReadData/specificdocs/documents/2023/mar/doc202337167601.pdf> accessed 12 June 2024.

empowerment in the recently negotiated India–EFTA Trade and Economic Partnership Agreement.[48]

5.5 Fears of Cultural Imperialism

A significant concern for a country could be the extent to which a legal provision related to gender might allow countries to further expand the already-stretched concept of gender equality. If country A justifies a measure that bans or restricts trade with country B because country B ranks poorly on the World Economic Forum's *Global Gender Gap Reports* or because it does not adhere to its commitments under International Labour Organization (ILO) conventions, country B can interpret this as country A's attempt to impose its cultural standards on country B. An actual WTO case demonstrates this problem. The WTO's ruling in *EC—Seals*[49] may be seen as legitimizing moral imperialism that was inherent in the EU seal regime as it could be viewed as an attempt by the EU to impose its moral values on foreign jurisdictions without any consideration for their moral interests.[50] In a way, this imposition also contradicted the traditions and cultural practices related to seal hunting in Canada and Norway. In other words, by giving legitimacy to animal welfare concerns as a public moral concern, both the WTO Panel and the Appellate Body subordinated the moral concerns of the indigenous sealing communities in other countries to those of the EU's animal welfare concerns. This is a classic example that reflects how justifying a trade measure under a vaguely defined value (eg 'morality' or 'gender equality') may allow the responding country to effectively define the moral concerns of foreign jurisdictions, disregarding the moral values of others and potentially also undermining their comparative advantage in a particular product or industry.

An attempt to address women-related concerns may be seen as an attempt to engage in 'cultural imperialism' as it could allow countries to export their own social or cultural model to those countries with a different set of values and concerns. However, the inclusion of stringent labour standards in the United States–Mexico–Canada Agreement (USMCA) to minimize the exploitation of workers and improve wages and working conditions in Mexico could also be seen as a strategy by the United States to impose its labour standards, not merely to help Mexican workers but rather as a new form of imperialism to reduce Mexico's comparative

[48] Trade and Economic Partnership Agreement between the EFTA States and the Republic of India (signed 10 March 2024) ch 11 Trade and Sustainable Development, art 11.6.

[49] WTO Appellate Body Report, Status report by the European Union—Addendum, *European Communities—Measures Prohibiting the Importation and Marketing of Seal Products* (16 October 2015) WT/DS400/16/Add.7 WT/DS401/17/Add.7.

[50] Whitsitt (n 20).

advantage in manufacturing automobiles due to its low labour costs and the labour-intensive nature of its automobile industry. However, no such concerns were raised during the negotiation. This example shows that trade policy instruments have developed an appetite for labour standards in part because they are trade-germane interests that directly impact countries' economic interests. However, this may not be the case for other supposedly non-trade-germane concerns, such as those related to women.[51]

Some European Parliamentary Members have openly voiced opposition against the incorporation of women's perspectives in trade agreements, fearing it will be perceived as 'colonialist behaviour'. Joachim Starbatty of the European Conservatives and Reformists Group stated: 'If we start putting forward clauses such as the one you are proposing, then we will be laughed at … We cannot impose our vision of gender on the world. It's colonialist behaviour.'[52] Fears of cultural imperialism and the use of gender standards for the protection of domestic industries are the main concerns that several countries have voiced when they have resisted or opposed any development in respect of trade and gender, for example signing the 2017 WTO Declaration or even joining the WTO's informal group on trade and gender to discuss these matters.

5.6 Sovereignty Cost, Cost of Compliance, and Probability of Compliance

A women-related provision could impose a significant cost on nations in terms of their sovereignty as it can allow other countries to interfere in their domestic affairs and place limits on their ability to deal with matters relating to their own social, political, economic, cultural, and even religious affairs.[53] This cost could vary as it depends on several factors including a given country's gender gap rating as per the

[51] Desiree LeClercq, 'The Disparate Treatment of Rights in US Trade' (2021) 90(1) Fordham Law Review 1 (the author notes that this appetite largely depends on whether the non-trade concerns are related to trade and whether they impact production or trade costs).

[52] Guyot (n 39).

[53] Kathryn Sikkink, 'Human Rights, Principled Issue-Networks, and Sovereignty in Latin America' (1993) 47(3) International Organization 411 (sovereignty cost refers to the amount of power or authority a sovereign country would otherwise have but needs to surrender it when it joins an international treaty that place limits on and encourages interference in its domestic affairs. Noting that the 'doctrine of internationally protected human rights offer[s] one of the most powerful critiques of sovereignty as currently constituted …'); Kenneth W Abbot and Duncan Snidal, 'Hard and Soft Law in International Governance' (2000) 54(3) International Organization 421 (Abbott and Snidal note that the 'sovereignty costs' are low when states 'simply make international commitments that limit their behavior in particular circumstances' but that these costs are higher when 'states accept external authority over significant decisions'). For a contrary view, see Christian Reus-Smit, 'Human Rights and the Social Construction of Sovereignty' (2001) 27(4) Review of International Studies 519 (the author observes that sovereignty and human rights are inter-related and should be seen as two contradictory values).

WEF's *Global Gender Gap Reports*[54] or the World Bank's *Women, Business and the Law Reports.*[55]

Often countries give in and accept this sovereignty cost and its resulting implications to uphold their economic or market access interests. The greater the economic significance of a country's market offering an inducement to influence changes in the domestic policies of another country in exchange for improved market access, the more prominent and attractive that inducement becomes. Andrew Moravcsik observes that countries' willingness to 'tolerate sovereignty costs increases insofar as the costs are outweighed by the benefits of reducing domestic political uncertainty'.[56] Rationalist scholars have asserted that material interests are likely to dominate other interests and concerns. However, countries' willingness and appetite for such inducements rely on their domestic conditions as they may be unwilling to join agreements containing obligations with which they cannot comply.[57] Hence, countries may not usually engage in cooperation efforts that require a significant departure from their domestic policies and practices or those that require countries to act differently than they otherwise would. Hence, the cost of compliance with the provisions in an agreement is fundamental to a country's decision to join an agreement that may require that country to change the status quo in respect of its laws, policies, and practices.

The more a country's practices and policies encourage and support women's concerns and adhere to universally accepted norms in this respect, the more likely it is that the country will be willing to accept women-related commitments in its trade agreements. The countries with practices and policies that do not discourage inequality against women and do not adhere to commonly accepted norms, such as the elimination of discrimination based on sex and hence are poorly ranked in gender-related indexes, might be less likely to accept such a provision or an interpretation that can favour women or address their barriers.[58] This is primarily because, in addition to the high cost of compliance, the probability of complying with such provisions might also be discouragingly low. Policymakers may find it

[54] WEF, 'Closing the Gender Gap Accelerators' <www.weforum.org/projects/closing-the-gender-gap-accelerators> accessed 21 May 2024.

[55] World Bank Group, 'Women, Business and the Law 2021' (World Bank 2021) <https://wbl.worldbank.org/en/wbl> accessed 21 May 2024.

[56] Andrew Moravcsik, 'The Origins of Human Rights Regimes: Democratic Delegation in Postwar Europe' (2000) 54(2) International Organization 217, 228.

[57] George W Downs, David M Rocke, and Peter N Barsoom, 'Is the Good News About Compliance Good News About Cooperation?' (1996) 50(3) International Organization 379; see also James C Murdoch and Todd Sandler, 'The Voluntary Provision of a Pure Public Good: The Case of Reduced CFC Emissions and the Montreal Protocol' (1997) 63(3) Journal of Public Economics 331; contrary view in Beth A Simmons, 'International Law and State Behavior: Commitment and Compliance in International Monetary Affairs' (2000) 94(4) The American Political Science Review 819 (the authors observe that 'international legal rules do alter governments' interests in compliant behavior').

[58] Oona A Hathaway, 'The Cost of Commitment' (2003) 55(5) Stanford Law Review 1821 (the author has referred to this as the 'sovereignty view', wherein countries take into account the cost of such a commitment to their national sovereignty).

difficult in their national parliaments to advocate for the ratification of an agreement that contains problematic provisions. The ratification of such agreements becomes unlikely because of the amount of criticism they may face by parliamentarians, primarily because of the high compliance costs and uncertainty regarding the interpretation or application of those provisions by their trade partners.[59] Such provisions can raise scepticism due to the vagueness with which they are generally drafted as countries might invoke them to justify values only remotely related to women's concerns or values not shared or observed by other countries.[60]

The case of Africa contradicts the 'cost of compliance' and 'probability of compliance' theories. Trade agreements in the African region generally do not have a stand-alone chapter on trade and women or exhaustive provisions on cooperation activities. However, they have employed several provisions with binding force and obligatory expressions. Some of the agreements even include women-explicit minimum legal standards. The African countries playing a pioneering role in this respect are Kenya, Rwanda, Tanzania, Uganda, and Zimbabwe, which have signed agreements with ambitious, binding women-related commitments in this region. These findings contradict the 'cost of compliance' and 'probability of compliance' theories as with their poor rating in the *Global Gender Gap Index* and the *Women, Business and the Law 2021* index, the cost of compliance with such provisions might be quite high for them and, on the contrary, the probability of compliance may be significantly low. Their poor ranking is mainly attributed to their gender unequal social, economic, political, and legal structures. However, it seems that the high cost of compliance and low probability of compliance have not discouraged them from negotiating and accepting women-responsive agreements, perhaps due to three main reasons.

First, many African countries have included women's empowerment as an issue related to their region's development; it seems that they have equated their need for growth and development with women´s empowerment and are thus attempting to enhance women's participation to further socio-economic transformation and sustainable growth.[61] Second, these countries might still be willing to assume such commitments as they may be committed to changing their domestic conditions using international policy instruments. The negotiation and ratification of these instruments can encourage the emergence of new norms or policies that may impact or even change a country's behaviour.[62] This reason is inferred from the

[59] Interview with trade negotiators from three developing countries (details withheld, on file with the author).

[60] Interview with trade negotiator (details withheld, on file with the author).

[61] Interview with trade negotiators from the African Continental Free Trade Area (AfCFTA) and Common Market for Eastern and Southern Africa (COMESA) Secretariats (details withheld, on file with the author).

[62] Martha Finnemore, *National Interests in International Society* (Cornell UP 1996) 87 (noting that states' preferences can change during international dialogues and negotiations, and international systems can change state action by changing their preferences).

normative view that countries might still be willing to assume such commitments, overlooking their high cost of compliance, if they are committed to achieving gender equality and changing their domestic conditions using international policy instruments. Finnemore, for instance, defends this 'norm emergence' view and argues that the negotiation and ratification of international policy instruments can encourage the emergence of new norms or policies that may impact or even change a country's behaviour.[63] Additionally, governments may have legitimate interests in the well-being of foreign citizens for various reasons that include promotion of international stability, minimization of wars and disorder, and furtherance of global economic growth.[64] Third, these countries may have found a safe abode in binding commitments since the agreements that have included such commitments in the region are mainly negotiated between African countries with similar domestic conditions and challenges. This confirms the finding that parties are more willing to accept binding commitments when they are negotiating these provisions with countries that are similarly situated in terms of their gender development levels, as having partners with similar domestic conditions minimizes fears of trade protectionism.

5.7 Lack of Understanding and Awareness

Amidst an ever-growing debate on which interests should or could be added to trade agreements, what is lacking is an understanding of the inclusion of such non-trade issues and the place of such concerns in global trade governance. In particular, the nexus between trade and women is far from straightforward. Moreover, what is now clear beyond doubt is that globalization and trade liberalization can have contradictory effects on women's employment and livelihoods. In some cases, they generate employment and business opportunities for women; in others, they create burdens by disrupting industries that employ women or are prevalent in small businesses run by women.[65] This complex and contradictory nexus is difficult to understand. Lack of understanding and awareness of how international

[63] Martha Finnemore and Kathryn Sikkink, 'International Norm Dynamics and Political Change' (1998) 52(4) International Organization 887, 900 (observing that the creation and adoption of international agreements and treaties can change a country's preference and shape its norms and domestic behaviour); Emilie M Hafner-Burton, 'Trading Human Rights: How Preferential Trade Agreements Influence Government Repression' (2005) 59(3) International Organization 593 (the author observes how international treaties are designed to regulate sovereign governments' behaviours towards individuals).

[64] Jack L Goldsmith and Eric A Posner, *The Limits of International Law* (OUP 2005) 109–10 (the authors observe that although countries are mainly interested in the well-being of their own citizens, they also have some interest in the well-being of others).

[65] Gender Equality & Trade Policy, 'UN Women Watch Resource Paper' (2011) <www.un.org/womenwatch/feature/trade/gender_equality_and_trade_policy.pdf> accessed 21 May 2024.

trade and women's concerns are related impede efforts to negotiate trade agreements through women's perspectives.

Lack of understanding may also manifest itself in disbelief in and indifference to this approach. Some observers, for instance, have suggested that 'references to gender in trade agreements are no more than nice rhetoric, and that they do not address the full range of gender equality issues at stake'.[66] In particular, one senior government aide has claimed that the efforts relating to women empowerment in the context of economic activities are 'nothing' and that '[i]t's just about being nice to women, which is fine, but is that it?'.[67] Such views reflect indifference, which may be borne out of a lack of understanding and paucity of research in this area.

In this sense, women-related provisions are not alone in facing such a critique as the inclusion of other sustainability issues has followed a very similar trajectory of opposition, understanding, capacity-building, and, finally, acceptance. For example, after a long-held rejection of the trade–labour linkage by the trade policy community, the inclusion of labour standards has now become a norm in trade agreements.[68] However, enforceable labour standards, such as the labour provisions included in USMCA that are made enforceable by its rapid response mechanism, are generally added into trade agreements as impositions on developing country partners at the insistence of developed country partners.[69]

Over time, trade policy instruments have accommodated both labour and women-related concerns, but they have developed a larger appetite for labour standards than for women's issues. This might be, in part, because labour, as one of three main manufacturing inputs, together with capital and raw materials, is seen as a trade-germane interest. That might not be the case for other 'supposedly' non-trade-germane social concerns such as those of women.[70] Another probable reason might be the long-held relationship between trade and labour standards, stretching as far back as the founding of the ILO and possibly back to the colonial slave trade.[71] Hence, these reasons show how preparing a business case for such inclusions and the presence of familiarity with negotiating them may also help with

[66] Valerie Hughes, 'Gender Chapters in Trade Agreements: Nice Rhetoric or Sound Policy?' (CIGI 9 October 2019) <www.cigionline.org/articles/gender-chapters-trade-agreements-nice-rhetoric-or-sound-policy/> accessed 21 May 2024.

[67] Tom Mctague, David M Herszenhorn, and Andrew Restuccia, 'Trump blows up G7 agenda' (Politico 30 March 2018) <www.politico.eu/article/donald-trump-blows-up-g7-summit-agenda-canada/> accessed 21 May 2024.

[68] Robert Howse, Brian Langille, and Julien Burda, 'The World Trade Organization and Labour Rights: Man Bites Dog' in Virginia A Leary and Daniel Warner (eds), *Social Issues, Globalisation and International Institutions* (Brill 2006) 157.

[69] Elisa Dávalos, 'Protectionism, USMCA and its Possible Effects on Mexico's Automotive Industry' (2020) 7(1) European Review of International Studies 81.

[70] LeClercq (n 51).

[71] Adrian Smith and others, *Free Trade Agreements and Global Labour Governance* (Routledge 2021); see also Marcus Gustafsson and Amrita Bahri, 'Progressive Trade: Labour and Gender' in Daniel Bethlehem and others (eds), *The Oxford Handbook of International Trade Law* (OUP 2022).

better acceptance of women-related concerns in trade agreements. Even though there is now increased international visibility being given to how trade agreements can enable women empowerment, policymakers in many countries are not familiar with the inclusion of women-related concerns in trade negotiations and they fail to understand how the two issues are interrelated. Several countries believe that FTAs are trade instruments only concerned with market access issues, and hence they are not appropriate forums to discuss women issues as these issues are not market access issues, and therefore countries should refrain from introducing non-trade issues to the agenda.[72]

To overcome this impediment, countries need to ensure that their policymakers and negotiators understand how trade agreements can have different gendered implications. The inclusion of women in their economies is not only the morally right thing to do but also has a compelling business case. Government officials at the negotiating table must understand the implications of all substantive issues they are negotiating on different vulnerable groups, including women. Enhancing this understanding and relevant expertise within the government ministries responsible for trade negotiations is vital, as policymakers' understanding and expertise on this subject are important triggers for such inclusions.

Even though multiple advances have been made in research on enhancing the understanding of this nexus, it has to some extent been held back by limited gender-disaggregated data. Multiple studies have shown a clear correlation between international trade and women as employees, business actors, and customers. However, what remains to be done is gathering concrete numbers that testify to this correlation. Hence, paucity of country-wise and industry-wise gender disaggregated data on how trade disciplines impact women is also perhaps slowing down mainstream efforts in this regard.

5.8 Paucity of Gender Disaggregated Data

The absence of gender disaggregated data that disentangles the effects of trade liberalization from other simultaneous changes on the situation of women makes it difficult to assess the empirical impact of trade agreements on women and whether the inclusion of women-related provisions makes a difference.[73] Data needs to show information on the social and economic situation of women concerning

[72] Suresh Prabhu, Indian Minister of Industry and Commerce (Indian Press Conference, WTO Ministerial Conference, Buenos Aires, 11 December 2017) (statement on file with the author).

[73] Kate Higgins, 'Gender and Free Trade Agreements: Best Practices and Policy Guidance' (The North-South Institute 2013) <https://cawtarclearinghouse.org/storage/AttachementGender/2013%20Gender%20and%20FTAs%20Best%20Practices%20and%20Policy%20Guidance.pdf> accessed 21 May 2024.

men affected or influenced by trade liberalization. This should include reciprocal-relationship information on costs and benefits of trade for men and women and costs and benefits of women empowerment on international trade and economic growth. This dual analysis can help establish a direct and practical linkage between trade and women.[74] This data, reflecting a reciprocal relationship between trade and women, is crucial to steer trade liberalization towards inclusive growth and to address existing inequalities for better and more inclusive trade outcomes. Moreover, since the relationship between women and trade is very country and industry specific, specific data analysis of the impact of trade on women and vice versa is needed on a case-by-case basis.

In addition, the lack of capacity to interpret data in a trade policy and gender context once such data is collected is another factor that limits mainstreaming efforts.[75] To enhance the understanding of the nexus between trade and women, data needs to be analysed to answer a range of questions: what is the direct impact of trade on female employment? What is the indirect impact of trade on female workforce? How are women employees, employers, and customers impacted by liberalization-triggered disruptions in the supply chain? How do global supply chains interact with and empower cross-border women traders? How do exports and imports impact affordability and the standard of living of women consumers? How would women employees in labour-intensive industries be impacted with the negotiation of a chapter or provision on digital commerce in a particular agreement? Has a cooperation provision on enhancing the access of women to productive resources or a stand-alone chapter added in previous agreements made any measurable impact on the position of women? We need to provide trade negotiators and policymakers with answers to these questions in the form of concrete numbers and their analysis before we can expect to see enforceable and implementable commitments in future trade agreements.

If gender-disaggregated data and its analysis are available, they can be used as concrete evidence for countries to see how trade and gender equality are not separate issues but intricately related and interdependent. The absence of the required gender-disaggregated data that can identify and measure the impact that the inclusion of women's concerns in trade agreements is having on the role and rights of women continues to impede concrete development in this respect as there is no evidence to see if such inclusions have actually helped.

[74] UNCTAD, UNECA, and UNECE, 'Desk study on the gender aspects of trade and trade policy for statistics, UNDA project 2023D: Data and statistics for more gender-responsive trade policies in Africa, Eastern Europe, Caucasus and Central Asia' <https://unctad.org/system/files/information-document/20201012_WebinarGender_DeskStudy_en.pdf> accessed 1 May 2024.

[75] UNCTAD, 'Better Data and Statistics For Gender-responsive Trade Policy' (2018) <https://unctad.org/system/files/official-document/presspb2018d7_en.pdf> accessed 1 May 2024.

5.9 Absence of Expertise

The lack of understanding and absence of data on trade and women can explain or perhaps even justify the lack of expertise within government offices in this respect. One trade negotiator notes that some trading partners just do not want to talk about women's issues while they are engaged in trade negotiations for various reasons.[76] They believe that trade is gender-neutral or that an FTA is not a tool to advance social issues or to develop women-focused considerations.[77] Countries holding these views have no incentive or motivation to create capacity and expertise in negotiating agreements with women's perspectives. The absence of expertise on trade and women's issues within government departments responsible for carrying out trade negotiations is therefore another impediment that needs to be overcome in this respect.

Going forward, negotiators need to develop expertise on how to apply an inclusive lens during negotiation, drafting, and implementation of trade agreements. To build this expertise, negotiators and policymakers should be provided with up-to-date knowledge and developments on these issues. They can be kept engaged through a range of measures such as carrying out debates on such issues in parliamentary discussions and high-level conferences, requiring negotiators to read relevant studies and participate in pertinent training courses, and carrying out exchange visits to discuss and share experiences with negotiators from other countries in this respect. Negotiators and policymakers can also receive hands-on training on the following aspects: (1) how are women-related considerations mainstreamed by other countries; (2) what are some best practice provisions in this respect; (3) what benefits have other countries realized from mainstreaming such concerns in the past few years; (4) what are the main arguments behind the inclusion of women's concerns in trade instruments; (5) what are the different ways of including women-related considerations in trade agreements; and (6) how can negotiators assess whether a given agreement is responsive to women's needs and concerns and, if needed, increase its responsiveness content?

In particular, the last two questions point to the absence of an indicator to measure and track progress in this respect. This is where the need to have a toolkit comes in—a methodology that can guide trade negotiators on how they can negotiate and draft women-responsive trade agreements. One such methodology is the International Trade Centre's (ITC) maturity framework, which can help negotiators gauge the gender-responsiveness of their trade agreements. This framework can help policymakers identify the level of gender-responsiveness a particular agreement may have and guide them on how they can increase this

[76] Interview with trade negotiator (details withheld, on file with the author).
[77] Interview with trade negotiator (details withheld, on file with the author).

gender-responsiveness. Trade negotiators and policymakers can also employ the framework in the renegotiation or modernization of existing trade agreements to enhance their potential to engage and empower women. The following chapter presents this framework—a new methodology—that helps measure gender-responsiveness in a trade agreement.

6
Measuring Gender-Responsiveness of Trade Agreements
Using the Maturity Framework

6.1 Introduction

If a negotiator is keen on negotiating a free trade agreement (FTA) that accommodates women's concerns or is responsive to their concerns, what provisions might that negotiator consider for such a negotiation? Is there a scale or framework to guide the negotiator on how to increase the responsiveness of a given agreement? For that matter, what does it take for a trade agreement to be gender responsive or for a negotiator to employ the approach of gender mainstreaming in the negotiation of a given trade agreement? This chapter situates the concepts of 'gender mainstreaming' and 'gender responsiveness' within an objective context with the help of a maturity framework. This framework allows trade negotiators and policymakers to objectively measure the extent to which the text of a particular trade agreement is gender-responsive.[1] In this chapter, the term 'gender mainstreaming' refers to the incorporation of concerns relating to women in the drafting and implementation of FTAs. This process ensures that women's perspectives are included in trade liberalization efforts and policies. Furthermore, the term 'gender responsiveness' refers to evaluating how sensitive, informed, or committed the provisions of a trade agreement are to women's issues. In other words, the degree to which an agreement mainstreams women's concerns determines its responsiveness to those concerns.

The findings in this chapter do not imply that every country must form new or revise existing FTAs in a specific manner nor do they suggest that all future FTAs

[1] For details, see International Trade Centre (ITC), 'Mainstreaming Gender in Free Trade Agreements' (ITC 2020) <www.intracen.org/publication/mainstreaming-gender-FTA/> accessed 25 August 2021. Also available in Spanish at ITC, 'La incorporación de la perspectiva de género en los tratados de libre comercio' (ITC 2020) <https://intracen.org/resources/publications/mainstreaming-gender-in-free-trade-agreements#:~:text=The%20recommendations%20include%20embedding%20gender,monitoring%20and%20dispute%20settlement%20mechanisms> accessed 12 May 2024. (Since 2020, the framework explained in this chapter has been employed by the ITC to assess trade agreements and their women-related provisions for the ITC's 'She Trades Outlook', a tool that uses pioneering data to explore and compare how countries are addressing gender in trade policies and practices. More details at ITC, 'She Trades Outlook' <https://outlook.shetrades.com/home> accessed 12 May 2024.)

Trade Agreements and Women. Amrita Bahri, Oxford University Press. © Amrita Bahri 2025.
DOI: 10.1093/9780198935759.003.0007

should prioritize or achieve the highest levels of gender-responsiveness as per the proposed framework. Instead, the chapter acknowledges the necessity of tailoring the incorporation of women's perspectives to the unique economic, political, social, and cultural contexts of the countries involved. This approach allows for flexibility and customization, ensuring that the integration of women-related concerns is relevant and effective for each situation. Nevertheless, using this diagnostic approach, this new methodology can allow countries to develop a roadmap to achieve the desired level of gender-responsiveness for their FTAs, following their needs, willingness, and resources. In this manner, it provides insights to policymakers and trade negotiators on how they can draft gender-responsive trade agreements. The impact of mainstreaming women's perspectives on women and trade will only become visible over time for the reasons discussed in the previous chapter. In the meantime, the framework can help countries move in that direction.

Working with and under the guidance of the ITC, I employed multiple methods to prepare this maturity framework. The framework was prepared using a triangulation of research methods, which started with an in-depth review of literature on trade and women and feminist economics to gain the initial conceptual understanding.[2] Together with the literature review, a review of selected FTAs was carried out to understand how women-related considerations have been included in existing FTAs.[3] Thereafter, I employed an empirical approach to gather practical insights. This empirical approach entailed group discussions, conference participations, and semi-structured interviews at various locations with trade negotiators, policymakers, gender studies scholars, and international diplomats.[4] Subsequently, I carried out content analysis of selected FTAs to identify

[2] Some of these leading works include: Adrian Wood, 'North–South Trade and Female Labour in Manufacturing: An Asymmetry' (1991) 27(2) Journal of Development Studies 168; Robert Baldwin, 'Trade Policies in Developed Countries' in Ronald Jones and Peter Kenen (eds), *Handbook of International Economics* (North-Holland 1984) vol 1, 571; James Levinsohn, 'Employment Responses to International Liberalization in Chile' (1999) 47(2) Journal of International Economics 321; Marzia Fontana, 'Gender Justice in Trade Policy—The Gender Effects of Economic Partnership Agreements' (One World Action 2009) <https://oneworldaction.org.uk/GendJustTrad.pdf> accessed 27 October 2022; Marzia Fontana and Cristina Paciello, 'Gender Dimensions of Agricultural and Rural Employment: Differentiated Pathways out of Poverty' (FAO, IFAD, and ILO 2010) <www.ilo.org/employment/Whatwedo/Publications/WCMS_150558/lang--en/index.htm> accessed 27 October 2022; Karen Melanson, 'An Examination of the Gendered Effects of Trade Liberalisation' (2005) 2(1) Policy Perspectives 10, 17; Remco Oostendorp, 'Globalization and the Gender Wage Gap' (2009) 23(1) World Bank Economic Review 141, 61; Philip Sauré and Hosny Zoabi, 'International Trade, the Gender Wage Gap and Female Labour Force Participation' (2014) 111(C) Journal of Development Economics 17; Cirila Quintero-Ramírez, 'The North American Free Trade Agreement and Women' (2002) 4(2) International Feminist Journal of Politics 240; Irene van Staveren and others, *The Feminist Economics of Trade* (Routledge 2007).

[3] This included a study of 74 FTAs signed by 25 Commonwealth countries. The countries included are: Australia, Bangladesh, Botswana, Canada, Fiji, Gambia, Ghana, Jamaica, Kenya, Lesotho, Malawi, Malaysia, Mauritius, Namibia, Nigeria, Rwanda, Samoa, Seychelles, Sierra Leone, South Africa, Sri Lanka, Swaziland-Eswatini, Trinidad and Tobago, Uganda, and Zambia.

[4] Geneva (July 2019), Mexico City (November 2018; April 2019; May 2019), Istanbul (September 2019), Delhi (February 2019), Stockholm (February 2019), Online (December 2018; April 2019; May 2019; July 2019; November 2019) (details on record with the author).

and categorize their explicit and implicit women-related provisions. This led to the formation of categories, dimensions, questions, and answer led-options included in the framework. I ran a pilot of this preliminary version in which selected negotiators were asked to carry out the assessment and suggest changes.[5] In parallel, the framework was applied to over 100 FTAs to measure their responsiveness to women's concerns and interests. The results gained during this pilot phase helped in refining the questions and their answer options. Methodological triangulation was used to ensure the comprehensiveness and credibility of the research that led to the creation of this framework.[6]

The framework is constructed in line with the maturity model; this model helps assess the current effectiveness of a subject and supports determining what capabilities or elements it needs to progress or improve in a certain aspect.[7] Section 6.2 introduces the maturity model, detailing both its definition and the advantages of employing this model for the task at hand. Following this, Section 6.3 delves into the intricacies of the ITC's framework, explaining its core components. Section 6.4 outlines the target audience for this framework and discusses the potential benefits they can expect to achieve from its application. Section 6.5 addresses several limitations of the framework, providing a balanced perspective. Finally, Section 6.6 wraps up the chapter with practical advice for negotiators, offering strategies on how they can effectively apply this framework in their negotiation efforts.

6.2 What is the Maturity Model and Why Use It?

The maturity model is an instrument to measure certain capabilities and identify appropriate actions to increase such chosen capabilities.[8] Its application areas typically range from cognitive science to business applications and engineering. This academic intervention introduces this approach to international trade and gender studies. The ITC framework, using a maturity model, can help measure and improve the gender-responsiveness of a given trade agreement.

The use of the maturity model allows us to benefit from three different approaches: dimensional, benchmark, and diagnostic. The use of the 'dimensional approach' helps us analyse the women-related content of a given FTA from

[5] Details of participants on record with the author.

[6] Wendy Olsen, 'Triangulation in Social Research: Qualitative and Quantitative Methods can Really be Mixed' in Martin Holborn (ed), *Developments in Sociology* (Causeway Press 2004).

[7] Details provided in the following section.

[8] For details on maturity model, see Gabriel Alberto García-Mireles, María Ángeles Moraga, and Félix García, 'Development of maturity models: a systematic literature review' (16th International Conference on Evaluation & Assessment in Software Engineering, 2012) 279 <https://digital-library.theiet.org/content/conferences/10.1049/ic.2012.0036> accessed 27 October 2022; John Bessant and Sarah Caffyn, 'High-Involvement Innovation through Continuous Improvement' (1997) 14(1) International Journal of Technology Management 14.

different angles and perspectives, such as location, scope, nature, and language. It enables the identification of dimensions in which a given FTA excels or falls short, allowing policymakers and negotiators to pinpoint areas that require modest or substantial enhancement to boost the agreement's overall gender-responsiveness. The use of the 'benchmark approach' allows policymakers to gain an independent perspective on how well a given FTA performs compared to other FTAs. With this approach, the framework develops a standardized set of metrics to achieve different levels of gender-responsiveness. These metrics can encourage a culture of account-taking and continuous improvement in learning amongst negotiators and policymakers. Using a 'diagnostic approach', policymakers can carry out an overall dimensional assessment of a given FTA, which they can use to decide if they want that FTA to progress to a more advanced level of gender-responsiveness. In light of this understanding, they can negotiate, revise, and renegotiate a given FTA.

6.3 An Introduction to ITC's Framework: Nuts and Bolts

Assessing the gender-responsiveness of FTAs requires a thorough and multifaceted evaluation to identify both strengths and areas that need improvement. This comprehensive assessment is essential to ensure that the agreement effectively addresses women-related issues across various aspects. To achieve these results, a detailed framework is proposed in this chapter and it is presented in the form of a comprehensive questionnaire. This questionnaire is organized into ten distinct dimensions, each designed to evaluate the agreement from different contextual angles. By systematically addressing these dimensions, policymakers and negotiators can gain a nuanced understanding of the agreement's performance in terms of its gender-responsiveness. The first dimension is 'frequency of relevant provisions' and it assesses whether and to what extent the given FTA mentions women-related expressions in the drafting of its main text, side instruments, and annexes. The second dimension is 'location of relevant provision' and it seeks to gauge whether the given FTA prioritizes or sidelines gender provisions by positioning them in the agreement's preamble, stand-alone chapters, side agreements, specific provisions, cross-cutting provisions or chapters, or annexes.

The third dimension is 'affirmations and reaffirmations'. This assesses whether the given FTA contains provisions that reflect members' commitments to address women's issues or reaffirmations wherein they reaffirm their commitments under other international instruments relating to women's interests. The fourth dimension, 'cooperation activities', seeks to determine whether the given FTA demonstrates members' commitments to cooperate nationally and internationally on issues relating to women's access to resources, elimination of trade barriers, and access to education. The fifth dimension pertains to 'institutional arrangements', which evaluates whether a given FTA establishes institutions dedicated to the implementation of the commitments related to gender equality. Such institutions may take the form of a committee, unit, council, network, or commission. The sixth dimension is 'procedural arrangements' and it seeks to determine whether the given FTA establishes procedures for the implementation of the relevant provisions in the agreement. These procedures may include the development of an action plan, the exchange of information, dialogues, and sharing of best practices, studies, and research.

The seventh dimension is 'review and funding' and it assesses whether a given FTA establishes provisions to review the implementation of women-related commitments and whether parties provide for or identify ways to finance this implementation, review, and assessment. The eighth dimension—'settlement of disputes'—focuses on investigating if a given FTA provides a system for the settlement of disputes that arise from women-related provisions. The methods to settle disputes could range from consultation, mediation, and arbitration to litigation. The ninth dimension is 'waivers, reservations, and exceptions' and it seeks to explore whether a given FTA provides for explicit women-favouring exceptions, reservations, and waivers. These provisions could be found in the form of right-to-regulate reservations, women-specific exceptions (drafted on the lines of General Agreement on Tariffs and Trade-like exceptions), supplier diversity programmes favouring supplies from women-owned or women-managed businesses, women-favouring reservations for provision of services, or women-favouring government procurement arrangements. The tenth dimension concerns 'minimum legal standards', examining whether a given FTA recommends or mandates its members to maintain or ensure legal standards that their domestic laws can use to eliminate or reduce inequality. As discussed in Chapter 4, these standards could include, inter alia, equal pay for equal work for women and men, women's representation in decision-making roles, gender-based anti-discrimination, and anti-violence requirements.

Figure 6.1 provides a comprehensive illustration of the ITC Maturity Framework, elucidating its structure and components. It groups the ten dimensions of the framework into three broad categories: awareness, affirmative action, and enforcement. By doing so, it demonstrates how each dimension contributes to the overall assessment of a trade agreement's gender-responsiveness, offering a more detailed insight into the framework's methodology and application.

As shown in Figure 6.1, the first three dimensions are employed to assess the parties' awareness and the importance they assign to the incorporation of women's concerns in each FTA. The fourth, fifth, sixth, and seventh dimensions are used to assess whether the parties to a given FTA consider or commit to any affirmative action to incorporate women's concerns. The last three dimensions are focused on investigating if the parties to an FTA consider or commit to the robust enforcement of women-related components included in that FTA.

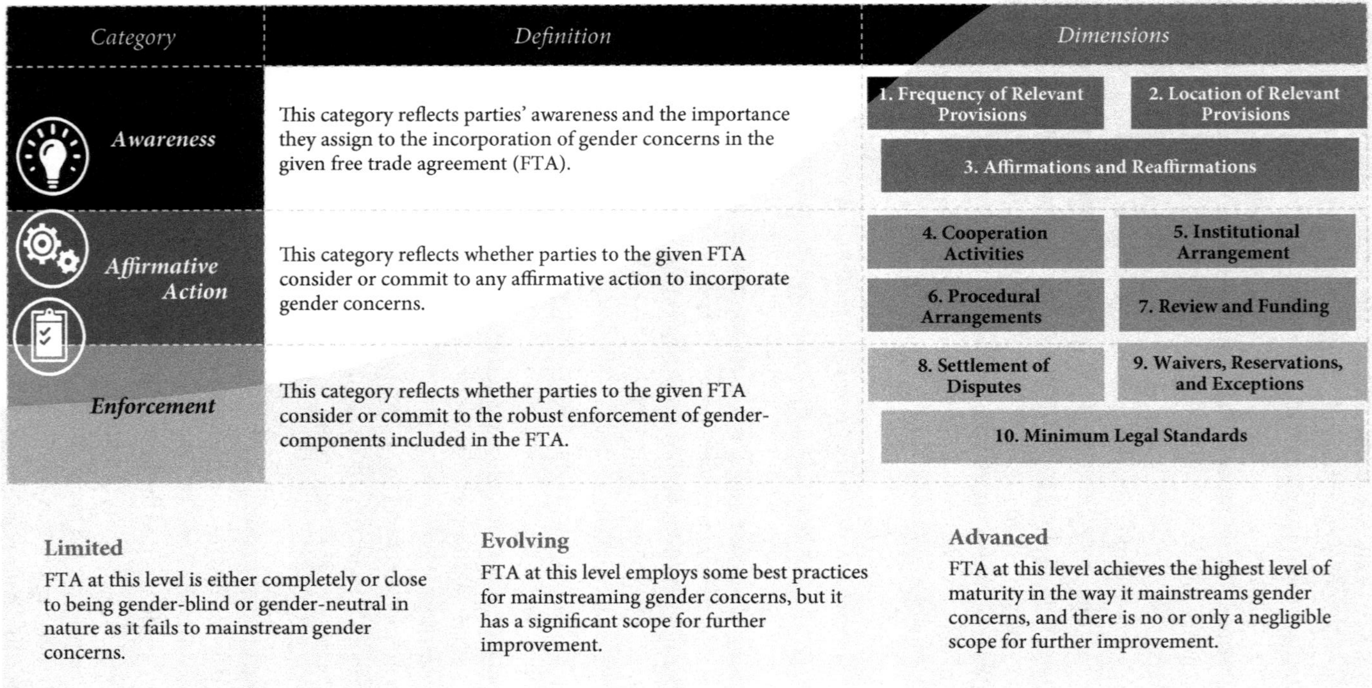

Figure 6.1 ITC Maturity Framework

The questionnaire in Table 6.1 contains 20 questions. Each question has the same impact factor and each has three answer options. Each answer option has a different weight assigned to it. For every question answered, the maximum score is '1 point' and the minimum is '0 point'. If you select an answer corresponding to:

(1) 'limited gender-responsiveness', you will receive '0 point' for that question;
(2) 'evolving gender-responsiveness', you will receive '0.5 point' for that question;
(3) 'advanced gender-responsiveness', you will receive '1 point' for that question.

All the questions in the questionnaire focus on assessing the text of an FTA. However, some of the questions also relate to the implementation potential of women-related provisions as they assess whether a given FTA has procedural, institutional, and dispute-settlement mechanisms to implement or enforce those provisions. The score obtained in each question contributes equally to the overall score and maturity level obtained by a given FTA. Once all questions are answered for a given FTA, the FTA receives a maturity score. This score corresponds to a maturity level. As can be seen in Figure 6.1, there are three maturity levels: Limited, Evolving, and Advanced. An agreement is:

(1) 'limited' if it has scored below or equal to 33.33%;
(2) 'evolving' if it has scored more than 33.33% and less than or equal to 66.66%;
(3) 'advanced' if it has scored more than 66.66%.

The first and the lowest level of maturity an agreement can attain is 'limited' gender responsiveness. An agreement at this level is either completely or close to being gender-blind or gender-neutral in its nature as it fails to mainstream women concerns in a significant or notable manner. The next level of maturity is 'evolving' gender responsiveness. An agreement at this level employs several best practices for mainstreaming women concerns but it has significant scope for further improvement either in terms of the scope, implementation, or enforcement requirements for women-related commitments. The third and highest level is 'advanced' gender responsiveness. An agreement at this level achieves the highest level of maturity in the way it mainstreams women concerns with the use of best practices and there might only be minor or negligible scope for further improvement as per its ten dimensional analyses.

The key benefit of using this approach is not merely to measure and identify the gender responsiveness level a particular agreement is at; it also helps in identifying the list of components that the agreement requires to improve and progress to the next level. The identification of levels is therefore an intermediate exercise that leads to the determination of elements that an agreement needs to improve its consideration towards the interests and needs of women. Hence, the underlying idea behind using this model is to help assess the current state of an agreement and then progress further. The aim is to make continuous improvements until a given agreement optimizes the level of maturity. The questionnaire can be answered either by a trade negotiator, policymaker, or a researcher assessing a given FTA.

6.4 Who Can Benefit From this Framework? Target Audience

(1) *Trade negotiators and policymakers* can use the ITC's framework to assess and understand the gender-responsiveness of preliminary texts under ongoing trade negotiations and draft FTAs accordingly in an informed manner. They can also assess the gender-responsiveness of existing FTAs that are undergoing the process of revision or renegotiation to determine whether and how the gender-responsiveness of those FTAs can progress to a higher level of maturity. Using the framework's diagnostic function, policymakers can identify the level at which a given agreement stands. Through dimensional assessment, they can gain an understanding of various dimensions that can be developed or improved to enhance the overall gender responsiveness of the agreement. In this manner, the framework can shape the way trade agreements are negotiated in the future.

(2) *Researchers and academics* can use this framework in their research and teaching. Researchers can apply the framework to future agreements and craft country-specific and agreement-specific recommendations on improving the gender responsiveness of trade agreements. This methodology also provides a new approach to teaching disciplines on international trade law and gender. For example, this could be a useful resource for teaching a sub-discipline on trade law and sustainable development (including gender equality) as part of an international economic law course at universities. Academics can employ the framework to design practical activities for students (or for policymakers in capacity-building training) aimed at reading FTAs and identifying women-related components in those agreements. Moreover, the approach may be employed to construct similar frameworks that could assess different components of sustainable development in trade instruments, such as environmental and labour provisions.

6.5 Limitations of the Framework

The framework is an evolving initiative and might undergo revisions as new examples of gender mainstreaming surface with the signing and enforcement of new agreements, and as progress is made on the understanding of this topic with the collection of data to better understand the interaction between trade and women. As of now, there are three main limitations of the current framework.

(1) The framework can gauge the gender responsiveness of agreements only by carrying out an agreement's textual analysis. It does not look at the enforcement, review, or implementation aspects that follow the signing and ratification of an agreement. The framework is limited to measuring the gender-responsive of the text or content of a given FTA. It does not include assessing in any way the actual impact a given FTA might have on women's concerns or women's empowerment. In this respect, it is very different in its scope and purpose from the United Nations Conference on Trade and Development (UNCTAD) trade and gender toolbox which provides a systematic framework to evaluate the impact of trade agreements on women and gender inequalities before their implementation.[9] In this sense, the ITC's framework helps mainstream women-related considerations and the UNCTAD toolbox helps with impact assessment.
(2) Some legal provisions might have a negative or positive impact on women and their engagement in trade and commerce even though they do not contain any women-explicit expressions. Cross-cutting disciplines like intellectual property rights, agriculture, fisheries, digital trade, government procurement, and small and medium-sized enterprise protection may have a significant impact on the participation of women in trade and commerce. However, the framework does not take these cross-cutting provisions into account in measuring responsiveness if they do not contain any women-explicit terminology; in other words, only women-explicit provisions are considered in the assessment. Women-explicit provisions are those that use terms relating to gender, women, females, or a similar expression (including but not limited to gender, women, female, girl, sex, mother, maternity, or childcare) in the provision in an explicit manner.
(3) The dimensions are not compatible with the mutually exclusive and collectively exhaustive (MECE) principle. The dimensions are not mutually exclusive as they can overlap and converge in several situations. The defining elements of these dimensions are not collectively exhaustive as it is possible to identify and incorporate new elements into the existing list. While a framework needs to be comprehensive, all frameworks must draw a balance between their comprehensiveness and manageability. As a framework becomes more comprehensive, it can often become less manageable; conversely, the more manageable a framework is, the less comprehensive it might be. The proposed framework strikes a balance between being comprehensive and manageable.

[9] UNCTAD, 'UNCTAD Trade and Gender Tool Box' (2017) <https://unctad.org/en/pages/PublicationWebflyer.aspx?publicationid=1877> accessed 27 October 2022.

6.6 Practical Instructions on Using the Framework

Here are some instructions that can guide a policymaker or a trade negotiator to assess the gender-responsiveness of a given agreement using the ITC framework.

Before you start:

- **Step 1:** Read the ITC Report, 'Mainstreaming Gender in Free Trade Agreements' (International Trade Centre 8 July 2020)
- **Step 2:** Open Annex 1: Maturity Framework Questionnaire (Table 6.1).
- **Step 3:** To understand the scope and purpose of the questions being asked, read the definitions of all dimensions before you start reading and answering the questions.

As you read and answer:

- **Step 4:** Start from Dimension I. Read again the definition of Dimension I. Read the first question.
- **Step 5:** Read all three answer options one by one, starting from the option corresponding to 'limited' all the way to 'advanced'. Read the requirements of each answer option carefully. While reading, pay attention to the conjunctions used such as 'or', 'and', and 'but'. They define the scope and requirements.
- **Step 6:** Select the answer option that best answers the question for the given FTA. You can only select one answer option for each question.
- **Step 7:** Repeat Step 4 to Step 6 when you move to the next question in this dimension and the subsequent nine dimensions. Keep repeating Step 4 to Step 6 until you answer all 20 questions.

After you answer:

- **Step 8:** Revise the answer sheet to ensure that you have answered all 20 questions. Ensure that you have only selected one answer option for each question.
- **Step 9:** Now you can calculate the score in the following manner. Each question has the same impact factor. Each question has three answer options. Each answer option has a different weight assigned to it. For every question answered, the maximum score is'1 point' and the minimum is '0 point'. If you have selected an answer corresponding to:
  (1) 'limited gender-responsiveness', you will receive '0 point' for that question;
  (2) 'evolving gender-responsiveness', you will receive '0.5 point' for that question;
  (3) 'advanced gender-responsiveness', you will receive '1 point' for that question.

- **Step 10:** Once you have secured the scores for each question, the total of these scores constitutes the overall maturity score the agreement at hand receives. This overall score corresponds to a maturity level. There are three maturity levels: Limited, Evolving, and Advanced. An agreement is:
  (1) 'limited' if it has scored below or equal to 33.33%;
  (2) 'evolving' if it has scored more than 33.33% and less than or equal to 66.66%;
  (3) 'advanced' if it has scored more than 66.66%.

How to read questions and answer-options?

- Each question and answer option is separate and individual. Read each question and answer option carefully.
- If you are unsure about a specific term or expression used in the question or answer option, consult the 'Glossary' provided in the ITC's paper.[10]
- Understand the meaning of each question and answer option in light of the dimension and category it belongs to.
- If a question belongs to the category of 'awareness', it will seek a response on a matter relating to members' awareness. If the question belongs to the category of 'affirmative action', it will seek a response on different affirmative actions contemplated in the FTA. If a question relates to the category of 'enforcement', it will seek a response on different aspects of enforcing the actions, activities, rights, obligations, and commitments contemplated in the FTA.
- If you are unsure of possible answers to a particular question or what type of provision could satisfy the requirements of a particular answer option, consult the 'List of examples for answer options' in the ITC paper.[11] Here you will find examples of provisions (actual or made up) to illustrate the kinds of provisions that will satisfy the requirements of a possible answer option.

6.7 The Questionnaire

The questionnaire is available in an Excel version to facilitate its use and calculation of scores. For access to the Excel version, please contact the book's author.

[10] ITC, 'Mainstreaming Gender in Free Trade Agreements' (n 1).
[11] ibid.

Table 6.1 The Questionnaire

I. Frequency of relevant provisions (This dimension assesses whether and to what extent the given FTA mentions gender-related expressions in the drafting of its main text, side instruments, and annexes)		
1. Does the given FTA (main text, side instruments, or annexes) mention the term gender/women/female/girl/sex/mother/maternity/childcare (referred to as a gender-related term, excluding mention as products or list of entities)?		
Limited responsiveness	Evolving responsiveness	Advanced responsiveness
There is no mention of any gender-related term but there is a mere mention of human rights, social or moral or labour concern that might include issues relating to gender	There is: (i) an explicit mention of gender-related terms, or (ii) an acknowledgement of the role of women in trade, commerce, or economy in general	The agreement does not: (i) mention any gender-related term, or (ii) mention human rights, social or moral or labour concern that might include issues relating to gender
2. How many times is a gender-related term (gender/women/female/girl/sex/mother/maternity/childcare) mentioned in the given FTA including side instruments, footnotes, and/or annexes (excluding mention as products or list of entities)?		
Limited responsiveness	Evolving responsiveness	Advanced responsiveness
These terms are not mentioned once in the entire agreement including side instruments, footnotes, and/or annexes	Any of these terms is mentioned less than ten times in the entire agreement including side instruments, footnotes, and/or annexes	Any of these terms is mentioned ten or more times in the entire agreement including side instruments, footnotes, and/or annexes
II. Location of relevant provisions (This dimension assesses whether the given FTA prioritizes or sidelines gender provisions by positioning them in the agreement's preamble, stand-alone chapters, side agreements, specific provisions, cross-cutting provisions or chapters, or annexes)		
1. Is there a mention of gender-related concerns in the given FTA's preamble?		
Limited responsiveness	Evolving responsiveness	Advanced responsiveness
There is no mention of: (i) gender, or (ii) related concerns in the given FTA's preamble	There is an explicit mention of gender-specific concerns in the given FTA's preamble, which merely shows members' awareness to address gender inequality and/or promote women's economic empowerment	There is an explicit mention of gender-specific concerns in the given FTA's preamble, which shows a commitment by members to address gender inequality and/or promote women's economic empowerment

2. In which part of the given FTA are 50% or more of gender-explicit provisions located?		
Limited responsiveness	Evolving responsiveness	Advanced responsiveness
There are no gender-explicit provisions in the given FTA	50% or more of gender-explicit provisions are mentioned in the FTA's preamble	50% or more of gender-explicit provisions are mentioned in the operative section (that includes the main text, annexes, side agreement, protocols, and post FTA decisions)
III. Affirmations and reaffirmations (This dimension assesses whether the given FTA contains provisions that reflect members' commitments to address gender issues or affirmations that reaffirm their commitments under other international instruments relating to gender)		
1. Does the agreement demonstrate members' willingness or commitment to incorporate gender perspective into their economic growth and development, policies, programmes, decision-making, policymaking, and practices at the national level?		
Limited responsiveness	Evolving responsiveness	Advanced responsiveness
There is no such demonstration in the agreement	The agreement shows members' awareness about the importance of incorporating gender perspective into their economic growth and development, policies, programmes, decision-making, policymaking, or practices at the national level	There are one or more provisions which contain members' commitments to incorporate a gender perspective into their economic growth and development, policies, programmes, decision-making, policymaking, or practices at the national level
2. Are there any references or affirmations or reaffirmations to existing international conventions or declarations or other international instruments directly or indirectly related to gender issues?		
Limited responsiveness	Evolving responsiveness	Advanced responsiveness
The agreement does not have any such references or affirmations or reaffirmations	There are explicit references to one or more international instruments that incorporate or include gender objectives but neither of these instruments are exclusively focused on gender objectives (eg CEDAW or 2017 Buenos Aires Declaration or ILO Convention 100 or 111)	There are explicit references to one or more international instruments that incorporate or include gender objectives and one of these instruments must have an exclusive focus on gender objectives (eg CEDAW or 2017 Buenos Aires Declaration or ILO Convention 100 or 111)

(continued)

Table 6.1 Continued

IV. Cooperation activities (This dimension assesses whether the given FTA demonstrates members' commitments to cooperate nationally and internationally on issues relating to women's access to resources, elimination of barriers to trade, and access to education)		
1. Does the given FTA contain provisions that prescribe cooperation activities aimed at the elimination or reduction of barriers to trade for women and enhancement of women's empowerment (eg cooperation on access to education, access to finance, formation of business networks, etc)?		
Limited responsiveness	Evolving responsiveness	Advanced responsiveness
The agreement does not have any such provision referring to women empowerment	The agreement has provisions that: (i) provide a list of cooperation activities directly related to women empowerment and inclusive trade, but these activities merely envisage women as an employee or labour, or (ii) the agreement indicates members' commitment to cooperate on areas and engage in activities that strengthen women's empowerment but it does not provide a list of cooperation activities	The agreement has provisions that: (i) provide a list of cooperation activities directly related to women empowerment and inclusive trade, and (ii) these activities envisage women not merely as an employee or labour but also as an entrepreneur, leader, decision-maker, scientist, engineer, and/or other high-paid professional
2. Does the given FTA amongst its cooperation activities incorporate women's access to education or skill development?		
Limited responsiveness	Evolving responsiveness	Advanced responsiveness
(i) The agreement does not contain any cooperation activity, or (ii) mentioned cooperation activities do not include women's access to education or skill development	(i) The cooperation activities contain specific commitments from members to work on enhancing or encouraging women's access to education or skill development, and (ii) these commitments are either made without outlining the type and nature of education and skill development or they only focus on traditional education and skill development opportunities (eg farming, fisheries, textiles, teaching, nursing, handloom, and so on)	(i) The cooperation activities contain specific commitments from members to work on enhancing or encouraging women's access to education or skill development, and (ii) these commitments focus on enhancing educational or skill development opportunities in the fields that can translate to high-paid job opportunities for women (eg science, technology, engineering, and mathematics(STEM) and information and communications technology (ICT)-focused education)

V. Institutional arrangements (This dimension assesses whether the given FTA establishes institutions to implement commitments or understandings related to gender. These could be in the form of a committee, council, network, or a commission)		
1. Is there a committee or any other institution to monitor the implementation or operation of gender-focused provisions?		
Limited responsiveness	Evolving responsiveness	Advanced responsiveness
(i) There is no committee or any other institution to monitor the implementation or operation of the whole agreement or for gender-specific provisions, or (ii) gender-focused provisions are excluded from the work of a general committee established for the whole agreement	The main or side agreement establishes a committee or any other institution to monitor the implementation or operation of provisions that include gender concerns among other areas	(i) The main or side agreement establishes a specialized committee or any other institution that specifically monitors the implementation or operation of only gender-focused provisions, and (ii) such an institution is created in a specialized chapter or a side agreement specific to gender or women in trade
2. Does the agreement define duties, functions, meeting frequencies, and other organizational requirements of the committee or any other institution created for the implementation or operation of gender-specific provisions?		
Limited responsiveness	Evolving responsiveness	Advanced responsiveness
(i) The agreement does not define any organizational requirement of the committee or any other institution, or (ii) the agreement does not create an institution to monitor the implementation or operation of gender-specific provisions	The agreement outlines: (i) the non-binding role, and (ii) functions of the committee or any other institution created for the implementation or operation of gender-specific provisions	The agreement outlines: (i) binding role and functions, and (ii) meeting frequencies of the committee or any other institution
VI. Procedural arrangements (This dimension assesses whether the given FTA establishes procedures to implement the commitments or understandings related to gender. These could be in the form of an action plan, exchange of information, dialogues, studies, and research)		

(continued)

Table 6.1 Continued

1. Does the agreement create procedural tools to address gender issues such as an action plan, frameworks, dialogues, information exchange, exchange of best practices and experiences, programmes, or legislations?		
Limited responsiveness	Evolving responsiveness	Advanced responsiveness
The agreement does not create any procedural tool to address gender issues	(i) The agreement shows some awareness of creating procedural tools to address gender issues, but (ii) it does not create or identify any such tool to address gender issues	The agreement creates or identifies procedural tools to address gender commitments such as action plan, frameworks, dialogues, information exchange, exchange of best practices and experiences, programmes, or legislations
2. Do the members encourage or seek to collaborate on study, research, or publication relating to gender and trade?		
Limited responsiveness	Evolving responsiveness	Advanced responsiveness
There is no demonstrated awareness or commitment to encourage or collaborate on study, research, or publication relating to gender and trade	There is an expression of will to encourage or collaborate on study, research, or publication relating to gender and trade among other social issues	There is a commitment to encourage or collaborate on study, research, or publication specifically relating to gender and trade
VII. Review and funding (This dimension assesses whether the given FTA establishes review and funding mechanisms that are needed to ensure the implementation of the commitments or understandings related to gender)		
1. Does the agreement contain a provision that requires: (i) the review of the implementation of gender provisions, and/or (ii) the assessment of gender impact of the agreement?		
Limited responsiveness	Evolving responsiveness	Advanced responsiveness
There is no such provision	There is an expression or statement of will to: (i) review the implementation of gender provisions, or (ii) assess the gender impact of agreement, but (iii) the agreement does not provide for members' commitment or any institution or procedure to carry out the same	There is a commitment to: (i) review the implementation of gender provisions, or (ii) assess the gender impact of the agreement, and (iii) either of the above-mentioned commitments is made along with the identification of a procedure or an institutional setting to facilitate the process of implementation review or impact assessment

2. Have members provided funding or identified measures to finance gender-related plans, processes, institutions, activities, and other related commitments?		
Limited responsiveness	Evolving responsiveness	Advanced responsiveness
There is no provision on financing gender-related plans, processes, institutions, activities, or other related commitments	There is a provision that demonstrates members' awareness on the importance of financing gender-related plans, processes, institutions, activities, or other related commitments	There is a provision that contains a commitment to: (i) finance gender-related plans, processes, institutions, activities, or other related commitments, or (ii) identify measures to finance gender-related plans, processes, institutions, activities, or other related commitments
VIII. Settlement of disputes (This dimension assesses whether the given FTA provides a system for the settlement of disputes that arise from gender-related provisions. The methods to settle disputes could range from consultation, mediation, and arbitration to litigation)		
1. Is there any consultation or discussion mechanism to resolve gender-specific conflicts (excluding the ones arising from cooperation activities)?		
Limited responsiveness	Evolving responsiveness	Advanced responsiveness
(i) There is no consultation or discussion mechanism, or (ii) gender provisions are excluded from the consultation or discussion mechanisms provided in the agreement, or (iii) there are no gender provisions in the agreement, or (iv) the only gender provisions in the agreement are mentioned as cooperation activities	(i) There is a consultation or discussion mechanism for conflicts arising generally out of the agreement including conflicts arising out of gender-related provisions, and (ii) gender provisions are not excluded from such consultation or discussion mechanisms	i) There is a specialized consultation or discussion mechanism for any conflicts arising out of several specific issues including gender provisions, and (ii) these provisions are located in specialised chapters or side agreements that incorporate several issues including gender

(continued)

Table 6.1 Continued

2. Are the majority of gender provisions (excluding the ones mentioned in cooperation activities) in the given FTA subject to a dispute-settlement mechanism?		
Limited responsiveness	Evolving responsiveness	Advanced responsiveness
(i) There is no dispute-settlement mechanism provided in the agreement for conflicts arising out of majority of gender provisions, or (ii) there are no gender provisions in the agreement, or (iii) gender provisions are excluded from the dispute-settlement mechanism	There is a non-binding and non-compulsory dispute -settlement mechanism for conflicts arising out of majority of gender provisions	There is a binding but not compulsory, or non-binding but compulsory dispute-settlement mechanism for conflicts arising out of majority of gender provisions
IX. Waivers, reservations, and exceptions (This dimension assesses whether the given FTA provides for explicit women-favouring exceptions, reservations, and waivers. These provisions could be found in the form of a gender exception (drafted on the lines of GATT-like exceptions), supplier diversity programmes favouring supplies from women-owned or women-managed businesses, and women-favouring government procurement arrangements)		
1. Does the agreement establish an exception referring to gender concerns?		
Limited responsiveness	Evolving responsiveness	Advanced responsiveness
The agreement does not establish an exception referring to gender	The agreement establishes a general public morals or human rights exception or merely incorporates general exceptions mentioned in GATT Article XX	The agreement establishes a gender-specific exception that any member can invoke to justify a possible FTA-inconsistent practice or law
2. Does the agreement allow parties to invoke a reservation or waiver explicitly favouring women or explicitly referring to gender concerns?		
Limited responsiveness	Evolving responsiveness	Advanced responsiveness
The agreement does not allow parties to have any reservation or waiver explicitly favouring women or explicitly referring to gender concerns	(i) The agreement does not confer a right on any party to invoke a reservation or waiver explicitly favouring women or explicitly referring to gender concerns, but (ii) it allows parties to negotiate such reservations or waivers in the future	(i) The agreement confers a right on the parties to invoke an identifiable reservation or waiver explicitly favouring women or explicitly referring to gender concerns, and (ii) it allows parties to negotiate additional reservations or waivers in the future

X. Minimum legal standards (This dimension assesses whether the given FTA recommends or mandates its members to maintain or ensure minimum legal standards in their domestic laws. These standards could include, inter alia, equal pay, reproductive rights, care work, representation, gender-based anti-discrimination, and anti-violence)		
1. Does the agreement establish minimum legal standards explicitly related to gender for the countries' respective domestic law?		
Limited responsiveness	Evolving responsiveness	Advanced responsiveness
The agreement does not establish minimum legal standards explicitly related to gender for countries' respective domestic law	The agreement establishes minimum legal standards explicitly related to gender for the countries' respective domestic law with the use of permissive language throughout such provision(s)	The agreement establishes minimum legal standards explicitly related to gender for the countries' respective domestic law with no use of permissive language in such provision(s)
2. Does the agreement contain provisions to encourage industries/enterprises to incorporate minimum standards on corporate social responsibility explicitly related to gender?		
Limited responsiveness	Evolving responsiveness	Advanced responsiveness
There is no such provision	(i) There is a provision which affirms the importance of corporate social responsibility explicitly related to gender, but (ii) it does not contain any expression to encourage its industries and enterprises (subject to its jurisdictions) to incorporate standards of corporate social responsibility explicitly related to gender into their internal policies and practices	(i) There is a provision which affirms the importance of corporate social responsibility explicitly related to gender, and (ii) it encourages its industries and enterprises (subject to its jurisdictions) to incorporate standards of corporate social responsibility explicitly related to gender into their internal policies and practices

7

Trade Agreements Can Empower Women

A Look at Practice Examples

7.1 Introduction

More and more countries are including provisions relating to various women's concerns in their trade agreements, albeit in different ways. As initially discussed in Chapter 4, some free trade agreements (FTAs) have a whole chapter on trade and women, but no legally binding obligations.[1] Some FTAs have a single provision on women concerns but that single provision creates a strong legal obligation.[2] Several agreements include these provisions in their main text;[3] others include them in a side agreement, annex, or protocol.[4] Some countries have sought to work on these concerns via cooperation actions;[5] others have reserved the right to regulate particular professions that most directly impact women or services related to nutrition or childcare, for instance.[6] In some agreements, general statements are found in which parties acknowledge the importance of the role of women in trade.[7] In other agreements, affirming and reaffirming provisions are found in which parties commit to engaging in concrete actions or reaffirm their commitments made under other international instruments.[8] Moreover, several

[1] Modernized Canada–Chile Free Trade Agreement (CCFTA) (in force 5 February 2019); Modernized Canada–Israel Free Trade Agreement (CIFTA) (in force 1 September 2019) (both include stand-alone chapters on gender); the Comprehensive and Progressive Agreement for Trans-Pacific Partnership (in force 30 December 2018) (it does not have a stand-alone chapter on gender and the provisions on gender are mainly included in the chapter on development).

[2] Stabilisation and Association Agreement between the European Communities and their Member States, of the one part, and the Republic of Montenegro, of the other part (in force 1 May 2010), art 101. (This obliges Montenegro to adjust its domestic legislation to provide for working conditions and equal opportunities for women and men.)

[3] The Agreement between the European Free Trade Agreement States and the Hashemite Kingdom of Jordan (in force 1 May 2002) and the North American FTA (in force 1 January 1994). (Gender-explicit provisions in these agreements are found in the main text of the agreements, in the cooperation and development sections.)

[4] The Canada–Panama FTA (in force 1 April 2002). (It establishes a provision on gender equality in the side agreement, ie the Agreement on Labour Cooperation, Appendix 1.)

[5] eg the CCFTA.

[6] Agreement on Trade in Goods Under the Framework Agreement on Comprehensive Economic Cooperation Among the Governments of the Member Countries of the Association of Southeast Asian Nations and the Republic of Korea (in force 1 January 2010) (ASEAN–Republic of Korea).

[7] The Canada–Honduras FTA (in force 1 October 2014). (It only contains a general statement on the importance of gender equality in Annex 1 which is a cooperation activity mentioned in best endeavour language.)

[8] The FTA between the United States of America and the Republic of Korea (in force 15 March 2012). (The parties reaffirm their commitments to ILO Conventions.)

Trade Agreements and Women. Amrita Bahri, Oxford University Press. © Amrita Bahri 2025.
DOI: 10.1093/9780198935759.003.0008

agreements are completely silent or merely make a single mention of expressions relating to women and yet others mention women-related expressions as many as 40 times or more in their main text (as in the case of the Canada–Chile FTA).

At one end of the spectrum, there are agreements that merely show parties' awareness in this respect as they acknowledge the importance of women empowerment as a social value amongst other non-economic concerns. For example, Article 9.3 of the Chile–Vietnam FTA mentions gender equality as one of the issues for cooperation and capacity building.[9] The Chile–Uruguay and Chile–Canada agreements go one step further. They do this not only by acknowledging the importance of gender issues for economic development but they also provide a list of cooperation activities and institutional mechanisms that can enable parties to carry out trade in an inclusive manner.[10] Another similar agreement, with some enforcement potential, is the Canada–Israel FTA. What makes this agreement unique in this respect is the possibility parties have to enforce the commitments they have assumed in respect of women as its relevant provisions are subject to the agreement's dispute-settlement mechanism with binding (but not compulsory) jurisdiction.[11] The parties to this FTA commit themselves to various activities directly related to women's empowerment and these activities envisage women not merely as employees or labourers but also as entrepreneurs, leaders, decision-makers, and scientists.[12] At the other end of the spectrum, we have the Interim Agreement on Trade between the European Union and the Republic of Chile in which parties have negotiated a stand-alone chapter entitled 'Trade and gender equality' with a vast scope and several commitments that can be enforced through the agreement's dispute-settlement provisions which have both binding as well as compulsory jurisdiction over the chapter.[13] This diverse and inconsistent inclusion of women's concerns in trade agreements, ranging from general acknowledgements to enforceable commitments, highlights the complexities and variations in how different countries approach women's issues in trade policies and agreements.

Provisions relating to women and their concerns are also drafted in different ways. Some are drafted in permissive language coupled with best-endeavour expressions;[14] others are either drafted in affirmative language or firmer styles, including the use of obligatory expressions.[15] The topics addressed in these provisions also vary from one region to another as some regions have included

[9] The FTA Between the Government of the Republic of Chile and the Government of the Socialist Republic of Viet Nam (in force 1 January 2014), art 9.3.

[10] See CIFTA (n 1) arts 13.3 and 13.4 and CCFTA (n 1) arts N *bis*-03 and N *bis*-04.

[11] CIFTA (n 1) art 13.6. (It provides a dispute-settlement mechanism for gender provisions with binding but not compulsory jurisdiction.)

[12] ibid art 13.3.

[13] (Signed 13 December 2023), ch 27.

[14] See eg CIFTA (n 1).

[15] Comprehensive Economic and Trade Agreement (CETA) between Canada, of the one part, and the European Union and its Member States, of the other part (in force 21 September 2017), art 8.10.

provisions on social and health-care concerns of women and others have covered purely economic- and market-oriented interests.[16] These differences reflect varied ways in which trade negotiations have dealt with the challenges relating to women's participation in trade and their economic empowerment.

The assessment of practice examples in this chapter is not limited to a certain type of agreement. It includes the assessment and analyses of all types of trade, cooperation, and partnership agreements. Trade agreements may comprise FTAs, preferential trade agreements (PTAs), comprehensive economic partnership agreements (CEPAs), or comprehensive economic cooperation agreements (CECAs). A free or preferential trade agreement involves two or more countries agreeing to offer preferential trade terms, rights of entry, or tariff concessions for specific products to the partner country. In contrast, partnership agreements or cooperation agreements are more extensive than FTAs or PTAs, addressing a broader range of issues. CECAs and CEPAs also consider regulatory aspects of trade, encompassing negotiations on services trade, investment, trade facilitation, customs cooperation, competition, and intellectual property rights. The other type consists of association or integration agreements, which are significantly broader than FTAs, PTAs, CECAs, or CEPAs. Association agreements (AAs) or integration agreements (IAs) establish associations or integrations between parties across various areas, including international trade. Additional areas of cooperation may include immigration, education and training, social cooperation, political dialogue, environmental management, and poverty alleviation.

Some regions, in particular the EU and Africa, have included women-related provisions in their broad association or integration agreements, even in sections that are not related directly to trade, such as political dialogue, social cooperation, immigration, and education.[17] Hence, it is not clear whether these inclusions in non-trade sections of such agreements form part of their trade discourse. In the case of the EU, since some of the provisions mentioned are not located within the trade regulation pillar of such agreements, EU negotiators do not engage with their partner countries on women-related issues in their trade policy context and they tend to view such provisions as separate from trade matters.[18] In one interview with an EU negotiator, it was affirmed that 'provisions on women's interests that are not located in the trade pillar, but are rather found in other pillars related to political dialogue and cooperation on social matters, cannot be seen as forming part of the EU's trade policy agenda. They are seen as a part of our broader foreign policy agenda instead.'[19] This approach, however, has certain problems. First, it is unclear

[16] Amrita Bahri, 'Gender Mainstreaming in Free Trade Agreements: A Regional Analysis and Good Practice Examples' (2022) Gender, Social Inclusion and Trade Knowledge Product Series, UK Aid.

[17] Euro-Mediterranean Agreement establishing an association between the European Communities and their Member States and the Hashemite Kingdom of Jordan (in force 1 May 2002).

[18] Interview with EU negotiator, EU Commission (online).

[19] ibid.

whether such provisions included in the general sections that apply to all parts of such agreements (eg preamble, objectives clause, exceptions, dispute settlement, institutions, and procedures) can be seen as being part of the trade or non-trade discourse. For example, Article 3 of the EU–Overseas Countries and Territories (OCT) FTA which is a general clause that outlines the objectives, principles, and values of the agreement, obliges parties to ensure the elimination of discrimination based on sex, among other things.[20] Such an inclusion, strictly speaking, is not directly included in the trade or non-trade sections of an agreement but it can guide the interpretation of all sections and provisions of said agreement. In that sense, these inclusions may be seen as a way of mainstreaming women's concerns in the trade policy context as well. Second, certain provisions in such agreements cross-cut and touch upon various other disciplines of the agreement and, hence, cannot be categorized as trade-centric or non-trade-centric. For instance, in the EU–Eastern and Southern Africa States Interim Economic Partnership Agreement (EPA), Chapter III regulates fisheries. Article 35 of that chapter is a provision on cooperation which states that the parties commit to cooperate on, among other things, 'encouraging participation of marginal groups in the fishing industry, for example, through the promotion of gender equality in fisheries by developing the capacity of women engaged in fisheries, as well as other disadvantaged groups with the potential to engage in fisheries for sustainable social economic development'.[21] Regulation of fisheries can be viewed as a trade matter but it does not form part of the agreement's section on trade regulation as it is included in a separate section entitled 'Inland fisheries and aquaculture development'. Hence, it is unclear whether the inclusion of this commitment in such a manner can be seen as a way of mainstreaming women's concerns in the trade policy context.

With due consideration to the gaps in understanding how such commitments may be situated in a trade, cooperation, partnership, or integration agreement, this book evaluates all such provisions as they are integrated into the same accord and hence their implementation is interconnected with the ratification and implementation of the entire agreement. No provision or part of an international treaty can be interpreted independently or in isolation from its surrounding provisions and parts. Savigny describes the 'systematic' (contextual) element as the 'inner linkage which connects all legal institutes and legal rules to form one unitary whole'.[22] As per Savigny, context presupposes that the law is unitary and systematic and not an aggregate of legal acts that can all be interpreted in isolation. This contextual interpretation is mandated by Article 31(1) of the Vienna Convention of the Law

[20] Association of the overseas countries and territories with the European Union (in force 1 January 1971; no longer in force).

[21] Interim Agreement establishing a framework for an Economic Partnership Agreement between the Eastern and Southern Africa States, on the one part, and the European Community and its Member States, on the other part (in force 14 May 2012), art 35.

[22] Odile Ammann, *Domestic Courts and the Interpretation of International Law* (Brill 2020) 191.

of Treaties (VCLT). Moreover, Article 32 of the VCLT prescribes that the circumstances surrounding the conclusion of a treaty are 'supplementary means of interpretation'.[23] Hence, the inclusion of women-related provisions in the non-trade sections of such comprehensive agreements can be considered as related to, or negotiated within, the broader spectrum of trade policies.

7.2 Ten Different Approaches

This section identifies and examines the ten most common ways in which women-related concerns are found in existing trade agreements. The discussions provided in each category explain the approach then outline practice examples that employ that approach and, finally, provide some reflections on the benefits (and pitfalls if any) of employing that particular approach.

7.2.1 Approach 1: inclusion of stand-alone chapters

The latest trend in adding women's perspective in trade agreements has been the addition of stand-alone and dedicated chapters on trade and women. Chile has taken the lead in this respect and has included stand-alone chapters in multiple FTAs that it has signed with its trade partners including Uruguay,[24] Argentina,[25] Brazil,[26] the EU,[27] the UK,[28] and Ecuador.[29] Chile is also negotiating a chapter on trade and women with Paraguay and, together with Colombia, Mexico, and Peru, it is considering the inclusion of a similar chapter in the agreement between the Pacific Alliance and associates.[30]

An interesting recent development in this respect can be observed in the amended Chile–Ecuador trade agreement, which contains a new, dedicated chapter on trade and women.[31] Chapter 18 of the agreement is quite comprehensive as it includes various affirmations, cooperation-based commitments, and reaffirmations. However, it is the first of its kind as the parties to the agreement have created a detailed and dedicated bilateral consultation procedure to resolve

[23] Vienna Convention on the Law of Treaties between States and International Organizations or between International Organizations (adopted 20 March 1986) 1155 UNTS 331, 8 ILM 679.
[24] FTA between Chile and Uruguay (in force 13 December 2018).
[25] FTA between Argentina and Chile (in force 1 May 2019).
[26] FTA between Brazil and Chile (in force 21 January 2022).
[27] Agreement Establishing an Association between the European Community and the Republic of Chile (in force 1 February 2003).
[28] Association Agreement between the Republic of Chile and the United Kingdom of Great Britain and Northern Ireland (in force 1 January 2021).
[29] Economic Complementation Agreement between Chile and Ecuador (in force 1 January 2010).
[30] Interview with trade negotiator (12 October 2022) (details withheld, on record with the author).
[31] Chile–Ecuador Complementation Agreement (n 29).

differences that may arise from the provisions included in the chapter. It is also the first agreement that requires its parties to set up a national consultative committee that is responsible for gathering views from the public (including representatives from women's organizations and business entities) on matters covered in the stand-alone chapter.

In 2023, the EU and Chile negotiated a stand-alone chapter entitled 'Trade and gender equality' in their Interim Agreement on Trade.[32] Its scope is vast and quite comprehensive. In the chapter, the parties reaffirm their commitment to women-specific international conventions such as the World Trade Organization's (WTO's) 2017 Joint Declaration on Trade and Women's Economic Empowerment,[33] the Beijing Declaration and Platform for Action,[34] and the Convention on the Elimination of All Forms of Discrimination against Women (CEDAW).[35] In addition to reaffirmations, the chapter contains a range of provisions on cooperation activities, minimum legal standards and common commitments relating to their laws and procedures, institutional arrangements, procedures for review and implementation, and procedures for dispute settlement.

As common commitments, the parties seek to ensure that they improve their relevant laws and policies for the promotion of equal rights and opportunities between men and women, promote public awareness in their territories, and consider the objective of equality between men and women when formulating or implementing relevant policies or measures. Moreover, in addition to featuring ambitious labour standards, the chapter also contains a commitment on gathering sex-disaggregated data to better understand the different impacts of trade policy instruments on women and men.[36] The parties have also incorporated cooperation activities but these activities, unlike most other agreements, go beyond the general traditional areas and include commitments on improving the capacity and conditions of women not only as workers but also as businesswomen, entrepreneurs, and leaders. The parties also endeavour to share experiences and best practices relating to policies and programmes aimed at promoting women's financial inclusion, women's leadership, and the development of women's networks. This includes their participation in decision-making positions in both the public and private sectors; education in areas where they are under-represented, such as science, technology, engineering, and mathematics (STEM), as well as innovation

[32] Interim Agreement on Trade between the European Union and the Republic of Chile (signed 13 December 2023), ch 27.

[33] Joint Declaration on Trade and Women's Economic Empowerment on the Occasion of the WTO Ministerial Conference in Buenos Aires in December 2017 <www.wto.org/english/thewto_e/minist_e/mc11_e/genderdeclarationmc11_e.pdf> accessed 12 May 2023.

[34] The Beijing Declaration and the Platform for Action: Fourth World Conference on Women (15 September 1995) Doc A/CONF. 177/20 (contains a progressive blueprint for advancing women's empowerment).

[35] Adopted and opened for signature, ratification, and accession by the General Assembly Resolution 34/180 (New York, 18 December 1979).

[36] EU–Chile Interim Agreement (n 32) art 27.3.

and business. Additionally, they aim to enhance the competitiveness of women-led enterprises to promote the internationalization of small and medium-sized enterprises (SMEs) led by women, to improve women's digital skills and access to online business tools and e-commerce platforms, to advance care policies and programmes, to implement work–life balance measures, and to develop gender-based analyses of trade policies.[37] The parties to the agreement also outline institutional arrangements to ensure the implementation and review of such commitments.[38] Notably, a first-ever and much-awaited inclusion is the application of the agreement's dispute-settlement provisions to these commitments, with both binding and compulsory jurisdiction.[39] This example shows that the inclusion of a dedicated chapter is a possible way forward to mainstream women's concerns in trade agreements as it can serve as an umbrella chapter for different types of provisions.

This is a comparatively much newer approach as most of the existing agreements with such chapters were negotiated six or seven years earlier. However, it is important to mention that some of the earlier agreements (negotiated as regional integration agreements) by countries in Africa had begun to include stand-alone chapters on women empowerment as early as the 1990s; in 1993, the Treaty Establishing the Common Market for Eastern and Southern Africa (COMESA) was negotiated as the first agreement to feature a stand-alone chapter on women in its main text (ie Chapter 24, entitled 'Women in Development and Business'). This was replicated in 1999 in the Treaty for the Establishment of the East Africa Community (EAC), which also included a chapter on women (ie Chapter 22, entitled 'Enhancing the Role of Women in Socio-Economic Development'). In all these chapters—old and now—one problematic factor remains common. With all these examples, countries have generally loaded commitments relating to women in a stand-alone chapter, which implies that with the adoption of this approach, such commitments usually remain absent from these agreements' other chapters or disciplines that directly relate to market access interests.

7.2.2 Approach 2: inclusion in chapters or provisions on sustainable development

The EU has taken a lead in respect of employing this approach as it has included women-centric provisions in its chapters or provisions on sustainable development in multiple FTAs. For example, Chapter 9 of Armenia–EU Comprehensive and Enhanced Partnership Agreement is entitled 'Trade and Sustainable

[37] ibid art 27.4.
[38] ibid art 27.5.
[39] ibid art 27.6.

Development'. It contains several affirmations where the parties seek to cooperate on activities to enhance sustainable development. It also contains affirmations to existing international conventions such as the International Labour Organization (ILO) Declaration on Social Justice for a Fair Globalization of 2008 and the UN 2030 Agenda for Sustainable Development entitled 'Transforming Our World: the 2030 Agenda for Sustainable Development'.[40] The EU–Georgia trade agreement also has a stand-alone chapter on trade and sustainable development.[41] Parties in this provision seek cooperation on various interests including labour, environment, human resource development, gender equality, and conservation of exhaustible resources such as forests and fisheries.

The EU–Republic of Korea FTA contains two explicit provisions, one of which is found in Chapter 13 entitled 'Trade and Sustainable Development', and the other is included in Annex 13 on 'Trade and Sustainable Development' with similar commitments and coverage.[42] The chapter contains commitments to productive employment and decent work for all, including men, women, and young people. It also includes commitments on effective recognition of the right to collective bargaining, elimination of all forms of forced or compulsory labour, effective abolition of child labour, and elimination of discrimination in respect of employment and occupation. The parties in this chapter reaffirm their commitments under the ILO Declaration on Fundamental Principles and Rights at Work and its follow-up. The annex focuses on corporate social responsibility and accountability, environmental protection, climate change and energy efficiency, cooperation on trade-related aspects of biodiversity, and sustainable fishing practices. Gender equality is mentioned as one of the possible areas of cooperation. The chapter and the annex are drafted without including any provision on how these affirmations or reaffirmations may be implemented or financed.

The benefit of this approach is that it allows parties to embrace various elements of sustainable development and undertake commitments to work on different activities focused on the environment, climate change, labour standards, child labour, poverty reduction, women empowerment, human resource development, and the fight against corruption. The fundamental problem with the approach is that because it includes a range of issues, women's empowerment is included as one concern amongst many others. Because they are overloaded with a range of concerns, such chapters, as compared to stand-alone chapters, leave significantly less space for the inclusion of concrete and detailed commitments, activities, and implementation plans to achieve the various goals. In other words, the ideas in

[40] Armenia–EU Comprehensive and Enhanced Partnership Agreement (CEPA) (in force 1 March 2021), art 272.

[41] Association Agreement between the European Union and the European Atomic Energy Community and their Member States, of the one part, and Georgia, of the other part (in force 1 July 2016), ch 13.

[42] FTA between the European Union and the Republic of Korea (in force 1 July 2011), Annex 13.

such chapters remain at a superficial level and the parties are generally unable to delve deep into understanding and addressing specific concerns.

The mainstreaming benefits may be even less pronounced in agreements that include women-related provisions in a stand-alone provision on trade and sustainable development. The EU–Singapore FTA, for example, contains a provision on labour cooperation in the context of trade and sustainable development, in which parties seek to cooperate on labour aspects of trade and sustainable development.[43] The provision identifies several procedures that may be used to carry out cooperation activities, such as the exchange of information and sharing of best practices; however, it does not precisely spell out the kind of activities on which countries can cooperate to target precise barriers or identify any particular actor in the respective territories that might be responsible for identifying these activities. Hence, while the inclusion of women-centric provisions within chapters or provisions on sustainable development allows for a comprehensive approach to various interconnected issues, it often results in broad commitments that lack specificity and enforceability, thereby diluting the focus on the concrete actions and detailed implementation plans that are necessary for empowering women through trade.

7.2.3 Approach 3: inclusion of cross-cutting explicit and implicit provisions

In some trade agreements, explicit and implicit women-centric provisions are often tied to other cross-cutting issues. The inclusion of these provisions in cross-cutting issues are found in two different forms: (1) provisions that contain explicit expressions relating to women and (2) provisions that do not contain explicit language or expressions relating to women but are nonetheless relevant to women. There are several provisions that may or may not be explicitly related to women but they hold the potential to benefit women either by dealing with the barriers they face or by creating new opportunities for them. These can include provisions on the protection of SMEs (or micro, small, and medium-sized enterprises (MSMEs)), access to e-commerce and digital trade, access to government procurement opportunities, trade finance and access to finance, foreign investment, fisheries and agriculture, market access barriers, trade facilitation, and so on.

The EU–Canada Trade Agreement offers an example of an explicit provision with respect to foreign investment. Article 8.10 of this FTA contains a binding obligation that prohibits sex-based discrimination against foreign investors. The provision encourages women businesses to engage in foreign investment without fear or uncertainty of being discriminated against on the basis of their

[43] FTA between the European Union and the Republic of Singapore (in force 21 November 2019), art 12.4.

sex. Moreover, there are many agreements that feature explicit and implicit provisions on the protection of micro enterprises (MEs) and SMEs. Even implicit provisions on the protection of SMEs' interests are directly beneficial to women because they own close to ten million of the world's SMEs.[44] This means that more than 30% of SMEs in the world are owned by women entrepreneurs. Globally, approximately 50% of working women are employed in service-based SMEs.[45] This number rise to 85% if we observe female employment in service sectors in advanced economies.[46] These numbers show how such a provision aimed at enhancing SMEs' market access can help women both as business stakeholders and employees.

One relevant agreement is the United States–Mexico–Canada Agreement (USMCA), wherein the parties commit to enhancing trade and investment opportunities for SMEs in the region.[47] Specifically, the agreement provides opportunities for SMEs in the region to increase their exports and participation in global and North American value chains. It seeks to achieve this through various means, including: (1) the promotion of cooperation between the parties' small businesses via dedicated SME centres, incubators, accelerators, and export assistance centres; (2) engaging in activities to support SMEs owned by under-represented groups, including women; (3) working on improving SMEs' access to capital and credit, their participation in covered government procurement opportunities, and helping them adapt to changing market conditions; and (4) encouraging SME participation in web-based platforms to share information and best practices, and facilitating connections with international suppliers, buyers, and other potential business partners. The parties to the agreement have also sought to facilitate the region's SME participation in government procurement, as they commit to providing notices of intended procurement in a single electronic portal and encouraging it by electronic means, thus increasing transparency and efficiency for SMEs and their businesses.[48] The agreement also eliminates local presence obligations for cross-border service providers, which benefits SMEs by removing the unnecessary burden of opening an international office as a requirement for doing business.[49]

[44] Usman Ahmed and others, 'Filling the Gap: How Technology Enables Access to Finance for Small- and Medium-Sized Enterprises' (2015) 10(3)–(4) Innovations: Technology, Governance, Globalization 35, 42.

[45] ILO, 'Global Employment Trends 2014: The risk of a jobless recovery' (21 January 2014) <www.ilo.org/wcmsp5/groups/public/---dgreports/---dcomm/---publ/documents/publication/wcms_233953.pdf> accessed 12 February 2020.

[46] ILO, 'Global Employment Trends for Women 2012' (11 December 2012) <www.ilo.org/wcmsp5/groups/public/---dgreports/---dcomm/documents/publication/wcms_195447.pdf> accessed 12 February 2020.

[47] Agreement between the United States of America, the United Mexican States, and Canada (in force 1 July 2020), art 25.2.

[48] ibid art 13.20.

[49] ibid art 15.10.

In the Australia–Chile FTA,[50] the parties commit to exchanging information on their respective approaches to enhance SMEs' access to the government procurement market.[51] Moreover, the protection of SMEs' interests with respect to business and employment opportunities also appears as an area of cooperation in the agreement, as the parties seek to work on enhancing the identification and development of innovative cooperation initiatives capable of providing added value to their bilateral relationship.[52] A similar commitment to cooperate is found in the Chile–Thailand FTA[53] and the EU–Chile FTA.[54]

Some agreements also seek to protect women's interests in particular industries such as fisheries and agriculture. One example is the EU–Eastern and Southern Africa States Interim Economic Partnership Agreement in which parties seek to encourage the participation of marginal groups (eg women) in the fishing industry through the 'promotion of gender equality in fisheries by developing the capacity of women engaged in fisheries'.[55] The fisheries sector is known for employing a significant female workforce as the low wages and poor working conditions suit its labour-intensive nature. Therefore, a provision for capacity building in this sector could be particularly beneficial for women, especially in the developing world.

In several other agreements, parties have included labour standards in dedicated labour chapters or provisions, labour annexes, or side agreements on labour. The Canada–Jordan Side Agreement on Labour Cooperation imposes a binding labour standard on the parties to eliminate discrimination in respect of employment and occupation (including equal pay for women and men) in its very first provision.[56] In the Eurasian Economic Union (EAEU) Treaty, parties seek to cooperate on labour migration concerns in various ways and, in particular, seek to enhance the social welfare of labour migrants by mandating compulsory insurance for maternity needs.[57] In the US–Colombia,[58] US–Panama,[59] and US–Peru[60] FTAs, parties have incorporated several labour standards that concern women in their annexes on labour cooperation. These annexes reflect parties' willingness to work on labour programmes related to women's issues, including the elimination of discrimination in respect of employment and occupation. They also show the parties' inclination to implement their labour standard commitments under ILO Conventions. These inclusions are important as women and labour concerns are

50 (In force 6 March 2009.)
51 Australia–Chile FTA, art 15.24.
52 ibid art 18.2.
53 FTA between the Government of the Republic of Chile and the Government of the Kingdom of Thailand (in force 5 November 2015), art 11.3.
54 ibid art 44.
55 (n 21) art 35.
56 Agreement on Labour Cooperation between Canada and Jordan (in force 1 October 2012), art 1.
57 Treaty on the Eurasian Union (in force 1 January 2015), art 96.
58 Colombia–United States Trade Promotion Agreement (in force 15 May 2012), Annex 17.6.
59 FTA between the United States and Panama (in force 31 October 2012), Annex 16.6.
60 FTA between the United States of America and Peru (in force 1 February 2009), Annex 17.6.

interrelated because labour standards such as workers' rights, reasonable working hours, parental leave or childcare, occupational safety and health, minimum wage, and anti-discrimination directly impact women as both workers and employers.[61]

Another relevant area for inclusion of such commitments is government procurement, as seen in Chapter 3. A few agreements include useful provisions in this respect; however, most of these inclusions are made implicitly. In the Australia–Chile FTA, for example, the parties commit to enhancing the exchange of information relating to the development and use of electronic communications in government procurement systems and make efforts to increase understanding of their respective government procurement systems. They also clarify that one of the main aims of information exchange is to maximize access for SMEs to the government procurement market.[62] A similar commitment is found in the European Free Trade Association (EFTA)–Central America FTA, where parties have sought to enhance the use of 'electronic means of communication to permit efficient dissemination of information on government procurement, particularly as regards tender opportunities offered by procuring entities, while respecting the principles of transparency and non-discrimination'.[63] These commitments, even though seemingly gender-neutral, can benefit women entrepreneurs who own or manage small businesses in these countries, as one of the major obstacles that women-owned businesses face is the lack of access to relevant information and understanding of the systems and processes. In the US–Colombia FTA, the parties provide for a Committee on Procurement that is responsible for ensuring that efforts are made to increase understanding of their respective government procurement systems, with a view to maximizing access to procurement opportunities, especially for small business suppliers. To achieve this, the Committee can foster trade-related technical assistance, including training of government personnel or interested suppliers on specific elements of that party's government procurement system, in coordination with the Committee on Trade Capacity Building.[64]

As these examples show, cross-cutting provisions in various areas (eg fisheries, labour standards, SME market access, government procurement, and foreign investment) make a considerable inroad for women businesses and their workforces in various sectors and markets. However, most of these provisions are couched in best endeavour language; they appear in a variety of places—in the main texts of FTAs or their side instruments—but almost none of them are binding or enforceable. Moreover, they mostly appear as implicit inclusions as they do not explicitly identify women as a potential beneficiary group. Hence, for them to work in favour

[61] Marcus Gustafsson and Amrita Bahri, 'Progressive Trade: Labour and Gender' in Daniel Bethlehem and others (eds), *The Oxford Handbook of International Trade Law* (2nd edn, OUP 2023).
[62] Australia–Chile FTA (n 50) art 15.24.
[63] FTA between the EFTA States and the Central American States (in force 19 August 2014), art 7.5.
[64] Colombia–United States TPA (n 58) art 9.15.

of women, policymakers need to interpret and implement them inclusively so that they can respond to women's needs and problems.

7.2.4 Approach 4: inclusion in the preamble or other general clauses

Several FTAs incorporate related commitments in their preamble, albeit in different ways. The European Economic Area (EEA) is the first example that recognizes in its preamble the importance of 'equal treatment of men and women' in the EEA to achieve social progress in the region and to 'promote full employment, an improved standard of living, and improved working conditions within the European Economic Area.'[65] Another example is the African Continental Free Trade Agreement (AfCFTA), as its preamble, amongst other things, recognizes the importance of gender equality 'for the development of international trade and economic cooperation.'[66] These two examples are very different as the first example seeks to ensure equal treatment of women and men as an instrument for 'social' development; the parties in the latter example recognize equality between women and men as an instrument of 'trade' to achieve 'economic' development.

The parties in the Comprehensive and Progressive Agreement for Trans-Pacific Partnership (CPTPP) explicitly and unambiguously mentions 'the importance of promoting ... gender equality ...' in its preamble.[67] This inclusion is made without stating the purpose behind the inclusion. 'Gender equality' is stated as a value parties reaffirm their commitment to, among others including environmental protection, labour rights, sustainable development, and indigenous rights. The preamble to the EU–Papua New Guinea/Fiji FTA incorporates gender equality in an indirect manner. It does not directly mention any explicit expression in its preamble, but incorporates it by reference the objectives of the Cotonou Agreement.[68] Article 1 of the Cotonou Agreement states its objectives, one of which is that a 'systematic account shall be taken of the situation of women and gender issues in all areas—political, economic, and social.'[69] These examples show that countries have opted for a number of ways to include such references in their agreements' preambles.

Including such commitments in the preamble is an important way to ensure that there is an option for policymakers and adjudicators to interpret a given trade agreement from a women's perspective. The preamble is a vital part of any international instrument or agreement as it can be instrumental in determining the

[65] Agreement Establishing the European Economic Area (in force 1 January 1994), Preamble.

[66] Agreement establishing the African Continental Free Trade Area (AfCFTA) (in force 30 May 2019), Preamble.

[67] CPTPP (n 1), Preamble.

[68] Interim Partnership Agreement between the European Community, of the one part, and the Pacific States, of the other part—Protocols—Final Act—Declarations (in force 20 December 2009).

[69] Cotonou Agreement (signed 23 June 2000).

intentions of its negotiators or drafters at the time it was concluded.[70] In disputes arising from a given agreement, decision-makers can consider the wording used in the preamble to identify the parties' objectives and the intentions underlying the agreement. Moreover, the three examples discussed above confirm that once the parties to an FTA frontload this concern in the preamble, they tend to include at least one other commitment relating to women in the agreement's main text. Hence, there are several benefits with such preambular inclusions.

Similar benefits can be seen with the inclusion of women's concerns in an agreement's 'general objectives' clause. Most FTAs contain a general clause in the initial provisions of the text, delineating the objectives that the parties aim to achieve through the agreement. Sometimes, parties include a commitment to gender equality in such general clauses. The East African Community is an example of such an inclusion. In Article 5, wherein parties set out the objectives of the Community, they also commit to adding women's perspectives in all their endeavours and enhance the 'role of women in cultural, social, political, economic, and technological development'. Another provision entitled 'Objectives, principles, and values' is Article 3 of the EU–Overseas Countries and Territories (OCT) FTA, which prohibits discrimination based on sex in the areas of cooperation the parties seek to engage in under the agreement.

These inclusions can also influence the way other provisions in an FTA are interpreted.[71] Article 31 of the Vienna Convention on the Law of Treaties (VCLT) establishes that 'a treaty shall be interpreted in good faith in accordance with the ordinary meaning to be given to the terms of the treaty in their context and in the light of its object and purpose'.[72] This principle confirms the purposive approach of interpretation. According to this approach, each of the covered agreements must be interpreted considering the purpose of the text and in a way that will give 'effect to all the terms of the treaty'.[73] Such an inclusion, as with an inclusion in a preamble, can help in resolving a dispute by allowing other provisions of that FTA to be interpreted in light of its objectives or principles. However, other than this benefit, general clauses or preambular inclusions do not contain any concrete commitments. They only include broad objectives that can neither be enforced nor implemented unless they are coupled with further inclusion of associated commitments in that agreement's text.

[70] Article 31 of the VCLT (n 23) requires that an agreement must be interpreted considering its context, object, and purpose.

[71] WTO Panel Report, *Russian Federation—Measures Concerning Traffic in Transit* (5 April 2019) WT/DS512/R, para 7.59.

[72] VCLT (n 23).

[73] WTO Appellate Body Report, *United States—Standards for Reformulated and Conventional Gasoline* (29 April 1996) WT/DS2/AB/R, 21; Panel Report, *Japan—Taxes on Alcoholic Beverages* (1 November 1996) WT/DS8/R, WT/DS10/R, WT/DS11/R as modified by the Appellate Body Report, WT/DS8/AB/R, WT/DS10/AB/R, WT/DS11/AB/R.

7.2.5 Approach 5: inclusion of provisions on cooperation activities

Explicit cooperation-styled provisions are those legal provisions in which parties assume positive affirmations to cooperate nationally with their public and private stakeholders and/or internationally with other parties on various matters that relate to women's concerns. This is an important approach, given the sheer number of agreements that have included such provisions on cooperation activities. Some FTAs include provisions that merely touch upon the prospect of strengthening women's empowerment or addressing their concerns without identifying precise activities for how that might be achieved. Other FTAs have delved into different aspects of women's empowerment as they have included provisions that focus on reducing various barriers that impede women's access to international trade. These provisions range from enhancing women's access to education, skill development, digital training, health services, and productive resources to increasing the representation of women in decision-making and policymaking roles.

Parties to some FTAs have employed a single focus for drafting such provisions. For example, FTAs such as the Turkey–Malaysia FTA and the EU–Ukraine FTA have a single focus on health care, particularly in maternal and child health and reproductive health-care services in their cooperation provisions.[74] The EU–Montenegro FTA in its cooperation provision seeks to enhance access to all levels of education and training.[75] Cooperation-based provisions in other FTAs have focused on multiple concerns. The parties in the CPTPP seek to cooperate on a range of activities to help women businesses and workers benefit from the opportunities the agreement creates.[76] These activities focus on information sharing, capacity building, and increasing market access for women. They include providing advice or training; exchanging information and experiences on programmes to help women build skills and capacity; improving women's access to markets, technology, and financing; developing women's leadership networks; and identifying best practices relating to workplace flexibility. The East African Community displays a slightly different trend in this respect. In this accord, parties seek to increase the participation of women in decision-making roles, eliminate regulations and customs that discriminate against businesswomen and their access to resources, and adopt technology to help women progress professionally.[77] In Articles 155 and 174 of the accord, the parties create various legislative,

[74] FTA between the Government of Malaysia and the Government of the Republic of Turkey (in force 1 August 2015) art 9.13; Association Agreement between the European Union and the European Atomic Energy Community and their Member States, of the One Part, and Ukraine, of the Other Part (in force 1 September 2017), art 427.

[75] Stabilisation and Association Agreement between the EU and Montenegro (in force 1 May 2010), art 102.

[76] CPTPP (n 1) art 23.4.

[77] Treaty for the Establishment of the East African Community (in force 7 July 2000), arts 154 and 155.

procedural, and institutional tools to carry out these commitments, providing the much needed implementation machinery for the activities they seek to undertake in the cooperation-based provisions.

The Chile–Argentina Agreement presents another, yet different, example in this respect. In the agreement, the parties agree to work on several cooperation activities that envision women not only as workers and entrepreneurs but also as leaders, decision-makers, and scientists.[78] The parties to this agreement seek to improve the educational or skills development opportunities that can translate to high-paid job opportunities for women (eg science, technology, engineering, and mathematics (STEM) and information and communication technology (ICT)). The FTA is exceptional in this respect as most trade pacts only focus on cooperation-oriented provisions in fields that have traditionally been reserved for women, often ignoring their participation in lucrative sectors. Other areas of cooperation included in the agreement are also highly beneficial as they address barriers commonly faced by women in the region. These areas encompass, but are not limited to, the following: promoting financial inclusion for women, including financial training, access to finance, and financial assistance; advancing women's leadership and developing women's networks in business and trade; fostering women's representation in decision-making and positions of authority in the public and private sectors, including on corporate boards; promoting female entrepreneurship and women's participation in international trade; conducting gender-based analysis; and sharing methods and procedures for the collection of sex-disaggregated data, the use of indicators, and the analysis of gender-focused statistics related to trade.[79]

The parties to the Canada–Israel FTA also commit themselves to similar activities directly related to women's empowerment.[80] However, they raise the bar as they provide a dedicated implementation mechanism through the creation of a Trade and Gender Committee that is responsible for organizing and facilitating the cooperation activities, reporting on progress, and making recommendations and all efforts for the implementation of the identified activities.[81] These attempts to identify institutions responsible for putting cooperation activities into action are welcome steps. However, the attempts fall short of various aspects required for effective implementation. This is due to the fact that the existing provisions generally fail to specify the precise functions of such committees, the manner in which their activities and meetings will be financed, the procedures they may employ in executing their functions, and timelines and action plans for their fulfilment. Moreover, the parties undertake these commitments in a rather modest and

[78] Argentina–Chile FTA (n 25) art 15.1.
[79] ibid art 12.9.
[80] CIFTA (n 1) art 13.3.
[81] ibid art 13.4.

non-binding manner as the implementation of the activities is contingent upon their available resources and willingness.

7.2.6 Approach 6: inclusion of domestic policy commitments

In several agreements, countries have sought to approximate their domestic laws or policies with other parties' laws or policies and assume commitments relating to their domestic laws, rules, regulations, policies, and practices. These have usually included commitments to maintain or improve labour standards, the protection of international standards, the elimination of discrimination, or the provision of benefits such as medical or life insurance for women. These commitments may be explicit or implicit in nature. The majority of such inclusions are presented in the form of non-derogation clauses wherein parties include a statement that indicates that a given provision should be interpreted in a manner that does not diminish or impact other existing rights or interests.

An example of an implicit non-derogation clause can be seen in the agreement between Japan and the Philippines in which the parties 'recognize that it is inappropriate to encourage investment by weakening or reducing the protections afforded in domestic labour laws'.[82] Each party has committed to ensuring that it does not waive or otherwise derogate from, or offer to waive or otherwise derogate from, such laws in a manner that weakens or reduces adherence to internationally recognized labour rights that includes prohibition and elimination of discrimination and promotes acceptable conditions of work with respect to minimum wages, hours of work, and occupational safety and health. A very similar commitment can be seen in the Japan–Switzerland agreement,[83] where parties simply recognize that 'it is inappropriate to encourage investment activities by relaxing domestic health, safety or environmental measures, or lowering labour standards'.[84] Another similar example can be seen in the South Korea–Peru agreement,[85] where parties undertake effective enforcement of their labour laws and regulations and commit not to derogate from their laws or regulations in a manner that is inconsistent with the principles established in the ILO Conventions.[86]

In other agreements, parties have included policy commitments in the form of minimum legal standards. For example, in the EU–Cameroon agreement,[87] parties

[82] Economic Partnership Agreement between Japan and Philippines (in force 11 December 2008), art 103.
[83] Agreement on Free Trade and Economic Partnership between Japan and the Swiss Confederation (in force 1 September 2009).
[84] ibid art 101.
[85] FTA between the Republic of Korea and the Republic of Peru (in force 1 August 2011).
[86] ibid art 18.2.
[87] Interim Agreement with a view to an Economic Partnership Agreement between the European Community and its Member States, of the one part, and the Central Africa Party, of the other part (in force 4 August 2014).

agree that the agreement's legal and regulatory regimes and administrative capacity shall be established on several selected legal standards. One such standard is the protection of sensitive data concerning sex. Furthermore, it calls for additional safeguards to be implemented if data related to sex and other personal information needs to be disclosed.[88] This could be seen as a useful provision, particularly for women-owned or managed businesses. This is because the protection of data relating to an owner's or manager's gender can help them to operate without facing gender-based discrimination or harassment.[89] For women, lack of protection of sensitive data is a real and imminent threat as they often face discrimination and social exclusion.[90] An explicit inclusion of a minimum legal standard in a standalone provision can be seen in the EU–Central America agreement,[91] which commits parties to pay special attention 'to sectoral reforms and to ensure an equitable access to quality health services, food, and nutritional security in particular for vulnerable groups such as the disabled, elderly people, women, children, and indigenous peoples'.[92]

Another example is the Canada–Jordan agreement in which the parties commit to ensuring that their labour laws and practices embody and provide protection for internationally recognized labour principles and rights. This includes the elimination of discrimination in respect of employment and occupation, such as ensuring equal pay for women and men.[93] In the Canada–Costa Rica FTA, parties seek to reflect in their laws, regulations, procedures, and practices, the principles and rights recognized in the ILO Declaration on Fundamental Principles and Rights at Work, in particular, the principle of equal pay for women and men.[94] It is unclear whether a commitment to 'reflect' can be seen as setting a minimum legal standard to harmonize domestic laws with such international standards.

These examples show that domestic policy commitments can be negotiated as minimum legal standards or non-derogation clauses and they can also be drafted with strict binding expressions or a combination of binding and non-binding expressions. In addition, these provisions are different from provisions that are styled as cooperation-based endeavours as they are mostly drafted with binding expressions. Most of these commitments require parties to revise or amend their domestic laws and policies and, thus, they could potentially impose a significant compliance cost on the countries accepting or assuming such commitments. It is

[88] ibid art 63.

[89] Similar provision in the Economic Partnership Agreement between the CARIFORUM States and the European Community (in force 1 January 2009), art 198; interview with a trade negotiator (details withheld).

[90] Interview with individuals (details withheld).

[91] Agreement establishing an Association between the European Union and its Member States, on the one hand, and Central America on the other (in force 1 August 2013).

[92] ibid art 44.

[93] Canada–Jordan FTA (in force 1 October 2012), art 1.

[94] FTA between the Government of Canada and the Government of the Republic of Costa Rica (in force 1 November 2002), Annex 1.

for this reason that such commitments regarding women's empowerment are uncommon in trade agreements. Even when they are included, they are often incorporated implicitly or indirectly.

7.2.7 Approach 7: reaffirmation to commitments in other international instruments

In many agreements, countries have reaffirmed or reiterated the legal commitments they have made under other international instruments. The most frequently incorporated instruments in such agreements include, but are not limited to: the United Nations 2030 Agenda and Sustainable Development Goals (UN SDG 2030),[95] the Convention on the Elimination of All Forms of Discrimination Against Women (CEDAW) 1979, the Universal Declaration of Human Rights,[96] the International Covenant on Civil and Political Rights,[97] the International Covenant on Economic, Social and Cultural Rights,[98] the Beijing Declaration of 1995 and Platform for Action, as well as the ILO Conventions (eg Convention 100 on equal pay,[99] Convention 111 on discrimination in employment and occupation,[100] and Convention 156 on workers with family responsibilities,[101] among others).

The Chile–Uruguay FTA has adopted an interesting approach in this respect. Instead of identifying a set of international instruments as is common in most agreements containing such provisions, the parties have reaffirmed their international commitments on gender issues in general terms without mentioning a specific list of instruments. The parties also specify that their priority agreements are those that relate to 'equal pay for men and women, maternity protection, reconciliation of work and family life, decent work for domestic workers, family responsibility, among others'.[102] In this sense, its reaffirmation-based provisions are much less specific than most of the similar inclusions in other agreements.

In other agreements, such reaffirmations are more specific as the parties spell out the precise instruments they want to recall or reaffirm their commitments to. The

[95] United Nations, 'Transforming Our World: The 2030 Agenda For Sustainable Development' (25–27 September 2015, New York) A/RES/70/1.

[96] Universal Declaration of Human Rights, Adopted and proclaimed by General Assembly Resolution 217 A (III) of 10 December 1948.

[97] International Covenant on Civil and Political Rights 1966, 999 UNTS 171, art 3 (which mentions women's right to equality).

[98] International Covenant on Economic, Social and Cultural Rights, 1966, 993 UNTS 3, arts 3 and 7 (which mentions women's right to equality and women's right to a fair wage).

[99] Richard Anker, Helinä Melkas, and A Korten, 'InFocus Programme on Promoting the Declaration on Fundamental Principles and Rights at Work' (2003) <www.researchgate.net/publication/321167476_InFocus_Programme_on_Promoting_the_Declaration_on_Fundamental_Principles_and_Rights_at_Work> accessed 12 May 2024.

[100] ibid.

[101] ibid.

[102] Chile–Uruguay FTA (n 24) art 14.2.

parties in the Argentina–Chile FTA,[103] for example, refer to specific international conventions that are directly related to women-related issues such as the UN SDG 2030 and CEDAW. Another interesting example is that of the EU–Chile Interim Agreement in which parties reaffirm their commitments to a range of general, as well as women-specific, international instruments such as the ILO Declaration on Fundamental Principles and Rights at Work, the ILO Declaration on Social Justice for a Fair Globalization, the Universal Declaration of Human Rights, the WTO's 2017 Joint Declaration on Trade and Women's Economic Empowerment, the Beijing Declaration and Platform for Action, and CEDAW.

By making these references, parties to these agreements recall their commitments to empower all women and girls. They also seek to acknowledge the importance of women's participation in the labour market and in sustainable and inclusive economic growth and prosperity. Even though these reaffirmations can send an important signal to the international community about the priorities of these countries, they are nevertheless instances where parties merely recall their already assumed commitments. These provisions do not identify or provide space for parties to undertake specific positive actions in respect of women empowerment. It is also worth noting that most of the existing trade agreements feature general instruments that are not specific to women's concerns and agreements that include direct references to women-specific instruments such as CEDAW are more of an exception. Moreover, such provisions are generally included without any effort to identify mechanisms that might be responsible for the implementation of these previously agreed promises. Nevertheless, these inclusions can provide parties with an indirect route to include values or concerns that they may not have otherwise been able to include in the main trade agreements for various negotiating complexities and reasons. Therefore, indirect inclusion of a commitment by referring to a relevant international instrument can help countries bring onboard a range of additional strategic issues in a diplomatically and politically viable manner, such as commitments to eliminate employment discrimination, provide anti-harassment procedures in the workplace, and protect maternity and childcare rights.

7.2.8 Approach 8: policy carve-outs such as reservations and exceptions

In trade agreements, parties include a range of policy carve-outs to protect their autonomy while liberalizing their markets. These policy carve-outs have taken two main forms with respect to women's interests: reservations and exceptions.

[103] Argentina–Chile FTA (n 25) art 15.1 para 2 and art 15.2.

Reservations, when typically drafted as the 'right to regulate' provisions, are styled as the act of keeping back, withholding, or setting apart a right to protect a certain social or public welfare interest. In reservation carve-outs, parties must first examine their markets, pinpoint the relevant domestic law which would have otherwise breached the obligations in the FTAs, and then pre-emptively carve-out those laws in either reservation lists or in the agreement's main text. However, in exceptions, instead of directly pinpointing the law, parties usually have mutual agreements on the necessity of pursuing certain policy objectives listed in the provisions of that agreement under certain predetermined conditions.

Exceptions are the express exclusion of something from an agreement's operation. They are generally added to provide support measures that may otherwise be legally inconsistent. Exceptions permit parties to have policy autonomy under certain conditions, including for the requirements that domestic law seeks to pursue in respect of policy objectives that have been previously agreed by the parties (eg public morals, public health, and national security) over trade liberalization, non-discrimination, and market access rules under certain conditions. So far, explicit exceptions in respect of women have not been negotiated in trade agreements. However, policymakers have included a range of implicit exceptions that may include or relate to women's interests. One such example is found in chapter 15 (on government procurement) of the Australia–Chile Trade Agreement.[104] Parties in this chapter include the following exceptions:

Article 15.23: exceptions

1. Provided that such measures are not applied in a manner that would constitute a means of arbitrary or unjustifiable discrimination between Parties where the same conditions prevail or a disguised restriction on trade between the Parties, nothing in this Chapter shall be construed to prevent a Party from adopting or maintaining measures:
   (a) necessary to protect public morals, order, or safety;
   ...
   (d) relating to goods or services of handicapped persons, of philanthropic or not for profit institutions, or of prison labour.

It is possible to argue that this exception can be invoked to justify measures that are taken in respect of protecting public morals that could include either women's empowerment or goods or services of non-profit institutions that can operate for the benefit of women. However, it is important to note that this exception is drafted with a broad scope as it 'relates' to goods or services 'of' non-profit institutions. It

[104] Australia–Chile FTA (n 50).

does not specify what kinds of goods or services are covered under the exception and it does not specify whether those goods or services are ones that are to be provided to or by non-profit institutions.

Reservations are a more accepted, common, and explicit form of provision negotiated in respect of women. Reservations that have appeared quite frequently in trade agreements are styled as 'right to regulate' provisions. By carving out such special reservations, countries generally reserve a right to engage in policies or activities that would otherwise be inconsistent with their obligations under that agreement. These reservations are mostly found in the agreement's annexes wherein parties include their schedules of specific commitments. For example, Article 10.2 of the Chile–South Korea FTA contains a right to regulate childcare services.[105] A similar reservation can be found in Annex II of the South Korea–Peru FTA.[106] In these agreements, countries reserve their policy space to regulate specific areas that may affect women's health and maternal concerns, such as health care, nutrition, childcare, and women's safety.[107] Other examples of such policy carve-outs include the right to subsidize social services for the protection of maternity needs, including childcare.[108] These examples show that such types of provisions in trade agreements generally seek to uphold women's role as mothers or caregivers. However, there are some agreements—though very few—in which the parties have sought to protect women's market access using such reservations.

One example that could be seen as focusing on women's market access interest is the US–Dominican Republic–Central America FTA.[109] In this agreement, parties reserve the right to craft government procurement schemes that may be favourable for certain groups, including women.[110] Another example is found in the USMCA,[111] an agreement which provides for a special reservation to protect market access for indigenous women engaged in cross-border trade in services. This cultural reservation aims to preserve the culture, languages, knowledge, traditions, and identity of indigenous women with a special focus on the economic integration of women and seeks to simplify women's market access across borders.

As these examples show, parties in such provisions reserve their right to ensure that trade liberalization under a given FTA does not limit their policy space to regulate areas of strategic importance such as public welfare including the provision of

[105] FTA between the Republic of Korea and the Republic of Chile (in force 1 April 2004).

[106] South Korea–Peru FTA (n 85).

[107] ibid.

[108] Economic Partnership, Political Coordination and Cooperation Agreement between the European Community and its Member States, of the one part, and the United Mexican States, of the other part (in force October 2000).

[109] FTA between Central America, the Dominican Republic, and the United States of America (in force 1 March 2006).

[110] ibid Annex 9.1.2(b)(i).

[111] USMCA (n 47), Annex 15-E.

social services or measures that may benefit minorities or marginalized groups. These are generally drafted with binding expressions and, hence, they seem to create legal obligations and rights for such parties. These provisions can help countries guarantee benefits and protections for women that they otherwise may not be able to extend either through their domestic laws or through a legal standard as that might require changes in their domestic laws.

7.2.9 Approach 9: negotiation of side instruments: protocols, recommendations, arrangements, and declarations

Countries have also adopted a side path to include women's concerns in their trade policy context by negotiating supplementary or independent instruments. These instruments can provide a second opportunity to include sustainability issues for parties that have not done so during the negotiation and drafting of the main trade agreement. So far, they have either taken the shape of protocols, recommendations, declarations, or stand-alone arrangements.

The Comprehensive Economic and Trade Agreement signed between the EU and Canada only includes a single explicit provision on women that prohibits sex-based discrimination against foreign investors, thereby protecting women's discrimination-free access to investment opportunities.[112] Even though this is the only explicit women-related commitment found in the entire agreement, the parties subsequently adopted a stand-alone recommendation on trade and gender.[113] In this recommendation, the parties created a work plan to gather and analyse gender-disaggregated data, carry out the agreement's gender impact assessment, add an inclusive lens to the implementation of the agreement, conduct webinars and capacity-building sessions on the subject, and provide regular reporting on those activities. It remains unclear whether the subsequent adoption of such a recommendation forms part of an FTA per se if it is not mentioned or incorporated by reference in the agreement's text. However, such developments allow parties to work together on activities that may bring about positive outcomes for women at the domestic level. Recommendations centred on the collection of data and the commissioning of research to better understand the nexus between women and trade, as well as the impact of trade agreements on women, can significantly inform future trade policymaking and negotiations.

Other examples worth considering are the Southern African Development Community (SADC) Protocol on Gender and Development (2008) and the

[112] CETA (n 15) art 8.10.

[113] 'CETA Trade and Gender Recommendation: EU–Canada Work Plan 2020–2021' <www.international.gc.ca/trade-commerce/trade-agreements-accords-commerciaux/agr-acc/ceta-aecg/CETA_work_plan-AECG_plan_travail-2020-2021.aspx?lang=en> accessed 12 June 2024.

Declaration on Gender & Development (1997).[114] In the SADC Treaty, parties identify 'gender mainstreaming in the process of community building' as one of the treaty's objectives.[115] However, the treaty itself, without taking into account its objectives, is silent on how parties might mainstream women-related considerations or take steps to include women in the process of community building. The parties have clarified this vision in the SADC Protocol on Gender and Development and the Declaration on Gender & Development. Again, these instruments are not mentioned or referenced in the treaty's text, but their content contains ambitious plans and concrete commitments in this respect.

Except for Botswana and Mauritius, SADC member states have adopted the SADC Protocol on Gender and Development, signed in August 2008. The main objectives of the protocol are to provide for the empowerment of women, to eliminate discrimination, and to achieve gender equality through the development and implementation of inclusive legislation, policies, and programmes. The protocol also reaffirms the SADC member states' commitments to other international instruments such as CEDAW, the Beijing Declaration, and its Platform of Action. In the protocol, SADC member states have identified the following priority areas to accelerate progress in the achievement of women's empowerment: (1) integration of women's perspective into all sectors of regional integration; (2) promoting women's representation and participation in all political and decision-making positions in the SADC; (3) elimination of gender-based violence; and (4) eradication of poverty and promotion of women's economic empowerment in the SADC region.

The will to include women's concerns dates to 1997 in the SADC region. In 1997, SADC member states signed the Declaration on Gender & Development to promote closer regional cooperation and collective action to foster women's empowerment.[116] The declaration reaffirms SADC member states' commitment to eliminate discrimination against women in Southern Africa. In the declaration, member states agree to establish policy and institutional frameworks for advancing gender equality, to set up governmental and non-governmental organizations to monitor issues relating to it, and to create a Gender Unit within the SADC Secretariat.[117] These measures were included in the instrument to compel reforms in domestic laws that discriminate against women and create obstacles for women to access productive resources. This development was followed by its Addendum on the Prevention and Eradication of Violence against Women and Children in

[114] SADC Protocol on Gender and Development (2008) and Declaration on Gender & Development (1997) <www.sadc.int/issues/gender/> accessed 12 June 2024.

[115] Treaty Establishing the Southern African Development Community (in force 30 September 1993), art 5.

[116] See n 114.

[117] Declaration on Gender & Development, art 17.

September 1998.[118] Thereafter, the SADC Council of Ministers in 2007 adopted the SADC Gender Policy.

Another example is the Joint Declaration on Fostering Progressive and Inclusive Trade in which New Zealand, Canada, and Chile confirmed their commitment to make trade policies more progressive and inclusive.[119] The declaration is not entirely focused on the need to foster women empowerment; it includes affirmations on human rights, labour standards, environment protection, cultural diversity, climate change, rights of indigenous people, elimination of discrimination against women, and empowerment of women and girls. In addition, the parties commit to examining the impact of the CPTPP (within three years of its entry into force) on various sustainable development concerns, including on women. Like the two previously mentioned examples, this declaration does not form part of the CPTPP's text. If the declaration were to be signed by all CPTPP member states, then it could be considered as an extension or a follow-up endeavour to the provisions on labour and women concerns included in the CPTPP's text itself. However, that is not the case. It is interesting to see that only three parties to the CPTPP came together to sign that declaration within the context of the agreement. The other eight CPTPP member countries chose to stay out of the declaration. Moreover, it is an instrument that solely contains affirmations and reaffirmations of the objectives of making trade progressive, sustainable, and inclusive. The countries joining the declaration do not identify any procedures or institutions that might be responsible for putting the affirmations or reaffirmations into action. It also sets an interesting precedent of a negotiating experience where 11 countries negotiate a trade agreement but only three of them chose to negotiate an additional instrument to work on sustainable development concerns. This example shows that waiting to achieve consensus is not always the right strategy to achieve results that are not commonly shared by all participating countries.

Another recent development is the Global Trade and Gender Arrangement (GTAGA) which is an independent cooperation agreement not annexed to any particular agreement.[120] It seeks to promote an inclusive approach towards international trade, to eliminate the barriers women face in accessing trade opportunities, and to increase the number of women entrepreneurs in trade. Seen as a groundbreaking landmark initiative which is both innovative and comprehensive in its scope, it is a non-binding arrangement and a cooperation-focused initiative strongly geared towards improving women's access to trading opportunities. The participants in the arrangement acknowledge that women's empowerment and

[118] Addendum on the Prevention of Violence Against Women & Children (1997).

[119] Joint Declaration on Fostering Progressive and Inclusive Trade <www.international.gc.ca/trade-commerce/trade-agreements-accords-commerciaux/agr-acc/cptpp-ptpgp/declaration_fpit-pcpi.aspx?lang=eng> accessed 12 June 2024.

[120] Global Trade and Gender Arrangement 2020 (as amended on 28 February 2024).

their enhanced participation as employees and entrepreneurs contribute to prosperity, competitiveness, and the well-being of society. The GTAGA participants also seek to encourage their private companies to assume voluntary sustainable standards by incorporating gender equality standards, guidelines, and principles in the workplace. Its parties identify a wide range of cooperation activities to enhance the 'ability of women, including workers, entrepreneurs, business women, and business owners, to fully access and benefit from the opportunities created by this Arrangement'.[121] The list of cooperation activities is comprehensive as it includes, but is not limited to, capacity building, access to education, including digital skills development, measures to foster leadership and entrepreneurship, business development, access to networks and trade missions, and government procurement.[122] Yet, the specific nature of the opportunities being referred to remains unclear as the arrangement is neither a stand-alone trade agreement nor appended to any existing trade agreement that might be perceived as fostering trade opportunities for women in these economies.

7.2.10 Approach 10: inclusion of voluntary sustainability standards for business stakeholders

Another possible way to include women's discourse within the trade policy context is to include provisions on voluntary sustainability standards (VSS) in trade agreements.[123] These are guidelines that encourage businesses to respect and accommodate human rights, animal welfare, labour standards, environmental impacts, and women-related considerations within their operations. Through these standards, countries can encourage or even require multinational enterprises (MNEs) operating within or subject to their jurisdiction to include gender equality considerations within their codes of conduct or in their contracts for the sale of goods and services. These standards can promote internal compliance (within a company, concerning owners and employees) and external compliance (for their suppliers, sub-suppliers, and consumers).

The use of VSS-based provisions can serve as a tool to articulate and encourage sustainable and inclusive practices in trade transactions and processes. To pursue women's interests through trade regulations and trade transactions, it is important

[121] ibid arts 8, 9.

[122] ibid art 8.

[123] VSS is defined as 'standards specifying requirements that producers, traders, manufacturers, retailers, or service providers may be asked to meet, relating to a wide range of sustainability metrics, including respect for basic human rights, worker health and safety, environmental impacts, community relations, land-use planning and others' ('Voluntary sustainability standards: today's landscape of issues & initiatives to achieve public policy objectives', (United Nations Forum on Sustainability Standards 2012) <https://unfss.org/wp-content/uploads/2012/05/unfss-report-issues-1_draft_lores.pdf> accessed 12 June 2024.)

to engage the business stakeholders as they are the victims and beneficiaries of trade sustainability. Businesses benefit from empowering women and businesses affect women's interests. While most standards are not designed to promote women interests, there are an increasing number of women-focused VSSs being developed within the trade policy space for private stakeholders. Global companies are now under increasing pressure from their customers and governments to accommodate these standards for various objectives.

Using FTAs, parties have encouraged public and private businesses to develop plans and internal procedures targeting such standards. Through corporate self-regulation provisions, governments have sought to push companies to include social and environmental sustainability standards in their business plans and procedures. This approach seems quite promising as enterprises are crucial actors in international trade and trade agreements in particular. FTAs that support companies' businesses through enhanced and frictionless market access can also encourage or require them to trade inclusively and sustainably.[124] Some recent FTAs have included such provisions in their text. In the Canada–Israel agreement, for example, the parties seek to encourage their businesses to use corporate social responsibility to address issues including labour, the environment, and gender equality.[125]

This example shows the growing influence of VSS in global trade and the role of governments in encouraging businesses to employ such inclusive policies that may help in reducing the barriers women employees currently face. However, one obstacle to the implementation of this approach may be the inadequate incentives and rewards for businesses that employ such VSSs in their operations and code of conduct, and lack of sanctions for those that behave irresponsibly. To some extent, this obstacle can be overcome if countries develop trade policies to enable suppliers with inclusive practices to get preferential access to markets, simplified registration or licensing procedures, or other trade incentives. However, such incentives will have to be designed in accordance with the trade law commitments that country has assumed under multilateral and bilateral trade agreements.

A fundamental problem with this approach is that its benefits may only extend to workforces in the formal sector and, hence, may not reach the majority of the female workforce which is employed in the informal sector, mainly in developing countries. Recent studies show that two billion people in the world work in the informal sector, the majority being in emerging and developing countries. This means that more than 61% of the world's employed population makes their living from the informal economy. If we only look at the world's informal employment

[124] International Trade Centre, 'From Europe to the World: Understanding Challenges for European Businesswomen' (September 2019) <https://intracen.org/file/fromeuropetoworldwomeneufinalweb pdf> accessed 12 June 2024.
[125] CIFTA (n 1) art 16.4. Similar provision in CCFTA (n 1) art G-14 *bis*.

sector in emerging and developing countries, the number increases to 93%.[126] Out of two billion workers in informal employment worldwide, over 740 million are women. In South Asia, over 80% of women in non-agricultural jobs are in informal employment. This number surpasses 74% in Sub-Saharan Africa and 54% in Latin America and the Caribbean.[127] Women in this sector, which is often referred to as the 'grey economy', frequently work without decent salaries, protection from labour laws, insurance or health cover, maternity benefits, or paid sick leave.[128] They are the ones who need the most protection. Yet, encouraging sustainability standards in business conduct may not reach those who are in need of better employment conditions and environment. Another downside of this approach is the increased cost of compliance with such standards that businesses may have to face. When this cost falls on businesses, it can further marginalize resource-constrained SMEs as they are less likely to have the expertise or human resource capacity to deal with such additional requirements.[129] They may also have insufficient financial capacity and resources to pay for audits and certifications that may not always be compensated for by higher prices or profit margins.

[126] ILO, *Women and men in the informal economy: A statistical picture* (3rd edn, International Labour Office 30 April 2018) <www.ilo.org/global/publications/books/WCMS_626831/lang--en/index.htm> accessed 21 April 2020.

[127] *Progress of the World's Women 2015–2016: Transforming economies, realizing rights* (UN Women 2015) ch 2, 71.

[128] Martha Alter Chen, 'Women in the Informal Sector: A Global Picture, the Global Movement' (2001) 21(1) SAIS Review 71.

[129] Raphael Kaplinsky and Mike Morris, 'How Regulation and Standards Can Support Social and Environmental Dynamics in Global Value Chains' (International Centre for Trade and Sustainable Development, Geneva December 2017).

8
Problems with the Existing Inclusions on Women and Trade

8.1 Introduction

The current inclusion of provisions on women's concerns in trade agreements is a step forward; however, what cannot be said with certainty is whether it is a step forward in the right direction. As previously discussed, more than 21% of free trade agreements (FTAs) include provisions relating to women's empowerment and several countries have opted to negotiate such provisions in their trade agreements. Moreover, as covered in the previous chapter, countries have employed different ways to include such provisions as they have negotiated them either as cooperation-based affirmations, reaffirmations, minimum standards, reservations, voluntary standards, etc. Each of these approaches has its benefits and challenges and their effectiveness and viability varies as per the domestic needs and conditions of the negotiating parties. After assessing in the previous chapter the ways in which such provisions are currently added, it is now important to critically assess the problems with the ways in which these provisions have so far been included.

The current inclusions have been criticized by scholars as well as policymakers for several reasons. They have mainly been criticized for being drafted as non-binding and with an imprecise scope, for their lack of enforcement potential, the absence of associated plans for their effective implementation, the disconnect between the solutions they offer and the barriers women face in trade, their focus on women in their traditional roles, and the protectionist fears they can invoke. This chapter elaborates on this critical assessment and presents eight fundamental problems with the current inclusion of such provisions.

8.2 Problem 1: Non-Binding Promises Drafted with Imprecision and Permissive Language

To assess the binding force of a legal provision, it is important to consider three specific aspects in which the provision is drafted or included in a specific agreement: first, the location of a given provision in the agreement; second, its degree of precision; and, third, the verbs used in its drafting.

Trade Agreements and Women. Amrita Bahri, Oxford University Press. © Amrita Bahri 2025.
DOI: 10.1093/9780198935759.003.0009

Although including women's empowerment as an objective within an agreement or as a value in its preamble underscores its significance to the participating countries, it does not typically indicate a binding commitment. Merely mentioning women's concerns in a list of areas of cooperation is also less likely to result in specific policy action to support women than an entire chapter on women that includes specific actions to be taken.[1] Moreover, if countries assume a commitment to increase women's access to financial resources in their respective jurisdictions, even if they draft the commitment with binding expressions using verbs such as 'shall' and 'must', it may still not have any binding force if they place the provision in the agreement's cooperation section. However, a reservation to regulate social services related to maternity or childcare added to a country's schedule of commitments, or a labour standard focused on women added in a labour chapter that falls under the jurisdiction of an agreement's dispute-settlement mechanism, could make the women-related provision binding. This can be seen in the Peru–Korea FTA (KPFTA) in Annex—II (Schedule of Peru), which mentions that 'Peru reserves the right to adopt or maintain any measure with respect to the provision of law enforcement and correctional services, and the following services to the extent that they are social services established or maintained for a public purpose: income security and insurance, social security, social welfare, public education, public training, health, and childcare.'[2] This example shows that the location of a provision in a given agreement has a bearing on its binding value on the parties.

Dedicated chapters on women, while conveying a high degree of concern, may not necessarily indicate a high degree of commitment—in such instances, the wording used can be more relevant in revealing the strength of a given commitment as the language of a provision also determines its binding value.[3] The verbs used can indicate the degree of binding force a provision might have on the agreement's parties. For example, the modal verbs 'shall' or 'must' indicate a higher binding force than 'may', 'could', 'consider', 'promote', 'encourage', or 'cooperate', which typically convey a degree of discretion in the enforcement of a given obligation. The vast majority of women-related provisions included in existing trade agreements are drafted with non-mandatory verbs and soft permissive grammatical constructions.[4]

[1] Maya Sophie Cohen, 'The Pink Trojan Horse: Inserting Gender Issues into Free Trade Agreements' (2021) 5(2) International and Public Affairs 75.

[2] FTA between the Republic of Korea and Peru (in force 1 August 2011).

[3] Lolita Laperle-Forget, 'Gender Provisions in African Trade Agreements: An Assessment of the Commitments for Reconciling Women's Empowerment and Global Trade' (July 2021) Tralac Working Paper No G21WP/2021 <www.tralac.org/publications/article/15242-gender-provisions-in-african-trade-agreements-an-assessment-of-the-commitments-for-reconciling-women-s-empowerment-and-global-trade.html> accessed 28 October 2023.

[4] Raj Bhala and Cody N Wood, 'Two Dimensional Hard–Soft Law Theory and the Advancement of Women's and LGBTQ + Rights Through Free Trade Agreements' (2019) 47(2) Georgia Journal of

Women-related provisions in trade agreements are also often criticized for being vaguely drafted. This ambiguity can make it challenging to properly implement or enforce these provisions, ultimately impacting their effectiveness. However, the value of aspirational and vaguely drafted provisions cannot be underestimated as these provisions can still change the normative environment of trade negotiations and can act as a starting point in negotiating women-related commitments for countries with less developed appetites or understandings of these matters. This is mainly because countries sometimes need flexibility and a somewhat large escape hatch before they can assume commitments they do not entirely understand and before using trade agreements to protect women when they do not know how those agreements will affect women in their economies.[5] One negotiator from a developing country expands on this concern in the following:

> We should start by holding each other's hands, we should cooperate, and give each other the time required to develop capacity on these issues, and then go ahead. Why use a stick and penalize each other? We need to help each other and hand-hold our trade partners, and developed countries should support us [developing countries] with their expertise and their capacity to help us [developing countries] get to the same page before thrusting upon us [developing countries] such binding requirements.[6]

In addition, a provision that sets out an obligation of results indicates a higher level of commitment than one that sets out an obligation of means. For instance, when countries commit to taking certain actions, such as eliminating discriminatory practices, they must take actions to achieve that result for the commitment to be fulfilled. On the other hand, when they agree to cooperate or promote, they are committing only to an obligation of means, not of results. Hence, the implementation of such provisions is at their discretion, making the potential benefits of such provisions for women less predictable. Most of the existing agreements set out obligations of means and not ends, which often leads to variability in the outcomes for women affected by these agreements.

International and Comparative Law (the authors point out that most gender-related commitments in the US–Mexico–Canada Agreement (USMCA) and the Comprehensive and Progressive Agreement for Trans-Pacific Partnership (CPTPP) are aspirational and non-binding, and hence non-enforceable. They also add that they are sometimes drafted with vagueness and ambiguity and so are susceptible to myriad interpretations).

[5] Meredith Kolsky Lewis, 'Human Rights Provisions in Free Trade Agreements: Do the Ends Justify the Means?' (2015) 12 Loyola University Chicago International Law Review 1, 12.

[6] Interview with a trade negotiator (details withheld, on file with the author).

8.3 Problem 2: Lack of Enforcement

Almost no FTA so far, with very few exceptions, contemplates how commitments to women can be enforced and countries have explicitly and unambiguously excluded women-related provisions and chapters from the application of their agreements' dispute-settlement mechanisms.[7]

The absence of applicable dispute-settlement procedures implies that a country's failure to comply with these obligations or commitments or affirmations has no direct legal implication. One exception to this trend is the Canada–Israel FTA (CIFTA), which for the first time includes a binding dispute-settlement procedure applicable to its chapter on trade and women.[8] Unfortunately, this also seems to be a cosmetic attempt to provide an enforcement mechanism because the parties have subjected the binding jurisdiction of that mechanism to their consent, making its jurisdiction non-compulsory in nature.[9] In relation to the agreement's women-related provisions, if Canada were to employ a trade policy measure that Israel believed hindered the participation of women in the workforce, Israel could bring a challenge against the measure. The dispute can be decided by a panel that can issue a legally binding decision on whether the measure in question violates the terms of the agreement's trade and women chapter. However, both countries would have to consent to take the matter to the agreement's dispute-settlement process and it is unlikely that a responding country whose measure is challenged will agree to the binding jurisdiction of such a panel.

Moreover, even though women-related provisions in some agreements are not explicitly excluded from the agreement's dispute-settlement processes, provisions related to women are often barely enforceable given the permissiveness with which they are drafted, their location in the agreement, and the low-level precision of the language used. These discussions show that there is half-open door in FTAs that countries need to push further open in order to enforce their commitments to women's empowerment.[10] Some recent agreements have endeavoured to push that door open. The investment chapter of the EU–Canada FTA (CETA) features a binding provision that explicitly addresses concerns specific to women. Article 8.10(d) of the agreement states that a party will breach its obligation to provide fair and equitable treatment to foreign investors if any of its measures constitutes 'targeted discrimination on manifestly wrongful grounds, such as gender ...'.[11] The provision is binding as well as enforceable as it comes under the agreement's

[7] Amrita Bahri, 'Measuring the Gender-Responsiveness of Free Trade Agreements: Using a Self-Evaluation Maturity Framework' (2019) 14(11) Global Trade and Customs Journal 517.

[8] CIFTA, ch 13.

[9] ibid art 13.6.

[10] Amrita Bahri, 'Women at the Frontline of COVID-19: Can Gender Mainstreaming in Free Trade Agreements Help?' (2020) 23(3) Journal of International Economic Law 563.

[11] EU–Canada Comprehensive Economic and Trade Agreement (CETA) (in force 21 September 2017), art 8.10.

dispute-settlement jurisdiction. Such developments represent a drastic change in the trade policymaking mindset. Yet, provisions like this are an exception as very few agreements have so far included binding as well as enforceable obligations. Hence, to ensure that the women-related commitments included in trade agreements become a 'game-changer' for women in the future, it is crucial to rethink how these commitments might be enforced.

Another example is the North American Free Trade Agreement 2.0 (NAFTA 2.0) now known as USMCA in which the parties have assumed binding and enforceable commitments relating to the protection of labour rights and enhancing trade and investment opportunities for small businesses, including those owned by women.[12] One of these binding commitments concerns the elimination of discrimination based on sex in respect of employment, occupation, and wages. The other aspects are the consideration of women's issues related to occupational safety, health, and other workplace practices including the prevention of occupational injuries and illnesses and the prevention of workplace violence and harassment based on sex.[13] This agreement is a milestone in the treatment of enforceable women's issues included in its labour chapter; the provisions are made enforceable through the new Facility-Specific Rapid Response Labour Mechanism that allows the United States, Mexico, and Canada to directly take action against facilities with labour standard failures.[14] However, the problems with these inclusions, even though the chapter in which they are included is subject to the Rapid Response Mechanism, are that most of them are located in the subsection on cooperation (which may not be considered binding) and that the United States has added a disclaimer in the chapter specifying that its existing policies are sufficient to meet these requirements and thus no additional action on the part of the United States is required for compliance.[15]

8.4 Problem 3: Women Envisioned in Their Traditional Roles, Mostly as Employees or Mothers

The previous chapter's assessment of relevant provisions reflects the varied roles that existing trade agreements attribute to women. Broadly speaking, trade agreements have so far incorporated provisions that have sought to focus on six different roles of women. We can categorize these roles as follows: (1) women as representatives and decision-makers; (2) women as mothers; (3) women as employees;

[12] (Signed 17 December 1992; termination date 1 July 2020.) This has been replaced by the US–Mexico–Canada Agreement (in force 1 July 2020), arts 25.2 and 23.12.

[13] ibid art 23.9.

[14] ibid ch 23.

[15] ibid.

(4) women as business owners; (5) women's role in growth and development; and (6) women as social and cultural stakeholders.

Countries in some trade agreements seek to foster women's representation in decision-making and positions of authority in both public and private sectors, including on corporate boards and legislative assemblies.[16] In the treaty establishing the Common Market for Eastern and Southern Africa (COMESA), for example, through legislation and other measures, the parties in Articles 154 and 155 have pledged to increase women's participation in decision-making, eliminate regulations and customs that discriminate against women entrepreneurs and their access to resources, and adopt technology for the professional progress of women.[17] Another example is the Treaty for the Establishment of the East African Community (EAC Treaty)[18] in which the parties, in Article 50, seek to ensure a balance between men and women in the appointment of staff for the composition of institutions for the Community and in the election of the members of the East African legislative assembly.

There are some legal provisions in existing trade agreements that can help encourage women's business potential and their capacity to own, manage, and expand their businesses. In the EU–South Africa FTA, for example, the parties seek to enhance the market access of micro enterprises (MEs) and small and medium-sized enterprises (SMEs) in South Africa.[19] Through this provision, the parties also seek to promote 'cooperation between SMEs in the Community and those in South Africa and the region in a manner that is sensitive to gender equality'.[20] In particular, the parties seek to work on increasing SMEs' access to finance, skills training, technology, and marketing, providing them with appropriate technical support, and establishing appropriate channels to improve the flow of information relating to business trends and opportunities, market access opportunities, and joint ventures. Article 8.10 of the EU–Canada agreement, which focuses on investment protection, contains a binding obligation that prohibits sex-based discrimination against foreign investors.[21] This provision facilitates women's access to investment opportunities as it encourages women's businesses to engage in foreign investment without fear or uncertainty of being discriminated against based on their owners' sex. However, these agreements are more of an exception as the

[16] Olayinka Bandele, 'An Equal Seat at the Table: Gendering Trade Negotiations' (2016) International Trade Working Paper No 2016/14, Commonwealth Secretariat <https://doi.org/10.14217/5jm0qglb1s9s-en> accessed 12 May 2024.

[17] (In force 8 December 1994), arts 154 and 155.

[18] (In force 7 July 2000), ch 22, arts 50 and 121.

[19] Agreement on Trade, Development and Cooperation between the European Community and its Member States, of the one part, and the Republic of South Africa, of the other part (EU–South Africa) (in force 1 May 2004), Title IV Economic cooperation, art 54.

[20] ibid.

[21] Comprehensive Economic and Trade Agreement between Canada, of the one part, and the European Union, of the other part (in force 21 September 2017), art 8.10.

prevailing majority of trade agreements include commitments that treat women in their traditional roles as mothers, cultural actors, or employees.

Many agreements have sought to improve the working conditions of women and increase their participation in the labour force. Several countries, for example, have included commitments to promoting women's empowerment in the workplace and eliminating discrimination based on sex, pregnancy, sexual orientation, gender identity, and caregiving responsibilities concerning employment, occupation, and wages.[22] Others have sought to provide equal wages for women and men by applying the principle of equal pay for equal work in the same establishment and sought to develop cooperation activities for the prevention of workplace violence and harassment against women.[23] For example, in the EU trade agreements with Korea, Ukraine, and Vietnam, the parties have sought to promote labour practices that integrate and retain women in the job market and build the capacity and skills of women workers, including on workplace challenges and in collective bargaining.[24] In these different forms, the majority of provisions that are vocal about women's concerns are incorporated as labour standards.

Countries in the Asia Pacific region have frequently opted to focus on women as mothers and child carers as they have negotiated provisions on eliminating discrimination in the workplace based on pregnancy and caregiving in respect of employment, occupation and wages, and reserving the right to maintain or adopt measures relating to social services for childcare, maternity, and services provided by midwives.[25] Countries in the Middle East have also sought to bolster and develop their countries' family planning and mother and child protection programmes through provisions drafted as minimum legal standards.[26] Childcare is a frequently found topic in existing trade agreements. Some trade agreements, such as the Australia–New Zealand Closer Economic Relations Trade Agreement

[22] USMCA (n 12) art 23.12; Canada–Jordan FTA (in force 1 October 2012), art 1.

[23] Dominican Republic–Central America–United States FTA (in force 1 March 2006), Annex 16.5; United States–Colombia Trade Promotion Agreement (in force 15 May 2012), Annex 17.6; United States–Peru FTA (in force 1 February 2009), Annex 17.6.

[24] FTA between the European Union and its Member States, of the one part, and the Republic of Korea, of the other part (in force 1 July 2011), ch 13 Trade and Sustainable Development, art 13.4; Association Agreement between the European Union and the European Atomic Energy Community and their Member States, of the One Part, and Ukraine, of the Other Part (in force 1 September 2017), Title IV Trade and Trade-Related Matters, ch 13 Trade and sustainable development, art 291; FTA between the European Union and the Socialist Republic of Viet Nam (in force 1 August 2020), ch 13 Trade and Sustainable Development, art 13.4.

[25] Euro-Mediterranean Agreement establishing an association between the European Communities and their Member States, of the one part, and the Republic of Tunisia, of the other part (in force 30 March 1998), Title VI Cooperation in social and cultural matters, ch 3 Cooperation in the social field, art 65; FTA between New Zealand and the Republic of Korea (in force 20 December 2015), Annex II.

[26] Euro-Mediterranean Agreement establishing an association between the European Communities and their Member States and the Hashemite Kingdom of Jordan (in force 1 May 2002), Title VI Cooperation in social and cultural matters, ch 2 Social cooperation actions, art 82.

(ANZCERTA),[27] the Peru–South Korea FTA,[28] and the South Korea–Central America FTA[29] contain explicit rights to regulate provisions relating to childcare. In Annex II of ANZCERTA, for example, New Zealand reserves the right to regulate certain social services including childcare. Childcare challenges pose a significant barrier to work, especially for mothers who disproportionately take on unpaid responsibilities when they cannot find affordable childcare.[30] The availability of affordable childcare facilities is crucial as the lack of such facilities often hinders women from advancing in their careers or pursuing their educational goals. This right-to-regulate provision, drafted in the form of a policy carve-out, seems to be a women-favouring commitment as it indicates that the liberalization of services under a given FTA will not affect its parties' right to regulate and provide for childcare services in its respective jurisdiction. Protection of maternity concerns can also enable women to participate in economic opportunities as it can help them delegate some of their household responsibilities and allocate that time to employment or business activities. However, these examples show that several provisions are limited to women's concerns as mothers or child caretakers.

Some agreements, such as the ones between the EU and Central America, seek to strengthen dialogue and awareness in communities on promoting women's empowerment and various other social issues and promote public knowledge of laws and practices supporting women's equality. In other agreements, such as COMESA and the EAC Treaty, countries seek to promote effective awareness programmes aimed at changing negative attitudes and stereotyping of women.[31] Countries in some agreements have also sought to construct policies to combat domestic violence against women and protect their physical safety.[32] These examples and these focus areas heavily dominate the current inclusion of women in trade agreements. These interests are vital and at the forefront of the protection of basic human rights, yet significant emphasis on these interests limits trade agreements to largely focus on women in their roles as mothers, employees, cultural actors, or social actors and not on their roles as entrepreneurs or decision-makers.[33]

[27] (In force 1 January 1983.)

[28] (In force 1 August 2011.)

[29] FTA between the Republic of Korea and the Republics of Central America (in force 1 October 2019).

[30] Kim Parker, 'Women more than men adjust their careers for family life' (Pew Research Center 1 October 2015) <www.pewresearch.org/fact-tank/2015/10/01/women-more-than-men-adjust-their-careers-for-family-life/> accessed 28 October 2023.

[31] COMESA (n 17); EAC Treaty (n 18).

[32] Agreement on Trade in Goods Under the Framework Agreement on Comprehensive Economic Cooperation Among the Governments of the Member Countries of the Association of Southeast Asian Nations and the Republic of Korea (in force 1 January 2010), Appendix; FTA between the Republic of Korea and the Republics of Central America (in force 1 October 2019), Annex I Schedule of Costa Rica.

[33] Caroline Dommen, 'Mainstreaming Gender in Trade Policy: Practice, evidence, and ways forward' (International Institute of Sustainable Development (IISD) November 2021), 11 <www.iisd.org/system/files/2021-11/mainstreaming-gender-in-trade-policy.pdf> accessed 29 October 2023.

8.5 Problem 4: Lack of Definitions

Except for the EAC Treaty, which offers a basic definition of 'gender', trade agreements generally lack explicit definitions for 'gender equality' and 'women empowerment'.[34] To date, no international organization has established a universally accepted definition of 'gender equality' or 'women empowerment' for global consideration. This absence of standardized definitions for these fundamental concepts is not a new issue within the realm of international trade law. Various other important concepts remain undefined in international trade agreements, in particular, in the agreements of the World Trade Organization (WTO). Three such examples are the lack of definition for crucial terms used frequently in those agreements, such as 'developing countries',[35] 'like products',[36] and 'national security exception'.[37] Another example is that of the 'public morality' exception as it also lacks a universally accepted definition. Scholars have raised concerns about the overbroad nature of the public morality exception that could provide a cloak for protectionism.[38] Likewise, as observed in Chapter 5, a women-related legal provision could impose a significant cost in terms of national sovereignty as it can allow other countries to interfere in the domestic affairs of a nation and place limits on its ability to manage matters related to its social, political, economic, cultural, and even religious affairs. The principal concern is the extent to which such an exception to an interpretation can allow countries to stretch the scope of women-related provisions beyond women's concerns, hence invoking protectionist fears. As seen in Chapter 5, an attempt to address women empowerment concerns may also be seen as a protectionist weapon for countries to take advantage of unequal market power or indirectly use those concerns to diminish other countries' comparative advantage by exporting their own social or cultural model to those countries with different sets of values and concerns. The fears of cultural imperialism and the use

[34] (n 18) art 1(1).

[35] See eg the General Agreement on Tariffs and Trade (GATT 1994), art XVIII and the Enabling Clause officially called the Decision on Differential and More Favourable Treatment, Reciprocity and Fuller Participation of Developing Countries. For details, see Aniekan Ukpe and Sangeeta Khorana, 'Special and Differential Treatment in the WTO: Framing Differential Treatment to Achieve (Real) Development' (2021) 20(2) Journal of International Trade Law and Policy 83.

[36] See eg GATT 1994, arts I and III. For details, see Won-Mog Choi, *Like Products in International Trade Law: Towards a Consistent GATT/WTO Jurisprudence* (OUP 2003).

[37] See eg GATT 1994, art XXI. For more details, see Daria Boklan and Amrita Bahri, 'The First WTO's Ruling on National Security Exception: Balancing Interests or Opening Pandora's Box?' (2020) 19(1) World Trade Review 123.

[38] Pelin Serpin, 'The Public Morals Exception after the WTO Seal Products Dispute: Has the Exception Swallowed the Rules?' (2016) 1 Columbia Business Law Review 219 (the author observes how this protectionist tool can undermine the progress made towards trade liberalization and agreements over the past few decades); WTO Appellate Body Report, *United States—Measures Affecting the Cross-Border Supply of Gambling and Betting Services* (signed 7 April 2005, adopted 20 April 2005) WTO doc WT/DS285/AB/R <www.wto.org/english/tratop_e/dispu_e/cases_e/ds285_e.htm> (This has left open the fundamental issue of what values or interests qualify as public morals and whether a state can unilaterally define its own public morals.)

of standards for the protection of domestic industries are, as previously discussed, the main concerns that several countries have voiced when they have resisted or opposed any development in respect of trade and women, such as with the signing of the WTO's Joint Declaration on Women and Trade.[39] Given these concerns, countries need to agree on a universal definition of 'women empowerment' or 'gender equality' and then incorporate that definitional agreement by reference in the text of their trade agreements.

8.6 Problem 5: Lack of Implementation Mechanisms or Procedures

Thus far, almost no FTA contemplates how women-related commitments can be implemented. As of today, even the most advanced FTAs in respect of women's concerns do not clarify precise procedures for the implementation of women-related commitments nor do they identify channels to finance those activities.[40] To ensure that trade agreements and policies work to create an inclusive trade environment, they need to be drafted with a responsive approach towards women's concerns; a responsive approach to women calls for the inclusion of commitments that go well beyond symbolic promises which are not meant or designed to be acted upon.

Most provisions are currently included without any associated provisions or clarification of how they might be implemented, financed, or monitored. With the majority of such inclusions, where no associated clarification is provided, it can be inferred that such provisions are considered to be under the supervision of the general monitoring institution of the agreement. There are some recent exceptions to this prevailing trend as some agreements have provided for the establishment of a 'technical body on trade and gender' that is solely responsible for overseeing the implementation of those provisions and monitoring their impact.[41] This body is usually composed of government representatives and its primary function is to coordinate and foster cooperation rather than conduct in-depth monitoring and evaluation activities on the impact of the provisions. One example is the Chile–Uruguay FTA, which provides for the creation of a gender committee.[42]

[39] Roberto Bissio, 'Is "Gender" a Trojan Horse to Introduce New Issues at WTO?' (Third World Network 11 December 2017) <https://twnetwork.org/wto/%E2%80%9Cgender%E2%80%9D-trojan-horse-introduce-new-issues-wto> accessed 12 November 2021.

[40] As per the author's calculations, using the ITC maturity toolkit: 'Mainstreaming Gender in Free Trade Agreements' (8 July 2020) www.intracen.org/publication/mainstreaming-gender-FTA/> accessed 12 November 2021.

[41] Lolita Laperle-Forget, 'WTO Database on Gender Provisions in RTAs' (WTO 2022) <www.wto.org/english/tratop_e/womenandtrade_e/gender_responsive_trade_agreement_db_e.htm> accessed 28 October 2023 (which maps 252 gender provisions under the supervision of a monitoring institution. Among others, 94 are under the supervision of the institution in charge of the whole agreement, 50 under a technical cooperation body, and 36 under a technical body on trade and gender (eg the Canada–Chile FTA establishes the Trade and Gender Committee (art N *bis*-04) and the UK–Japan FTA establishes the Working Group on Trade and Women's Economic Empowerment (art 21.3)).

[42] (In force 13 December 2018), art 14.4.

It establishes that the committee is to be composed of representatives from government institutions responsible for the relevant gender and trade matters from each concerned party. However, what is still missing in most of these attempts is an effort to clarify how such an institutional mechanism would work. Therefore, it would be advantageous to delineate the detailed functions, milestones, and objectives expected to be achieved along with timelines for accomplishing such milestones and the actors who will constitute such units or divisions. Such a provision is more of an exception, as most of the current commitments in this respect are assumed without the parties having given any thought in the agreement's text to how such commitments might be implemented or monitored. In addition, the currently created dedicated bodies do not benefit from different perspectives and insights as their members are usually government officials.

Going forward, future trade negotiators could consider establishing a technical body on trade and women, composed not only of party representatives but also of external stakeholders that can take up the monitoring and review exercise. Trade negotiations in this respect could also benefit from a wider exchange between the public and private stakeholders. Trade negotiators are often not aware of the specific barriers faced by women in their various economic roles and, as a result, they can face challenges in promoting provisions that can successfully address those barriers. In addition, private industries and companies are generally the key beneficiaries and victims of international trade policies and hence some form of public–private coordination in the conduct of trade negotiations is embedded in the very nature of such agreements.[43] For these reasons and more, efforts are needed to create a channel of communication between public and private stakeholders before, during, and after negotiations.

Moreover, if provisions on women empowerment are meant to be acted upon, parties need to consider and clarify different aspects of implementation which include but may not be limited to the procedures for implementation, the stakeholders responsible for the implementation, the timelines and benchmarks, the possibility to monitor the implementation and impact of such commitments, and the mobilization of resources that might be required for such implementation or monitoring. This institutional set-up also requires an associated set of procedures that the responsible actors can use to implement the commitments. To operationalize the institutional and procedural set-ups, it is important to identify funding arrangements that can finance gender-related activities and ways to mobilize the other resources that are required for the envisioned tasks. As of today, none of the FTAs assessed clarify this aspect of funding and resource mobilization. This

[43] Hyun-jung Je, 'Public–Private Relationships in Trade Policy-Making' (2018) World Scientific 81; Amrita Bahri and Nadia Hasham, 'Trade negotiation dialogue and capacity building: applying the PXA Framework' (WTO 1 September 2023) 255 <https://wtochairs.org/mexico/research/trade-negotiation-dialogue-and-capacity-building-applying-pxa-framework-world-trade> accessed 12 May 2024.

becomes a crucial challenge, mainly for developing countries that may not have the resources that are required to implement the commitments they might have assumed in this context.

8.7 Problem 6: The Whole-of-the-Agreement Approach is Missing

When we turn to the location and nature of these provisions, we find that they are generally located in sections on objectives, general principles, or cooperation-based activities and they are largely absent from the substantive provisions or chapters, such as those on market access, technical barriers to trade, investment, digital trade, trade facilitation, government procurement, or cross-border trade in services.

It is important to note that the location of explicit women-focused provisions varies significantly across agreements. While some agreements integrate these provisions directly into their main text, others relegate them to side agreements, annexes, or protocols. Those that include them in the main text typically position them in the preamble, objectives, general principles clause, or in cooperation-based chapters of their operative sections, in areas such as social and cultural development and sustainable development. Some countries have also placed them in dedicated trade and women chapters in the agreement's main text. Moreover, some countries have preferred to negotiate side instruments alongside or subsequent to the negotiation of the main agreement.[44] However, it is important to consider that stand-alone chapters or side instruments, by virtue of their nature, do not carve out any positive commitment for women in substantive areas of international trade. With few exceptions, agreements have so far not included explicit cross-cutting commitments directly related to market access, for example those on increasing women businesses' market access to lucrative and booming industries such as textiles and apparel, manufacturing, financial services, and cross-border trade in services. This seems to be a significant omission as cross-cutting provisions with explicit commitments relating to women can make some inroads for women's businesses in various sectors and markets.

Women play various roles in international trade and, accordingly, face different kinds of barriers. It is therefore important that trade negotiations consider women's role and their barriers with a multifaceted approach. A 'whole-of-the-agreement approach' to including such commitments can support more inclusive outcomes and address more effectively the barriers that women face in accessing

[44] Global Affairs Canada, 'CETA Trade and Gender Recommendation: EU–Canada Work Plan 2020–2021' (Government of Canada 2020) <www.international.gc.ca/trade-commerce/trade-agreements-accords-commerciaux/agr-acc/ceta-aecg/CETA_work_plan-AECG_plan_travail-2020-2021.aspx?lang=eng> accessed 29 October 2023.

international trade opportunities. To achieve this, trade negotiations in the future can employ a sectoral approach to the inclusion of such commitments.[45] However, for this approach to work, it will be important for policymakers to identify the structural barriers to women's empowerment and inequalities that impact women in their multiple economic roles and, more specifically, in the individual sectors of trade.

8.8 Problem 7: Disconnect between Barriers and Policy Solutions

Despite advancements and lofty goals, which were discussed in detail in the previous chapters, long-standing distributional issues remain unaddressed in the current inclusion of women-related provisions.[46] As shown in the previous subsections, trade agreements have so far covered a wide range of concerns but those provisions have (with very few exceptions) focused on women mainly as employees or social and cultural actors and not on their roles as entrepreneurs or decision-makers. In addition, the current inclusions have not covered issues that directly relate to the barriers exacerbated by international trade. In other words, there is a disconnect between the barriers that have been exacerbated by the distributive impacts of trade liberalization and the policy solutions currently offered in trade agreements. The barriers that are left largely unaddressed in existing trade agreements are those that relate to women's access to finance, access to productive resources, access to e-commerce and digital trade opportunities, and their effective participation in opportunities offered by international trade.[47]

Women tend to be disproportionately impacted by the negative effects of trade liberalization and face greater barriers when engaging in economic activity. Some of this is due to bias against women in education and training, along with inequality in wages, distribution of resources, and unequal access to productive inputs such as credit, land, and technology.[48] Because of the changing dynamics of employment and businesses caused by trade, women's jobs, businesses, and livelihoods

[45] Nadira Bayat, 'A Whole Agreement Approach to Gender Mainstreaming in the AfCFTA: Forging a New Path in Post-COVID Response and Recovery' (UNCTAD April 2022) <https://elearning.unctad.org/pluginfile.php/34245/mod_page/content/10/Nadira%20Bayat_Presentation_5%20April_Randa_Final.pdf> accessed 29 October 2023.

[46] Jakob Engel and others, 'The Distributional Impacts of Trade: Empirical Innovations, Analytical Tools, and Policy Responses' (The World Bank 2021) <https://documents1.worldbank.org/curated/en/976331621501704900/pdf/The-Distributional-Impacts-of-Trade-Empirical-Innovations-Analytical-Tools-and-Policy-Responses.pdf> accessed 29 October 2023.

[47] This idea was initially discussed in Katrin Kuhlmann and Amrita Bahri, 'Gender Mainstreaming in Trade Agreements: "A Potemkin Façade"?' in *Making Trade Work for Women: Key Findings from the 2022 World Trade Congress on Gender* (WTO 2023) 235 <https://doi.org/10.30875/9789287042712> accessed 12 May 2024.

[48] International Trade Centre, *Unlocking Markets for Women to Trade* (2015) <https://intracen.org/file/womenintradeweb1pdf> accessed 29 October 2023.

can be put at risk, especially when industries that predominantly employ women are disrupted. In particular, women face many challenges due to the uncertain and precarious nature of their work, the lack of social safety nets and affordable finance and credit, inadequate physical and reputational collateral, and their role in unpaid and informal work.[49]

Moreover, although digital trade has given rise to new opportunities for women, they are also particularly affected by the digital divide[50] which, when combined with legal issues, impacts women's ability to leverage new opportunities offered by digital trade or e-commerce. Women also face several regulatory barriers (or 'regulatory gateways')[51] that limit their participation in markets. These include domestic rules and regulations that fall within the category of non-tariff measures, for example sanitary and phytosanitary (SPS) measures, standards, and border measures, many of which are not responsive to women's issues. In terms of border measures, women traders continue to face procedural challenges and safety issues at the border,[52] although the implementation of the WTO's Trade Facilitation Agreement[53] has simplified measures and encouraged digitalization of border procedures. Women traders also often lack information on cross-border regulations and procedures,[54] putting them at a disadvantage and subjecting them to costly and sometimes dangerous delays at border crossings. These barriers, or their acknowledgement, remain visibly missing from the current trade agreements as the relevant provisions have, with very few exceptions, largely ignored such concerns.

Distributional challenges are not only limited to trade in goods as they also include discriminatory practices in services sectors where women tend to be heavily

[49] UNCTAD, 'Impact of the COVID-19 Pandemic on Trade and Development: Transitioning to a New Normal' (United Nations Conference on Trade and Development, 2020) <https://unctad.org/system/files/official-document/osg2020d1_en.pdf> accessed 29 October 2023.

[50] AfCFTA Secretariat and United Nations Development Programme (UNDP), 'The Futures Report: Making the AfCFTA Work for Women and Youth' (3 December 2020) <www.undp.org/africa/publications/futures-report-making-afcfta-work-women-and-youth> accessed 29 October 2023.

[51] Katrin Kuhlmann, 'Mapping Inclusive Law and Regulation: A Comparative Agenda for Trade and Development' (2021) 2 African Journal of International Economic 48. ('Legal and regulatory gateways' are the decision points and hurdles contained within a legal or regulatory process (licence, registration or permit, for example) that 'correspond with practical steps that enterprises and other stakeholders encounter in navigating a particular aspect of the legal and regulatory system.' They also 'signify intervention points to make the rules more equitable, inclusive and efficient'.)

[52] Philomena Apiko, Sean Woolfrey, and Bruce Byiers, 'The promise of the African Continental Free Trade Area (AfCFTA)' (December 2020) European Centre for Development Policy Management (ECDPM) Discussion Paper No 287 <https://ecdpm.org/application/files/3116/5546/8595/Promise-African-Continental-Free-Trade-Area-AfCFTA-ECDPM-Discussion-Paper-287-December-2020.pdf> accessed 12 May 2024.

[53] Protocol Amending the Marrakesh Agreement Establishing the World Trade Organization (28 November 2014) WTO doc WT/L/940.

[54] Taku Fundira, 'Informal Cross-border Trading: Review of the Simplified Trade Regimes in East and Southern Africa' (March 2018) Tralac Trade Brief No US18TB03/2018 <www.tralac.org/documents/publications/trade-briefs/2018-1/1816-us18tb032018-fundira-informal-cross-border-trading-review-of-simplified-trade-regimes-esa-08032018-fin/file.html> accessed 12 May 2024.

involved.[55] The services sector has increasingly become a focal point in global trade, offering new avenues for economic growth and development. Notably, women constitute a significant portion of the workforce in this sector. However, they continue to face numerous challenges that limit their full participation and benefits from trade in services. Yet trade agreements have failed to address or include provisions that can deal with the barriers that impede women's access to trade in services. The digital revolution presents a plethora of opportunities for women in the services sector, particularly in overcoming their traditional trade barriers. Online platforms and digital marketplaces have democratized access to international markets, allowing women entrepreneurs to showcase their services to a global audience without the need for intermediaries or substantial capital investment. Yet current agreements remain silent on how trade can help women leverage such opportunities.

Women are also disproportionately involved in the informal sector, which, while sometimes more flexible, may offer little security and room for advancement.[56] Within the informal sector, migrant women face some of the most significant challenges as the Covid-19 pandemic has underscored.[57] However, the women-focused discourse in FTAs has largely been confined to formal sectors of the economy, thereby overlooking a significant portion of women who are engaged in informal employment. This omission is particularly glaring given the disproportionately high representation of women in the informal sector, especially in developing economies. In South Asia, for instance, over 80% of women in non-agricultural jobs are informally employed; the figure stands at 74% in Sub-Saharan Africa and 54% in Latin America and the Caribbean.[58] The informal sector, often referred to as the 'grey economy', presents a myriad of challenges for women. These range from the absence of labour law protections and social benefits, such as pensions and health insurance, to unsafe working conditions and vulnerability to sexual harassment. The ramifications of this lack of social protection are long term and deeply entrenched. Given this context, FTAs must extend their scope beyond the formal sectors and address the unique challenges faced by women in the informal economy.

These examples reflect a disconnection between the barriers women face and the solutions that the current FTAs offer through their provisions. Moreover, important concerns and aspects remain weakly integrated into current FTAs. All of

[55] Viral V Acharya and others, 'Whatever It Takes: The Real Effects of Unconventional Monetary Policy' (2019) 32(9) The Review of Financial Studies 3366.

[56] UN Women, 'Progress of the World's Women 2015–2016: Transforming economies, realizing rights' (2015) <www.unwomen.org/en/digital-library/publications/2015/4/progress-of-the-worlds-women-2015> accessed 29 October 2023.

[57] Joan Fitzpatrick and Katrina R Kelly, 'Gendered Aspects of Migration: Law and the Female Migrant' (1998) 22(1) Hastings International and Comparative Law Review 47.

[58] UN Women, 'Women in informal economy' <www.unwomen.org/en/news/in-focus/csw61/women-in-informal-economy> accessed 29 October 2023.

these aspects speak to and raise questions on whether FTAs adequately incorporate equity and inclusion, particularly to address distributional issues and promote women's economic opportunities, enhanced skills, entrepreneurship, access to finance, and bridging the digital divide, among others.

8.9 Problem 8: Lack of Innovation and Use of Previous Templates

One important reason for the disconnection between barriers and policy solutions is perhaps the lack of innovation in the inclusion of women-related provisions. This is mainly because the current inclusions are in most cases based on the common practice of copying and pasting provisions from previously negotiated agreements without any attempt to adapt them to the countries' and stakeholders' unique needs. This is predominantly the case for developed countries as they negotiate such provisions with a predetermined template possibly used in their previous negotiations. Generally, these templates are designed by and for the developed world, spearheaded by the EU, the UK, Canada, and the United States.[59] Hence, many provisions focused on women are deliberately copied from previous agreements.[60] Studies have found that at least 100 FTAs take 80% or more of their content—word for word—from existing agreements.[61] Furthermore, it is important to note that both developed countries (with significant negotiation capacity) and developing countries (with limited negotiation capacity) copy and paste quite extensively as governments with low negotiation capacity search for existing templates and countries with high negotiation capacity repeatedly push for their templates and preferred language.

Copying provisions from existing agreements is beneficial for a number of reasons as it reduces the costs of bargaining, has a lower compliance cost and higher probability of compliance as those commitments have already been agreed to in a different agreement, and, finally, it reduces the challenges of arriving at domestic consensus over specific issues that may require changing domestic laws and procedures. It also means that the cost of negotiation is lower as the clause is adapted from an earlier agreement and the substantive costs are also lower since the concession has already been made on a previous occasion. Countries additionally tend to develop certain templates for agreements and provisions over a number of years for the sake of convenience and familiarity.[62]

[59] Leonardo Baccini, Andreas Dür, and Yoram Z Haftel, 'Imitation and Innovation in International Governance: The Diffusion of Trade Agreement Design' in Andreas Dür and Manfred Elsig (eds), *Trade cooperation: The Purpose, Design, and Effects of Preferential Trade Agreements* (CUP 2015) 167.

[60] Todd Allee and Manfred Elsig, 'Are the Contents of International Treaties Copied and Pasted? Evidence from Preferential Trade Agreements' (12 July 2019) 63(3) International Studies Quarterly 603.

[61] ibid.

[62] Lisa Lechner, 'The Domestic Battle over the Design of Non-Trade Issues in Preferential Trade Agreements' (2016) 23(5) Review of International Political Economy 840.

Another benefit of this approach is that it can drive a process of change, where a partner country may try to imitate the approach of its other trade partner countries in respect of certain issues they do not fully comprehend or on which they have no expertise.

However, using a different template can motivate a government to add issues it has traditionally not included in its trade agreements or within the scope of its trade policy agenda.[63] The main downside of this 'copy and paste' approach is that it reduces innovation and makes the inclusion of new issues or policy solutions more difficult. The repetition and copying practices of such provisions not only involve women-related provisions but are also found in provisions related to other social concerns, such as disability inclusion or labour standards. These practices obstruct innovation in the negotiation and inclusion of more ambitious commitments that can effectively help marginalized groups overcome their barriers. A recent study[64] has shown that this practice is very much prevalent in the provisions on disability inclusion as countries have most commonly opted for replicating and copying the North American Free Trade Agreement's (NAFTA's) minimal disability provision which was borrowed from the WTO Agreement on Government Procurement (GPA)—a provision that places no further responsibilities on the assuming states and does not create any affirmative commitment in any respect.[65] The same can be said for women-explicit provisions as the majority of trade agreements have included such provisions in the form of labour standards or as cooperation-based provisions. Some new-generation trade agreements, such as the Canada–Chile FTA (CCFTA)[66] and the Canada–Israel FTA (CIFTA),[67] feature stand-alone chapters on trade and gender that are drafted with very similar provisions, structures, and scope. Other examples of such repetitions are found in general provisions, reaffirmations, and cooperation-styled affirmations in the Argentina–Chile, Chile–Brazil, Chile–Ecuador, Canada–Jordan, and Canada–Peru agreements.[68] The underlying basis of such inclusions in these agreements includes repetition of statements on the importance of enhancing opportunities for women in the domestic and global economy, affirmations on cooperation activities

[63] Karolina Milewicz, James Hollway, and Duncan Snidal, 'Beyond Trade: The Expanding Scope of the Non-Trade Agenda in Trade Agreements' (2018) 62(4) Journal of Conflict Resolution 743.

[64] Amrita Bahri, 'Trade Agreements and Disability Inclusion: Demystifying the Disconnect between Barriers and Policy Solutions' (2023) United Kingdom Foreign, Commonwealth and Development Office and Cowater International Inc.

[65] Agreement on Government Procurement, Marrakesh Agreement Establishing the World Trade Organization (15 April 1994) 1915 UNTS 103, Annex 4(b).

[66] Articles N *bis*-02, N *bis*-03, and N *bis*-04.

[67] Articles 13.2, 13.3, and 13.4.

[68] FTA between Argentina and Chile (in force 1 May 2019) arts 15.1, 15.2, and 15.3; FTA between Brazil and Chile (in force 25 January 2022), ch 18, arts 18.1, 18.2, and 18.3; Economic Complementation Agreement between Chile and Ecuador (in force 25 January 2010), ch 18, arts 18.1, 18.3, and 18.4; Canada–Jordan FTA (in force 1 October 2012), Annex 1, art 1(K); Canada–Peru FTA (in force 1 August 2009), Annex 1, art 9 (K); Canada–Panama FTA (in force 1 April 2013), Appendix 1, art 1(J).

aimed at improving the access of women to markets, and developing women's leadership and business networks.[69]

The frequent repetition of templated provisions within FTAs, especially those addressing concerns of marginalized communities, raises significant doubts about the efficacy of international trade policies in championing the causes of those who are traditionally overlooked, such as women. Despite advancements in recognizing and articulating the need to empower women within the trade policy context, the translation of theoretical acknowledgements or affirmations into actionable commitments and negotiations of barrier-responding policy solutions remains a looming challenge. The reluctance for change or to try out new provisions in this respect not only stifles progression towards a more inclusive trade environment but also critically undermines the depth and impact of dialogue between the public and private sectors. Hence, the practice of using a pre-used template reduces the motivation of policymakers to investigate the actual problems that marginalized groups in their jurisdictions face and engage in discussions with them as that would require them to look beyond their current templates. It is against this backdrop that the need for a strategic overhaul emerges, propelling nations towards drafting policies that are reflective of the actual challenges faced by women in the multifaceted arena of international trade.

8.10 Conclusion

The problems discussed in this chapter show that the current inclusion of women-related provisions in trade agreements is not sufficiently revolutionary and a lot more remains to be done. Moving forward will not be easy and, as usual, the devil lies in the detail of the viability and implementation potential of current inclusions. Progress on this matter will require a change of mindset, enhanced understanding, and the will to experiment with new methods and provisions on the part of trade negotiators. The following chapter proposes some policy recommendations that trade negotiators can consider in respect of negotiating women-related provisions in future trade agreements.

[69] Amrita Bahri, 'Gender Mainstreaming in Trade Agreements: Best Practice Examples and Challenges in the Asia-Pacific' in Amrita Bahri, Dorotea López, and Jan Remy (eds), *Trade Policy and Gender Equality* (CUP 2023).

9

The Pentagon Roadmap for Trade and Gender Negotiations

Five-Dimensional Policy Recommendations

9.1 Introduction

This chapter presents a set of recommendations aimed at enhancing the integration of women's concerns into future trade negotiations to make them more meaningful and effective. These recommendations are adaptable to the diverse political, economic, social, and legal contexts of different countries. The primary short-term objective is to equip policymakers and trade negotiators with recommendations on negotiating women-related concerns in trade agreements. The long-term objective is to ensure that trade agreements foster an environment conducive to women's empowerment, thus making women-related considerations a fundamental aspect of trade policy instruments.

The proposed 'Pentagon Roadmap', as shown in Figure 9.1, is structured in five distinct dimensions, each addressing critical facets of trade agreements that can be leveraged to support women's empowerment.

9.2 Dimension I: Resolve Drafting Dilemma

Dimension I of the Pentagon Roadmap addresses the complexities of legal drafting in trade agreements. It aims to guide policymakers through the drafting challenges they face, including the use of clear, precise, and inclusive language; the choice between aspirational and obligatory terms; the definition of gender-related terms; and the balance between rigid and flexible legal language. It also emphasizes the importance of cultural sensitivity and simplicity in crafting provisions that effectively reflect diverse needs.

9.2.1 Know the decisive parameters: best endeavour or binding provisions?

With the help of five proposed parameters, this recommendation can help trade policymakers determine whether they should draft a given commitment as a best

Trade Agreements and Women. Amrita Bahri, Oxford University Press. © Amrita Bahri 2025.
DOI: 10.1093/9780198935759.003.0010

Pentagon Roadmap for Trade and Gender Negotiations

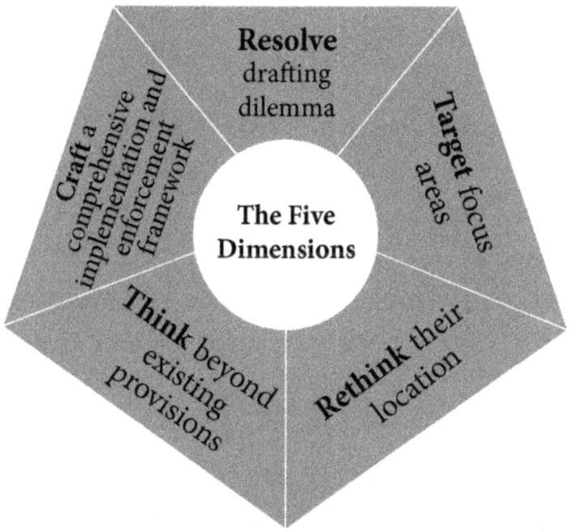

Dimension I: Resolve Drafting Dilemma

01 Know the decisive parameters: Best endeavour or binding provisions?

02 Decide and define: Gender equality or gender equity?

03 Prefer precision and clarity but consider flexibility as well.

04 Evaluate drafting options: hard, soft, or a mix and match of hard and soft.

05 Use culturally sensitive and plain language.

Dimension II: Target Focus Areas

01 Provide support for women entrepreneurs.

02 Include commitments on access to productive resources.

03 Protect women's access to health care.

04 Increase representation of women in international trade.

05 Include commitments on access to education, skill development, and technology.

Dimension III: Rethink Their Location

01 Frontload women concerns in the agreement's preamble.

02 Utilize objectives clause and set clear objectives.

03 Negotiate a stand-alone chapter on trade and women.

04 Assess negotiating options for follow-up or supplementary policy instruments.

05 Consider a whole-of-the-agreement approach with cross-cutting provisions.

Dimension IV: Think Beyond Existing Provisions

01 Include reservations and waivers to positively discriminate in favour of women.

02 Consider commitments on voluntary sustainability standards.

03 Craft an explicit exception for women or employ existing public morality exception.

04 Spell-out the cooperation-styled affirmations and keep them realistic.

05 Collaborate on study, research, or publication relating to women and trade.

Dimension V: Craft a Comprehensive Implementation and Enforcement Framework

01 Create institutions and procedures, and spell out their operations.

02 Mobilize resources for funding and engage private stakeholders.

03 Provide for monitoring, review, and impact assessment.

04 Identify transparency and accountability mechanisms.

05 Consider soft enforcement through consultation and non-punitive remedies.

Figure 9.1 The proposed framework of policy recommendations
Source: Author's work.

endeavour or a binding provision. The five parameters proposed in this chapter relate to implementation complexity vs value of the provision. The 'value' parameter depends on the anticipated short-term and long-term strategic benefits and the commitment's importance determined in light of the relevant barriers that women in a given country face. The four factors relating to 'implementation complexity' depend on several interdependent and interconnected factors, including the resources required to implement a given provision, the compliance cost of implementing that provision, the political readiness and level of agreement that member countries to that trade agreement have in relation to the relevant commitment under consideration, and the risks associated with the adoption of a given provision as a binding and enforceable commitment. The five parameters are explained in the following sections.

9.2.1.1 Resources required

The resources required to implement a given provision can impact and shape the drafting of that provision. This parameter includes every single resource that is needed to implement that commitment including finances, human resources, expertise and understanding, institutional set-up, information, and relevant data.[1] Some commitments are less resource-demanding than others and so may be more readily accepted as binding commitments. One such commitment is where the parties to an agreement commit to encourage their businesses to adopt women-centric corporate social responsibilities and provide flexible working arrangements for women workers. In this commitment, the government does not face any resource complications as it delegates the investment of resources to its business stakeholders. Another low-cost provision could relate to the parties' commitment to comply with the obligations they have assumed under the United Nations Sustainable Development Goals (UN SDG) 2030 Framework. The resources required to implement this commitment may be quite significant but this is a commitment the parties have already assumed therefore the inclusion of another provision in a trade agreement would not impose any additional demand on resources.

An example of a more resource-demanding commitment would be when parties commit to offering financial benefits to businesses owned by women in the form of subsidies and bailouts during crisis situations. With such a commitment, countries assume a responsibility to dedicate a significant portion of their revenue to strengthening women's entrepreneurship and thus assume a direct financial obligation. Another high-cost implication provision would be where the parties seek to enhance women's access to digital learning and infrastructure. Governments implementing such a commitment will need to invest considerable resources in providing training and skill development opportunities for women, subsidized smart phones or tablets, internet access for women, helping women entrepreneurs design their e-commerce web portals, and other related benefits.

[1] Based on interviews the author carried out with multiple trade negotiators (online, details withheld, on file with the author).

9.2.1.2 Compliance cost (legal, social, cultural, and economic)

A binding provision related to women's concerns could impose a significant cost on nations in terms of their sovereignty as it could allow countries to interfere in the domestic affairs of other countries and place limits on their ability to deal with matters relating to their own legal, social, political, economic, cultural, and even religious affairs.[2] However, this cost would vary due to several factors, including a country's domestic conditions.

Countries' willingness and appetite for binding provisions may rely heavily on their domestic conditions as countries may not be willing to assume binding commitments that contain obligations with which they cannot comply.[3] Hence, in respect of such commitments, countries could consider engaging in cooperation efforts and drafting provisions using permissive language especially for commitments that require a significant departure from their domestic laws, policies, conditions, and practices or those that require countries to act differently than they would otherwise do. Hence, the cost of compliance should be fundamental to a country's determination of whether to draft a particular commitment as a best endeavour or a binding obligation. The more a country's practices and policies align with universally accepted norms on women's empowerment and equality, the more likely that country is to accept those commitments as binding provisions. Countries with practices and policies that do not discourage inequality between women and men and do not adhere to commonly accepted norms (eg the elimination of discrimination based on sex) might be more inclined to negotiate such commitments as best endeavour provisions.[4]

9.2.1.3 Political readiness and level of agreement

The lack of political will to leverage trade agreements to empower women is one of the key factors that can keep policymakers away from considering language that is legally binding. As seen in Chapter 5, if matters concerning women do not enjoy political priority in the trade agendas of a country, then these issues fall down the priority list. To see real advancement in this respect, the trigger to negotiating binding women-related commitments needs to come from the highest levels of administration, that is, the political stakeholders including legislators and parliamentary members. The political salience of a particular concern plays a vital role in determining how that concern is addressed in the negotiating room as the views of the a country's lawmakers may factor into the calculus of the negotiators when

[2] Kenneth Abbot and Duncan Snidal, 'Hard and Soft Law in International Governance' (2000) 54(3) International Organization 421.

[3] Beth Simmons, 'International Law and State Behavior: Commitment and Compliance in International Monetary Affairs' (2000) 94(4) The American Political Science Review 819.

[4] Oona A Hathaway, 'The Cost of Commitment' (2003) 55(5) Stanford Law Review 1821 (the author referred to this as the 'sovereignty view' whereby countries take into account the cost of such commitment to their national sovereignty).

considering the content and scope of an agreement's language as the agreement will require the lawmakers' approval for its ratification.[5]

9.2.1.4 Risk of protectionism and fears of cultural imperialism

As seen in Chapter 5, fears of protectionism and cultural imperialism can deter countries from assuming commitments in respect of women that can have certain legal implications for them. This is especially the case if a given legal provision relating to women is drafted with so much flexibility and imprecision that it allows countries to extend the already-stretched concept of women's empowerment to concerns that are only remotely related. Hence, countries, particularly developing countries, may hesitate in assuming binding commitments relating to women's empowerment in their trade agreements as such commitments can allow developed countries to use their more forward gender policies to obstruct imports coming from developing countries.

9.2.1.5 Commitment's importance and expected benefits

Another parameter that can shape a country's decision to assume binding or best endeavour-styled commitment relates to the overall importance of that measure and its benefits in terms of helping women overcome the barriers they currently face in their given countries. The importance of a measure could be symbolic or intrinsic in nature. A measure could be important from a normative point of view, advocating that a country might be willing to assume a binding commitment if it is dedicated to achieving women's empowerment and changing its domestic conditions using international policy instruments.[6] The importance of a measure may also be symbolic in nature if a country agrees to enter into negotiations on women-related provisions to keep up with the ongoing trend of gender mainstreaming, to be recognized as a country making efforts towards women empowerment, or to please a trade partner which might be a pioneer of mainstreaming women's concerns in its trade agreements. The importance of a measure may also be defined in substantive terms if a country might be willing to assume a binding commitment for a concern that is significant for the women in its country. Hence, the language and level of commitment of a measure may also be determined based on the practical benefits that can be assessed in light of the barriers women face and the opportunities needed to create a level playing field. For example, in a country with significant disparities that favour men in access to education or digital skills, a provision to enhance women's access to education and digital learning would yield substantial benefits. Conversely, in a country where women have equal access to

[5] William Alan Reinsch, Jasmine Lim, and Ally Brodsky, 'Negotiating Trade Agreements: Gender as a Priority?' (Centre for Strategic and International Studies 24 May 2021) <www.csis.org/analysis/negotiating-trade-agreements-gender-priority> accessed 11 October 2023.

[6] Martha Finnemore, *National Interests in International Society* (Cornell UP 1996) 87.

productive resources such as land, finance, and bank accounts, a provision to further enhance women's access to those resources may be less impactful. Therefore, the level of commitment of a specific provision must be determined in light of the expected benefits assessed by the country's domestic conditions and state of affairs.

Balancing and weighing exercise: to determine the level of binding force in the language of a given provision, the concern or commitment being embedded in that provision should be assessed by considering the systemic weighing and balancing of these five parameters. If the anticipated short- and long-term strategic benefits and the importance of a commitment are generally higher than the complexity of its implementation, policymakers can consider using a higher level of commitment when drafting the provision. Conversely, if the benefits and importance are lower than the implementation complexity, policymakers should be cautious about adopting high-commitment language. Instead, they should push for language that reflects a lower level of commitment to avoid potential legal repercussions from trade partners in the case of non-compliance.

9.2.2 Decide and define: gender equality or gender equity?

As seen in the previous chapter, drafting a legal provision using vague and broad expressions can only escalate the already existing hesitations that countries have against such inclusions and can also weaken the case for making trade agreements work for the benefit of women. It is therefore important that policymakers consider adopting precise definitions associated with gender-related terminology in the agreement's text. In this respect, policymakers need to answer two questions: first, would they consider defining the scope and meaning of terms they are using, such as 'gender', 'gender equality', or 'women empowerment'; if the answer to that question is affirmative, whether they are seeking to enhance 'gender equality' or 'gender equity' through commitments they are considering in a given agreement.

In respect of the first question, policymakers need to determine whether they would like to define the precise scope of the provisions they are including in respect of women or whether they would prefer to retain flexibility and escape hatches by being vague about the provisions. If there is an intention to define the scope, then policymakers need to consider including definitions of terms that are of fundamental importance. If an agreement uses the term 'gender', which is the case with a large number of existing trade agreements, it must be accompanied by clarification of whether that only refers to *cisgender* or whether it includes non-traditional non-*cisgenders* too. In the Peru–Australia Fręe Trade Agreement (FTA), the parties have clarified that they seek to undertake cooperation and capacity-building activities in areas of common interest, which may include but are not limited to areas including gender equality.[7] However, it is unclear how the parties intend to define the term 'gender equality'. 'Gender equality' has not been defined in any multilateral or regional trade agreements with the exception of the Treaty for the Establishment of the East African Community Treaty (EAC Treaty) which has defined 'gender' as the 'the role of women and men in society'.[8] It is probably time for countries to agree on a universally accepted definition of 'gender equality' or 'women empowerment' and then incorporate that definitional agreement into the text of their trade agreements by reference. This could be done through multilateral negotiations; however, given the current negotiation deadlock at the World Trade Organization (WTO), this could be done either in the form of a plurilateral declaration or a joint statement initiative.

In respect of the second question, the terms 'gender equality' and 'gender equity' serve distinct purposes in trade policy formulation. Gender equality refers to equal treatment and access to resources and opportunities regardless of gender, aiming for uniformity in outcome. Gender equity, on the other hand, recognizes the different needs, preferences, and histories of individuals based on their gender, advocating for the provision of resources and opportunities according to those needs, to achieve fairness in treatment and outcomes. In drafting trade agreements, deciding whether to focus on gender equality or equity depends on the specific goals of the agreement and the domestic contexts of the parties involved. For example, provisions aimed at gender equality might be suitable for contexts where the primary concern is removing legal and formal barriers to women's participation in trade. On the other hand, gender equity might be more appropriate in situations where different starting points for women and men need to be acknowledged and addressed through a range of differentiated measures.

When countries intend to use trade agreements to correct the disproportionate distributive impacts of trade liberalization on women, they are essentially intending to do so by including special provisions that are based on differential treatment in favour of women. If that is the case, then countries need to reconsider the appropriateness of 'gender equality' as a common expression used in their agreements and consider using the term 'gender equity' instead, which may be more appropriate to refer to the use of temporary special measures to compensate for historical or systemic bias or discrimination against women.[9] Gender equity is

[7] (In force 11 February 2020.)

[8] (In force 7 July 2000), art 1.

[9] United Nations Children's Fund (UNICEF), Regional Office for South Asia, 'Gender equality: Glossary of terms and concepts' (November 2017) <www.unicef.org/gender/training/content/resources/Glossary.pdf> accessed 12 June 2024. UNICEF defines 'gender equity' as the:

> process of being fair to men and women, boys, and girls, and importantly the equality of outcomes and results. Gender equity may involve the use of temporary special measures to compensate for historical or systemic bias or discrimination. It refers to differential treatment that is fair and positively addresses a bias or disadvantage that is due to gender roles or norms or differences between the sexes. Equity ensures that women and men and girls and boys have

essential to achieve gender equality as it is a means to balance the playing field between women and men and empower women to benefit from equal opportunities. Gender equity in trade requires ensuring equal access to trade opportunities, reducing gender inequalities in access to resources, and creating conducive conditions for women to access opportunities created by trade agreements. Gender equity is difficult to achieve without economic, social, or political equity and favourable policies for the empowerment of women are needed to ensure that trade agreements can contribute to women empowerment. Defining these terms clearly within trade agreements is crucial to avoid ambiguity and ensure that all parties have a shared understanding of the goals. This clarity also helps in the implementation phase as it can direct the development of specific policies and practices that may align with the chosen approach.

9.2.3 Prefer precision and clarity but consider flexibility as well

The language used in drafting a provision is the result of a trade-off between the countries' preference for precision or ambiguity as vaguely worded treaty provisions can create flexibility by giving countries more room to manoeuvre. However, the vaguer the rules, the more power countries may have in interpreting them and, hence, in the end these vague rules may not foster much of the needed flexibility. Greater precision of provisions also increases the level of commitment because it implies that the countries concerned have limited discretion in the implementation of specific actions in an identified area.[10] A similar tension is seen between rigidity and flexibility. Rigidity here refers to the drafting of provisions using mandatory constructions and flexibility refers to such drafting with permissive expressions and in the form of best-endeavour promises that are not legally binding.

Excessive rigidity in drafting provisions can limit an agreement's practical applicability over time and in varying contexts. Flexibility allows agreements to adapt to unforeseen circumstances and evolving socio-economic landscapes, particularly with women-specific provisions. This can be achieved through mechanisms like review clauses, which mandate regular reassessment, and conditional or opt-out clauses for adjustments. Balancing precision with flexibility ensures that agreements are actionable and adaptable, evolving within robust frameworks without the need for renegotiation or amendment.

an equal chance, not only at the starting point, but also when reaching the finishing line. It is about the fair and just treatment of both sexes that considers the different needs of the men and women, cultural barriers and (past) discrimination of the specific group.

[10] Amrita Bahri, 'Making Trade Agreements Work for Women Empowerment' (2021) 4(11) Latin American Journal of Trade Policy 6.

Most of the women-related provisions today are drafted in imprecise language with a large amount of flexibility in respect of how they might be interpreted. This ambiguity and lack of clarity can make it challenging to properly implement or enforce such provisions, ultimately impacting their effectiveness. To address this issue, there is a growing need for more clarity and specificity to ensure that such considerations are adequately incorporated and prioritized. Using specific, precise, and actionable language in such provisions within trade agreements can bring several benefits for the negotiating parties. Some of these benefits may be related to legal certainty, effective implementation, enhanced accountability and enforcement potential, and the avoidance of a symbolic tokenism-based approach.

Precise language leaves less room for ambiguity, ensuring that the rights and obligations regarding women-related concerns are clearly defined and understood by all parties involved. Clear language helps prevent misinterpretations and disputes over the meaning of terms and obligations. Specific language is also needed to clearly outline concrete actions that need to be taken to promote women's empowerment, making it easier for countries to implement and monitor the implementation of those provisions. Moreover, clear and actionable language enhances accountability mechanisms, making it easier to hold parties accountable for meeting the women-related commitments they have assumed under trade agreements. With precise language and the use of expressions that have a specific connotation, these provisions stand a better chance of bringing about tangible and meaningful changes that can promote women's interests. Detailed language can also help policymakers move these promises beyond token gestures that may not lead to any concrete promises as it can encourage the inclusion of actionable and concrete commitments.

However, there are certain perceived reasons or arguments for drafting such provisions in a vague and imprecise manner, although these reasons may be subject to critique. One argument is that the vague language of such provisions can allow countries much-needed flexibility in their interpretation and implementation. Such flexibility is crucial for two reasons: first, there is insufficient evidence and data on the impact of such provisions in trade agreements on women; and, second, since such provisions infringe on a range of domestic interests and conditions, some flexibility may be deemed necessary to accommodate domestic contexts and diverse stakeholder perspectives. Additionally, without clear global standards or norms on gender provisions in trade agreements, vague and imprecise language may serve as a starting point for building consensus and initiating discussion on the topic.

In some cases, negotiating detailed and precise provisions may face resistance from certain parties and it may also be difficult to have them ratified by the parliaments back home; in such situations, vague language might be seen as a compromise to avoid such political resistance and still include women considerations in a trade agreement. However, it is crucial to recognize that vague and imprecise provisions can lead to challenges in terms of their enforcement, effectiveness, and accountability. Therefore, if a country is keen to negotiate trade agreements that can lead to an inclusive trading environment and more opportunities for women in their country, their policymakers can push their trade partners for more specific and actionable language in trade agreements to ensure that such considerations are meaningfully integrated and then eventually realized.

9.2.4 Evaluate drafting options: hard, soft, or a mix and match of hard and soft

In legal drafting, particularly in international agreements, 'hard' and 'soft' law provisions represent a spectrum of enforceability and formality. 'Hard law' refers to legally binding commitments with clear, enforceable obligations and established dispute-resolution mechanisms. 'Soft law', while not legally binding, can influence behaviour through norms, guidelines, and recommendations that can lead to the formation of customary practices and eventually hard law.

The previous discussions have shown that the current provisions have mainly used soft law language and expressions in their drafting. The value of provisions drafted in soft law language should not be underrated as these provisions can still change the normative environment of trade negotiations and can act as a starting point in negotiating gender-related commitments for countries with less developed appetites or understanding of these matters. Hence, voluntary provisions provide a safe haven for countries that have hesitations and doubts in respect of employing hard language for such commitments. It is therefore important that countries understand the pace of their trade partners and the need for them to take own time to develop their own willingness before they are expected to negotiate commitments that are legally binding and enforceable in nature. Countries that have an appetite for assuming binding commitments in this respect are able to include such commitments in the agreements they negotiate with partners who are at a similar level of appetite and readiness, but they should refrain from imposing such commitments on their partners which are probably not yet at that point and need more time to develop their understanding, appetite, and expertise in that respect.[11]

Binding provisions on women's concerns drafted with hard law language are more of an exception in trade agreements. However, in some agreements, parties have come closer to such language as they have used a combination of binding and

[11] Amrita Bahri and Renata Amaral, 'Gender Equality Provisions in Trade and Investment Agreements: Are They Widening the Negotiation Capacity Gap?' (2024) 23(1) World Trade Review 47.

non-binding expressions, which perhaps indicates a stronger yet symbolic binding force or a higher importance of the provision to the parties, but the use of soft expressions entwined in the language ensures that the given provision remains non-binding in nature. This is seen in a couple of provisions in which parties use 'shall' before or after 'cooperate' or 'may', 'consider', 'endeavour', or 'prioritize'.[12] This composite approach may be used by policymakers if there is an appetite to assume commitments beyond best endeavours but the country is still not willing to assume the associated risks that may come with the incorporation of hard obligations.

These observations show that the use of hard or soft law language in the drafting of such provisions is directly related to the level of commitment a country may want to demonstrate towards a given concern in their trade agreements. This level of commitment may vary according to the focus area and scope of each provision as a country may be willing to demonstrate a high commitment towards women's access to education or health-care services but it may not be ready to show a similar commitment towards women's access to international markets.

Policymakers can consider the following verb constructions and combinations depending upon the level of commitment they would like to employ for a specific legal provision:

(1) Low level of commitment verb combinations (combinations of non-binding and permissive expression, keeping the provision as plainly non-binding):
  - use of 'may' and 'cooperate' or 'endeavour' together, followed or preceded by encourgage(ing)/promote(ing)/foster(ing)/advance(ing)/develop(ing)/conduct(ing)/share(ing)/undertake(ing)/consolidate(ing)/strength(ening);
  - remove 'may' and combine 'cooperate' or 'endeavour' with encourgage(ing)/promote(ing)/foster(ing)/advance(ing)/develop(ing)/conduct(ing)/share(ing)/undertake(ing)/consolidate(ing)/strength(ening);
  - remove 'cooperate' or 'endeavour' and combine 'may' with encourgage(ing)/promote(ing)/foster(ing)/advance(ing)/develop(ing)/conduct(ing)/share(ing)/undertake(ing)/consolidate(ing)/strength(ening).

(2) Medium level of commitment verb combinations: the usage of 'shall' before or after 'cooperate' or 'may', 'consider', 'endeavour', 'prioritize' (combination of binding and non-binding expressions, keeping the provision non-binding in nature, but has a stronger symbolic force).

(3) High level of commitment verb combinations: the use of 'shall' or 'should' or 'must' or 'undertake' without the use of accompanying non-binding

[12] Examples of such provisions are the Modernized Canada–Chile Free Trade Agreement (CCFTA) (in force 5 February 2019), art N *bis*-03 and the Economic Partnership Agreement between the CARIFORUM States and the European Community (in forced 1 January 2009), art 41(4).

expressions (making the provision binding in nature, which makes it enforceable if it is subjected to that agreement's dispute-settlement mechanism).

Choosing between hard, soft, or mixed approaches in drafting such provisions depends on several factors including the political will of the parties, their existing legal frameworks, and the specific objectives of the provisions. Hard law provisions are essential when the goal is to establish firm commitments that require specific actions or omissions, accompanied by the assurance of compliance through legal recourse. Soft law constructions, while less coercive, offer flexibility and easier consensus among the parties, which can be particularly useful in complex or sensitive areas such as domestic policies relating to women where nations may have different cultural perspectives or readiness levels. Soft law can pave the way for gradual adaptation to norms and prepare the ground for harder legal commitments in the future. A mixed approach can often be pragmatic, blending the enforceability of hard law with the adaptability of soft law. This can be achieved by framing core obligations in hard law while accompanying them with soft law guidelines that provide advice on best practice and flexible implementation strategies.

9.2.5 Use culturally sensitive and plain language

The use of culturally sensitive, gender-neutral, and plain language in trade agreements is crucial for ensuring their inclusivity and accessibility for a wide range of stakeholders. Culturally sensitive language can help policymakers respect the diverse social norms and practices of different countries, helping to prevent cultural resistance that such trade agreements or provisions may face from domestic stakeholders. Cultural awareness and recognition of different values and beliefs are crucial to arrive at mutually acceptable outcomes, and trade negotiations are no exception to this norm. If a specific provision or the way it is drafted or the use of a certain expression in it does not align with the cultural or religious norms or beliefs a country or a specific community in that country may have, then such inclusions could lead to significant opposition and challenges during its ratification process. Hence, to promote the acceptance of such provisions, policymakers need to be culturally aware and reflect that awareness in their drafting proposals.

Policymakers should also consider the use of plain and simple language to draft such provisions. The legal community has made a move away from legal jargon. This movement towards plain English or plain language in legal writing began in the 1970s as an effort to make legal documents more accessible to the public. According to Richard C Wydick, documents written in plain language can reduce costs and increase profits for businesses.[13] For lawyers, using plain English can help improve relations with clients, communicate better, and win cases.[14] So what is plain and simple language? Garner defines it as 'the idiomatic and grammatical use of language that most effectively presents ideas to the reader'.[15] One way to do that is to avoid using legal jargon which unnecessarily complicates language as it is used to impress, rather than to inform, readers. Avoidance of legal jargon does not mean the avoidance of the use of technical terms which can be crucial for an agreement (eg technical barriers to trade or most favoured nation) but policymakers can avoid the use of unnecessary expressions in the drafting of a trade agreement or a provision that makes it complicated to understand or interpret. Such unnecessary terms may include but are not limited to: 'hereinafter', 'heretofore', 'wherefore', 'whereas', 'aforesaid', 'aforementioned', 'herewith', 'herein', 'therein', 'thereinafter', 'to wit', 'witnesseth', and the like. They can simply be omitted from the drafting of such provisions as they are not needed.

Plain language makes the text more accessible to non-specialists, including stakeholders and the general public, facilitating a broader understanding and engagement with the trade agreement's goals and mechanisms. This approach can enhance transparency and promote wider support of and compliance with such commitments, which are essential for the successful implementation of women-focused provisions. Engaging with linguistic and cultural experts during the drafting process can provide valuable insights about drafting options that may enhance the effectiveness and acceptability of such provisions.

9.3 Dimension II: Target Focus Areas

Dimension II of the Pentagon Roadmap deals with the key areas that are essential for enhancing women's empowerment within the realm of international trade. This dimension outlines specific focus areas—that are generally ignored in current agreements—and so they require concentrated efforts and commitments to support and empower women through trade agreements. By providing support for women entrepreneurs, ensuring access to productive resources, safeguarding health and safety, enhancing women's representation in trade, and facilitating their access to education and technology, trade agreements can directly address gender disparities and promote an inclusive economic environment. This strategic focus can create multiple entry points for women's empowerment and participation;

[13] Barbara Yonemura, 'Plain English for Lawyers by Richard C Wydick–eScholarship' (1981) 7(2) National Black Law Journal 384.

[14] Paulina Meza and others, 'Plain Writing in the Legal Field: An Approach from the Discourse of Specialists' (2020) 22 Discourse Studies 356.

[15] Bryan A Garner, *Legal Writing in Plain English: A Text with Exercises* (University of Chicago Press 2001).

however, the focus areas need to be tailored to the diverse needs and challenges faced by women in individual countries or sectors.

9.3.1 Provide support for women entrepreneurs

Supporting women entrepreneurs is a vital focus area, aimed at fostering an inclusive economic environment where women can thrive as business owners and innovators. However, as discussed in the previous chapter, it has largely been ignored by trade agreements as the majority of the existing provisions have focused on women as employees or labourers. Very few agreements, mainly those of the new generation, have been vocal about the need to enhance women's business interests. The EU–Canada FTA is such an exception as Article 8.10 of the agreement contains a binding obligation that prohibits sex-based discrimination against foreign investors.[16] This provision can encourage women businesses to engage in foreign investment without fear or uncertainty of being discriminated against on the basis of the owners' sex. In the EC–South Africa Cooperation Agreement, Article 54 seeks to enhance the market access of micro enterprises (MEs) and small and medium-sized enterprises (SMEs) in South Africa.[17] Another relevant agreement is the recently negotiated United States–Mexico–Canada Agreement (USMCA) in which parties commit to work on enhancing trade and investment opportunities for SMEs.[18] Globally, approximately 50% of working women are employed in service-based SMEs.[19] This number shows how such a provision aimed at enhancing SME market access can help women both as business stakeholders and as employees.

Although these market-access-enhancing commitments are good practices as they seek to foster women's access to entrepreneurial opportunities, it is also important that future trade agreements consider expanding women's access to lucrative sectors such as e-commerce, digital trade, and manufacturing. Another useful initiative that policymakers can consider in this respect is in the form of financial initiatives that should be accessible and designed to overcome the traditional barriers women's businesses face in securing capital. For example, countries can consider establishing dedicated funds or financial products that are specially tailored

[16] EU–Canada Comprehensive Economic and Trade Agreement (CETA) (in force 21 September 2017), art 8.10.

[17] Agreement on Trade, Development and Cooperation between the European Community and Its Member States, of the One Part, and the Republic of South Africa, of the Other Part with Protocol 1 and 2 (in force 1 May 2004).

[18] Agreement between the United States of America, the United Mexican States, and Canada (in force 1 July 2020), art 25.2.

[19] International Labour Organization, 'Global Employment Trends 2014: The risk of a jobless recovery' (21 January 2014) <www.ilo.org/wcmsp5/groups/public/---dgreports/---dcomm/---publ/documents/publication/wcms_233953.pdf> accessed 23 November 2022.

for women-led businesses, including grants, loans with favourable terms, and venture capital.

Future policymaking can also focus on capacity-building programmes to enhance business skills, including management, financial literacy, digital literacy, and specific trade-related knowledge. These programmes can be accompanied by efforts to enhance business networks and mentorship opportunities for women entrepreneurs as these opportunities can help connect women entrepreneurs with mentors, peers, and industry leaders who can provide crucial support, advice, and opportunities for collaboration and market expansion. It may also be useful for trade agreements to include provisions that can facilitate women entrepreneurs' access to new and existing markets through trade fairs, e-commerce platforms, and direct links with international buyers and suppliers.

9.3.2 Include commitments on access to productive resources

Various barriers impede women's access to productive resources, including their access to finance and other assets. Access to finance, as seen in Chapter 1, is a critical factor for business initiation and survival. Very few FTAs have accommodated provisions that focus on enhancing women's access to finance. In the Canada–Israel FTA, parties seek to work on enhancing women's involvement in international trade through their financial inclusion, including financial training, access to finance, and financial assistance. They also seek to work on promoting female entrepreneurship and women's participation in international trade by improving women's access to, participation in, and leadership in science, technology, and innovation.[20]

In Article 155(1) of the Common Market for Eastern and Southern Africa (COMESA),[21] parties agree to increase women's access to finance as it seeks to eliminate domestic laws and regulations that hinder women's access to credit. However, these provisions are more of an exception as in most trade agreements in which the parties have included resource-related commitments they have not clarified the kind of resources on which they would like to focus. This is problematic because enhancing resource access to productive assets such as finance or land are commitments that can require significant investment of capital by the government. Going forward, resource-access-related provisions can be made more robust by defining the kind of resource access the parties intend to work on, identifying procedures to implement such promises and, perhaps, drafting those provisions as legal standards and not merely as cooperation-based provisions.

[20] Modernised Canada–Israel FTA (CIFTA) (in force 1 September 2019), art 13.3.
[21] (In force 8 December 1994.)

9.3.3 Protect women's access to health care

Insufficient provision of health requirements such as maternity needs and medical insurance cover has traditionally impeded women's empowerment. Countries in the Asia Pacific region and the EU have signed several agreements with provisions on health-related concerns. The EU–Ukraine FTA is one such example where parties seek to cooperate on addressing the major health concerns of women such as maternity needs, mental health care, and child health.[22] In the Eurasian Economic Union, parties mandate employers to provide compulsory medical insurance to pregnant women and mothers if they are migrant labourers or if they are involved in the production and process of goods that may have health risks.[23] This provision seeks to protect pregnant women and nursing mothers if they are involved in processes of production, design, manufacture, construction, installation, and operation as such activities may have a high degree of health risk.

A common thread that links these provisions is their language, specifically the binding expressions and verb constructions used in drafting them. Through such provisions in trade agreements, countries can impose binding obligations on their business stakeholders to provide health coverage and maternity benefits to their female employees. Alternatively, countries can draft these provisions as voluntary standards that enterprises operating within their territory or subject to their jurisdiction may be encouraged to adhere to. Such commitments can also take the shape of 'right to regulate' provisions which can serve to ensure that trade agreements do not interfere with a government's ability to regulate health care and that health interests are not damaged by the pursuit of potential economic gains. Hence, these provisions can ensure that if governments take measures to protect and promote women's access to health or maternity services, those measures cannot be subject to legal challenge through an investor–state dispute settlement (ISDS) or a similar mechanism. To be better prepared to operate in the post-Covid-19 world and to engage women in the economic recovery process, future trade agreements must embrace this focus on health requirements and assume binding commitments in that respect.

9.3.4 Increase representation of women at trade policy forums

We have recently witnessed various developments in women in trade occupying leadership roles. The appointment of women as leaders of international

[22] Association Agreement between the European Union and the European Atomic Energy Community and their Member States, of the One Part, and Ukraine, of the Other Part (in force 1 January 2016), art 427.

[23] (In force 1 January 2015), art 96.

organizations such as the World Trade Organization (WTO), the International Trade Centre (ITC), and the United Nations Conference on Trade and Development (UNCTAD) has shown how women's representation in leadership positions is on the rise. However, this increase has happened at a slow pace. While the WTO has recently achieved parity among men and women in its Secretariat administrative staff, the number of women serving in senior positions in the Secretariat, as chairs of WTO governing bodies, panellists, chairs of panels, and Appellate Body members remains visibly low.[24] This is not only the case with the WTO as similar asymmetries can be seen in other international organizations and at regional or bilateral trade negotiation forums.[25] Women are significantly under-represented at various tables where trade reforms or policies are discussed and negotiated.

The forums where trade negotiations take place involve large numbers of public and private stakeholders and hence they are prone to reproduce existing inequalities against women at different policymaking and decision-making levels. This is mainly because women are often under-represented in higher roles in politics, government offices, and businesses.[26] The higher the decision-making forum, the more likely it is that women will be absent or under-represented. Hence, women are largely absent from important high-level decision-making processes at trade negotiating forums. One effective way to add women's perspectives to future trade negotiations is to appoint more women to negotiating and policymaking roles.[27]

Appointment of women in negotiating roles in trade policy forums may be vital for ensuring that future trade agreements are considerate towards women's concerns for several reasons. First, women on negotiating tables may offer unique perspectives, making the process more responsive towards the needs of women negotiators who at the same time may have childcare or other family responsibilities. Second, increasing the number of senior female trade negotiators can prioritize the frontloading of women empowerment concerns on the trade negotiation agenda. Third, female trade negotiators in high-responsibility roles within global-trade-negotiating forums have a higher motivation to understand and address women's concerns and gain the technical skills required for the job. This, in turn, means that they are more likely to bring these concerns to the negotiating table and seek

[24] Debra Steger, 'Gender Equality in the WTO: The Need for Women Leaders' (CIGI 2018) <www.cigionline.org/articles/gender-equality-wto-need-women-leaders> accessed 22 November 2022.

[25] Maria V Sokolova, Alisa DiCaprio, and Nicole Bivens Collinson, 'Is it time for women leaders in international organizations?' (TradeExperttes 2020) <www.tradeexperettes.org/blog/articles/is-it-time-for-women-leaders-in-international-organizations> accessed 22 November 2022.

[26] One World Action and Commonwealth Secretariat, Advocacy Tool, 'Gender Justice in Trade Policy: The Gender Effects of Economic Partnership Agreements' (OECD 2009) <www.oecd.org/social/gender-development/47566754.pdf> accessed 22 November 2022.

[27] Olayinka Bandele, 'An Equal Seat at the Table: Gendering Trade Negotiations' (2016) International Trade Working Paper 2016/14 (Commonwealth Secretariat) <https://doi.org/10.14217/5jm0qglb1s9s-en.> accessed 22 November 2022.

trade outcomes that are equitable in favour of women. Studies have shown how 'women's increased voice and agency in parliaments and national development processes confirm that gender-equitable targeted interventions typically increase with women's greater involvement, leading to transformative change . . . '.[28] Finally, having women in leadership roles may contribute to changing the narrative of how women have been perceived in traditional and conservative societies.[29]

Several existing FTAs contain provisions that seek to enhance women's representation in decision- and policymaking roles. In Article 13.3 of the Canada–Israel FTA, parties commit to fostering women's representation in decision-making and positions of authority in the public and private sectors, including on corporate boards. In Article 45 of the EU–Palestine Association Agreement, parties seek to give priority to measures aimed at 'the promotion of the equality of women and a balanced participation in the decision-making process in the economic and social sphere'.[30] These examples show that, through FTAs, countries can encourage their trade partners to promote diversity in decision-making roles by the participation of women not merely in the public sector but also on the corporate boards of private companies. However, future FTAs should be more vocal about increasing women's representation in trade policymaking, trade agenda-setting, and negotiating roles. In addition, countries in these FTAs can also assume commitments to increasing women's representation on dispute-settlement panels, including by appointing more women to ISDS panels. Finally, it is important to consider that women's inclusion is the responsibility of everyone and it is the ideal to have both men and women involved in the crafting of inclusive trade policies.

9.3.5 Include commitments on access to education, skill development, and technology

Despite decades of progress, there remains a visible gap in women's and men's access to education, skill development, and technology. Women remain significantly under-represented in the science, technology, engineering, and math (STEM) disciplines.[31] Lack of access to STEM education, coupled with the digital divide, reduces potential job and business opportunities for women, mainly in lucrative sectors. These inequalities present significant barriers to women's

[28] ibid.

[29] Interview with trade negotiator (details withheld, on record with the author).

[30] Euro-Mediterranean Interim Association Agreement on Trade and Cooperation between the European Community, of the One Part, and the Palestine Liberation Organization (PLO) for the Benefit of the Palestinian Authority of the West Bank and the Gaza Strip (in force 1 July 1997).

[31] UNESCO, 'Boosting gender equality in science and technology: a challenge for TVET programmes and careers' (2020) <https://unesdoc.unesco.org/ark:/48223/pf0000374888> accessed 22 November 2022.

economic empowerment as STEM and ICT-based education can offer access to the new digital economy, financial inclusion opportunities through financial technologies such as open banking, training, and educational opportunities, inclusion in political processes, and, particularly during pandemics and other crisis, continued access to e-commerce opportunities, health care, and medical information.

Hence, improving women's access to education is a good practice provision that policymakers should consider. Many FTAs already include cooperation provisions on enhancing women's access to education and skill development. For example, in Article 102 of the EU–Montenegro Association Agreement, the parties seek cooperation on ensuring equal access to all levels of education and training which is 'free from discrimination on the grounds of gender ...'.[32] In Article 78 of the Algeria–EC Association Agreement, the parties seek to cooperate on placing special emphasis on 'giving the female population access to education, including technical training, higher education, and vocational training'.[33] These agreements include commitments to enhance women's access to education; however, the fundamental problem with most of these provisions is that they do not spell out the type of education or skill development. Therefore future FTAs should contain provisions that spell out the kind of education and skill development that the parties seek to work on. Through such commitments, the parties can create incentives to encourage women to undertake studies in the fields of science, technology, engineering, mathematics, and skill-based training that can prepare them for professions such as aerospace, rail, information technology, system design, engineering, business services, leadership roles, and professional services.[34] These new roles will enable women to move away from the traditional, low-paid, stereotyped jobs that societies have imposed on them in the fields of agriculture, fisheries, nursing, or invisible household responsibilities.

Policymakers should also consider negotiating provisions on access to technology and digital learning. Technology has taken up a large space in our lives. The onset of a global pandemic in the recent past has made it clear that digital access is no longer a luxury but an absolute necessity. In this era, it has become imperative to increase women's participation and expertise in this sector. Ensuring that women develop the requisite skills to use these technologies can open new employment and business opportunities for them. Better access to technology can also improve access to foreign markets for women entrepreneurs as it can enhance their access to external finance and other digital trade opportunities.

[32] Stabilisation and Association Agreement between the EU and Montenegro (in force 1 May 2010).

[33] Euro-Mediterranean Agreement Establishing an Association between the European Communities and Their Member States, of the One Part, and Algeria, of the Other Part (in force 1 September 2005).

[34] CIFTA (n 20) art 13.3; CCFTA (n 12) art N (*bis*-03). The recently modernized CIFTA and CCFTA focus on enhancing educational or skill development opportunities in fields that can translate into high-paid job opportunities for scientists women (eg STEM and ICT-focused education).

9.4 Dimension III: Rethink Their Location

Dimension III of the Pentagon Roadmap deals with the strategic placement of women-related provisions within the structure of trade agreements. This placement is crucial as it can significantly impact the prominence, enforceability, implementation, and effectiveness of these provisions. By thoughtfully positioning such concerns at various locations throughout a trade agreement, policymakers can ensure that the issues receive the necessary attention and commitment from all parties involved. This dimension explores various strategic locations within an agreement where such issues can be integrated, such as the preamble, objectives clauses, specific chapters, side instruments, and cross-cutting provisions, each contributing to an important approach to inclusivity.

9.4.1 Frontload women concerns in the agreement's preamble

Frontloading a women-specific provision in the preamble is a useful way to mainstream women's perspectives. Although an agreement's preamble is not legally binding, it helps in setting the tone for that agreement as international agreements can be interpreted in light of their preambles. A recent example is the Agreement establishing the African Continental Free Trade Area (AfCFTA), as its preamble amongst other things recognizes the importance of 'gender equality ... for the development of international trade and economic cooperation'.[35]

The preamble is a vital part of any international instrument or agreement as it can be instrumental in determining the intentions of the negotiators or drafters of the agreement at the time it was concluded. In disputes arising out of a given agreement, decision-makers can consider the wording used in the preamble to identify the parties' objectives and the intentions underlying the agreement. Hence, the inclusion of concerns related to women in the preamble implies that its provisions must be read and implemented to reconcile those concerns with international trade. Moreover, the examples discussed earlier confirm that once parties to an FTA frontload this concern in the preamble, they tend to include at least one other commitment relating to women's empowerment in the agreement's main text.

9.4.2 Utilize objectives clause and set clear objectives

Similar benefits as those discussed for the inclusion of concerns in the preamble may also be seen with their inclusion in an agreement's 'general objectives' clause.

[35] AfCFTA (in force 30 May 2019), Preamble.

Most FTAs in their first few provisions lay down a general clause that spells out the objective parties seek to achieve through that agreement. For example, in EAC Treaty, the parties set out the objectives of the Community and also commit to 'mainstreaming of gender in all its endeavours and the enhancement of the role of women in cultural, social, political, economic, and technological development'.[36]

These inclusions can influence the way other provisions of the given FTA are interpreted. Article 31 of the Vienna Convention on the Law of the Treaties (VCLT)[37] establishes that 'a treaty shall be interpreted in good faith in accordance with the ordinary meaning to be given to the terms of the treaty in their context and in the light of its object and purpose'.[38] This principle confirms the purposive approach of interpretation. According to this approach, each of the covered agreements must be interpreted considering the purpose of the text and in a way that will give 'effect to all the terms of the treaty'.[39] Such an inclusion, like an inclusion in the preamble, can therefore help in resolving a dispute by allowing other provisions of an agreement to be interpreted in accordance with the agreement's objectives. However, such general clauses do not contain any concrete commitments; they only include broad objectives that can neither be enforced nor implemented unless they are coupled with the further inclusion of related commitments in the agreement's text. Moreover, the goals in such an objectives clause need to be defined and stated clearly, which is not usually the case as such inclusions in agreements objectives' clauses are found to be quite vague and imprecise. Going forward, policymakers should define clear, measurable objectives related to gender equality, for example increasing women's participation in trade by a specific percentage or ensuring equitable access to resources for women-owned businesses. Moreover, policymakers should clarify at this location whether their goal is to achieve gender equality or equity through the added commitments. Clearly stated and explicitly defined objectives can serve as a roadmap for subsequent sections of the agreement, guiding policy actions and ensuring consistency in the interpretation and application of trade terms.

9.4.3 Negotiate a stand-alone chapter on trade and women

A stand-alone chapter on trade and women can serve as an umbrella chapter for all kinds of provisions on women's interests, including cooperation activities, legal standards, reservations, affirmations, and reaffirmations. This approach translates

[36] EAC Treaty (n 8) art 5.

[37] Article 31 of the VLCT requires that an agreement must be interpreted in light of its context, object, and purpose.

[38] ibid.

[39] WTO Appellate Body Report, *United States—Standards for Reformulated and Conventional Gasoline* (1996) WTO doc WT/DS2/AB/R, 21.

into something specific as it has four clear benefits: visibility, room for exploration, implementation machinery, and capacity building.

First, such chapters raise the profile and visibility of women-related concerns in trade discourse and trade policy instruments. Giving higher visibility to the 'problem' that such commitments can resolve means that trade negotiators and policymakers have an incentive to gain more awareness in that respect. It also helps negotiators justify the time and resources they spend on bilaterally negotiating these commitments with their counterparts.[40] Second, they justify the creation of institutions and the mobilization of funds for putting such commitments into action.[41] In the existing FTAs that have included such stand-alone chapters, parties have gone ahead to create a specialized committee or unit that is responsible for implementing or overseeing the implementation of commitments contained in the umbrella chapter. As seen in the Canada–Chile FTA (CCFTA), Article N *bis*-04 entitled 'Trade and gender committee' provides for dedicated committees overseeing the work, providing advice, and preparing reports, forming concrete action plans, and eventually tracking the progress of efforts and activities in the respective countries. Moreover, with a whole chapter to work on, the experts can probably engage in bilateral negotiations with dedicated counterparts on the issues; and this separate branch of negotiation can provide the required legitimacy to mobilize funds for their meetings and activities.

The third benefit is that it gives parties much more room to include different, concrete commitments and outline precise activities and procedures the specialized committees might work on and employ to implement the commitments. It also allows room for putting in writing various 'nuts and bolts' including: what is the purpose of empowering women? What activities will be engaged in? How exactly will these commitments be implemented or financed? Who will be responsible for their implementation, review, or monitoring? The space for including different categories of provisions in a chapter allows agreements to address these pertinent questions. Such chapters may not overcome deeply engrained social, cultural, and legal barriers but they can comprise provisions that may touch on the barriers that impede women from accessing trade opportunities.[42]

The fourth benefit is that such chapters can strengthen capacity building, especially when one of the countries is still in the early phases of understanding the interrelation between trade and women. A specific chapter on trade and women will require, or at least motivate, countries negotiating that chapter to appoint dedicated negotiators with the required understanding to engage with their counterparts. This incentivizes countries to develop their awareness and expertise in respect of negotiating issues relating to women within their trade policy context.

[40] Interview with a trade negotiator (15 September 2022) (details withheld, on file with the author).
[41] Interview with a trade negotiator (2 March 2022) (details withheld, on file with the author).
[42] Interview with a trade negotiator (18 November 2021) (details withheld, on file with the author).

Hence, the need to negotiate such a chapter can encourage the appointment of expert officials for the negotiation of trade and women's issues. Negotiators responsible for this chapter can have their own table to discuss, share experiences, exchange best practices, and understand better each other's domestic conditions.[43]

These benefits can, to some extent, also be realized with the inclusion of specific provisions but it does not allow the same room for exploring the inclusion of different kinds of provisions as a whole chapter would provide. However, the inclusion of such chapters must not be used as a window-dressing exercise to avoid the inclusion of such concerns in other chapters that are directly related to market access. A simple glance through the existing agreements that contain such standalone chapters reinforces this concern, as in most of these agreements women-explicit concerns are loaded into those chapters but remain completely absent from the substantive chapters on technical barriers to trade, agriculture, fisheries, e-commerce, financial technology, intellectual property rights, competition, etc.

9.4.4 Assess negotiating options for follow-up or supplementary policy instruments

In some agreements, as seen in Chapter 7, countries have adopted a side path to include women's concerns in the trade policy context by negotiating supplementary or follow-up instruments such as protocols, recommendations, declarations, or stand-alone arrangements. Negotiating such instruments can have several benefits. First, they can provide a second opportunity to include sustainability issues if the parties have not done so during the negotiation and drafting of the main trade agreement. Second, they can allow parties to explore and set in writing the operative details of the commitments they have assumed in the main agreement, such as the institutional and procedural arrangements for the implementation of women-related provisions or how parties intend to mobilize resources for their implementation, review, and monitoring. Follow-up mechanisms and supplementary policy instruments can also ensure that the commitments made in the main agreement can adapt over time and remain effective as they can allow for the negotiation of additional agreements or annexes that can be updated or added as needed without renegotiating the entire trade agreement.

One recent development in this respect is the AfCFTA Protocol on Women and Youth in Trade, which was negotiated as a stand-alone protocol by the AfCFTA parties to enhance the participation of women in the region.[44] It specifies the roles

[43] Interview with a trade negotiator (details withheld, on file with the author).

[44] AfCFTA (n 35), Protocol on Women and Youth in Trade to the Agreement Establishing the African Continental Free Trade Area (Draft) <www.bilaterals.org/IMG/pdf/women_and_youth_in_trade_protocol.pdf> accessed 12 May 2024.

and responsibilities of the parties in facilitating trade for women through several commitments such as improving women's access to finance, capacity building, digital trade, and protection against harassment. Additionally, it contains institutional arrangements for monitoring, evaluation, review, and implementation of the commitments assumed in the Protocol and the main agreement.

9.4.5 Consider whole-of-the-agreement approach with cross-cutting provisions

A whole-of-the-agreement approach in terms of locating women-related provisions—which entails the inclusion of women-explicit provisions in substantive market-access-related chapters—can support more inclusive outcomes and address more effectively the barriers that women face in accessing trade opportunities. Women play various roles in international trade and, accordingly, they face different barriers. It is therefore important that trade negotiations consider women's roles and their barriers with a multifaceted approach. To achieve this, trade negotiations in the future can employ a sectoral approach for the inclusion of such commitments. However, for this approach to work, it will be important for policymakers to identify the structural barriers to women's economic empowerment and the inequalities that impact women in their multiple economic roles, and more specifically in the individual sectors of trade.

Going forward, negotiators can consider including explicit commitments to increasing women businesses' market access to lucrative and booming industries, for example textiles and apparel, manufacturing, financial services, and e-commerce. Such cross-cutting provisions with explicit commitments can make some inroads for women businesses in lucrative sectors and markets. Future policymakers can consider incorporating such commitments in substantive chapters of their agreements that have a direct bearing on market access, such as those on trade facilitation, intellectual property rights, tariff and non-tariff barriers to trade, trade in services, trade finance, cross-border investment, government procurement, and other areas. Incorporation of women-related provisions in some sectors and disciplines may be more important than others depending upon the demographics of women's participation in these sectors in different countries and, hence, policymakers need first to identify the areas where women participate the most, the barriers they face, and then accordingly devise policy solutions responding to their barriers in specific sectors of trade.

One useful sectoral innovation in this respect could be the inclusion of such commitments in the agreement's chapter on digital trade as the digital economy is an area that cannot be overlooked if we want trade to enhance the business interests of women entrepreneurs, especially amidst the current surge in digital trade. There are very few examples of recently concluded trade agreements where parties have assumed such commitments. The Digital Economy Partnership Agreement (DEPA)[45] between Chile, New Zealand, and Singapore (South Korea has just initiated the process of joining) is a leading example as it includes specific language that emphasizes digital inclusion for marginalized groups including women. This is an agreement wherein the parties recognize 'the importance of expanding and facilitating digital economy opportunities by removing barriers' and cooperating 'on matters relating to digital inclusion'.[46] Further, Joint Committees and Contact Points are established to oversee the implementation of the provisions.[47] The UK–Australia FTA[48] is another recent example that merits consideration. In this FTA, the parties recognize the global nature of digital trade and the need to facilitate women's participation in digital trade and technology.[49] They also commit to undertaking cooperation activities that support women entrepreneurs to access the full benefits and opportunities created by the agreement and identify that one of the priority areas will be enhancing women's access to online business tools and opportunities to strengthen their digital skills.[50] Although these provisions are cooperation-based and are explicitly left outside the scope of the agreement's dispute-settlement mechanism,[51] they are not included without accompanying procedures of implementation. Parties to this FTA outline various procedures that include collection of sex-disaggregated data, use of indicators, monitoring and evaluation methodologies, analysis of statistics related to trade and women, and undertaking research on trade and women's empowerment.

It is important to note that increasing women's participation in the digital economy and increasing their e-commerce entrepreneurial capacity requires bringing together three related aspects: (1) access to digital learning; (2) access to digital infrastructure; and (3) access to e-commerce platforms and opportunities.[52] In this sense, two problems can be seen with the existing inclusions. First, recent FTAs focus on enhancing women's access to digital learning or infrastructure but remain silent on how to implement these promises. Second, most FTAs are not vocal about the need to increase access to e-commerce platforms and digital financial services, which is also crucial for women's economic participation. Most of the existing agreements do not include concrete commitments, including the means countries can employ to enhance women's access to digital financial wallets, e-banking, and e-commerce platforms, which could lead to an overall increase in

[45] DEPA (in force 7 January 2021).
[46] ibid art 11.1.
[47] ibid art 12.1.
[48] FTA between the United Kingdom of Great Britain and Northern Ireland and Australia (signed 15 December 2021).
[49] ibid arts 14.21, 24.1, and 24.2.
[50] ibid art 24.2.
[51] ibid art 24.4.
[52] Francesca Borgonovi and others, 'Bridging the Digital Gender Divide: Include, Upskill, Innovate' (OECD 2018) <www.oecd.org/digital/bridging-the-digital-gender-divide.pdf> accessed 29 October 2023.

women's participation in the economy. The use of digital platforms, for example, may offer women with many additional opportunities including the possibility to overcome challenges related to mobility restrictions, accessing new markets and knowledge, connecting with potential markets and customers, and enjoying flexible work hours and modes.

Policymakers should also consider incorporating such commitments into substantive chapters such as trade finance as existing trade finance mechanisms do not often cater to the unique needs of women entrepreneurs. This could include developing gender-sensitive trade finance options such as microloans, credit guarantees, or export insurance tailored to women-led businesses. Another useful area of intervention could be non-tariff barrier reductions as non-tariff barriers (eg complicated paperwork, discriminatory regulations or technical trade barriers) often disproportionately affect women traders.

A whole-of-the-agreement approach can ensure that women-related considerations are woven through all relevant sections of a trade agreement not just isolated in specific chapters or clauses. It may also call for an intersectional analysis, which may require policymakers to apply an intersectional lens to analyse how different provisions might interact to affect women differently based on other identities (eg race, colour, region, and socio-economic status). Moreover, policymakers can consider cross-referencing such provisions in a given agreement to reinforce and highlight the interconnections between gender provisions and other trade issues.

9.5 Dimension IV: Think Beyond Existing Provisions

Dimension IV of the Pentagon Roadmap encourages a forward-thinking approach that transcends traditional trade agreement frameworks to integrate and prioritize women's concerns more effectively. This dimension proposes innovative ways of drafting women-centric provisions in the form of reservations and waivers, sustainability standards, special exceptions, detailed cooperative affirmations, and collaborative research efforts.

9.5.1 Include reservations and waivers to positively discriminate in favour of women

Reservations and waivers are legal tools that allow countries to set aside or exempt themselves from certain obligations under a trade agreement in specific circumstances. Utilizing these tools to positively discriminate in favour of women can provide the necessary space for implementing women-focused policies.

These policy carve-outs can help women deal with situations of hardship such as a crisis. For example, many observed that the Covid-19 relief packages offered by governments when the pandemic struck formally or informally excluded women-owned businesses from their lists of beneficiaries.[53] Going forward, governments may consider offering various support schemes to small businesses in their respective countries that can particularly impact women entrepreneurs. These schemes could take the shape of state aid, government bailouts, loans, or subsidies. In addition, countries may consider mandating or encouraging the relevant industries to employ supplier-diversity programmes.[54] Through these programmes, they can obligate or somehow incentivize multinational companies to ensure that a certain percentage of their purchases are sourced directly from marginalized vendors such as women entrepreneurs.

Several existing FTAs allow their parties to extend favourable measures. In the South Korea–Singapore FTA, the parties in chapter 9 on cross-border trade in services reserve the right to regulate and provide financial benefits (in the form of loans, guarantees, tax waivers, and so so) to small businesses owned by women.[55] One of the measures that parties may be allowed to employ under the provision could be the waiver of sales tax payment for domestically produced goods by women-owned small businesses. This measure could be taken to support those businesses that are most severely hit by a crisis and to help them to sustain or revive their operations.[56]

Another support measure that could help women businesses sustain or revive from a pandemic or another crisis relates to government procurement. Public procurement accounts for around one-fifth of global gross domestic product (GDP).[57] Governments are both market regulators and market participants and, hence, they are best placed to make procurement procedures considerate of women by minimizing the barriers that impede women's access to this market. Using existing reservations in their FTAs, governments can take several steps in this direction. Governments can provide procurement-related assistance to SMEs to encourage their participation in public tenders. Such measures may help to increase the participation of women-owned enterprises in bidding processes, which in turn could

[53] Anoush Der Boghossian and Amrita Bahri, 'Finding Feet on Trade Agreements: Empowering Women Entrepreneurs Amidst a Pandemic' (2023) 50(1) Legal Issues of Economic Integration 13.

[54] Deborah Abrams Kaplan, 'Walmart's sourcing from women-owned suppliers drives business' (Supply Chain Dive 8 March 2018) <www.supplychaindive.com/news/sourcing-procurement-women-diverse-business/518624/> accessed 1 July 2020. (Supplier diversity programmes can allow multinational companies to make a percentage amount of their purchases from marginalized vendors such as women entrepreneurs: eg Walmart US and the supplier diversity initiative it has employed.)

[55] Free Trade Agreement between the Republic of Korea and Singapore (in force 2 March 2006), art 9.2.

[56] Alabama Department of Revenue (ADOR), 'Alabama Department of Revenue Responds to the COVID-19 Outbreak' (17 March 2020) <www.revenue.alabama.gov/ador-responds-to-the-covid-19-outbreak/> accessed 2 July 2021. (The ADOR has extended relief to small retail businesses that are unable to pay their sales tax liabilities. This includes tax exemption, late payment penalty waivers, and extension of deadlines.)

[57] Keric Chin, 'Empowering women through public procurement' (ITC 2014) <https://intracen.org/file/womenprocurementguidefinalwebpdf> accessed 24 November 2022.

help to revive women-owned SMEs that might have had to scale down or face closure during the most recent health pandemic.[58] One FTA where parties have accommodated such a provision is the EU–Canada FTA in which the parties reserve the right to offer favourable government procurement programmes for the provision of social services or grants such as childcare.[59] This waiver can allow countries to carve out procurement schemes that are favourable for women and thereby enhance their market access.

Beyond such inclusions in trade agreements, multiple WTO members in their Trade Policy Review Reports have reported the introduction of preference schemes that aim to enhance women-owned small businesses' access to government procurement opportunities. These countries have reserved a specific percentage of quota allocation for small businesses owned by women and, on average, the quota has ranged at around 20%. Some of these quota policies focus only on local procurement to facilitate the economic development of rural areas as they target rural women.[60] Other countries have employed a different approach. Some have developed specific provisions in government procurement laws to generally prohibit discrimination against women in the allocation of contracts;[61] others have given preference to companies that implement equality and equal wage policies for men and women.[62] One country is combining both options: while introducing quotas for women-owned companies, the government awards 'points'-based incentives to companies applying women-friendly policies and practices.[63] To strengthen such policies going forward, countries need to define a precise definition of women-owned enterprises. This is where the International Standards Organization's (ISO's) latest attempt at defining women-owned companies can come in useful[64]

[58] Members may need to assess the proposal's compatibility with the WTO Agreement on Government Procurement if they are party to this plurilateral agreement.

[59] CETA (n 16) art 9.2.

[60] Trade Policy Review, *Trade Policy Review for Guyana* (28 July 2015) WTO doc WT/TPR/G/320, 3 <https://docs.wto.org/dol2fe/Pages/SS/directdoc.aspx?filename=q:/WT/TPR/G320.pdf&Open=True> accessed 24 November, 2022; Trade Policy Review, *Trade Policy Review for Paraguay* (2 August 2017) WTO doc WT/TPR/G/360, 20, 21 <www.wto.org/english/tratop_e/tpr_e/tp460_e.htm> accessed 24 November 2022; Trade Policy Review, *Trade Policy Review for Gambia* (21 November 2017) WTO doc WT/TPR/G/365, 6, 9, 13 <www.wto.org/english/tratop_e/tpr_e/g365_e.pdf> accessed 24 November 2022.

[61] Patric Aeberhard, 'WTO Workshop on Enhancing the Participation of Women Entrepreneurs and Traders in Government Procurement' (2018) Federal Office for Gender Equality <www.wto.org/english/tratop_e/womenandtrade_e/s02_03_patric_aeberhard.pdf> accessed 24 November 2022; see also Anoush der Boghossian, 'Trade Policies Supporting Women's Economic Empowerment: Trends in WTO Members' (WTO Economic Research and Statistics Division 25 April 2019) WTO Staff Working Paper ERSD-2019-07 <www.wto.org/english/res_e/reser_e/ersd201907_e.pdf> accessed 24 November 2022.

[62] Trade Policy Review, *Trade Policy Review for Iceland* (30 August 2017) WTO doc WT/TPR/G/361, 7, 8 <www.wto.org/english/tratop_e/tpr_e/g361_e.pdf> accessed 24 November 2022; see also Trade Policy Review, *Trade Policy Review for Mozambique* (29 March 2017) WTO doc WT/TPR/G/354, 7 <www.wto.org/english/tratop_e/tpr_e/g354_e.pdf> accessed 24 November 2022.

[63] Boghossian (n 61).

[64] ISO, 'IWA 34:2021 Women's entrepreneurship—Key definitions and general criteria' (International Standard, edn 1, 2021) <www.iso.org/standard/79585.html> accessed 9 July 2021.

and it may be helpful to integrate this definition into current trade and procurement policies.

9.5.2 Consider commitments on voluntary sustainability standards

Another possible way to include the discussion on women's empowerment within the trade policy context is to include provisions on voluntary sustainability standards (VSS).[65] These are guidelines that encourage businesses to respect and accommodate within their operations different non-economic interests such as human rights, animal welfare, labour standards, environmental impacts, and women's empowerment considerations. VSS can be used as a tool to articulate and encourage sustainable and inclusive practices in trade transactions and processes.[66] Global companies are now under increasing pressure from their customers and their governments to accommodate these standards for various objectives. While most standards are not designed to promote equality among men and women, there is now an increasing number of women-focused VSSs that are being developed within the trade policy space.

Through corporate self-regulation provisions in trade agreements, governments can push companies to include social and environmental sustainability standards in their business plans and procedures. FTAs that support companies' businesses through enhanced and frictionless market access can also encourage or require them to trade inclusively and sustainably. Various agreements, such as the United States–Peru FTA[67] and the EU–Georgia FTA,[68] contain provisions on corporate social responsibility. However, these provisions do not explicitly mention women's concerns. Very few agreements include explicit corporate social responsibility (CSR) provisions about women. One such FTA is the Canada–Israel agreement in which the parties seek to encourage their businesses to use CSR to address issues including 'labour, environment and gender equality'.[69] These examples show that policymakers can identify opportunities to engage with VSS initiatives to deliver on women's empowerment commitments while also promoting trade liberalization. Policymakers and trade negotiators should recognize the growing influence

[65] United Nations Forum on Sustainability Standards (UNFSS), 'Voluntary Sustainability Standards: Today's Landscape of Issues & Initiatives to Achieve Public Policy Objectives' (2012) <https://unfss.org/wp-content/uploads/2012/05/unfss-report-issues-1_draft_lores.pdf> accessed 24 November 2022.

[66] Sally Smith, 'Advancing Gender Equality through Voluntary Standards for Trade' (Gender, Social Inclusion and Trade Working Group 2020) <www.bkp-development.com/images/reports/Voluntary_Standards_for_Trade_bkp_final.pdf> accessed 23 November 2022.

[67] FTA between the United States of America and Peru (in force 1 February 2009), art 17.6.

[68] Association Agreement between the European Union and the European Atomic Energy Community and their Member States, of the one part, and Georgia, of the other part (in force 1 July 2016), art 348.

[69] CIFTA (n 20) art 16.4; similar provision in CCFTA (n 12) art G-14(*bis*).

of VSS in global trade and the role of governments in encouraging businesses to employ such inclusive policies that may help in reducing the barriers women employees currently face. Countries create incentives by allowing suppliers with women-inclusive practices to receive preferential market access, simplified procedures, or other trade benefits. Agreements can also include provisions to offer other incentives for products meeting gender-sensitive standards. While options are numerous, it is crucial to advance VSS-focused provisions in trade agreements to offer guidance and ideas to companies. However, those incentives must align with trade law commitments under existing bilateral and multilateral agreements.

9.5.3 Craft an explicit exception for women or employ existing public morality exception

It is very common to find various General Agreement on Tariffs and Trade (GATT)-like exceptions in existing FTAs; these range from the protection of public morals, human health, or life to environment or national security.[70] These exceptions have allowed parties to escape the liability of violating their trade obligations for the protection of their legitimate non-trade interests. The first option for countries that are keen to implement exceptions is to justify favourable measures under Article XX(a) of GATT 1994.[71] The public morals exception operates as a 'catch-all' exception for measures that may relate to or affect any value that a country may view as a matter of its public morals.[72] This exception is not only found in the WTO's agreements but also in nearly all FTAs.[73]

Public morals range from views related to religion, human rights, consumption of alcohol, drug trafficking and corruption, gambling, consumer protection, and protection of animals. Certain moral interests are shared more commonly than others as opposed to being country-specific.[74] Women's empowerment is one such interest as it is recognized as a fundamental moral norm by the majority of WTO members in multiple international conventions and treaties.[75] Hence, a country

[70] USMCA (n 18) art 32.1.

[71] General Agreement on Tariffs and Trade (Marrakesh Agreement Establishing the World Trade Organization) (1994) 1867 UNTS 187, 33 ILM 1153 (GATT 1994), Annex 1A; Marrakesh Agreement Establishing the World Trade Organization (1994) 1869 UNTS 183, 33 ILM 1167 (General Agreement on Trade in Services (GATS)), Annex 1B.

[72] Liane Jarvis, 'Women's Rights and the Public Morals Exception of GATT Article 20' (2000) 22(1) Michigan Journal of International Law 219.

[73] Author's calculations; country-wise reports (on record with the author).

[74] Mark Wu, 'Free Trade and the Protection of Public Morals: An Analysis of the Newly Emerging Public Morals Clause Doctrine' (2008) 33(1) Yale Journal of International Law 237, 240.

[75] eg the WTO Ministerial Conference, 'Buenos Aires Joint Declaration on Trade and Women's Economic Empowerment' (2017) <www.wto.org/english/tratop_e/womenandtrade_e/buenos_aires_declaration_e.htm> accessed 18 October 2022, which outlines actions to empower women; the Convention on the Elimination of All Forms of Discrimination Against Women (CEDAW) 1979 UNTS 1249; etc.

may invoke this exception in a trade dispute to argue that the imposition of a support measure or a trade restriction to protect women's economic interests amounts to the protection of that country's moral interests. This is an ambitious interpretation of the morality exception and it can face intense scrutiny.[76]

Alternatively, countries can consider crafting new women-specific exceptions, although no such exception yet exists in multilateral and regional trade agreements. An exception specific to women can allow countries to provide favourable support in the form of government bailouts, loans, and subsidies (that may otherwise be inconsistent with their trade obligations) for industries that particularly impact women employees and businesses.[77] Such an exception can also allow parties to create favourable conditions for investment and growth in sectors that are particularly relevant for women (eg agriculture, tourism, hospitality, and education services). It can also allow countries to employ measures that can help them minimize the disproportionate harm women employees and businesses face in disrupted industries in situations of hardship or crisis such as a pandemic.

9.5.4 Spell-out cooperation-styled affirmations and keep them realistic

Cooperation-styled affirmations in trade agreements are commitments to work collaboratively to achieve certain goals, which are particularly useful for addressing complex issues such as gender inequality.[78] However, if they are the only location in an agreement where women-related concerns are accommodated, then those provisions need to be clearly set out and the commitments embedded need to be realistic and achievable for the countries assuming them. In number of agreements, as seen in Chapter 7, the provisions on cooperation are added ambiguously where parties merely indicate their interest to cooperate in certain areas and engage in activities that strengthen women's empowerment, but such provisions usually do not provide a list of specific cooperation activities or the focus areas those provisions are meant to target.

Going forward, it is important to consider three advances in respect of cooperation-based provisions. First, these provisions should set out specific collaborative goals in which countries can identify specific areas where they can collaborate, such as technology transfer, educational exchanges, or joint ventures that promote women's participation in trade. Second, parties should clarify the

[76] Amrita Bahri and Daria Boklan, 'Not Just Sea Turtles, Let's Protect Women Too: Invoking Public Morality Exception or Negotiating a New Gender Exception in Trade Agreements?' (2022) 33(1) European Journal of International Law 237.

[77] This recommendation was originally proposed in Caroline Dommen, 'Mainstreaming Gender in Trade Agreements: A New Approach' (ITC 2020) <www.iisd.org/publications/mainstreaming-gender-trade-policy> accessed 22 November 2022.

[78] Jeffrey Kucik and Eric Reinhardt, 'Does Flexibility Promote Cooperation? An Application to the Global Trade Regime' (2008) 62(3) International Organization 477.

objectives they seek to achieve through such inclusions, for example whether the provisions are aimed at the elimination or reduction of barriers to trade for women in general or whether they are more focused on enhancing specific women's access to opportunities created by the given trade agreement. Third, for these cooperation-based commitments to be more than just 'Cinderella promises', negotiators need to set realistic goals with measurable targets to ensure that the affirmations lead to tangible outcomes in the future. For example, in some agreements, countries have assumed commitments that are heavily resource-demanding such as increasing women's access to finance or other productive resources.[79] It is doubtful whether parties to those agreements have considered the resources they would be required to invest to bring those commitments into reality. Trade agreements are practical and operational policy instruments; they are not documents that contain a wish list. Hence, before countries go on to assume broad and ambitious commitments, they need to assess whether they have the capacity, intention, and will to implement them.

9.5.5 Collaborate on study, research, or publication relating to women and trade

Knowledge is a critical component of effective policymaking. Collaborations on research and studies about women in trade can provide data and explanations that are necessary to understand these issues and craft effective solutions. Many efforts at the multilateral level currently encourage research and study on women and trade. One prominent initiative is the WTO Gender Research Hub which was launched in May 2021 to deepen understanding of the impact of trade on women and gender equality. The Hub now serves as a knowledge-gathering platform where the latest research on the topic is shared and discussed. The Hub includes trade and gender researchers and experts from the WTO Secretariat, international and regional organizations, think tanks, and universities, and its members are encouraged to present recent findings from their research, share new perspectives, and expand multidisciplinary research on trade and gender issues.[80] Such initiatives can be incorporated into the framing of trade agreements as policymakers can consider adding commitments on consultations with experts from the Hub during negotiations or for implementation, review, or monitoring of such provisions.

Where available resources allow, countries may also endeavour to create funds to promote research and publication on trade and gender. Research and publications

[79] See eg the Comprehensive and Progressive Agreement for Trans-Pacific Partnership (CPTPP), art 23.4.

[80] More details on the WTO database, 'Gender Research Hub' <www.wto.org/english/tratop_e/womenandtrade_e/gender_research_hub_e.htm> accessed 12 June 2024.

on this topic are on a steep rise; however, most of the publications are available with significant cost repercussions. There is, therefore, a need for countries or international organizations to support research and publication efforts to allow authors to publish on an open-access basis. This will ensure that findings on trade and women are widely published and accessible, helping them to inform policy decisions and public awareness. Moreover, going forward, policymakers can use research as a feedback mechanism to continually refine trade policies and practices thus ensuring that they remain relevant and effective in promoting gender equality.

9.6 Dimension V: Craft a Comprehensive Implementation and Enforcement Framework

Dimension V of the Pentagon Roadmap addresses the critical aspect of implementation and enforcement of provisions related to gender equality and women's empowerment. Effective implementation and robust enforcement mechanisms are crucial for the practical realization of these commitments laid out in trade agreements. This dimension focuses on establishing comprehensive institutions and procedures, mobilizing necessary resources, ensuring continuous monitoring and assessment, upholding transparency and accountability, and incorporating soft enforcement measures. Each of these points is designed to ensure that women-focused provisions are not included as symbolic acknowledgements but as concrete and actionable commitments that are actively and effectively integrated in a country's trade practices and policies.

9.6.1 Create institutions and procedures and spell-out their operations

Most of the relevant provisions are currently included without any associated provisions or clarifications on the institutions or actors who will be responsible for their implementation. For the majority of such inclusions in which no such associated clarification is provided, it can be inferred that such provisions are considered to be included under the supervision of a general monitoring institution in a given agreement. There are some recent exceptions to this prevailing trend as agreements have more recently provided for the establishment of a 'technical body on trade and gender' which is solely responsible for overseeing implementation or monitoring of the impact of such provisions. One example is the Chile–Uruguay FTA,[81] which provides for the creation of a trade and gender committee (Art 14.4).

[81] (In force 13 December 2018.)

This provides that this committee is to be composed of representatives from government institutions responsible for relevant gender and trade matters from each concerned party but it falls short of prescribing its functions and operational requirements. The CCFTA raises the bar higher as it provides for some operational requirements and functions of the trade and gender committee (Art N *bis*-04). The committee is supposed to meet at least once a year and review the implementation of the trade and gender chapter every two years. However, what remains somewhat missing in most of these attempts is an effort to clarify how such an institutional mechanism will work, that is, to outline its detailed functions, the milestones and objectives they are expected to achieve, a timeline by which they are expected to be achieved, and which actors will form part of such units or divisions. It is also important to ensure that these institutions are staffed with individuals who are trained in both trade and gender issues so that they can bridge the gaps between these typically separate areas of expertise.

This institutional set-up requires an associated set of procedures that the responsible actors can use to implement the commitments. These procedures could include exchanging best practices and experiences to conduct field visits, commissioning of research, conducting training workshops and capacity-building sessions, participating in relevant conferences, engaging in collaborative projects and publications, and consulting with private stakeholders including civil society, companies, representative associations, and subject matter experts. A very recent and interesting example is the Interim Agreement on Trade between the European Union and the Republic of Chile, as parties in its stand-alone chapter, entitled 'Trade and gender equality', include detailed provisions on institutions and procedures for the implementation of gender-related provisions. In terms of procedural arrangements, the parties clarify that they seek to work on cooperation activities through a range of procedures including the sharing of experiences and best practice relating to their policies and programmes. They also outline the means through which such cooperation may take place, including workshops, seminars, conferences, collaborative programmes, and projects; and the exchange of subject matter experts (Art 27.4). In addition, the parties also clarify in that chapter that the Sub-Committee on Trade and Sustainable Development will be responsible for the implementation of the gender-related commitments contained in the chapter. The parties agree on the importance of monitoring and assessing the impact of the implementation of the agreement on equality between men and women and opportunities provided for women concerning trade. The chapter also features a commitment to review, whereby the parties agree to review the chapter in light of experiences gained from its implementation. However, there remains a gap in these provisions as they do not specify how the outlined procedures and activities will be financed or how parties will mobilize other resources (in addition to finance) such as subject matter expertise, organizational and logistic support, management of technological means, and so on. Such an understanding may not be very relevant for a developed country partner with sufficient resources required for the purpose but it is crucial for developing country partners to have identified resources or have identified ways to mobilize such resources before they assume commitments which can at times be quite resource-demanding.

9.6.2 Mobilize resources for funding and engage private stakeholders

Securing adequate funding and engaging private stakeholders are crucial for the sustainable implementation of women-centric trade policies. To operationalize institutional and procedural set-ups, it is important to identify funding arrangements that can be used to finance gender-related activities and to mobilize other resources that are required for the envisioned tasks. As yet, none of the FTAs assessed clarify this aspect of their funding and resource mobilization. This becomes a crucial challenge mainly for developing countries that may not have the resources required to implement the commitments they might have assumed in this context. One way to mitigate this challenge is to foster consultation with the private sector (ie civil society, companies, representative associations, and subject matter experts) that can provide relevant information and evidence on several issues to the policymakers during negotiations.

Another possibility for developing countries is to leverage the institutional strength and expertise that existing international organizations have in respect of different trade and trade-germane concerns.[82] Enhanced exchange and dialogue between developed and developing country partners could also help developing countries gain capacity and expertise on relevant issues that they can then utilize not only for trade negotiations but also for the implementation of commitments they assume in such agreements. For example, international organizations can conduct capacity-building workshops or workshops to exchange ideas and experiences between developed and developing country members and can also hold training sessions to regularly share ongoing research and data on the subject with their members.

9.6.3 Provide for monitoring, review, and impact assessment

Regular monitoring, through review processes and impact assessments, is essential to evaluate the effectiveness of trade policies and their impact on women. With limited understanding of the trade–gender nexus, countries need to consider negotiating associated provisions on monitoring and review of trade agreements

[82] Takashi Hattori, 'Building the Institutional Capacity for Trade and the Environment' (2006) 8(2) Interdisciplinary Environmental Review 70.

and the performance of women-related provisions in such agreements. Future negotiations could include forming a technical body on trade and women, comprising both party representatives and external stakeholders to handle these tasks.

The importance of monitoring and review of trade agreements and the impact or implementation of their relevant provisions to assess their impact on women is crucial. As proposed by the Organisation for Economic Co-operation and Development (OECD), agreements should set periodic dates for monitoring and review of a trade agreement's impact and the implementation of the relevant gender-related provisions. These should include clear indications on which actors are responsible for such exercises and countries should also make an effort to ensure that the relevant actors have the means to access the required data, expertise, and other resources needed for carrying out such monitoring and review activities.[83] The committees and institutions overseeing the implementation of international policy instruments such as the CEDAW Committee and the WTO's Trade Policy Review Mechanism, as well as the concerned international organizations, can help in gathering and providing the data needed to carry out monitoring and review tasks. It is equally important that countries identify the actors or institutions that will receive and assess the reports from monitoring and review exercises so that remedial action can be taken if an exercise demonstrates that an agreement is accentuating the inequalities between women and men (or other vulnerable groups).

Given the scant data on how trade agreements have impacted women, countries can undertake a comprehensive analysis of such impacts in the form of an ex-ante impact assessment exercise. Such exercises could assess the direct effects of changes in market access and trade reforms as well as the indirect effects that show how women may be impacted by different chapters and provisions in each trade agreement. Ex-ante impact assessments can help policymakers gather gender-disaggregated data and can also inform the negotiating processes and strategies.[84] Trade negotiators could adapt their negotiating plans to findings that are of particular importance for women workers or traders or consumers. Ex-ante assessment is important for negotiators because if there are potential negative impacts an agreement can have on women, they can include buffer provisions or change those provisions to mitigate their negative impact.

There is no shortage of enthusiasm in finding different methods and tools to carry out ex-ante assessments. Some examples of the most recently developed

[83] Jane Korinek and others, 'Trade and Gender Review of New Zealand' (OECD 1 June 2022) <www.oecd.org/publications/trade-and-gender-review-of-new-zealand-923576ea-en.htm> accessed 13 June 2024.

[84] Clemens Striebing, Evanthia Kalpazidou Schmidt, and Rachel Palmén, 'Pragmatic Ex-Ante Evaluation Using an Innovative Conceptual Framework: The Case of a High-Tech Entrepreneurship Program for Women' (December 2019) Evaluation and Program Planning 77 <https://doi.org/10.1016/j.evalprogplan.2019.101714> accessed 13 June 2024.

tools in this respect are Canada's Gender-Based Analysis Plus (GBA Plus) and UNCTAD's Gender and Trade Toolbox.[85] The UNCTAD Trade and Gender Toolbox is an important attempt in this respect as it helps to measure the impact and identify the intended and unintended consequences of trade agreements. It seeks to provide a systematic framework to evaluate the impact of trade policies and agreements on women before implementation of such agreements. The toolbox has four main components: (1) descriptive analysis of gender inequalities and the economic context of the country at stake; (2) quantitative analysis of the expected consequences of the trade reform on the economy and women's participation in the economy in particular; (3) a checklist for gender-sensitive accompanying measures and monitoring indicators; and (4) a Trade and Gender Index. The key question this ex-ante gender analysis aims to answer is what could happen to women if a given trade policy or an agreement is implemented in a specific country and a specific industry.

As noted, another method designed by Canada to assess how diverse groups of women, men, and gender-diverse people may experience policies, programmes, and initiatives is GBA Plus. Using GBA Plus involves taking a gender- and diversity-sensitive approach to trade negotiations. When trade agreements are assessed using the GBA Plus assessment, the results can help inform negotiators and policymakers of ways to incorporate relevant considerations in trade negotiations and draft agreements. This can help policymakers identify the negative effects of various provisions and the possible opportunities and benefits created through the application of a given FTA. Canada has applied this method to assess several agreements and trade negotiations. For example, Canada conducted a comprehensive chapter-by-chapter GBA Plus of its ongoing FTA negotiations with the Mercosur bloc (Argentina, Brazil, Paraguay, and Uruguay) and documented its analysis in a summary report.[86] It has also applied this method following the conclusion of its negotiation of the USMCA to evaluate the outcome and its potential effects and opportunities for people in Canada.

Policymakers and trade negotiators are encouraged to employ the available tools; however, these tools can be most effective when they are applied with the help of data related to, among other things, industries, economic structure, participation of women, and the impact of policies and trade reforms. This data can feed into effective policymaking for countries advancing the pursuit of women empowerment through their trade policies and agreements. Better understanding of how trade impacts women in their different roles can also create

[85] Cecilia Viscarra Moser, 'Photo Special: Trading for a Better Tomorrow' (2016) 1 International Trade Forum 8.

[86] Government of Canada, 'Summary of Initial Gender-based Analysis Plus (GBA+) for Canada–Mercosur Free Trade Agreement Negotiations' (4 March 2021) <www.international.gc.ca/trade-commerce/gender_equality-egalite_genres/gba_plus_summary-acs_plus_resume.aspx?lang=eng> accessed 24 November 2022.

evidence for policymakers on why and how trade agreements can be made to work for women. However, these methodologies only become relevant if they are put into application by policymakers and the output of those assessments are considered by policymakers and negotiators in a timely manner. The recent example of the EU's unsuccessful attempt to employ UNCTAD's Trade and Gender Toolbox exemplifies this point. On 28 June 2019, after two decades of negotiation, a historic trade agreement was struck between the EU and the Mercosur trading bloc. During the negotiations, the EU commissioned a Sustainability Impact Assessment of the agreement. For the component of women's concerns in that assessment, the EU used UNCTAD's toolbox; however, the negotiations leading to the agreement were finalized and a draft was agreed by the parties before the group of impact assessment experts could provide its final assessment.[87] This example shows that even if the technical tools are available, it is important to employ them during negotiations and initiate such assessment in a timely manner so that the results of the assessments can be considered during the negotiations themselves.

9.6.4 Identify transparency and accountability mechanisms

Embedding transparency and accountability mechanisms for such provisions in trade agreements has several benefits. If policymakers include explicit provisions on women's concerns in their trade agreements, transparency and accountability mechanisms can ensure that such considerations are reflected in the design and implementation of trade policies and agendas of the negotiating countries. This assessment can help countries better understand how trade policies interact with women and their interests in their jurisdictions and it can also help mitigate any negative distributional impact that trade liberalization may have on women in respect of their employment, entrepreneurship, and access to markets. These mechanisms can also assist in ensuring that trade policies and agreements are aligned with the goals and commitments that the countries have assumed in other international policy instruments in respect of women empowerment, human rights, labour rights, and sustainable development. This helps to create a more coherent and integrated approach towards women empowerment at the domestic level. These mechanisms can additionally provide opportunities for different stakeholders, including women organizations, civil society groups, businesses, and gender experts to participate in the policymaking and implementation processes. This interaction and exchange is essential as it can ensure that diverse perspectives and voices are

[87] Directorate-General for Trade, European Commission publishes final Sustainability Impact Assessment and Position Paper on the EU–Mercosur Trade Agreement' (29 March 2021) <https://trade.ec.europa.eu/doclib/press/index.cfm?id=2260> accessed 24 November 2022.

heard and considered during the negotiation and implementation stages, leading to more effective and inclusive trade policies.

Transparency and accountability mechanisms can enable the monitoring and evaluation of the implementation of such provisions and the impact they may have on women in their jurisdictions. This helps to identify gaps, challenges, and areas for improvement, allowing for evidence-based policy adjustments and ensuring accountability for achieving outcomes that can address the barriers women face. These mechanisms can also facilitate capacity-building initiatives and knowledge-sharing platforms to enhance understanding in this area and how trade agreements can better uphold women's interests.

Several procedures can be considered in this respect. Policymakers can create reporting and monitoring mechanisms for assessing the implementation and impact of such provisions. They can consider regular reporting requirements from signatory countries as well as the establishment of independent monitoring bodies or committees responsible for monitoring compliance with women-related provisions. It is also important to utilize independent audits to verify the accuracy of such reports and their effectiveness. Governments and relevant stakeholders can collaborate to collect data on various dimensions (eg women's participation in trade, gender wage gaps, and access to markets) to inform evidence-based policy decisions. What could also help in this respect is raising public awareness of the importance of women-related provisions in trade agreements to foster support and accountability. Public education campaigns, awareness-raising initiatives, and targeted communication strategies can help generate understanding and support for making trade agreements work for women.

9.6.5 Consider soft enforcement through consultations and non-punitive remedies

Successful outcomes for the enforcement of provisions relating to women require a move away from the zero-sum mercantilist 'give-and-take' approach—that is traditionally used in multilateral trade negotiations—to inclusive interstate engagement through cooperative and non-contentious efforts. Some FTAs provide for softer enforcement procedures in the case of disputes on matters relating to such commitments. For example, in the case of conflict, parties can try to resolve the matter through consultation, dialogue, and cooperation as seen in the Argentina–Chile FTA (Art 15.5).[88] These procedures are voluntary and do not invoke any sanction or legal action for non-compliance. Policymakers can choose to invoke such voluntary procedures or go beyond them to consider how they can make such

[88] (In force 1 May 2019.)

provisions somewhat more enforceable. One option could be the appointment of an expert panel that is entitled to make non-binding recommendations to guide countries on how to comply with such provisions. There are advantages for opting for an expert panel to resolve certain issues, such as short timelines to reach a final decision and the wealth of expertise and enthusiasm of relevant experts from which the proceedings can benefit.[89] This procedure would also increase the parties' accountability as a panel of experts can closely assess compliance with the provisions and make recommendations accordingly. The responding party can then report after a certain period on measures taken to implement the relevant provisions.

Countries can consider alternative remedies that are not as punitive as traditional remedies and, hence, exclude the possibility of suspending trade concessions or seeking financial compensation as temporary remedial measures thus outlining a hierarchy of remedies.[90] The traditional remedies have already proven ineffective on several occasions in the multilateral trading system, especially when the interests of a developing or least developed country have been at stake.[91] It is also debatable whether a sanctions-based approach is better than a best-endeavour approach for implementing women-related provisions, especially given the lack of evidence on how trade agreements and women's concerns interact and intersect.[92]

Countries that are willing to negotiate enforceable commitments in this respect can experiment with innovative non-punitive remedies. For example, an agreement can require a responding country to take additional women-favouring steps (pending full compliance) such as introducing a government procurement procedure or a supplier diversity programme that favours women. This is not an enforcement remedy as such, but it can be considered a secondary obligation that the offending party may be asked to fulfil pending full compliance with the arbitral or expert panel that determines a violation. Such options could be seen as a way to offset the harm caused by the agreement in one industry or sector by creating an advantage for women in the same or a different industry or sector.

Policymakers can also consider remedies based on gender-based conditionality, referring to gender equality outcomes within trade agreements. These conditions incentivize or penalize compliance based on performance in achieving gender equality goals. The rewards or penalties could involve access to preferential trade terms, financial incentives, or other trade-related benefits. As an example,

[89] Economic Partnership Agreement between the CARIFORUM States, of the one part, and the United Kingdom of Great Britain and Northern Ireland, of the other part (in force 20 October 2021), art 209 (Eg a panel of experts established that they had 150 days to issue their report after the date of its establishment.)

[90] ibid arts 191, 212, and 213.

[91] Marco Bronckers and Naboth van den Broek, 'Financial Compensation in the WTO: Improving the Remedies of WTO Dispute Settlement' (2005) 8(1) Journal of International Economic Law 101, 105.

[92] Kate Perry, 'Better for Whom? Sanction Type and the Gendered Consequences for Women' (2021) 36(2) International Relations 151.

countries in an agreement could offer reduced tariffs on agricultural products, conditional on both parties achieving a pre-determined level of female representation in agricultural management. If one party does not meet that level, it can lose its preferential tariff status. Such conditionality can incentivize a country to improve the status and conditions of women in the sector. Alternatively, the agreement might provide financial bonuses for achieving specific outcomes, such as increasing the number of women-owned farms or ensuring equitable access to agricultural training for women. These proposals may violate other trade obligations that a country may have assumed in a given trade agreement and, hence, policymakers should assess their legal consistency with their other obligations before considering employing such measures.

Another example would be an agreement setting up gender equality funds and incentives that provide resources to support initiatives such as gender-responsive budgeting. The funding could be tied to certain progress indicators or enforceable commitments to promote gender equality. If a trade agreement disproportionately impacts women in a particular industry or sector, finance from the gender equality fund could be directed towards initiatives that support women's economic empowerment and entrepreneurship in the affected industry or in alternative sectors. Countries which fail to meet enforceable commitments could face a reduction or temporary suspension of funding.

Bibliography

Books

Adrian Smith, James Harrison, Liam Campling, Ben Richardson, and Mirela Barbu, *Free Trade Agreements and Global Labour Governance* (Routledge 2021)
Amrita Bahri, Weihuan Zhou, and Daria Boklan (eds), *Rethinking, Repackaging, and Rescuing World Trade Law in the Post-Pandemic Era* (Hart Publishing 2023)
Anh-Nga Tran-Nguyen and Americo Beviglia Zampetti (eds), *Trade and Gender: Opportunities and Challenges for Developing Countries* (United Nations 2004)
Anthea Roberts and Nicolas Lamp, *Six Faces of Globalization: Who Wins, Who Loses and Why It Matters* (Harvard UP 2021)
Berta Esperanza Hernández-Truyol and Stephen Joseph Powell, *Just Trade* (New York UP 2009)
Colette Dowling, *The Cinderella Complex: Women's Hidden Fear of Independence* (Summit Books 1981)
Cosimo Beverelli, Jürgen Kurtz, and Damian Raess, *International Trade, Investment, and the Sustainable Development Goals* (World Trade Forum 2020)
Debra Nelson and James Campbell Quick, *Principles of Organizational Behavior: Realities and Challenges* (South-Western 2012)
Gudrun Greve, Markéta Hronková, Karolina Kerplová, Michal Krebs, Evelyn Probst, Zaklina Radosavljevic, Paula Riedemann, Klaudia Rottenschlager, Tereza Šimonová, and Miruna Beatrice Toda, *Migrant Women and Human Trafficking: Handbook for Professionals* (La Strada Česká Republika 2016)
Hyun-jung Je, *Public–Private Relationships in Trade Policy-Making* (World Scientific Publishing 2018)
Irene Van Staveren, Diane Elson, Caren Grown, and Nilüfer Çağatay (eds), *The Feminist Economics of Trade* (Routledge 2007)
Jack L Goldsmith and Eric A Posner, *The Limits of International Law* (OUP 2005)
Jean G Jones and Herbert W Simons, *Persuasion in Society* (Routledge 2017)
Jean-Pierre Chauffour and Jean-Christophe Maur, *Preferential Trade Agreement Policies for Development: A Handbook* (World Bank 2014)
Julie A Nelson, *Gender and Risk-Taking: Economics, Evidence, and Why the Answer Matters* (Routledge 2018)
Linda D Molm, *Coercive Power in Social Exchange* (CUP 1997)
Martha C Nussbaum, *Women and Human Development: The Capabilities Approach* (CUP 2007)
Martha Finnemore, *National Interests in International Society* (Cornell UP 1996)
Naila Kabeer, *Gender Mainstreaming in Poverty Eradication and the Millennium Development Goals: A Handbook for Policymakers and Other Stakeholders* (Commonwealth Secretariat 2003)
Odile Ammann, *Domestic Courts and the Interpretation of International Law* (Brill 2020)
Olga Sasunkevich, *Informal Trade, Gender, and the Border Experience* (Routledge 2015)
Won-Mog Choi, *Like Products in International Trade Law: Towards a Consistent GATT/WTO Jurisprudence* (OUP 2003)
Zo Randriamaro, *Gender and Trade* (Institute of Development Studies 2006)

Book Chapters

Amrita Bahri, 'Blockchaining International Trade: A Way Forward for Women's Economic Empowerment?' in Maarten Smeets (ed), *Adapting to the Digital Trade Era: Challenges and Opportunities* (WTO Publications 2021)

Amrita Bahri, 'Gender Mainstreaming in Trade Agreements: Best Practice Examples and Challenges in the Asia-Pacific' in Amrita Bahri, Dorotea López, and Jan Remy (eds), *Trade Policy and Gender Equality* (CUP 2023)

Anoush der Boghossian, 'Gender Responsive WTO: Trade Rules and Policies Work for Women' in Amrita Bahri, Dorotea López, and Jan Remy (eds), *Trade Policy and Gender Equality* (CUP 2023)

Beate Rudolf, 'Freedom from Violence, Full Access to Resources, Equal Participation, and Empowerment: The Relevance of CEDAW for the Implementation of the SDGs' in Markus Krajewski (ed), *Interdisciplinary Studies in Human Rights* (Springer 2019)

Gary Gereffi and Olga Memedovic, 'The Global Apparel Value Chain: What Prospects for Upgrading by Developing Countries' in Leila Choukroune and James J Nedumpara (eds), *International Economic Law: Text, Cases and Materials* (CUP 2021)

Ghada Ahmed, 'Global Value Chains, Economic Upgrading and Gender in the Call Center Industry' in Cornelia Startiz and José G Reis (eds), *Global Value Chains, Economic Upgrading and Gender in the Call Center Industry* (Duke 2013)

Irene van Staveren, Diane Elson, Caren Grown, and Nilüfer Çağatay, 'The Feminist Economics of Trade' in Irene van Staveren, Diane Elson, Caren Grown, and Nilüfer Çağatay (eds), *The Feminist Economics of Trade* (Routledge 2007)

Isaiah Berlin, 'Two Concepts of Liberty' in Henry Hardy (ed), *Liberty* (OUP 2002)

John Ruggie, 'Embedded Liberalism Revisited: Institutions and Progress in International Economic Relations' in Emanuel Adler and Beverly Crawford (eds), *Progress in Postwar International Economic Relations* (Columbia UP 1991)

Judit Fabian, 'Global Economic Governance and Women: Why Is the WTO a Difficult Case for Women's Representation?' in Amrita Bahri, Dorotea López, and Jan Remy (eds), *Trade Policy and Gender Equality* (CUP 2023)

Katrin Kuhlmann and Amrita Bahri, 'Gender Mainstreaming in Trade Agreements: "A Potemkin Façade"?' in Anoush der Boghossian (ed), *Making Trade Work for Women: Key Findings from the 2022 World Trade Congress on Gender* (World Trade Organization 2023)

Leonardo Baccini, Andreas Dür, and Yoram Z Haftel, 'Imitation and Innovation in International Governance: The Diffusion of Trade Agreement Design' in Andreas Dür and Manfred Elsig (eds), *Trade Cooperation: The Purpose, Design, and Effects of Preferential Trade Agreements* (CUP 2015)

Marcus Gustafsson and Amrita Bahri, 'Progressive Trade: Labour and Gender' in Daniel Bethlehem, Donald McRae, Rodney Neufeld, and Isabelle Van Damme (eds), *The Oxford Handbook of International Trade Law* (OUP 2022)

Maria V Sokolova and Matthew Wilson, 'Setting Up the Table Right: Women's Representation Meets Women's Inclusion in Trade Negotiations' in Amrita Bahri, Dorotea López, and Jan Yves Remy (eds), *Trade Policy and Gender Equality* (CUP 2023)

Robert Baldwin, 'Trade Policies in Developed Countries' in Ronald Jones and Peter Kenen (eds), *Handbook of International Economics* (North-Holland 1984)

Robert Howse, Brian Langille, and Julien Burda, 'The World Trade Organization and Labour Rights: Man Bites Dog' in Virginia A Leary and Daniel Warner (eds), *Social Issues, Globalisation* (Brill 2005)

Wendy Olsen, 'Triangulation in Social Research: Qualitative and Quantitative Methods Can Really Be Mixed' in Martin Holborn (ed), *Developments in Sociology* (Causeway Press 2004)

Yin-Zu Chen and Hiromi Tanaka, 'Women's Empowerment' in Alex C Michalos (ed), *Encyclopedia of Quality of Life and Well-Being Research* (Springer 2014)

Journal Articles

Adrian Wood, 'North–South Trade and Female Labour in Manufacturing: An Asymmetry' (1991) 27(2) Journal of Development Studies 168

Albert Bandura, 'Self-Efficacy: Toward a Unifying Theory of Behavioral Change' (1977) 84(2) Psychological Review 191

Alessandro Nicita and Simonetta Zarrilli, 'Trade Policy and Gender—Unfolding the Links' (2010) 44(1) Journal of World Trade 203

Allan Winters, Neil McCulloch, and Andrew McKay, 'Trade Liberalization and Poverty: The Evidence So Far' (2004) 42(1) Journal of Economic Literature 72

Amrita Bahri, 'Making Trade Agreements Work for Women Empowerment: How Does It Help, What Has Been Done, and What Remains Undone?' (2021) 4(11) Latin American Journal of Trade Policy 6

Amrita Bahri, 'Women at the Frontline of COVID-19: Can Gender Mainstreaming in Free Trade Agreements Help?' (2020) 23(3) Journal of International Economic Law 563

Amrita Bahri, 'Measuring the Gender-Responsiveness of Free Trade Agreements: Using a Self-Evaluation Maturity Framework' (2019) 14 (11) Global Trade & Customs Journal 517

Amrita Bahri and Daria Boklan, 'Not Just Sea Turtles, Let's Protect Women Too: Invoking Public Morality Exception or Negotiating a New Gender Exception in Trade Agreements?' (2022) 33(1) European Journal of International Law 237

Amrita Bahri and Renata Amaral, 'Gender Equality Provisions in Trade and Investment Agreements: Are They Widening the Negotiation Capacity Gap?' (2024) 23(1) World Trade Review 47

Amy K Kiefer and Denise Sekaquaptewa, 'Implicit Stereotypes, Gender Identification, and Math-Related Outcomes: A Prospective Study of Female College Students' (2007) 18(1) Psychological Science 13

Andrew Guzman, 'The Design of International Agreements' (2005) 16(4) European Journal of International Law 579

Andrew Lang, 'Reconstructing Embedded Liberalism: John Gerard Ruggie and Constructivist Approaches to the Study of the International Trade Regime' (2006) 9(1) Journal of International Economic Law 81

Andrew Moravcsik, 'The Origins of Human Rights Regimes: Democratic Delegation in Postwar Europe' (2000) 54(2) International Organization 217

Aniekan Ukpe and Sangeeta Khorana, 'Special and Differential Treatment in the WTO: Framing Differential Treatment to Achieve (Real) Development' (2021) 20(2) Journal of International Trade Law and Policy 83

Anna Hutchens, 'Empowering Women through Fair Trade? Lessons from Asia' (2010) 31(3) Third World Quarterly 449

Anoush Der Boghossian and Amrita Bahri, 'Finding Feet on Trade Agreements: Empowering Women Entrepreneurs Amidst a Pandemic' (2023) 50(1) Legal Issues of Economic Integration 13

Arlo Poletti, Daniela Sicurelli, and Aydin B Yildirim, 'Promoting Sustainable Development Through Trade? EU Trade Agreements and Global Value Chains' (2020) 51(3) Italian Political Science Review/ Rivista Italiana di Scienza Politica 339

Arthur Alderson, 'Explaining the Upswing in Direct Dnvestment: A Test of Mainstream and Heterodox Theories of Globalization' (2004) 83(1) Social Forces 81

Asma Hyder and Jere R Behrman, 'International Trade Openness and Gender Gaps in Pakistani Labor Force Participation Rates over 57 Years' (2012) 17(3) Journal of the Asia Pacific Economy 367

Aurora Rubio, 'Factors that Impact Girls' Education in Ghana' (2018) 9(1) Leadership Research <https://viurrspace.ca/bitstream/handle/10613/6204/Rubio.pdf?sequence=1> accessed 18 September 2022

Axel Marx, Nicolás Brando, and Brecht Lein, 'Strengthening Labour Rights Provisions in Bilateral Trade Agreements: Making the Case for Voluntary Sustainability Standards' (2017) 8(3) Global Policy 78

Ayelet Makaros and Haya Itzhaky, 'Work-Related Stress and Social Workers' Perceptions of Effectiveness in Light of the Recent Changes in Social and Economic Policies in Israel' (2008) 30(2) Social Development Issues 45

Barbara Yonemura, 'Plain English for Lawyers by Richard C Wydick—eScholarship' (1981) 7(2) National Black Law Journal 384

Bart Kerremans and Myriam Martins-Gistelinck, 'Interest Aggregation, Political Parties, Labour Standards and Trade: Differences in the US and EU Approaches to the Inclusion of Labour Standards in International Trade Agreements' (2009) 14(5) European Foreign Affairs Review 683

Bedri Kamil Onur Tas, Kamala Dawar, Peter M Holmes, and Sübidey Togan, 'Does the WTO Government Procurement Agreement Deliver What It Promises?' (2018) 18 World Trade Review 609

Beth A Simmons, 'International Law and State Behavior: Commitment and Compliance in International Monetary Affairs' (2000) 94(4) The American Political Science Review 819

Brandon J Hill, Kris Rosentel, Trevor Bak, Michael Silverman, Richard Crosby, Laura Salazar, and Michele Kipke, 'Exploring Individual and Structural Factors Associated with Employment Among Young Transgender Women of Color Using a No-Cost Transgender Legal Resource Center' (2017) 2(1) Transgender Health 29

Charlotte May-Simera, 'Reconsidering Sheltered Workshops in Light of the United Nations Convention on the Rights of Persons with Disabilities' (2006) (2018) 7(1) Laws 6

Christian Broda and David E Weinstein, 'Globalization and the Gains from Variety' (2006) 121(2) Quarterly Journal of Economics 541

Christian N Thoroughgood, Katina Sawyer, and Jennica R Webster, 'Creating a Trans-Inclusive Workplace', Harvard Business Review (March-April 2020) <https://hbr.org/2020/03/creating-a-trans-inclusive-workplace> accessed 6 June 2024

Christian Reus-Smit, 'Human Rights and the Social Construction of Sovereignty' (2001) 27(4) Review of International Studies 519

Cirila Quintero-Ramírez, 'The North American Free Trade Agreement and Women' (2002) (4)2 International Feminist Journal of Politics 240

Constance Z Wagner, 'Looking at Regional Trade Agreements through the Lens of Gender' (2012) 31 St Louis University Public Law Review 497

Dale H Schunk and Maria K DiBenedetto, 'Motivation and Social Cognitive Theory' (2020) 60 Contemporary Educational Psychology 101832

Daria Boklan and Amrita Bahri, 'The First WTO's Ruling on National Security Exception: Balancing Interests or Opening Pandora's Box?' (2020) 19(1) World Trade Review 123

Daria Boklan, Olga Starshinova, and Amrita Bahri, 'Joint Statement Initiatives: A Legitimate End to "Until Everything is Agreed"?' (2023) 57(2) Journal of World Trade 339

Deborah M Wilson, Jessica D Davis, Carol Parker, and Candy Ratliff, 'The Self-Esteem of African American Women: The Impact of Black Church Attendance' (2022) 23(2) The Journal of the Research Association of Minority Professors 224

Deniz Kagniciouglu, 'The Role of Women in Working Life in Turkey' (2017) 226 WIT Transactions on Ecology and the Environment 349

Desirée LeClercq, 'The Disparate Treatment of Rights in Trade' (2021) 90(1) Fordham Law Review 1

Don Flynn and Eleonore Kofman, 'Women, Trade, and Migration' (2004) 12 Gender & Development 66

Edmé Domínguez Reyes, 'Women Organizing against Free Trade in Latin America, Latin American Policy' (2014) 5(2) Latin American Policy 193

Elina Viilup, 'EU Trade Policy: Gender-Sensitive or Gender Blind?' (2016) 5(6) GREAT Insights 1

Elisa Dávalos, 'Protectionism, USMCA and its Possible Effects on Mexico's Automotive Industry' (2020) 7(1) European Review of International Studies 81

Elizabeth Evatt, 'Finding a Voice for Women's Rights: The Early Days of CEDAW' (2002) 34(3) George Washington International Law Review 515

Elizabeth Whitsitt, 'A Comment on the Public Morals Exception in International Trade and the EC—Seal Products Case: Moral Imperialism and Other Concerns' (2014) 3(4) Cambridge Journal of International and Comparative Law 1376

Emezat Mengesha, 'Rethinking the Rules and Principles of the International Trade Regime: Feminist Perspectives' (2008) 22(78) Engendering National & Global Economic Policies 13

Emilie M Hafner-Burton, 'Trading Human Rights: How Preferential Trade Agreements Influence Government Repression' (2005) 59(3) International Organization 593

Esther Ann Bøler, Beata Javorcik, and Karen Helene Ulltveit-Moe, 'Working Across Time Zones: Exporters and the Gender Wage Gap' (2018) 111 Journal of International Economics 122

Esther Duflo, 'Women Empowerment and Economic Development' (2012) 50(4) Journal of Economic Literature 1051

Evgeny Postnikov and Ida Bastiaens, 'Does Dialogue Work? The Effectiveness of Labor Standards in EU Preferential Trade Agreements' (2014) 21(6) Journal of European Public Policy 923

Evgeny Postnikov and Ida Bastiaens, 'Social Protectionist Bias: The Domestic Politics of North–South Trade Agreements' (2020) 22(2) The British Journal of Politics and International Relations 347

Fiona Colgan and Sue Ledwith, 'Diversity, Identities and Strategies of Women Trade Union Activists' (2000) 7(4) Gender, Work and Organization 242

Flavia Jurje and Sandra Lavenex, 'Trade Agreements as Venues for "Market Power Europe"?' (2013) 52(2) Journal of Common Markets and Studies 320

George Prince, 'Education Inequality: How Patriarchy and Policy Collide in Ghana' (2015) 5(7) International Journal of Humanities and Social Science 11

George W Downs, David M Rocke, and Peter N Barsoom, 'Is the Good News About Compliance Good News About Cooperation?' (1996) 50(3) International Organization 379

Gregory Shaffer and Mark A Pollack, 'Hard vs Soft Law: Alternatives, Complements and Antagonists in International Governance' (2009) 94 Minnesota Law Review 706

Gunman Mishra, 'The Psychological Facets of Women Empowerment at Workplace' (2016) 2(1) International Journal of Recent Trends in Engineering & Research <www.semanticscholar.org/paper/The-Psychological-Facets-of-Women-Empowerment-at-Mishra/a938a5169abcf8a9b1b3f85062f85b50bf0e34d0#citing-papers> accessed 18 June 2024

Günseli Berik, 'Mature Export-Led Growth and Gender Wage Inequality in Taiwan' (2000) 6(3) Feminist Economics 1

Gurushri Swamy, 'International Trade and Women' (2004) 39(45) Economic and Political Weekly 4885

Guy Standing, 'Global Feminization through Flexible Labor: A Theme Revisited' (1999) 27(3) World Development Elsevier 583

Hayet Kerras, 'The Impact of the Gender Digital Divide on Sustainable Development: Comparative Analysis between the European Union and the Maghreb' (2020) 12(8) Sustainability 3347

Herminia Ibarra, Robin J Ely, and Deborah M Kolb, 'Women Rising: The Unseen' (2013) 91(9) Harvard Business Review 60

Ida Bastiaens and Evgeny Postnikov, 'Greening Up: The Effects of Environmental Standards in EU and US Trade Agreements' (2017) 26(5) Environmental Politics 847

Ida Bastiaens, Evgeny Postnikov, and Anne-Kathrin Kreft, 'Labour Provisions in Trade Agreements and Women's Rights in the Global South' (2023) 14(5) Global Policy 702

Inge Ropke, 'Trade, Development and Sustainability—a Critical Assessment of the "Free Trade Dogma"' (1994) 9 (1) Ecological Economics 13

J Allister McGregor and Nicky Pouw, 'Towards an Economics of Well-Being' (2017) 41(4) Cambridge Journal of Economics 1123

James Atta Peprah, Eric Atsu Avorkpo, and Evans Kulu, 'People with Disability and Access to Financial Services: Evidence from Ghana' (2023) 15(6) Regional Science Policy & Practice 1198

James C Murdoch and Todd Sandler, 'The Voluntary Provision of a Pure Public Good: The Case of Reduced CFC Emissions and the Montreal Protocol' (1997) 63(3) Journal of Public Economics 331

James Harrison, Mirela Barbu, Liam Campling, Franz Christian Ebert, Deborah Martens, Axel Marx, Jan Orbie, Ben Richardson, and Adrian Smith, 'Labour Standards Provisions in EU Free Trade Agreements: Reflections on the European Commission's Reform Agenda' (2019) 18 World Trade Review 635

James Levinsohn, 'Employment Responses to International Liberalization in Chile' (1999) 47(2) Journal of International Economics 321

Jayati Ghosh, 'Globalization, Export-Oriented Employment for Women and Social Policy: A Case Study of India' (2002) 30(11) Social Scientist 17
Jean-Frédéric Morin and Myriam Rochette, 'Transatlantic Convergence of PTAs' Environmental Clauses' (2017) 19(4) Business and Politics 621
Jean-Frédéric Morin, Andreas Dür, and Lisa Lechne 'Mapping the Trade and Environment Nexus: Insights from a New Data Set' (2018) 18(1) Global Environmental Politics 122
Jeffrey Kucik and Eric Reinhardt, 'Does Flexibility Promote Cooperation? An Application to the Global Trade Regime' (2008) 62(3) International Organization 477
Jiekun Huang and Darren J Kisgen, 'Gender and Corporate Finance: Are Male Executives Overconfident Relative to Female Executives?' (2013) 108(3) Journal of Financial Economics 822
Joan Fitzpatrick and Katrina R Kelly, 'Gendered Aspects of Migration: Law and the Female Migrant' (1998) 22(1) Hastings International and Comparative Law Review 47
John Bessant and Sarah Caffyn, 'High–Involvement Innovation through Continuous Improvement' (1997) 14(1) International Journal of Technology Management 14
John Ruggie, 'International Regimes, Transactions and Change: Embedded Liberalism in the Postwar Economic Order' (1982) 36(2) International Organization 379
Karen Melanson, 'An Examination of the Gendered Effects of Trade Liberalisation' (2005) 2(1) Policy Perspectives 10
Karin Ulmer, 'Are Trade Agreements with the EU Beneficial to Women in Africa, the Caribbean, and the Pacific?' (2004) 12(2) Gender & Development 53
Karolina Milewicz, James Hollway, and Duncan Snidal, 'Beyond Trade: The Expanding Scope of the Non-Trade Agenda in Trade Agreements' (2018) 62(4) Journal of Conflict Resolution 743
Kate Perry, 'Better for Whom? Sanction Type and the Gendered Consequences for Women' (2021) 36(2) International Relations 151
Kathryn Sikkink, 'Human Rights, Principled Issue-Networks, and Sovereignty in Latin America' (1993) 47(3) International Organization 411
Katrin Kuhlmann, 'Mapping Inclusive Law and Regulation: A Comparative Agenda for Trade and Development' (2021) 2 African Journal of International Economic 48
Kenneth W Abbot and Duncan Snidal, 'Hard and Soft Law in International Governance' (2000) 54(3) International Organization 421
Krista M Perreira, Joshua Wassink, and Kathleen Mullan Harris, 'Beyond Race/Ethnicity: Skin Color, Gender, and the Health of Young Adults in the United States' (2019) 38(2) Population Research and Policy Review 271
Kristi E Gamarel, Laura Jadwin-Cakmak, Wesley M King, Lilianna A Reyes, Racquelle Trammell, Torsten B Neilands, Maureen D Connolly, and Larissa Jennings Mayo-Wilson, 'Community-Led Response to Address Economic Vulnerability due to COVID-19 with, for, and by Transgender Women of Color: A Qualitative Pilot Evaluation' (2023) 8(2) Transgender Health 195
Kristoffer Marslev and Cornelia Staritz, 'Towards a Stronger EU Approach on the Trade–Labor Nexus? The EU–Vietnam Free Trade Agreement, Social Struggles and Labor Reforms in Vietnam' (2023) 30(3) Review of International Political Economy 1125
Leslie Kurshan, 'Rethinking Property Rights as Human Rights: Acquiring Equal Property Rights for Women Using International Human Rights Treaties' (2000) 8(2) Journal of Gender, Social Policy & the Law 353
Liane M Jarvis, 'Women's Rights and the Public Morals Exception of GATT Article 20' (2000) 22(1) Michigan Journal of International Law 219
Lilia Domínguez-Villalobos and Flor Brown-Grossman, 'Trade Liberalization and Gender Wage Inequality in Mexico' (2010) 15(4) Feminist Economics 53
Linda Shields, Jenny Hall, and Abdulla A Mamun, 'The "Gender Gap" in Authorship in Nursing Literature' (2011) 104(11) Journal of the Royal Society of Medicine 457
Linda Stevenson, 'The Bachelet Effect on Gender-Equity Policies' (2012) 39(4) Latin American Perspectives 129
Lisa Lechner, 'The Domestic Battle over the Design of Non-Trade Issues in Preferential Trade Agreements' (2016) 23(5) Review of International Political Economy 840

Maaike van der Vleuten, Stephanie Steinmetz, and Herman van de Werfhorst, 'Gender Norms and STEM: The Importance of Friends for Stopping Leakage from the STEM Pipeline' (2019) 24(3) Educational Research and Evaluation 1

Mackenzi Lafferty, 'The Pink Tax: The Persistence of Gender Price Disparity' (2019) 11 Midwest Journal of Undergraduate Research 56

Manuel Santos Silva and Stephan Klasen, 'Gender Inequality as a Barrier to Economic Growth: A Review of the Theoretical Literature' (2021) 19 Review of the Economics of the Household 581

Marc Zimmerman, 'Taking Aim on Empowerment Research: On the Distinction between Individual and Psychological Conceptions' (1984) 18(1) American Journal of Community Psychology 169

Marco Bronckers and Naboth van den Broek, 'Financial Compensation in the WTO: Improving the Remedies of WTO Dispute Settlement' (2005) 8(1) Journal of International Economic Law 101

Maria Floro, 'Economic Restructuring, Gender and the Allocation of Time' (1995) 23(11) World Development 1913

Mark Wu, 'Free Trade and the Protection of Public Morals: An Analysis of the Newly Emerging Public Morals Clause Doctrine' (2008) 33 Yale Journal of International Law 215

Martha Alter Chen, 'Women in the Informal Sector: A Global Picture, the Global Movement' (2001) 21(1) SAIS Review 71

Martha Finnemore and Kathryn Sikkink, 'International Norm Dynamics and Political Change' (1998) 52(4) International Organization 887

Mary Wilson, 'Lean In: Women, Work, and the Will to Lead: Sheryl Sandberg' (2014) 30 Asian Women 1

Matthias Doepke and Fabian Kindermann, 'Bargaining over Babies: Theory, Evidence, and Policy Implications' (2019) 109(9) American Economic Review 3264

Maya Sophie Cohen, 'The Pink Trojan Horse: Inserting Gender Issues into Free Trade Agreements' (2021) 5(2) International and Public Affairs 75

Mehraj Ahmad Sheikh, Mushtaq Ahmad Malik, and Rana Zehra Masood, 'Assessing the Effects of Trade Openness on Sustainable Development: Evidence from India' (2020) 5(1) Asian Journal of Sustainability and Social Responsibility

Mélika Ben Salem and Chahir Zaki, 'Revisiting the Impact of Trade Openness on Informal and Irregular Employment in Egypt' (2019) 34(3) Journal of Economic Integration 465

Mellanie C Steffens, Petra Jelenec, and Peter Noack, 'On the Leaky Math Pipeline: Comparing Implicit Math-Gender Stereotypes and Math Withdrawal in Female and Male Children and Adolescents' (2010) 102(4) Journal of Educational Psychology 947

Meredith Kolsky Lewis, 'Human Rights Provisions in Free Trade Agreements: Do the Ends Justify the Means?' (2015) 12 Loyola University Chicago International Law Review 1

Naila Kabeer, 'Globalization, Labor Standards, and Women's Rights: Dilemmas of Collective (In) Action in an Interdependent World' (2004) 10(3) Feminist Economics 35

Nanette Page and Cheryl E Czuba, 'Empowerment: What Is It?' (1999) 37(5) Journal of Extension 24

Nickolas B Davis and Stephen T Yeung, 'Transgender Equity in the Workplace: A Systematic Review' (2022) 12(1) Sage Open <https://journals.sagepub.com/doi/10.1177/2158244022 1082863> accessed 6 June 2024

Nicolas F Diebold, 'The Morals and Order Exceptions in WTO Law: Balancing the Toothless Tiger and Undermining Mole' (2007) 11(1) Journal of International Economic Law 43

Oona A Hathaway, 'The Cost of Commitment' (2003) 55(5) Stanford Law Review 1821

Pallavi Panda, 'COVID-19, Trade Disruptions, and Gender: A Survey of the Potential Interactions and Consequences for Economic Development in Sub-Saharan Africa' (2022) 23 (2) Journal of African Development 347

Paulina Meza, Felipe González-Catalán, Carmen López-Ferrero, and Israel Gutiérrez, 'Plain Writing in the Legal Field: An Approach from the Discourse of Specialists' (2020) 22 Discourse Studies 356

Pauline Rose Clance and Suzanne Imes, 'The Imposter Phenomenon in High Achieving Women: Dynamics and Therapeutic Intervention' (1978) 15(3) Psychotherapy Theory, Research and Practice 241

Pelin Serpin, 'The Public Morals Exception After the WTO Seal Products Dispute: Has the Exception Swallowed the Rules?' (2016) 1 Columbia Business Law Review 219

Petia Topalova, 'Immobility and Regional Impacts of Trade Liberalization: Evidence on Poverty from India' (2010) 2(4) American Economic Journal: Applied Economics 1

Philip Sauré and Hosny Zoabi, 'International Trade, the Gender Wage Gap and Female Labour Force Participation' (2014) 111(C) Journal of Development Economics 17

Popoola Sulaiman Akorede and others, 'Abuses of Women in Inheritance Across Cultures: An Exploratory Study of Its Prevalence and Religious Panacea' (2017) 16(12) Chinese Business Review 620

Puyang Sun, Yong Tan, and Guang Yang, 'Export, FDI and the Welfare Gains from Trade Liberalization' (2020) 92 Economic Modelling 230

PX Francina and Mary Venus Joseph, 'Women Empowerment: The Psychological Dimension' (2013) 5(2) Rajagiri Journal of Social Development 163

Raj Bhala and Cody N Wood, 'Two Dimensional Hard–Soft Law Theory and the Advancement of Women's and LGBTQ + Rights Through Free Trade Agreements' (2019) 47 Georgia Journal of International and Comparative Law 2

Rajesh Barik and Pritee Sharma, 'What Constraints Financial Inclusion for the Transgender Community? Field-Based Evidences from Odisha (India)' (2021) 13(1) Contemporary Voice of Dalit 66

Regis Y Simo, 'Trade and Morality: Balancing between the Pursuit of Non-Trade Concerns and the Fear of Opening the Floodgates' (2019) 51(3) George Washington International Law Review 407

Remco Oostendorp, 'Globalization and the Gender Wage Gap' (2009) 23(1) World Bank Economic Review 141

Renata Vargas Amaral and Lillyana Daza Jaller, 'The Role of Regulation and MNEs in Ensuring Equal Opportunities for Women' (2020) 27(3) Transnational Corporations 183

Roger P Alford, 'The Self-Judging WTO Security Exception' (2011) 697 Utah Law Review 698

Rohini Acharya, Olga Falgueras Alamo, Salma Mohamed Thabit Al-Battashi, Anoush der Boghossian, Naghm Ghei, Tania Parcero Herrera, Lee Ann Jackson, Ulla Kask, Claudia Locatelli, Gabrielle Marceau, Ioana-Virginia Motoc, Anna Caroline Müller, Nora Neufeld, Simon Padilla, Josefita Pardo de Léon, Stella Perantakou, Nadezhda Sporysheva, and Christiane Wolff, 'Trade and Women—Opportunities for Women in the Framework of the World Trade Organization' (2019) 22(3) Journal of International Economic Law 323

Ryan Abman and Clark Lundberg, 'Does Free Trade Increase Deforestation? The Effects of Regional Trade Agreements' (2020) 7(1) Journal of the Association of Environmental and Resource Economists 35

Sally M Reiss, 'External Barriers Experienced by Gifted and Talented Girls and Women' (2001) 4 Gifted Child Today 24

Sharon Wolf and others, 'Barriers to School Attendance and Gender Inequality: Empirical Evidence From a Sample of Ghanaian Schoolchildren' (2016) 11(2) Research in Comparative & International Education <https://journals.sagepub.com/doi/10.1177/1745499916632424> accessed 6 June 2024

SN Nyeck, '(Out)bidding Women: Public Procurement Reform Diffusion and Gender Equality in Africa' (2015) 13 Wagadu 24

Steve Charnovitz, 'The Moral Exception in Trade Policy' (1998) 38 Virginia Journal of International Law 689

Steve Charnowitz, 'The Law of Environmental PPMs in the WTO: Debunking the Myth of Illegality' (2002) 27(1) Yale Journal of International Law 59

Takashi Hattori, 'Building the Institutional Capacity for Trade and the Environment' (2006) 8 Interdisciplinary Environmental Review 70

Talajeh Livani, Nadeem Rizwan, and Sanjay Kathuria, 'Inclusive Regional Trade: Promoting the Economic Empowerment of Women in the BBIN Region' (2019) 4(1) ANTYAJAA: Indian Journal of Women and Social Change 33

Thi Anh-Dao Tran, 'The Feminization of Employment through Export-Led Strategies: Evidence from Viet Nam' (2019) 25 Revue de la regulation 1

Todd Allee and Manfred Elsig, 'Are the Contents of International Treaties Copied and Pasted? Evidence from Preferential Trade Agreements' (2019) 63(3) International Studies Quarterly 603

Tyler M Smith, 'Much Needed Reform in the Realm of Public Morals: A Proposed Addition to the GATT Article XX(A) Public Morals Framework, Resulting from China—Audiovisual' (2011) 19 Cardozo Journal of International and Competition Law 733

Usman Ahmed, Thorsten Beck, Christine McDaniel, and Simon Schropp, 'Filling the Gap: How Technology Enables Access to Finance for Small- and Medium-Sized Enterprises' (2015) 10 (3)–(4) Innovations: Technology, Governance, Globalization 35

Viral V Acharya, Tim Eisert, Christian Eufinger, and Christian Hirsch, 'Whatever It Takes: The Real Effects of Unconventional Monetary Policy' (2019) 32(9) The Review of Financial Studies 3366

Von Rudolf Adlung and Marta Soprana, 'SMEs in Services Trade—A GATS Perspective' (2013) 48(1) Intereconomics 4

Studies, Reports, and Periodicals

A4AI, 'Affordability Report 2019' (World Wide Web Foundation 2019) <https://a4ai.org/research/affordability-report/affordability-report-2019/> accessed 18 September 2022

Al Jazeera and Reuters, 'India: Banning women from owning mobile phones' (Al Jazeera 2016) <www.aljazeera.com/news/2016/02/26/india-banning-women-from-owning-mobile-phones/> accessed 18 September 2022

Alan V Deardorff and Robert M Stern, 'Measurement of Non-Tariff Barriers' (1997) OECD Working Paper 179 <www.oecd.org/economy/growth/1863859.pdf> accessed 17 August 2021

Amrita Bahri, 'Trade Agreements and Disability Inclusion: Demystifying the Disconnect between Barriers and Policy Solutions' (United Kingdom Foreign, Commonwealth and Development Office and Cowater International Inc., forthcoming 2024)

Amrita Bahri, 'Making Trade Agreements Work for People with Disabilities: What's been Achieved and What Remains Undone?' (UK FCDO and Cowater International Inc 2023) <www.genderandtrade.com/_files/ugd/86d8f7_a4ebc789a1ae4c81b51d725cbc31bfa3.pd> accessed 6 June 2024

Amrita Bahri, 'Gender Mainstreaming in Free Trade Agreements: A Regional Analysis and Good Practice Examples', Gender, Social Inclusion and Trade Knowledge Product Series (FCDO and the UK Government 2021) <https://wtochairs.org/sites/default/files/7.%20Gender%20mainstreaming%20in%20FTAs_final%20%286%29.pdf> accessed 13 August 2023

Anoush der Boghossian, 'Trade Policies Supporting Women's Economic Empowerment: Trends in WTO Members' (2019) WTO Staff Working Paper ERSD-2019-07 <www.wto.org/english/res_e/reser_e/ersd201907_e.pdf> accessed 18 October 2022

Anoush der Boghossian, 'Women's economic empowerment: an inherent part of Aid for Trade' (World Trade Organization: Economic Research and Statistics Division 2019)

Arthur Gailes, Tamara Gurevich, Serge Shikher, and Marinos Tsigas, 'Gender and Income Inequality in United States Tariff Burden' (US International Trade Commission 2018) <www.usitc.gov/publications/332/working_papers/ggst_-_gender_and_income_inequality_in_tariffs.pdf> accessed 18 September 2022

AS Shan, '50 Malayali women enmeshed in sex racket stranded in Bahrain' *The New Indian Express* (2019) <www.newindianexpress.com/states/kerala/2019/feb/23/50-malayali-women-enmeshed-in-sex-racket-stranded-in-bahrain-1942440.html> accessed 18 September 2022

Asli Demirgüç-Kunt, Leora Klapper, Dorothe Singer, and Saniya Ansar, 'The Global Findex Database, 2021: Financial Inclusion, Digital Payments, and Resilience in the Age of Covid-19' (World Bank Publications 2021)

Balakrishnan Rajagopal, 'Women and Trade at the WTO: Pink Herring, Trojan Horse or Historic Advance?' (CIGI Reshaping Trade Through Women's Economic Empowerment 9 April 2018)

Ben Shepherd and Susan Stone, 'Trade and Women', ADBI Working Papers 648, Asian Development Bank Institute <https://ideas.repec.org/p/ris/adbiwp/0648.html> accessed 25 September 2023

Betsey Stevenson and Justin Wolfers, 'Economic Growth and Subjective Well-Being: Reassessing the Easterlin Paradox' (2008) NBER Working Papers 14282 <http://www.nber.org/papers/w14282>

Caroline Dommen, 'Mainstreaming Gender in Trade Policy: Practice, evidence, and ways forward' (International Institute of Sustainable Development November 2021) <www.iisd.org/system/files/2021-11/mainstreaming-gender-in-trade-policy.pdf> accessed 29 October 2023

CEDAW, 'Concluding observations of the Committee on the Elimination of Discrimination against Women (Kuwait)' (United Nations Committee on the Elimination of Discrimination against Women 2011) <www2.ohchr.org/english/bodies/cedaw/docs/co/KUWAITCO30.pdf> accessed 18 September 2022

Centre for International Governance Innovation, 'Reshaping Trade through Women's Economic Empowerment: Mainstreaming Gender in the Face of Pervasive Inequality' (2018) <www.cigionline.org/sites/default/files/documents/Women%20and%20Trade.pdf> accessed 18 September 2022

Chatham House and Vivid Economics, 'Evidence for Action: Gender Equality and Economic Growth' (Chatham House 2010) <http://www.chathamhouse.org.uk/files/17416_0910gender.pdf> accessed 1 September 2021

Chelsea Ruiter, Lance Hadley, and Queena Li, 'Impacts of Non-Tariff Barriers for Women Small Scale Cross-Border Traders on the Kenya–Uganda Border' (Sauti Africa 2017) <https://sautiafrica.org/wp-content/uploads/2017/03/REV-4-Web-Impacts-of-Non-Tariff-Barriers-for-Women-Small-Scale-Cross-Border-Traders-on-the-Kenya-Uganda-Border.pdf> accessed 18 September 2022

Chinhui Juhn, Gergely Ujhelyi, and Carolina Villegas-Sanchez, 'Men, Women, and Machines: How Trade Impacts Gender Inequality' (2012) Working Paper 18106 <https://papers.ssrn.com/sol3/papers.cfm?abstract_id=2066403> accessed 19 October

Committee on Trade and Development, 'Aid-For-Trade Work Programme 2018–2019: Supporting Economic Diversification and Empowerment for Inclusive, Sustainable Development through Aid for Trade' (World Trade Organisation Committee on Trade and Development, Aid for Trade 7 May 2018) WT/COMTD/AFT/W/75

Communication from Canada, 'Working to Ensure Benefits from the GATS for Members' Small and Medium Sized Enterprises (SMEs)' (2005) TN/S/W/36, Council for Trade in Services Special Session

Council of Europe, 'Reflections on the Concept and Practice of the Council of Europe Approach to Gender Mainstreaming and Gender Equality' (1998)

Deutsche Gesellschaft für Internationale Zusammenarbeit (GIZ) GmbH, 'Trade and Gender—exploring a reciprocal relationship: Approaches to mitigate and measure gender-related trade impacts' (German Cooperation 2014) <www.oecd.org/dac/gender-development/GIZ_Trade%20and%20Gender_Exploring%20a%20reciprocal%20relationship.pdf> accessed 18 September 2022

Diane Whitmore Schanzenbach and Ryan Nunn, 'The 51%: Driving Growth Through Women's Economic Participation' (Brookings 2017) <www.brookings.edu/multi-chapter-report/the-51-percent-driving-growth-through-womens-economic-participation/> accessed 4 October 2022

ECLAC, 'Repository of information on time use in Latin America and the Caribbean' (2019) <https://oig.cepal.org/sites/default/files/2019-10_repositorio_uso_del_tiempo_eng.pdf> accessed 21 April 2020

Eddy Lee, 'Trade liberalization and employment' (2005) DESA Working Paper No 5, UN.org <chrome-extension://efaidnbmnnnibpcajpcglclefindmkaj/https://www.un.org/en/ecosoc/meetings/2005/docs/Eddy%20Lee.pdf> accessed 5 October 2023

Edward E Leamer, 'The Heckscher-Ohlin Model in Theory and Practice' (1995) 77 Princeton Studies in International Finance <https://ies.princeton.edu/pdf/S77.pdf> accessed 17 August 2020

Elisa Gamberoni and José Guilherme Reis, 'Gender-Informing Aid for Trade: Entry Points and Initial Lessons Learned from the World Bank' (The World Bank July 2011)

Employment and Social Development Canada, 'Employment and Social Development Canada 2018–2019 Departmental plan—Supplementary information—Annex 1.7: Gender-Based Analysis (GBA+)' <www.canada.ca/en/employment-social-development/corporate/reports/departmental-plan/2018-2019/gender-based-analysis.html> accessed 12 June 2024

Erin Kepler and Shane Scott, 'Are Male and Female Entrepreneurs Really That Different?' (SBA Office of Advocacy September 2007) <https://cmapsconverted.ihmc.us/rid=1225646682718_310554911_6940/Erin%20kepler%26scotte%20Shane%20-%20are%20male%20and%20female%20entrepreneurs%20really%20that%20different.pdf> accessed 18 September 2021

European Parliament, 'Implementation of the Generalized Scheme Preferences (GSP) Regulation (EU) No 978/2012 (2018/2109(INI))' (2019) European Parliament Resolution 9 <www.europarl.europa.eu/doceo/document/TA-8-2019-0207_EN.pdf> accessed 1 September 2021

Food and Agriculture Organisation, 'The State of Food and Agriculture, Women in Agriculture—Closing the Gender Gap for Development' (2011) <http://www.fao.org/3/a-i2050e.pdf> accessed 11 April 2020

FreshMinds, 'Evaluating SME Experiences of Government Procurement' (2008) <http://shared.freshminds.co.uk/marketing/SME_Procurement_Report.pdf> accessed 18 September 2021

GATT, 'Decision on differential and more favourable treatment reciprocity and fuller participation of developing countries' (1979) L/4903 <www.wto.org/gatt_docs/English/SULPDF/90970166.pdf> accessed 1 September 2021

Gender Digital Divide Index (GDDI), Report 2022 <https://gddindex.com/wp-content/uploads/2022/02/GDDI-Report-2022.pdf> accessed 18 September 2022

Gender Equality & Trade Policy, 'UN Women Watch Resource Paper' (2011) <www.un.org/womenwatch/feature/trade/gender_equality_and_trade_policy.pdf> accessed 21 May 2024

Global Entrepreneurship Monitor, '2018/2019 Women's Entrepreneurship Report' (2019) <www.gemconsortium.org/report/gem-20182019-womens-entrepreneurship-report> accessed 8 September 2022

Human Rights Council, 'Report of the Working Group on the issue of discrimination against women in law and in practice on its mission to Kuwait' (United Nations Office of the High Commissioner for Human Rights 2017) <www.refworld.org/docid/5947d4ec4.html> accessed 18 September 2022

Human Rights Watch, 'World Report 2017: Iran' (2017) <www.hrw.org/world-report/2017/country-chapters/iran> accessed 18 September 2022

Identification for Development, '2019 Annual Report' (World Bank Group 2019) 2 <http://documents1.worldbank.org/curated/en/566431581578116247/pdf/Identification-for-Development-ID4D-2019-Annual-Report.pdf> accessed 18 September 2022

IFC, 'Women-Owned SMEs: A Business Opportunity for Financial Institutions' <www.ifc.org/wps/wcm/connect/44b004b2-ed46-48fc-8ade-aa0f485069a1/WomenOwnedSMes+Report-Final.pdf?MOD=AJPERES&CVID=kiiZZDZ> accessed 17 September 2022

ILO, 'Maternity Protection Convention' 183 (2000) <www.ilo.org/dyn/normlex/en/f?p=NORMLEXPUB:55:0::NO::P55_TYPE,P55_LANG,P55_DOCUMENT,P55_NODE:REV,en,C183,/Document> accessed 17 September 2022

ILO, 'Women and Men in the Informal Economy: A Statistical Picture' (2018) <www.ilo.org/wcmsp5/groups/public/---dgreports/---dcomm/documents/publication/wcms_626831.pdf> accessed 17 August 2021

ILO, 'Beyond the Glass Ceiling: Why Businesses Need Women at the Top' (2019) <www.ilo.org/infostories/en-GB/Stories/Employment/beyond-the-glass-ceiling> accessed 17 August 2021

ILO, 'World Employment and Social Outlook Trends 2020' (2020) <www.ilo.org/wcmsp5/groups/public/---dgreports/---dcomm/publ/documents/publication/wcms_734455.pdf> accessed 17 August 2023

ILO, 'A Compendium of National Law and Practice' <www.ilo.org/public/english/standards/relm/ilc/ilc89/pdf/rep-iii-1b-c3.pdf> accessed 17 September 2020

Immaculate Martínez-Zarzoso, 'Assessing the Effectiveness of Environmental Provisions in Regional Trade Agreements: An Empirical Analysis' (2018) 2018/02 OECD Trade and Environment Working Papers <www.oecd-ilibrary.org/environment/assessing-the-effectiven

ess-of-environmental-provisions-in-regional-trade-agreements_5ffc615c-en> accessed 12 November 2021

India Centre for Migration and UN Women, 'Towards Safe Migration for Aspiring Women Domestic Workers' (UN Women 2018) <https://asiapacific.unwomen.org/en/digital-library/publications/2018/01/for-aspiring-women-domestic-workers> accessed 18 September 2022

Ingrid Brudvig, Chenai Chair, and Adriane van der Wilk, 'Covid-19 and increasing domestic violence against women: The pandemic of online gender-based violence' (World Wide Web Foundation) <http://webfoundation.org/docs/2020/07/WWWF-Submission-COVID-19-and-the-increase-of-domestic-violence-against-women-1.pdf> accessed 18 September 2022

Inter-agency Network on Women and Gender Equality, 'Gender Equality & Trade Policy' (Women Watch 10 2011) <www.un.org/womenwatch/feature/trade/gender_equality_and_trade_policy.pdf> accessed 1 April 2020

International Labour Organization, 'Women Work More, But are Still Paid Less' (ILO/95/22, ILO Press Release 25 August 1995) <www.ilo.org/global/about-the-ilo/newsroom/news/WCMS_008091/lang--en/index.htm> accessed 18 September 2021

International Labour Organization, 'Global Employment Trends for Women 2012' (11 December 2012) <www.ilo.org/wcmsp5/groups/public/---dgreports/---dcomm/documents/publication/wcms_195447.pdf> accessed 12 February 2020

International Labour Organization, 'Global Employment Trends 2014: The risk of a jobless recovery' (21 January 2014) <www.ilo.org/wcmsp5/groups/public/---dgreports/---dcomm/---publ/documents/publication/wcms_233953.pdf> accessed 12 February 2020

International Labour Organization, 'Labour Provisions in Trade Agreements don't Hurt Business' (18 July 2016) <www.ilo.org/global/about-the-ilo/newsroom/news/WCMS_499348/lang--en/index.htm> accessed 23 December 2021

International Labour Organization, 'Employer–Migrant worker relationships in the Middle East: Exploring scope for internal labour market mobility and fair migration' (2017) <www.ilo.org/beirut/publications/WCMS_552697/lang--en/index.htm> accessed 18 September 2022

International Labour Organization, 'Gender in employment policies and programmes: What works for women?' (2017) Working Paper No 235 <www.ilo.org/wcmsp5/groups/public/---ed_emp/documents/publication/wcms_613536.pdf> accessed 5 October 2023

International Labour Organization, 'Employment in agriculture, female (% of female employment) (modeled ILO estimate)' (2020) <https://data.worldbank.org/indicator/SL.AGR.EMPL.FE.ZS> accessed 11 April 2020

International Labour Organization, 'Statistics on Women' <https://ilostat.ilo.org/topics/women/> accessed 21 April 2024

International Trade Centre, 'Unlocking Markets for Women to Trade' (2015) <https://intracen.org/file/womenintradeweb1pdf> accessed 29 October 2023

International Trade Centre, 'Trade and Gender Issue Brief Series' (2016) <https://static.un.org/esa/ffd/wp-content/uploads/2016/01/Gender-and-trade_ITC_IATF-Issue-brief.pdf> accessed 19 October 2022

International Trade Centre, 'From Europe to the World: Understanding Challenges for European Businesswomen' (September 2019) <https://intracen.org/file/fromeuropetoworldwomeneufinalwebpdf> accessed 12 June 2024

International Trade Centre, 'Mainstreaming Gender in Free Trade Agreements' (2020) <https://intracen.org/resources/publications/mainstreaming-gender-in-free-trade-agreements> accessed 17 August 2021

International Trade Centre, 'Women Entrepreneurs: An Action Plan to "Build Back Better"' (2020) <https://edse.org.za/wp-content/uploads/2020/11/W20-Policy-brief_Bejing25_20201021_web.pdf> accessed 19 October 2022

Ipek Ilkkaracan, 'Analysis of Istanbul Labour Market from a Gender Equality Perspective' (International Labour Organization 2016) <www.ilo.org/wcmsp5/groups/public/---europe/---ro-geneva/---ilo-ankara/documents/publication/wcms_490144.pdf> accessed 18 September 2022

Jakob Engel, Deeksha Kokas, Gladys Lopez-Acevedo, and Maryla Maliszewska, 'The Distributional Impacts of Trade: Empirical Innovations, Analytical Tools, and Policy

Responses' (The World Bank 2021) <https://documents1.worldbank.org/curated/en/976331621501704900/pdf/The-Distributional-Impacts-of-Trade-Empirical-Innovations-Analytical-Tools-and-Policy-Responses.pdf> accessed 29 October 2023

James Harrison, 'Human Rights Impact Assessments of Free Trade Agreements: What is the State of the Art?' (University of Warwick 6 November 2013) <https://warwick.ac.uk/fac/soc/law/research/centres/chrp/governance/2010-hria-background-paper-harrison.pdf> accessed 28 October 2023

Jane Korinek, 'Trade and Gender: Issues and Interactions' (2005) 24 OECD Trade Policy Papers <www.oecd-ilibrary.org/docserver/826133710302.pdf?expires=1663237033&id=id&accname=guest&checksum=6321C322B67874ECFAD5FCC35C20D2A8> accessed 10 September 2022

Jane Korinek, Evdokia Moïsé, and Jakob Tange, 'Trade and Gender: A Framework of Analysis' (2021) OECD Trade Policy Papers No 246, 39 <https://doi.org/10.1787/6db59d80-en> accessed 4 April 2024

Janneke Pieters, 'Can Free Trade Policies help to reduce Gender Equalities in Employment and Wages' (IZA World of Labour 2018) <https://wol.iza.org/uploads/articles/455/pdfs/trade-liberalization-and-gender-inequality.pdf> accessed 17 August 2021

Jean-Baptiste Velut and others, 'Comparative Analysis of Trade and Sustainable Development Provisions in Free Trade Agreements' (LSE Consulting 2022) <www.lse.ac.uk/business/consulting/assets/documents/TSD-Final-Report-Feb-2022.pdf> accessed 16 May 2022

Jessica Jacobson and Susan Joekes, 'Violence Against Women Traders at Border Crossings' (UK Aid Work and Opportunities for Women 2019) <chrome-extension://efaidnbmnnnibpcajpcglclefindmkaj/https://assets.publishing.service.gov.uk/government/uploads/system/uploads/attachment_data/file/876256/Query-31-VAW-Traders.pdf> accessed 24 September 2023

John Schneider, 'Global State of Small Business Report' (Data for Good, Facebook 2021) <https://about.fb.com/wp-content/uploads/2021/04/Global-State-of-Small-Business-Report-March-2021.pdf> accessed 9 July 2021

José-Antonio Monteiro, 'Gender-related provisions in Regional Trade Agreements' (World Trade Organisation: Economic Research and Statistics Division 2018) <hrome-extension://efaidnbmnnnibpcajpcglclefindmkaj/www.wto.org/english/res_e/reser_e/ersd201815_e.pdf> accessed 6 October 2023

Kate Higgins, 'Gender and Free Trade Agreements: Best Practices and Policy Guidance' (The North-South Institute 2013) <https://cawtarclearinghouse.org/storage/AttachementGender/2013%20Gender%20and%20FTAs%20Best%20Practices%20and%20Policy%20Guidance.pdf> accessed 21 May 2024

Kate Higgins and Liz Turner, 'Brief 3: Integrating poverty and social analysis into Aid for Trade programmes: trade facilitation and trade-related infrastructure' (UK DFID Aid for Trade: Promoting Inclusive Growth and Poverty Reduction Programme 2010) <https://assets.publishing.service.gov.uk/media/57a08b1f40f0b652dd000aee/trade-brief3.pdf> accessed 18 September 2022

Katrin Kuhlmann, Tara Francis, Indulekha Thomas, Malou Le Graet, Mushfiqur Rahman, Fabiola Madrigal, Maya Cohen, and Ata Nalbantoglu, 'Re-conceptualizing Free Trade Agreements Through a Sustainable Development Lens' (UNESCAP 27 July 2020) <www.unescap.org/sites/default/files/145%20Final-Team%20Katrin%20Kuhlmann-USA.pdf> accessed 10 October 2023

Kimberly Weisul, 'Report: Female Entrepreneurs Much More Likely to Employ Women' (Women Entrepreneurship Report 2018) <www.inc.com/kimberly-weisul/these-entrepreneurs-hired-very-few-men.html> accessed 1 September 2021

Lolita Laperle-Forget, 'Gender Provisions in African Trade Agreements: An Assessment of the Commitments for Reconciling Women's Empowerment and Global Trade' (July 2021) Tralac Working Paper No G21WP/2021 <www.tralac.org/publications/article/15242-gender-provisions-in-african-trade-agreements-an-assessment-of-the-commitments-for-reconciling-women-s-empowerment-and-global-trade.html> accessed 28 October 2023

London Chamber of Commerce and Industries, 'Inclusion of Women in the Negotiation of Free Trade Agreements' <www.londonchamber.co.uk/LCCI/media/media/Inclusion-of-Women-in-the-Negotiation-of-Free-Trade-Agreements.pdf> accessed 12 June 2024

Marzia Fontana, 'The Gender Effects of Trade Liberalization in Developing Countries: A Review of Literature' (University of Sussex 2003) <www.ciedur.org.uy/adm/archivos/publicacion_200.pdf> accessed 12 September 2022

Marzia Fontana, 'Gender Justice in Trade Policy: The Gender Effects of Economic Partnership Agreements. Synthesis Report' (One World Action 2009) <www.oecd.org/social/gender-development/47566754.pdf> accessed 9 July 2023

Marzia Fontana, 'Implications of Current Trade Policies for Gender Equality' (10 November 2009) United Nations Expert Paper EGM/BPFA–MDG/2009/EP.9 <www.un.org/womenwatch/daw/egm/impact_bdpfa/EP9%20-%20FontanaREV.pdf> accessed 29 October 2023

Marzia Fontana, 'Women's Work: The Impact of Trade on Gender Equality' (World Politics Review 2014) <www.worldpoliticsreview.com/insights/13687/womens-work-the-impactof-trade-on-gender-equality> accessed 1 September 2021

Marzia Fontana, 'Gender Equality in Trade Agreements' (2016) Study for the FEMM Committee, Brussels, European Parliament <www.europarl.europa.eu/RegData/etudes/STUD/2016/571388/IPOL_STU(2016)571388_EN.pdf> accessed 10 September 2022

Marzia Fontana with Cristina Paciello 'Gender dimensions of rural and agricultural employment: Differentiated pathways out of poverty—A global perspective' (Rome, 31 March–2 April 2009) Food and Agriculture Organization of the United Nations (FAO), International Fund for Agricultural Development (IFAD), International Labour Office <https://citeseerx.ist.psu.edu/document?repid=rep1&type=pdf&doi=1ad2751713992b696f0f2ca70531ec73381642f2> accessed 12 May 2024

McKinsey & Co, 'The Power of Parity: How Advancing Women's Equality Can Add $12 Trillion To Global Growth' (2015) <www.mckinsey.com/~/media/mckinsey/featured%20insights/employment%20and%20growth/how%20advancing%20womens%20equality%20can%20add%2012%20trillion%20to%20global%20growth/mgi%20power%20of%20parity_full%20report_september%202015.pdf> accessed 17 August 2021

Migrant Forum in Asia Secretariat, 'Reform of the Kafala (sponsorship) system' (International Labour Organization) <www.ilo.org/dyn/migpractice/docs/132/PB2.pdf> accessed 18 September 2022

Nadira Bayat, 'A Whole Agreement Approach to Gender Mainstreaming in the AfCFTA: Forging a New Path in Post-COVID Response and Recovery' (UNCTAD April 2022) <https://elearning.unctad.org/pluginfile.php/34245/mod_page/content/10/Nadira%20Bayat_Presentation_5%20April_Randa_Final.pdf> accessed 29 October 2023

National Board of Trade Sweden, 'Trade and Social Sustainability: An Overview and Analysis' (2017) <www.kommerskollegium.se/globalassets/publikationer/rapporter/2017/publ-trade-and-social-sustainability-webb.pdf> accessed 8 September 2022

New York City Department of Consumer Affairs, 'From Cradle to Cane: The cost of being a female consumer, a study of gender pricing in New York City' (2015) <www1.nyc.gov/assets/dca/downloads/pdf/partners/Study-of-Gender-Pricing-in-NYC.pdf> accessed 1 September 2021

Niaz Asadullah and Zaki Wahhaj, 'Missing from the Market: *Purdah* Norm and Women's Paid Work Participation in Bangladesh' (IZA Institute of Labour Economics 2016) <www.iza.org/publications/dp/10463/missing-from-the-market-purdah-norm-and-womens-paid-work-participation-in-bangladesh> accessed 18 September 2022

Nisha Taneja, Sanjana Joshi, Shravani Prakash, and Samridhi Bimal, 'Trade Facilitation Measures to Enhance Participation of Women in Cross-border Trade in BBIN' (Crier 2018) <chrome-extension://efaidnbmnnnibpcajpcglclefindmkaj/https://www.icrier.org/pdf/Cross-border_Trade_in_BBIN-Jan-2018.pdf> accessed 24 September 2023

OECD, 'Women's Entrepreneurship: Issues And Policies' (2nd OECD Conference of Ministers Responsible for Small and Medium-Sized Enterprises 2004) <www.oecd.org/cfe/smes/31919215.pdf> accessed 24 September 2023

OECD, 'Bridging the Digital Gender Divide' (2018) <www.oecd.org/digital/bridging-the-digital-gender-divide.pdf> accessed 17 August 2021

OECD, 'Women's Political Participation in Jordan: Barriers, Opportunities And Gender Sensitivity Of Select Political Institutions' (2018) <www.oecd.org/mena/governance/womens-political-participation-in-jordan.pdf> accessed 6 June 2024

OECD, 'Trade and Gender: A Framework of Analysis' (2021) OECD Trade Policy Papers No 246 <www.oecd-ilibrary.org/docserver/6db59d80-en.pdf?expires=1663215197&id=id&accname=guest&checksum=2251E66982BBB62F6D4AF9E9340C66D5> accessed 24 September 2023

Olayinka Bandele, 'An Equal Seat at the Table: Gendering Trade Negotiations' (2016) International Trade Working Paper 2016/14 Commonwealth Secretariat, London <www.oecd-ilibrary.org/content/paper/5jm0qglb1s9s-en> accessed 22 November 2022

One World Action and Commonwealth Secretariat, 'Gender Justice in Trade Policy: The Gender Effects of Economic Partnership Agreements' (OECD.org 2009) <www.oecd.org/social/gender-development/47566754.pdf> accessed 22 November 2022

Owen Pinnell and Jess Kelly, 'Slave markets found on Instagram and other apps' (BBC News 2019) <www.bbc.com/news/technology-50228549> accessed 18 September 2023

Patric Aeberhard, 'WTO Workshop on "Workshop on Enhancing the Participation of Women Entrepreneurs and Traders in Government Procurement"' (Federal Office for Gender Equality, Switzerland 2018) <www.wto.org/english/tratop_e/womenandtrade_e/s02_03_patric_aeberhard.pdf> accessed 24 November 2022

Peter Draper, Nkululeko Khumalo, and Faith Tigere, 'Sustainability Provisions in Regional Trade Agreements: Can they be Multilateralised?' (International Centre for Trade and Sustainable Development, Geneva 2017) <https://e15initiative.org/wp-content/uploads/2015/09/RTA-Exchange-Sustainability-Provisions-Draper-Khumalo-Tigere-Final.pdf> accessed on 16 May 2022

Philomena Apiko, Sean Woolfrey, and Bruce Byiers, 'The promise of the African Continental Free Trade Area (AfCFTA)' (December 2020) European Centre for Development Policy Management (ECDPM) Discussion Paper No 287, ECDPM African Institution and Regional Dynamics, 'Political Economy Dynamics of Regional Organisations in the time of COVID-19 (PEDRO II)' <https://ecdpm.org/application/files/3116/5546/8595/Promise-African-Continental-Free-Trade-Area-AfCFTA-ECDPM-Discussion-Paper-287-December-2020.pdf> accessed 12 May 2024

Rae Lesser Blumberg, Joyce Malaba, and Lis Meyers, 'Women Cross-border Traders in Southern Africa: Contributions, Constraints, and Opportunities in Malawi and Botswana' <www.agrilinks.org/sites/default/files/resource/files/ICBT%20Gender%20Assessment%20Report_Final_4-30-2016.pdf> accessed 18 September 2022

Raphael Kaplinsky and Mike Morris, 'How Regulation and Standards Can Support Social and Environmental Dynamics in Global Value Chains' (International Centre for Trade and Sustainable Development, Geneva 2017)

Remco H Oostendorp, 'Does Globalization Reduce the Gender Wage Gap?' (World Bank workshop on 'Gender, growth and poverty', 2002) <https://openknowledge.worldbank.org/handle/10986/13887> accessed 19 October 2022

Sally Smith, 'Advancing Gender Equality through Voluntary Standards for Trade' (Gender, Social Inclusion and Trade Working Group 2020) <www.bkp-development.com/images/reports/Voluntary_Standards_for_Trade_bkp_final.pdf> accessed 23 November 2022

Sebastian Benz and Alexander Jaax, 'The costs of regulatory barriers to trade in services: New estimates of ad valorem tariff equivalents' (2020) OECD Trade Policy Papers no 238

Sharon Anglin Treat, 'Trade agreements and sustainability: innovations and illusions in EU and US agreements' (Institute for Agriculture & Trade Policy 23 September 2021) <www.iatp.org/documents/trade-agreements-and-sustainability-innovations-and-illusions-eu-and-us-agreements> accessed 12 May 2024

Sheba Tejani and William Milberg, 'Global Defeminization? Industrial Upgrading, Occupational Segmentation and Manufacturing Employment in Middle-Income Countries' (2010) Schwartz Center for Economic Policy Analysis Working Paper

Simonetta Zarrilli, 'Moving professionals beyond national borders: mutual recognition agreements and the GATS' (UNCTAD 2005) <https://unctad.org/system/files/official-document/ditctncd20052_en.pdf> accessed 18 September 2022

Social Institutions and Gender Index (SIGI), 'SIGI 2019 Global Report: Transforming Challenges into Opportunities' (8 March 2019) <www.oecd.org/dev/sigi-2019-global-report-bc56d212-en.htm> accessed 6 June 2024

Stephanie Barrientos and Charlotte Pallangyo, 'Global Value Chain Policy Series: Gender' (World Economic Forum September 2018) <www3.weforum.org/docs/WEF_51129_WP_Global_Value_Chain_Policy_Series_Gender_report_2018.pd> accessed 12 May 2024

Sununtar Setboonsarng, 'Transport Infrastructure and Poverty Reduction', Policy Brief No 21 Asian Development Bank

Susan Harris Rimmer (ed), 'Gender-smart Procurement Policies for Driving Change' (Global Economy and Finance Department, Chatham House December 2017)

The Japan Times Editorial, 'Social norms hinder women's career growth' *The Japan Times* (2019) <www.japantimes.co.jp/news/2019/03/22/national/social-norms-hinder-womens-career-growth/> accessed 18 September 2022

The Public Interest (ITPI), 'How Privatization Increases Inequality' (2016) <www.inthepublicinterest.org/wp-content/uploads/InthePublicInterest_InequalityReport_Sept2016.pdf> accessed 17 August 2021

The World Bank, 'Hashemite Kingdom of Jordan: Understanding how gender norms in MNA impact female employment outcomes' (2018) <https://openknowledge.worldbank.org/bitstream/handle/10986/30947/ACS25170-PUBLIC-FULL-REPORT-Jordan-Social-Norms-June-1-2018-with-titlepg.pdf?sequence=1&isAllowed=y> accessed 17 September 2022

The World Bank, 'Women's Financial Inclusion and the Law' <http://pubdocs.worldbank.org/en/610311522241094348/Financial-Inclusion.pdf> accessed 17 September 2022

The World Bank, FAO, and IFAD, 'Gender in Agriculture: Sourcebook' (2009) <http://siteresources.worldbank.org/INTGENAGRLIVSOUBOOK/Resources/CompleteBook.pdf> accessed 18 September 2021

Thomas Baum, 'International perspectives on women and work in hotels, catering and tourism' (International Labour Organization 2013) <www.ilo.org/wcmsp5/groups/public/@dgreports/@gender/documents/publication/wcms_209867.pdf> accessed 21 March 2020

Tina Power, 'The gender digital divide and COVID-19: Towards feminist internet regulations in Southern Africa' (African Declaration on Internet Rights and Freedoms 2020) <https://africaninternetrights.org/sites/default/files/Tina_Power.pdf> accessed 18 September 2022

Titan Alon and others, 'The Impact of Covid-19 on Gender Equality' (2020) NBER Working Paper 26947 <www.nber.org/system/files/working_papers/w26947/w26947.pdf> accessed 19 October 2022

UN, 'World Economic Situation and Prospects 2014: Country Classification' (2014) <www.un.org/en/development/desa/policy/wesp/wesp_current/2014wesp_country_classification.pdf> accessed 9 July 2021

UN, 'Transforming Our World: The 2030 Agenda For Sustainable Development' (25–27 September 2015, New York) A/RES/70/1

UN, 'Repository of information on time use in Latin America and the Caribbean' (ECLAC 2019) <https://oig.cepal.org/sites/default/files/2019-10_repositorio_uso_del_tiempo_eng.pdf> accessed 21 April 2020

UN Women, 'Innovation for Gender Equality' (2019) 5 <http://www.unwomen.org/-/media/headquarters/attachments/sections/library/publications/2019/innovation-for-gender-equality-en.pdf?la=en&vs=733> accessed 17 September 2022

UNCTAD, 'Mainstreaming Gender in Trade Policy' (2009) Note by the UNCTAD Secretariat TD/B/C.I/EM.2/2/Rev.1 <http://www.unctad.org/en/docs/ciem2d2_en.pdf> accessed 1 September 2021

UNCTAD, 'The New Way of Addressing Gender Equality Issues in Trade Agreements: Is It A True Revolution?' (October 2017) Policy Brief No 53 <https://unctad.org/en/PublicationsLibrary/presspb2017d2_en.pdf> accessed 13 August 2019

UNCTAD, 'Better Data and Statistics For Gender-responsive Trade Policy' (2018) <https://unctad.org/system/files/official-document/presspb2018d7_en.pdf> accessed 1 May 2024

UNCTAD, 'BORDERLINE: Women in informal cross-border trade in Malawi, the United Republic of Tanzania and Zambia' (2018) UNCTAD/DITC/2018/3 <https://unctad.org/en/PublicationsLibrary/ditc2018d3_en.pdf> accessed 18 September 2022

UNCTAD, 'Impact of the COVID-19 Pandemic on Trade and Development: Transitioning to a New Normal' (United Nations Conference on Trade and Development, 2020) <https://unctad.org/system/files/official-document/osg2020d1_en.pdf> accessed 29 October 2023

UNCTAD, 'The Effects of Trade on Women's Well-Being and Economic Empowerment: Evidence and Research Methodologies' (2021) <https://vi.unctad.org/tag/docs/vol1/vol1m2.pdf> accessed 17 August 2021

UNCTAD, UNECA, and UNECE, 'Desk study on the gender aspects of trade and trade policy for statistics, UNDA project 2023D: Data and statistics for more gender-responsive trade policies in Africa, Eastern Europe, Caucasus and Central Asia' <https://unctad.org/system/files/information-document/20201012_WebinarGender_DeskStudy_en.pdf> accessed 1 May 2024

UNESCO, 'Accountability in Education: Meeting Our Commitments', Global Education Monitoring Report (2017) <https://unesdoc.unesco.org/ark:/48223/pf0000259338> accessed 18 September 2022

UNESCO, 'Global Education Monitoring Report Gender Review: Meeting our commitments to gender equality in education' (2018) <https://en.unesco.org/gem-report/2018_gender_review> accessed 18 September 2022

UNESCO, 'I'd blush if I could. Closing Gender Divides in Digital Skills through Education' (2019) <https://2b37021f0f4a464083520a3c1b7c2aab.filesusr.com/ugd/04bfff_06ba0716e0604f51a40b4474d4829ba8.pdf> accessed 18 September 2022

UNFSS, 'Voluntary Sustainability Standards: Today's Landscape of Issues & Initiatives to Achieve Public Policy Objectives' (2012) <https://unfss.org/wp-content/uploads/2012/05/unfss-report-issues-1_draft_lores.pdf> accessed 24 November 2022

United Nations Economic and Social Council, 'Draft Training Materia on streamlining formalities and documentary procedures connected with importation, exportation and transit' (Centre for Trade Facilitation and Electronic Business, 25th Session, 2019) ECE/TRADE/C/CEFACT/2019/20

UNODC, 'Global Report on Trafficking in Persons 2018' (2018) <www.unodc.org/documents/data-and-analysis/glotip/2018/GLOTiP_2018_BOOK_web_small.pdf> accessed 18 September 2022

USAID, 'Toolkit for Integrating GBV Prevention and Response into Economic Growth Projects' (2014) <www.usaid.gov/sites/default/files/documents/1865/USAID%20Toolkit%20GBV%20EG%20Final%209-22-14.pdf> accessed 18 September 2022

USDOS, '2019 Trafficking in Persons Report: Saudi Arabia' (2019) <www.ecoi.net/en/document/2010898.html> accessed 18 September 2022

Wendy Cukier, Suzanne Gagnon, Jaigris Hodson, Tania Saba, Gina Grandy, Samantha Morton, Mohamed Elmi, Kevin Stolarick, and Zohreh Hassannezhad Chavoushi, 'The State of Women's Entrepreneurship in Canada: 2020' (Women Entrepreneurship Knowledge Hub 2020) <https://wekh.ca/wp-content/uploads/2020/10/WEKH_State_of_Womens_Entrepreneurship_in_Canada_2020_EN-1.pdf> accessed 7 October 2023

World Bank, 'Labour force participation rate, female (% of female population ages 15+) (modelled ILO estimate)—Japan, OECD members' (2020)

World Bank Group, 'Women, Business and the Law 2019: A Decade of Reform' (2019) 11 <https://thedocs.worldbank.org/en/doc/702301554216687135005002 2019/original/WBLDECADEOFREFORM2019WEB0401.pdf> accessed 17 September 2022

World Bank Group, 'Women and Trade: The Role of Trade in Promoting Women's Equality' (30 July 2020) <www.worldbank.org/en/topic/trade/publication/women-and-trade-the-role-of-trade-in-promoting-womens-equality> accessed 12 May 2024

World Customs Organization, 'WCO promotes Gender Equality and Diversity' <http://www.wcoomd.org/en/topics/capacity-building/activities-and-programmes/gender-equality.aspx> accessed 18 September 2021

World Economic Forum, 'Closing the Gender Gap Accelerators' <www.weforum.org/projects/closing-the-gender-gap-accelerators> accessed 21 May 2024

World Economic Forum, 'The Industry Gender Gap' (2016) 5 <http://www3.weforum.org/docs/WEF_FOJ_Executive_Summary_GenderGap.pdf> accessed 21 April 2020

World Trade Organization, 'Recommendations of the Task Force on Aid for Trade' (Aid for Trade Task Force 27 July 2006) WT/AFT/1 <https://docs.wto.org/dol2fe/Pages/FE_Search/FE_S_S009-DP.aspx?language=E&CatalogueIdList=58379&CurrentCatalogueIdIndex=0&FullTextHash=&HasEnglishRecord=True&HasFrenchRecord=True&HasSpanishRecord=True> accessed 18 September 2021

World Trade Organization, 'Aid for Trade at a Glance 2011: Showing Results' (2011) <www.wto.org/english/res_e/publications_e/aid4trade11_e.htm> accessed 18 September 2021

World Trade Organization, 'Gender Aware Trade Policy: A Springboard for Women's Economic Empowerment' (2016) <chrome-extension://efaidnbmnnnibpcajpcglclefindmkaj/https://www.wto.org/english/news_e/news17_e/dgra_21jun17_e.pd> accessed 6 October 2023

World Trade Organization, 'Trade Policies Supporting Women's Economic Empowerment: Trends in WTO Members' (20 May 2019) Economic Research and Statistics Division Staff Working Paper ERSD-2019-07

World Trade Organization, 'Interim Report Following the Buenos Aires Joint Declaration on Trade and Women's Economic Empowerment' (25 September 2020) WT/L/1095/Rev.1 <https://docs.wto.org/dol2fe/Pages/SS/directdoc.aspx?filename=q:/WT/L/1095R1.pdf&Open=True> accessed 7 October 2023

World Trade Organization, 'Enhanced Integrated Framework' <www.wto.org/english/tratop_e/devel_e/teccop_e/if_e.htm> accessed 18 September 2021

World Trade Organization, 'Informal Working Group on Trade and Gender' <www.wto.org/english/tratop_e/womenandtrade_e/iwg_trade_gender_e.htm> accessed 6 October 2023

World Trade Organization, 'Movement of natural persons' <www.wto.org/english/tratop_e/serv_e/mouvement_persons_e/mouvement_persons_e.htm> accessed 18 September 2021

World Trade Organization, 'Women and trade' <www.wto.org/english/tratop_e/womenandtrade_e/womenandtrade_e.htm> accessed 18 September 2021

World Trade Organization, 'WTO Action Plan On Trade And Gender 2021–2026' <chrome-extension://efaidnbmnnnibpcajpcglclefindmkaj/https://www.wto.org/english/tratop_e/womenandtrade_e/action_plan_21-26.pdf> accessed 6 October 2023

WTO, 'Financial Inclusion and the GATS: Barriers to Financial Inclusion and Trade in Services', Note by the Secretariat, Committee on Trade in Financial Services (2014) S/FIN/W/88/Add.1 <https://docs.wto.org/dol2fe/Pages/SS/directdoc.aspx?filename=q:/S/FIN/W88.pdf&Open=True> accessed 18 September 2022

WTO, 'Levelling the Trading Field for SMEs' (2016) World Trade Report 58 <www.wto.org/english/res_e/booksp_e/world_trade_report16_e.pdf> accessed 9 July 2021

WTO, 'Interim Report Following the Buenos Aires Joint Declaration on Trade and Women's Economic Empowerment' (25 September 2020) WT/L/1095/Rev.1 <https://docs.wto.org/dol2fe/Pages/SS/directdoc.aspx?filename=q:/WT/L/1095R1.pdf&Open=True> accessed 9 September 2022

WTO, 'Women and Trade 2020' (2020) <www.wto.org/english/tratop_e/womenandtrade_e/womenandtrade_e.htm> accessed 18 September 2022

WTO, 'Making trade work for women: key findings from the World Trade Congress on Gender' (2023)

WTO, 'Gender Aware trade policy: A Springboard for Women's Economic Empowerment', 4 <www.empowerwomen.org/en/resources/documents/2019/10/gender-aware-trade-policy-a-springboard-for-womens-economic-empowerment?lang=en> accessed 10 September 2022

WTO Gender Research Hub, <www.wto.org/english/tratop_e/womenandtrade_e/gender_research_hub_members_e.htm> accessed 7 May 2024

Xavier Jaravel and Erick Sager, 'What are the Price Effects of Trade? Evidence from the U.S. and Implications for Quantitative Trade Models' (Finance and Economics Discussion Series 2019) 068 <https://doi.org/10.17016/FEDS.2019.068> accessed 10 September 2022

Zornitsa Kutlina-Dimitrova, José M Rueda-Cantuche, Antonio F Amores, and M Victoria Román, 'How Important are EU Exports for Jobs in the EU?' (2018) 4 DG Trade Chief Economist Note <https://ideas.repec.org/p/ris/dgtcen/2018_004.html> accessed 9 September 2022

Electronic Resources

'Export Strategy: supporting and connecting businesses to grow on the world stage' (21 August 2018) gov.uk Policy Paper <www.gov.uk/government/publications/export-strategy-supporting-and-connecting-businesses-to-grow-on-the-world-stage/export-strategy-supporting-and-connecting-businesses-to-grow-on-the-world-stage> accessed 9 July 2021

'Facts and Figures 2021' (ITU 2021) <www.itu.int/en/mediacentre/Pages/PR-2021-11-29-FactsFigures.aspx> accessed 18 September 2022

'Gender sensitive trade policy' (UK Policy Briefings September 2019) <https://wbg.org.uk/analysis/uk-policy-briefings/gender-impacts-of-trade-and-investment-agreements/> accessed 9 July 2021

'If at First You Do Not Succeed, Try Women's Economic Empowerment through Trade' (Trade Experettes) <www.tradeexperettes.org/blog/articles/if-at-first-you-do-not-succeed-try-womens-economic-empowerment-through-trade?rq=simonetta> accessed 18 September 2023

'Labour force participation rate, female (% of female population ages 15+) (modelled ILO estimate)—Japan, OECD members' (World Bank) <https://data.worldbank.org/indicator/SL.TLF.CACT.FE.ZS?locations=JP-OE> accessed 1 October 2020

'Mainstreaming Gender in Free Trade Agreements' (ITC) <www.intracen.org/publication/mainstreaming-gender-FTA/> accessed 25 August 2021

'Women and Trade at the WTO: Pink Herring, Trojan Horse, or Historic Advance?' (CIGI 2023) <www.cigionline.org/articles/women-and-trade-wto-pink-herring-trojan-horse-or-historic-advance/> accessed 9 July 2023

'Women's Rights Groups Call on Governments to Reject the WTO Declaration on Women's Economic Empowerment' (APWLD 12 December 2017) <https://apwld.org/press-release-164-womens-rights-groups-call-on-governments-to-reject-the-wto-declaration-on-womens-economic-empowerment/> accessed 9 July 2021

Accenture, 'COVID-19: Consumer Change How They Shop, Work and Live' (2020) <www.accenture.com/us-en/insights/retail/coronavirus-consumer-behavior-research> accessed 19 October 2022

Adelina Mendoza, Gaurav Nayyar, and Roberta Piermartini, 'Are the "Poor" Getting Globalized?' (World Bank 2018) <https://openknowledge.worldbank.org/handle/10986/30576> accessed 18 September 2022

AfCFTA Secretariat and United Nations Development Programme, 'The Futures Report: Making the AfCFTA Work for Women and Youth' (UNDP 3 December 2020) <www.undp.org/africa/publications/futures-report-making-afcfta-work-women-and-youth> accessed 29 October 2023

Alessandro Cigno, 'Trade, Foreign Investment, and Wage Inequality in Developing Countries' (IZA World of Labour 2015) 193 <https://wol.iza.org/articles/trade-foreign-investment-and-wage-inequality-in-developing-countries/long> accessed 17 August 2021

Alexander Muravyev, Dorothea Schäfer, and Oleksandr Talavera, 'Entrepreneurs' gender and financial constraints: Evidence from international data' (2009) <https://econpapers.repec.org/article/eeejcecon/v_3a37_3ay_3a2009_3ai_3a2_3ap_3a270-286.htm> accessed 17 September 2022

Alianza del Pacífico, 'With Declaration on Gender Equality and the Digital Market of the bloc concludes the Pacific Alliance Summit' (11 December 2020) <https://alianzapacifico.net/en/with-declaration-on-gender-equality-and-the-digital-market-of-the-bloc-concludes-the-pacific-alliance-summit/> accessed 12 June 2024

Amit Kapoor and Bibek Debroy, 'GDP is Not a Measure of Human Well-Being' (HBR 4 October 2019) <https://hbr.org/2019/10/gdp-is-not-a-measure-of-human-well-being> accessed 10 September 2022

Amnesty International, 'Their House is My Prison: Exploitation of Migrant Domestic Workers in Lebanon' (2019) <www.amnesty.org/en/documents/mde18/0022/2019/en/#:~:text=Careers-,Lebanon%3A%20'Their%20house%20is%20my%20prison'%3A%20Exploitation%20of,migrant%20domestic%20workers%20in%20Lebanon&text=Lebanon%20is%20home%20to%20over,of%20these%20workers%20are%20women> accessed 18 September 2022

Ananya Singh, 'Explained: India's refusal to back WTO declaration on gender equality in trade' (QRIUS 15 December 2017) <https://qrius.com/explained-india-refusal-gender-equality-trade/> accessed 18 September 2021

Brittany Anthony, 'On-Ramps, Intersections, and Exit Routes: A roadmap for Systems and Industries to Prevent and Disrupt Human Trafficking' (Polaris 2018) <https://polarisproject.org/resources/on-ramps-intersections-and-exit-routes-a-roadmap-for-systems-and-industries-to-prevent-and-disrupt-human-trafficking/> accessed 18 September 2022

Cathy Morrow Roberson, 'Global parcel volumes expected to double by 2026 on e-commerce boom' *Journal of Commerce Online* (2020) <www.joc.com/international-logistics/global-parcel-volumes-expected-double-2026-e-commerce-boom_20201012.html> accessed 9 July 2021

Center for Human Rights in Iran, 'Married Women in Iran Still Need "Permission" to Travel Abroad Under Amendment to Passport Law' (2017) <www.iranhumanrights.org/2017/07/married-women-in-iran-still-need-permission-to-travel-abroad-under-amendment-to-passport-law/> accessed 5 October 2020

Centre for Human Rights in Iran, 'Gender Segregation Violates the Rights of Women in Iran' <www.iranhumanrights.org/2014/09/gender-segregation/> accessed 18 September 2022

CETA, 'Trade and Gender Recommendation: EU–Canada Work Plan 2020–2021' <www.international.gc.ca/trade-commerce/trade-agreements-accords-commerciaux/agr-acc/ceta-aecg/CETA_work_plan-AECG_plan_travail-2020-2021.aspx?lang=eng> accessed 13 August 2023

Claire Guyot, 'EP wants to include gender equality in free-trade agreements' (EURACTIV.fr 14 March 2018) <www.euractiv.com/section/politics/news/ep-wants-to-include-gender-equality-in-free-trade-agreements/> accessed 12 June 2024

Claire Guyot, 'Free trade agreements struggle to convince on social, environmental standards' (EURACTIV 23 March 2018) <www.euractiv.com/section/ceta/news/free-trade-agreements-struggle-to-convince-on-social-environmental-standards/> accessed 12 June 2024

Communication from Antigua and Barbuda, United States – Measures Affecting the Cross-Border Supply of Gambling and Betting Services (25 April 2013) WTO doc WT/DS285/26 <www.wto.org/english/tratop_e/dispu_e/cases_e/ds285_e.htm> accessed 12 May 2024

Deborah Abrams Kaplan, 'Walmart's sourcing from women-owned suppliers drives business' (Supply Chain Dive 8 March 2018) <www.supplychaindive.com/news/sourcing-procurement-women-diverse-business/518624/> accessed 1 July 2020

Debra Steger, 'Gender Equality in the WTO: The Need for Women Leaders' (CIGI 2018) <www.cigionline.org/articles/gender-equality-wto-need-women-leaders> accessed 22 November 2022

Dotcom Distribution, '2020 Dotcom Distribution eCommerce Consumer Study: Adapting to the Rapidly Changing eCommerce Landscape' (2020) <https://dotcomdist.com/2020-dotcom-distribution-ecommerce-consumer-study-adapting-to-the-rapidly-changing-ecommerce-landscape/> accessed 26 October 2022

Eliza Niewiadomska, 'Facilitating participation of women-owned small and medium-sized enterprises in local and global public procurement markets' (Workshop on Enhancing the Participation of Women Entrepreneurs and Traders in Government Procurement, 25 June 2018) <www.wto.org/english/tratop_e/womenandtrade_e/programme_workshop_e.htm> accessed 18 September 2021

Empower Women, 'Freedom of movement and women's economic empowerment' (2016) <www.empowerwomen.org/en/who-we-are/news/2016/2/freedom-of-movement-and-womens-economic-empowerment> accessed 7 October 2020

EU Monitor, 'EP Press conference Gender Equality in EU trade agreements report vote' (INTA/FEMM 13 March 2018) Strasbourg <www.eumonitor.eu/9353000/1/j9vvik7m1c3gyxp/vkmmbscygkt7?ctx=vhekc59myknp&tab=1> accessed 13 August 2023

European Parliament, 'Gender equality in EU trade agreements' (13 March 2018) 2017/2015(INI) <www.europarl.europa.eu/doceo/document/TA-8-2018-0066_EN.html> accessed 8 April 2020

European Parliament, 'Gender mainstreaming in EU trade agreements' <www.europarl.europa.eu/thinktank/en/document/EPRS_BRI(2024)760388> accessed 8 April 2020

Fiona David and others, 'Migrants and their vulnerability to human trafficking, modern slavery and forced labour' (IOM Publications 2019) <https://publications.iom.int/books/migrants-and-their-vulnerability-human-trafficking-modern-slavery-and-forced-labour> accessed 18 September 2022

France 24, 'In Saudi Arabia, domestic workers are auctioned online' (2018) <https://observers.france24.com/en/20180315-saudi-arabia-domestic-workers-are-auctioned-online> accessed 18 September 2022

Gabriel Alberto García-Mireles, María Ángeles Moraga, and Félix García, 'Development of maturity models: a systematic literature review' (16th International Conference on Evaluation & Assessment in Software Engineering, *IET Seminar Digest*, 2012) <https://digital-library.theiet.org/content/conferences/10.1049/ic.2012.0036> accessed 27 October 2022

GATS Mode 4, see 'Movement of natural persons (mode 4)', WTO <www.wto.org/english/tratop_e/serv_e/mouvement_persons_e/mouvement_persons_e.htm#:~:text=Under%20the%20General%20Agreement%20on,in%20the%20territory%20of%20another> accessed 6 June 2024

Gaurav Vivek Bhatnagar, 'At Passport Office, Women Encounter Discriminatory, Humiliating Procedures' (The Wire 2016) <https://thewire.in/gender/passport-procedures-discriminatory-humiliating-especially-women> accessed 18 September 2022

Global Affairs Canada, 'CETA Trade and Gender Recommendation: EU-Canada Work Plan 2020–2021' (Government of Canada 2020) <www.international.gc.ca/trade-commerce/trade-agreements-accords-commerciaux/agr-acc/ceta-aecg/CETA_work_plan-AECG_plan_travail-2020-2021.aspx?lang=eng> accessed 29 October 2023

Global Alliance for Trade Facilitation, 'The World Trade Organization's Trade Facilitation Agreement through a Gender Lens' (tradefacilitation.org) <www.tradefacilitation.org/global-alliance-publications/the-tfa-through-a-gender-lens/> accessed 18 September 2021

Global Alliance for Trade Facilitation, 'Who we are: The Alliance' (tradefacilitation.org) <www.tradefacilitation.org/who-we-are/about-us/> accessed 18 September 2021

Government of Canada, 'Canada's Feminist International Assistance Policy' <www.international.gc.ca/world-monde/issues_development-enjeux_developpement/priorities-priorites/policy-politique.aspx?lang=eng> accessed 8 May 2022

Government of Canada, 'Summary of Initial GBA+ for Canada-Mercosur FTA Negotiations' (international.gc.ca) <www.international.gc.ca/trade-commerce/gender_equality-egalite_genres/gba_plus_summary-acs_plus_resume.aspx?lang=eng> accessed 24 November 2022

Heidi Stensland Warren, Maria Liungman, and Aileen Yang, 'What's it like for women to trade across borders?' (World Bank 2019) <https://blogs.worldbank.org/trade/whats-it-women-trade-across-borders> accessed 18 September 2022

IMF Staff, 'Global Trade Liberalization and the Developing Countries' (IMF 2001) <www.imf.org/external/np/exr/ib/2001/110801.htm#ii> accessed on 7 October 2023

Ina Opartyová and Justin Lindeboom, 'Towards a gender-sensitive EU external trade policy' (*EJIL Talk*, 9 November 2023) <www.ejiltalk.org/towards-a-gender-sensitive-eu-external-trade-policy/> accessed 12 June 2024

International Bank for Reconstruction and Development, 'Achieving Universal Access to ID: Gender-based legal barriers against women and good practice reforms' (World Bank Group 2019) <https://openknowledge.worldbank.org/handle/10986/32474> accessed 18 September 2022

International Organization for Migration, 'Harnessing Knowledge on the Migration of Highly Skilled Women' (2014) <https://publications.iom.int/books/harnessing-knowledge-migration-highly-skilled-women> accessed 18 September 2022

International Telecommunications Union (ITU), 'Bridging the Gender Divide' <www.itu.int/en/mediacentre/backgrounders/Pages/bridging-the-gender-divide.aspx> accessed 9 July 2021

International Trade Centre, 'Unlocking Markets for Women to Trade' (2015) <www.un-ilibrary.org/content/books/9789210579407/read> accessed 9 July 2021

International Trade Centre, 'Empowering women through public procurement' (2014) <www.empowerwomen.org/en/resources/documents/2014/9/empowering--women-through--public-procurement?lang=en> accessed 24 November 2022

International Trade Centre, 'TFA Implementation' <www.intracen.org/itc/trade-facilitation-programme/TFA-Implementation/> accessed 18 September 2021

ISO, 'IWA 34:2021 Women's entrepreneurship—Key definitions and general criteria' (ido.org) <www.iso.org/standard/79585.html> accessed 9 July 2021

IWA 34:2021, 'Women's entrepreneurship—Key definitions and general criteria' (ISO.org 2021) <www.iso.org/obp/ui/#iso:std:iso:iwa:34:ed-1:v1:en> accessed 1 September 2021

Jagdish Bhagwati and 102 Other Signatories, 'Third World Intellectuals and NGOs', Statement against Linkage (TWIN-SAL) (CUTS 6 September 1999) <https://cuts-inter national.org/third-world-intellectuals-and-ngos-statement-against-linkage/> accessed 17 May 2022

Jan Yves Remy, 'Closing the Digital Gender Divide through Trade Rules' (Centre for International Governance Innovation 2019) <www.cigionline.org/articles/closing-digital-gender-divide-through-trade-rules> accessed 28 April 2020

Jane Korinek, Annabelle Mourougane, and Elisabeth van Lieshout, 'Women are less engaged in trade: Why, and what to do about it' (2023) <https://cepr.org/voxeu/columns/women-are-less-engaged-trade-why-and-what-do-about-it#footnote2_0tkosln> accessed 21 April 2024

Jeni Klugman and Elisa Gamberoni, 'Gender and Trade: A Fresh Look at the Evidence' *International Trade Forum Magazine* (1 July 2012) <http://www.tradeforum.org/Gender-and-trade-A-fresh-look-at-the-evidence> accessed 20 April 2020

Joan Faus, 'This is how coronavirus could affect the travel and tourism industry' (World Economic Forum 2020) <www.weforum.org/agenda/2020/03/world-travel-coronavirus-covid19-jobs-pandemic-tourism-aviation/> accessed 21 April 2020

Johnny Wood, '104 Countries have laws that prevent women from working in some jobs' (World Economic Forum 2018) <www.weforum.org/agenda/2018/08/104-countries-have-laws-that-prevent-women-from-working-in-some-jobs/> accessed 18 September 2022

José-Antonio Monteiro, 'The evolution of gender-related provisions in Regional Trade Agreements' (WTO.org 2021) <www.wto.org/english/res_e/reser_e/ersd202108_e.htm> accessed 11 October 2023

Joy Ezeilo, 'Law and practices relating to women's inheritance rights in Nigeria: an overview' (WomenAid Collective) <https://silo.tips/download/laws-and-practices-relating-to-womens-inheritance-rights-in-nigeria-an-overview> accessed 17 September 2022

Judi Chamberlin, 'A working definition on empowerment' (1997) <https://psycnet.apa.org/record/1997-05758-006> accessed 16 September 2022

Kim Parker, 'Women more than men adjust their careers for family life' (Pew Research Center 1 October 2015) <http://www.pewresearch.org/fact-tank/2015/10/01/women-more-than-men-adjust-their-careers-for-family-life/> accessed 28 October 2023

Lucia Hanmer, 'Refugee women face complex barriers to proving identity' (*World Bank Blogs*, 2020) <https://blogs.worldbank.org/dev4peace/refugee-women-face-complex-barriers-proving-identity> accessed 7 October 2020

Lucia Hanmer and Mariana Dahan, 'Identification for Development: Its Potential for Empowering Women and Girls' (*World Bank Blogs*, 2015) <https://blogs.worldbank.org/voices/identification-development-its-potential-empowering-women-and-girls> accessed 18 September 2022

Maïa De La Baume, 'Malmström urges "male-dominated" OECD to do better on gender' (Politico 8 March 2021) <www.politico.eu/article/cecilia-malmstrom-male-dominated-oecd-better-on-gender/> accessed 12 June 2024

Maria V Sokolova, Alisa DiCaprio, and Nicole Bivens Collinson, 'Is it time for women leaders in international organizations?' (Tradeexperttes 2020) <www.tradeexperettes.org/blog/articles/is-it-time-for-women-leaders-in-international-organizations> accessed 22 November 2022

Marianne Musumeci and Kaori Miyamoto, 'Strengthening the gender dimension of aid for trade in the least developed countries' (Enhanced Integrated Framework 2019) <https://trade4devnews.enhancedif.org/en/news/strengthening-gender-dimension-aid-trade-least-developed-countries> accessed 8 May 2022

Markus Goldstein and others, 'The Global State of Small Business during COVID-19: Gender Inequalities' (*World Bank Blogs*, 2020) <https://blogs.worldbank.org/developmenttalk/global-state-small-business-during-covid-19-gender-inequalities> accessed 9 July 2021

Martha Chen and others, 'Progress of the World's Women' (UNIFEM 2005) <www.unwomen.org/en/digital-library/publications/2005/1/progress-of-the-world-s-women-2005-women-work-and-poverty#view> accessed 1 April 2020

Maxime Houinato 'AfCFTA: Upcoming Protocol on Women and Youth in Trade a chance to empower women' (UN Africa Renewal 22 February 2024) <www.un.org/africarenewal/magazine/february-2024/afcfta-upcoming-protocol-women-and-youth-trade-chance-empower-women> accessed 8 April 2024

Media Institute of Southern Africa Zimbabwe, 'Internet access a fundamental human right—data must fall!' (MISA Zimbabwe 2020) <http://zimbabwe.misa.org/2020/04/08/internet-access-a-fundamental-human-right-data-must-fall> accessed 29 September 2020

Megan O'Donnell, 'Why Registration and ID Are Gender Equality Issues' (Center for Global Development 2016) <www.cgdev.org/blog/why-registration-and-id-are-gender-equality-issues> accessed 7 October 2020

Michelle Lonnquist, 'Hardships for Lebanon's Migrant Domestic Workers Rise' (Human Rights Watch 2020) <www.hrw.org/news/2020/09/14/hardships-lebanons-migrant-domestic-workers-rise> accessed 6 October 2020

Nilüfer Çagatay, 'Trade, Gender and Poverty' (United Nations Development Programme 2001) <www.researchgate.net/publication/49464683_Trade_Gender_and_Poverty> accessed 8 September 2022

OECD, 'Unlocking Markets for Women to Trade' (2015) <www.oecd-ilibrary.org/content/publication/aa9eaa55-en> accessed 18 September 2022

OECD, 'Closing the Gender Gap: Act Now' (2016) <www.oecd-ilibrary.org/social-issues-migration-health/close-the-gender-gap-now_9789264179370-en> accessed 18 September 2022

OECD, 'Bridging the Digital Gender Divide: Include, Upskill, Innovate' (2018) <www.oecd.org/digital/bridging-the-digital-gender-divide.pdf> accessed 18 September 2022

OECD, 'Covid-19 and International Trade: Issues and Actions' (2020) <www.oecd.org/coronavirus/policy-responses/covid-19-and-international-trade-issues-and-actions-494da2fa/> accessed 17 August, 2021

OECD, 'How are trade and environmental sustainability compatible?' <www.oecd.org/trade/topics/trade-and-the-environment/> accessed 18 September 2022

OED and Facebook, '2020 Global State of Small Businesses' (World Bank 2021) <https://dataforgood.fb.com/global-state-of-smb/> accessed 9 July 2021

Olivia Rumble, 'No Place to Discuss the CBAM, not even the WTO' (African Climate Wire 11 March 2024) <https://africanclimatewire.org/2024/03/no-place-to-discuss-the-cbam-not-even-the-wto/> accessed 9 July 2023

Oxfam America and the Tahirih Justice Centre, 'Surviving Deterrence: How US Asylum Deterrence Policies Normalise Gender-Based Violence' (2023) <www.tahirih.org/news/transgender-asylum-seekers-the-impact-of-gender-based-violence-and-deterrence-policies-at-the-border/> accessed 18 September 2023

Pete Pattisson, 'Women from Sierra Leone "sold like slaves" into domestic work in Kuwait' *The Guardian* (2015) <www.theguardian.com/global-development/2015/apr/02/women-sierra-leone-sold-like-slaves-domestic-work-kuwait#:~:text=Women%20from%20Sierra%20Leone%20formerly,and%20then%20resold%20multiple%20times.> accessed 18 September 2022

Pew Research Center, 'Among 41 countries, only US lacks paid parental leave' <www.pewresearch.org/fact-tank/2019/12/16/u-s-lacks-mandated-paid-parental-leave/> accessed 17 September 2022

Press release, ITU, '2.9 billion people still offline' <www.itu.int/hub/2021/11/facts-and-figures-2021-2-9-billion-people-still-offline/#:~:text=An%20estimated%2037%20per%20cent,still%20never%20used%20the%20Internet.> accessed on 30 November 2021

Ranja Sengupta, 'Addressing Gender and Trade Issues in Trade Agreements: Creating more problems than solutions?' (DAWN Publications 2018) <https://dawnnet.org/publication/addressing-gender-and-trade-issues-in-trade-agreements-creating-more-problems-than-solutions/> accessed 4 June 2024

Richard Anker, Helinä Melkas, and A Korten, 'InFocus Programme on Promoting the Declaration on Fundamental Principles and Rights at Work' (2003) <www.researchgate.net/publication/

321167476_InFocus_Programme_on_Promoting_the_Declaration_on_Fundamental_Principles_and_Rights_at_Work> accessed 12 May 2024

Roberto Bissio, 'Is "gender" a Trojan horse to introduce new issues at WTO?' (Third World Network 11 December 2017) <https://twnetwork.org/wto/%E2%80%9Cgender%E2%80%9D-trojan-horse-introduce-new-issues-wto> accessed 18 September 2021

Roshan De Stone and David L Suber, 'Women migrant workers come together against the kafala system in Lebanon' (Middle East Monitor 2018) <www.middleeastmonitor.com/20180508-women-migrant-workers-come-together-against-the-kafala-system-in-lebanon/> accessed 18 September 2022

Samira Rafaela, 'Incorporating gender in trade policy to benefit all Stakeholder' (EUobserver 12 April 2021) <https://euobserver.com/stakeholders/151507> accessed 12 June 2024

Semiray Kasoolu and others, 'Female Labor in Jordan: A Systematic Approach to the Exclusion Puzzle' (Center for International Development at Harvard University) <https://growthlab.cid.harvard.edu/publications/female-labor-jordan-systematic-approach-exclusion-puzzle> accessed 17 Sept 2022

Simonetta Zarilli, 'The gender chapters in trade agreements: A true revolution?' (ICTSD 14 November 2017) <http://www.ictsd.org/opinion/the-gender-chapters-in-trade-agreements-a-true-revolution> accessed 13 August 2019

Simonetta Zarrilli, 'International Trade Is at Risk of Leaving Women Behind' (CIGI 2018) <www.cigionline.org/articles/international-trade-risk-leaving-women-behind/> accessed 4 April 2024

Simonetta Zarrilli, Online Webinar Series: 'The role of IOs in gender mainstreaming with respect to trade policies' (6 September 2021) <www.youtube.com/watch?v=fHiglFpkrMs> accessed 4 April 2024

Simonetta Zarrilli, 'If at First You Do Not Succeed, Try Women's Economic Empowerment Through Trade' <www.tradeexperettes.org/blog/articles/if-at-first-you-do-not-succeed-try-womens-economic-empowerment-through-trade> accessed 4 April 2024

Soo Yeon Kim and Raymond Hicks, 'Credible Commitment Through PTAs and their Effects on Trade: A Study of Asia's Reciprocal Trade Agreements' (2009) APSA 2009 Toronto Meeting Paper <https://ssrn.com/abstract=1449204> accessed 11 October 2023

Souad Adnane, 'Moving freely: Moving closer to gender equality' (*World Bank Blogs*, 2019) <https://blogs.worldbank.org/opendata/moving-freely-moving-closer-gender-equality> accessed 28 September 2020

Soyoung Han and Marcus Noland, 'Companies with women in leadership positions are more profitable than those without' (PIIE 2020) <www.piie.com/research/piie-charts/companies-women-leadership-positions-are-more-profitable-those-without> accessed 1 September 2021

Susan Ariel Aaronson and Jean Pierre Chauffour, 'The Wedding of Trade and Human Rights: Marriage of Convenience or Permanent Match?' (nd) WTO Research and Analysis <www.wto.org/english/res_e/publications_e/wtr11_forum_e/wtr11_15feb11_e.htm> accessed 4 April 2024

Sustainability Impact Assessment and Position Paper on the EU-Mercosur Trade Agreement' (European Commission Trade 29 March 2021) <https://trade.ec.europa.eu/doclib/press/index.cfm?id=2260> accessed 24 November 2022

Taku Fundira, 'Informal Cross-border Trading: Review of the Simplified Trade Regimes in East and Southern Africa' (March 2018) Tralac Trade Brief No Taku Fundira, 'Informal Cross-border Trading: Review of the Simplified Trade Regimes in East and Southern Africa', Tralac Trade Brief No US18TB03/2018 <www.tralac.org/documents/publications/trade-briefs/2018-1/1816-us18tb032018-fundira-informal-cross-border-trading-review-of-simplified-trade-regimes-esa-08032018-fin/file.html> accessed 12 May 2024

The World Bank, 'Financial Access' (2016) <www.worldbank.org/en/publication/gfdr/gfdr-2016/background/financial-access> accessed 23 September 2023

The World Bank, 'Women and Trade: The role of trade in promoting gender equality' (World Bank Group & World Trade Organization 2020) <www.worldbank.org/en/topic/trade/publication/women-and-trade-the-role-of-trade-in-promoting-womens-equality> accessed 18 September 2021

The World Bank, 'Women, Business and the Law 2022' (2022) <https://openknowledge.worldbank.org/handle/10986/36945> accessed 6 June 2024

The World Bank and the World Trade Organization, 'The Role of Trade in Promoting Gender Equality' (World Bank Publications 2020) <www.worldbank.org/en/topic/trade/publication/women-and-trade-the-role-of-trade-in-promoting-womens-equality> accessed 17 August 2023

Tom Mctague, David M Herszenhorn, and Andrew Restuccia, 'Trump blows up G7 agenda' (Politico 30 March 2018) <www.politico.eu/article/donald-trump-blows-up-g7-summit-agenda-canada/> accessed 21 May 2024

UN General Assembly, 'Transforming our world: the 2030 Agenda for Sustainable Development' (21 October 2015) A/RES/70/1 <www.refworld.org/docid/57b6e3e44.html> accessed 13 November 2020

UN Women, 'Progress of the World's Women 2015–2016: Transforming economies, realizing rights' (2015) <www.unwomen.org/en/digital-library/publications/2015/4/progress-of-the-worlds-women-2015> accessed 29 October 2023

UN Women, 'On the 25th Anniversary of landmark Beijing Declaration on Women's rights, UN Women calls for accelerating its unfinished business' (2020) <www.unwomen.org/en/news/stories/2020/9/press-release-25th-anniversary-of-the-beijing-declaration-on-womens-rights> accessed 17 August 2021

UN Women, 'Women in informal economy' <www.unwomen.org/en/news/in-focus/csw61/women-in-informal-economy> accessed 29 October 2023

UNCTAD, 'Global Initiative Towards Post-Covid-19 Resurgence of the MSME Sector' <https://unctad.org/project/global-initiative-towards-post-covid-19-resurgence-msme-sector> accessed 9 July 2021

UNCTAD, 'UNCTAD Trade and Gender Tool Box' (2017) <https://unctad.org/en/pages/PublicationWebflyer.aspx?publicationid=1877> accessed 27 October 2022

UNCTAD, 'Making Trade Agreements Work For Gender Equality—Data and Statistics', Policy Brief No 81 <https://unctad.org/en/pages/PublicationWebflyer.aspx?publicationid=2795> accessed 1 July 2020

UNCTAD, 'Trade and Gender Linkages: The Gender Impact of Technological Upgrading in Agriculture' (2020) UNCTAD/DITC/2020/1 <https://unctad.org/webflyer/gender-impact-technological-upgrading-agriculture> accessed 17 September 2022

UNESCO, 'Boosting gender equality in science and technology: a challenge for TVET programmes and careers' (UNESCO International Centre for Technical and Vocational Education and Training 2020) <https://unesdoc.unesco.org/ark:/48223/pf0000374888> accessed 22 November, 2022

UNESCO, 'COVID-19 Educational Disruption and Response' (2020) <https://en.unesco.org/covid19/educationresponse> accessed 21 April 2020

UNESCO, 'Girls' education Gender equality in education benefits every child' <www.unicef.org/education/girls-education> accessed 18 September 2022

UNFPA, 'Gender Inequality and Women's Empowerment Ethiopian Society of Population Studies, In-depth Analysis of the Ethiopia Demographic and Health Survey' (2008) UNFPA: Addis Ababa <www.semanticscholar.org/paper/Gender-Inequality-and-Women-%E2%80%99-s-Empowerment-1-of-%E2%80%99-Ababa/17c3a0548b1942b868b03fc51dee22817dbabfcd> accessed 17 September 2024

UNICEF, 'Child marriage around the world' <www.unicef.org/stories/child-marriage-around-world> accessed 18 September 2022

UNICEF Regional Office for South Asia, 'Gender equality: Glossary of terms and concepts' <www.unicef.org/gender/training/content/resources/Glossary.pdf> accessed 17 September 2024

United Nations Food and Agriculture Organization, 'Women could feed millions more people if given access to means of production—UN' (UN News 7 March 2011) <https://news.un.org/en/story/2011/03/368252-women-could-feed-millions-more-people-if-given-access-means-production-un> accessed 18 September 2021

US Department of State, 'Saudi Arabia Country Specific Information' <https://web.archive.org/web/20131211183846/http://travel.state.gov/travel/cis_pa_tw/cis/cis_1012.html> accessed 18 September 2022

Valerie Hughes, 'Gender Chapters in Trade Agreements: Nice Rhetoric or Sound Policy?' (CIGI 9 October 2019) <www.cigionline.org/articles/gender-chapters-trade-agreements-nice-rhetoric-or-sound-policy/> accessed 21 May 2024

Victor Lavy and Edith Sand, 'On the origins of gender gaps in human capital: Short- and long-term consequences of teachers' biases' (2018) <www.sciencedirect.com/science/article/abs/pii/S0047272718301750> accessed 18 September 2022

WBG and WTO, 'Women and Trade: The Role of Trade in Promoting Gender Equality' (World Bank 2020) <https://openknowledge.worldbank.org/handle/10986/34140> accessed 1 September 2021

William Alan Reinsch, Jasmine Lim, and Ally Brodsky, 'Negotiating Trade Agreements: Gender as a Priority?' (CSIS 24 May 2021) <www.csis.org/analysis/negotiating-trade-agreements-gender-priority> accessed 12 June 2024

Index

For the benefit of digital users, indexed terms that span two pages (e.g., 52–53) may, on occasion, appear on only one of those pages.

References to figures are indicated by an italic *f* following the page number.